"While sculptor Clark Mills's name may be known to historians, relatively little has been published about his life. John Colletta has filled that gap with a lively and vivid account of Mills's rise to prominence and his creation of the celebrated Jackson statue in Lafayette Square, Washington, D.C. Colletta is a master storyteller and a scrupulously thorough researcher."

John DeFerrari, author of *Lost Washington, D.C.*,
co-author of *Sixteenth Street NW, Washington, DC's Avenue of Ambition*s

"Colletta's *Clark Mills* is a rare combination of engaging narrative and deep scholarship. *Clark Mills* is full of fresh information and new insight into this uniquely American genius."

Peter R. Penczer, author of
Washington, D.C.: Past and Present and *The Washington National Mall*

"In this first of a planned trilogy of books, Colletta begins to chronicle the life of Clark Mills, who transformed American sculpture by casting the first monumental bronze statue in the United States. In his signature 'you are there' style, Colletta captures the zeitgeist of several decades preceding the statue's 1853 installation, when Mills lived among the slaveholding elites in Charleston, South Carolina, and the city of Washington. Unlike similar histories that gloss over the presence of people of color, Colletta takes pains to acknowledge them, particularly Mills's enslaved assistant, Philip Reid. Colletta offers deeply researched and enthralling descriptions of antebellum social and political life."

LaBrenda Garrett-Nelson, JD, LLM,
CG®, CGL(SM), FASG,
author of *A Guide to Researching African American Ancestors in Laurens County, South Carolina*

Clark Mills

FOUNDER OF MONUMENTAL BRONZE SCULPTURE IN AMERICA

A STORY OF THE SLAVEHOLDING SOUTH
IN WASHINGTON, D.C.

TOLD IN THREE BOOKS

John Philip Colletta, Ph.D.

ALSO BY JOHN PHILIP COLLETTA

Only a Few Bones:
A True Account of the Rolling Fork Tragedy and Its Aftermath

Finding Italian Roots:
The Complete Guide for Americans

They Came in Ships:
A Guide to Finding Your Immigrant Ancestor's Arrival Record

Discovering Your Roots:
An Introduction to Genealogy
(CD, DVD or streaming from The Teaching Company)

Clark Mills

FOUNDER OF MONUMENTAL BRONZE SCULPTURE IN AMERICA

A STORY OF THE SLAVEHOLDING SOUTH
IN WASHINGTON, D.C.

BOOK 1:
1815–1853
PORTRAIT BUSTS AND
THE JACKSON EQUESTRIAN

John Philip Colletta, Ph.D.

Copyright © 2025 John Philip Colletta, Ph.D.

All rights reserved. Except as permitted under US Copyright Act of 1976, no part of this publication may be reproduced, distributed by any means, or stored in a database or retrieval system, without the prior written permission of the publisher.

ISBN-13: 978-1-939472-50-2

Library of Congress Control Number: 2025917541

Cover and interior design by Joan Keyes, Dovetail Publishing Services

Published by LifeStory Publishing, a division of
Writing Your Life
P.O. Box 541527
Orlando, Florida 32854
WritingYourLife.org

Cover photo credits:

Lithographic print, *Mill's* [sic] *Colossal Equestrian Statue of General Andrew Jackson,* 1853, photo courtesy of the Library of Congress

Engraving, *Clark Mills, the Sculptor,* [N.Y.] *Illustrated News,* Jan. 29, 1853, p. 72

Photographic print, "Picking Cotton, Savannah, Ga.," 1867–1890, photo courtesy of the Library of Congress

First Edition: November 2025
10 9 8 7 6 5 4 3 2 1
Printed in the USA

Note to Readers

This is a work of nonfiction. It tells a true story. All of the people depicted in this book really lived, every event really happened, and every description of a person or place is derived from original historical sources cited in the Notes section at the end of each chapter. To tell the story most vividly, rather than simply relate the facts, I have re-created the settings and narrated the action that those facts denote. A person's thoughts, opinions, temperament, or feelings are expressed only when documentable evidence warrants it. I introduce no fictional characters and I portray no action that is not implied by factual circumstances. Where there are gaps or contradictions in the historical record, I note them, and where speculation is introduced, I identify it as such and state the grounds for it. Dialogue in quotation marks is copied verbatim from original sources; dialogue not in quotation marks is insinuated based on the factual situation.

Readers may be offended by the racist language, attitudes, and practices common in Clark Mills's day, which are retained in this book to depict accurately the reality of his life and times.

Contents

(notes follow each chapter)

PROLOGUE	January 8, 1853	1
CHAPTER 1	1815–Spring 1836	18
CHAPTER 2	Spring–Summer 1836	31
CHAPTER 3	Fall 1836–Fall 1838	44
CHAPTER 4	February 1839–February 1844	54
CHAPTER 5	Ca. 1839/40–August 1844	67
CHAPTER 6	December 9, 1844	82
CHAPTER 7	December 1844–June 1845	84
CHAPTER 8	April 1845–January 1846	93
CHAPTER 9	June–October 1845	108
CHAPTER 10	January–June 1846	121
CHAPTER 11	June–July 1846	128
CHAPTER 12	November 1846–January 1847	139
CHAPTER 13	February 1847	148
CHAPTER 14	February 1847	154
CHAPTER 15	February–March 1847	161
CHAPTER 16	March 1846–March 1847	176
CHAPTER 17	March 1847–March 1848	189
CHAPTER 18	February 23, 1848	202
CHAPTER 19	March–April 1848	203
CHAPTER 20	April–July 1848	212
CHAPTER 21	June–December 1848	220

CHAPTER 22	March 1849	234
CHAPTER 23	March–May 1849	244
CHAPTER 24	May 1849	254
CHAPTER 25	June–December 1849	268
CHAPTER 26	December 1849–February 1850	278
CHAPTER 27	March–April 1850	283
CHAPTER 28	April 1850	297
CHAPTER 29	April 1850	302
CHAPTER 30	May–June 1850	315
CHAPTER 31	September 1850	330
CHAPTER 32	July–October 1850	331
CHAPTER 33	October 1850–August 1851	343
CHAPTER 34	September 1851–August 1852	360
CHAPTER 35	September–November 1852	370
CHAPTER 36	December 1852–January 7, 1853	377
EPILOGUE	January 8, 1853	385
ACKNOWLEDGMENTS		402
INDEX		405

PROLOGUE
January 8, 1853

A bright clear sky, a warm, mild, and spring-like atmosphere, and the almost entire absence of mud in the streets, all combined to render the day upon which the eighth of January fell this year the loveliest and most beautiful of the season. All nature, as it were, seemed anxious to assist art in commemorating the deeds of the illustrious dead.

"Inauguration of the Jackson Equestrian Statue," [Washington] *Evening Star*, Jan. 8, 1853, p. 2.

Twilight had already darkened to dusk when riders on horseback began trotting up to Jackson Hall. Dapper in formal attire, members of the Jackson Democratic Association, U.S. Senators and Representatives, federal and state judges, distinguished attorneys, businessmen and civil officials of Washington City, and the "reportorial corps" arrived. Military officers came, too, some retired but still impressive in their old dress uniforms. The men reined hard in front of 339 Pennsylvania Avenue, dismounted, and hitched their fine mares and geldings. After pulling on white gloves and removing their high hats, the ticket holders strolled into the Greek Revival building.[1]

A procession of carriages also rolled up to the address. Gentlemen descended first, then offered a hand to "their ladies." Hoop skirts of silk or velvet, festooned profusely with ribbons and lace, rustled. As the Negro hacks roused their teams to "Get ye up!" the elegant couples strolled arm-in-arm through the door to the upper floors. Some of the men stepped with an ivory-headed walking stick. All of the ladies wore fashionable bonnets and dangled a reticule from a gloved wrist. The guests climbed the long staircase and passed into a vast hall. The ceiling soared to 20 feet. Gas chandeliers blazed. Stoves glowed with heat.

> Flags of all kinds, representing the various nations of the world, prominent amongst which was our own star-spangled Banner, displayed their graceful folds in every part of the immense room. In the centre of the west side of the room was the picture of the President elect [Franklin Pierce], executed for the Jackson Democratic Association by that justly eminent artist, Mr. Healy. Opposite to this picture hung an engraving of the painting of General Jackson, made by the celebrated Tully.[2]

Attendees gasped with approval. The dashing Philip Barton Key, Esq., chairman of the Committee of Arrangements, had outdone himself![3]

It was the banquet of the Jackson Democratic Association. The event was held every "Eighth of January" to commemorate "the illustrious dead"—Andrew Jackson—and his victory at the Battle of New Orleans on January 8, 1814. The offer of tickets had appeared in the *Daily Union*:

> Tickets can be purchased at all the principal book stores and hotels and at Jackson Hall. A limited number of tickets for ladies will be sold. Price of gentlemen's tickets $3, ladies $2. The number of tickets will be limited to 400, and all persons desirous of attending will confer a favor by purchasing tickets before Friday next.[4]

This year, however, the Association's notice had elicited a less enthusiastic response than usual.[5] Evidently, people knew they would be too exhausted after attending the day's celebration to enjoy an evening affair. Today, commemorative "art" had been unveiled in Lafayette Square—a colossal bronze statue of General Jackson on horseback. The grand procession and dedicatory ceremony had drawn thousands of participants and spectators from out-of-town. Washington in all its stunning patchwork had turned out: government officials, professional men, White and free Black mechanics and laborers, and enslaved residents given the holiday—husbands and

Casimir Bohn's lithographic print of Mills's ground-breaking statue, *Jackson*, published shortly after the sculpture's unveiling in Washington, D.C., on January 8, 1853. Mills labored for six years to create the first monumental bronze statue ever cast in the United States and the first colossal equestrian statue balanced solely on its hind legs anywhere in the world. (Library of Congress)

wives and children. For years the nation's newspapers had stoked public excitement by tracking the trouble-beset making of the sculpture. The editor of the *Daily Union* estimated that 20,000 people filled the square.[6]

Preceding the climactic moment, Senator Stephen A. Douglas had mesmerized the throng for nearly an hour with his rousing oratory. Then the creator of the 15-ton sculpture, Clark Mills, stepped forward on the speakers' platform, stretched out an arm, and the enormous canvas curtain concealing the statue tumbled down. Suddenly, there he was, "Old Hickory," larger than life, hearty in the saddle of a gigantic, rearing charger, waving his cocked hat in the air. Fanfares blared from the gleaming brass of military bands. A volley of artillery blasts rippled the ground. A tremendous uproar of cheering, hollering, whistling and applause filled Lafayette Square. It had been a long, memorable, exhausting day of pageantry, pride and patriotism.[7]

By dusk, though, the city was peaceful again, except for Jackson Hall. Light from the blazing chandeliers of the upper chamber streamed from the huge windows, creating a brilliant patch in the long sweep of the Avenue. It gilded the flurry of ticket holders arriving on horseback and in carriages. The heartiest of Washingtonians and out-of-towners—"scarcely a hundred and fifty"—having caught their second wind and changed to evening attire—had no trouble spotting the address of the "Eighth of January Banquet." Not a few of them, too, came on foot from the many hotels along the Avenue. One of these, very likely, was the guest of honor, who kept a room at the Willard, the man of the hour, Clark Mills.[8] He showed up escorting two ladies.

> The banquet, which was spread out on four rows of tables, decorated in the most handsome manner, was got up by Mr. Walker.

Mssrs. Walker & Shadd were the mulatto chefs at the National Eating House in the basement of the National Hotel.[9]

> At eight o'clock the company sat down and proceeded to discuss the many good things that were placed before them.
>
> Amongst the distinguished gentlemen present, we noticed the Hon. Stephen A. Douglas and the Hon. Solomon W. Downs, of the Senate; the Speaker of the House; Clark Mills, the artist of the statue; Colonel George W. Hughes; Chief Justice Legrand and the Hon. James M. Buchanan, of Maryland; the Hon. David L. Seymour, of the House; Mr. Carrigan, of Philadelphia; General Armstrong; Amos Kendall, and Thos. Ritchie. . . . A number of ladies were present, who shed a beautiful effect upon the magnificent entertainment.[10]

All heads bowed as the Reverend James Gallaher, Chaplain of the House of Representatives, invoked a blessing. Then, for over an hour, while the Marine Band played, the hall echoed with the clatter of silver forks and knives on china and the din of many conversations proclaimed over the music. Wine was served. The room warmed. After the feast, all of the women and two-thirds of the men took their leave and a snappy corps of Black servants cleared the tables and removed the cloths for the toasting. The ritual was familiar to the 38 high-spirited gentlemen who remained. First would come the "regular toasts," then the "complimentary toasts," and lastly the "volunteer sentiments." The men had taken great care in composing the tributes they would read.

Jonah D. Hoover, president of the Association—and at 31 one of the younger members—stood at the head of one of the tables.[11] Francis McNerhany, vice president—a clerk in the Capitol ("clerk" designated a professional position in the 19th century)—stood at the foot.[12] Their voices alternated, American elocution and Irish brogue, as the two officers read the regular toasts. After each toast, the Marine Band played a tune. Thirteen tributes were declared:

> to the victorious Battle of New Orleans (followed by "Jackson's March")
> to the memory of George Washington ("Washington's March")
> to the memory of Andrew Jackson (a dirge)
> to President Millard Fillmore ("President's March")
> to the American Constitution ("Star-spangled Banner")
> to the Union ("Hail Columbia")
> to the Army, Navy and Militia ("Yankee Doodle")
> to the President-elect, Franklin Pierce ("Hail to the Chief")
> to the Vice President-elect, William R. King ("Auld Lang Syne")
> to the Democratic Party ("Wait for the Wagon")
> to the press (the Marseilles Hymn)
> to the triumph of Democratic principle ("Old Folks at Home") and
> to the ladies ("Heaven's Last, Best Gift to Man" and "Still So Gently O'er Me Stealing").

Jonah D. Hoover and Francis McNerhany retook their chairs. Stepping forward then, Philip Barton Key, the urbane chairman, presented the Association's president with "a beautiful rosewood walking stick, with a gold head," eliciting three robust cheers for Hoover from the assembly. Then Key held up his glass—the men encircling the tables lifted their glasses—and proclaimed:

> "To Clark Mills, of South Carolina: The artist whose inventive genius has given to immortality the form and features of Andrew Jackson."

The revelers bellowed three cheers. Then three more. Mills remained seated. The company shouted, "Mills! Mills! Mills!" and drank at last from their goblets as the guest of honor reluctantly rose to his feet. He was 37 years old and stood about five feet, ten inches tall.

A man in whose personal appearance there is nothing to strike an ordinary observer as remarkable; plain in his manners and dress, . . . well and strongly made—not stout. . . . He has a searching light grey eye, good regular Caucasian features, and gray hair, turned gray during the period of his labor and anxiety over the great work he has accomplished.[13]

So ran the description in the *Daily Union*. But an *Evening Star* reporter would call Mills's eyes "bluish grey," while a *Brooklyn Eagle* piece would describe them as "blue:"

and small but intelligent. . . .; thin lips and small mouth. . . .; cheek rather sunken. . . .; his hair gray and combed up and off from his forehead.[14]

An engraved portrait of Mills published in the New York *Illustrated News* would show a handsome man: thick, wavy locks; trim mustache; prominent chin.[15] He was, indeed, by his own fulsome profession, "of South Carolina," as Key pronounced, but not by birth—though it was understandable that most people assumed as much.

Five years prior to tonight's banquet, Mills had appeared in Washington from Charleston carrying his small model for the Jackson memorial. At that time no American, including Mills, had any idea how to cast a large bronze statue. Nor did the United States have a foundry equipped to make one. Such a feat could only be accomplished by a handful of specialized foundries in Europe. But the members of the Jackson Monument Committee—the group sponsoring the memorial project—were excited by Mills's exuberant statuette and won over by his self-assurance. They hired the inexperienced sculptor.

Since then Mills had labored doggedly, straining body and mind, overcoming repeated setbacks and mishaps, to keep his commitment. Through five ferocious years, doubted, then scoffed, then dismissed, he persevered, sinking deeper and deeper into debt. He disregarded his health. He neglected the welfare of his wife, Eliza, and their four sons—which state of affairs remained unresolved. (Neither of the lady companions seated to Mills's left and right this evening was his wife. Eliza's story was to play out in tragedy, but her husband's role in that tragedy would be unintended, however woeful.)

Through it all, Mills's belief in himself sustained him. Ultimately, he achieved what no other sculptor in history had ever been able to achieve: a colossal bronze horse poised on its hind legs with no external support. It was a world first. But wringing that marvel into existence had taken more than Mills's single-minded fixation. It had taken the unflagging support and repeated infusions of personal funds from a succession of southern men of immense wealth, power and influence.

It benefitted Mills immeasurably that his metamorphosis from house plasterer to sculptor occurred during the 1840s and '50s, when "the South" rose to dominance in Washington. During those years he garnered—in addition to dozens of admirers who signed surety bonds for him—14 benefactors. For the eight from South Carolina, one from North Carolina, one from Tennessee, and three from Virginia, success for Mills represented a satisfying poke in the eye of the North. These men used their money and social status, as well as their official positions, to ensure the continuance of their "home boy's" efforts. Thirteen of them owned enslaved men, women and children. One patron alone hailed from New England, a cultured man who appreciated Mills's mental acuity and physical stamina, all the while decrying the fact that the sculptor's assistant, Philip Reid, was his chattel property by law.[16] Without these mighty backers, Mills, on multiple occasions, would have had to slink back to Charleston, a braggard and a failure.

What the story of "Clark Mills, the Sculptor," makes manifest is this: the lifestyle of these mighty backers, the opulence and leisure that allowed them to finance a struggling sculptor, was provided by a multitude of forced, unremunerated Black workers. Untold lives spent in unpaid compulsory service enabled Mills to realize his potential and bring his fanatical efforts to fruition in the Jackson equestrian.

Nor would his story end there. On this watershed day for American art, it was already "bruited about" the city that Mills was about to receive from a thankful Congress not only generous compensation for his statue, but a contract for another one as well. And those would not be the last of the benefices accorded him by the nation's legislators. It was Mills's good fortune that the blossoming of his creativity coincided with the South's heyday in Washington. Upon its collapse and the liberation of the African American workforce, his prospects would change.

He was entirely self-taught. That's what he asserted throughout his life. The boast strains credibility, but it is, in a sense, true. Mills had a brilliant, analytical mind. He was a keen observer, a quick learner, and an inventor several times over. Nevertheless, he did have teachers, a string of them over the course of his unlikely career: a journeyman plasterer, Charlestonian stone carvers, a machinist from Baltimore.... Without the collaboration of one young man in particular, Mills could never have succeeded. The man was a bronze founder from Prussia named Carl Ludwig Richter. Richter designed and built Mills's foundry and taught him how to cast a huge statue in bronze. Never, though, did Mills acknowledge publicly any debt to Richter or to anyone else.

He did admit that a phrenologist whom he allowed on a lark to "read" his skull, and an itinerant Italian bust maker whom he encountered subsequently by chance, had prompted him to try his hand at sculpting. But he never named them. More flattering to Mills's vanity was the mystique of "genius," which epithet he did not disdain. It validated not only his self-perception, but the image of the United States cherished by his contemporaries. Newspapers lauded Mills as the epitome of the American spirit, the quintessential product of a free republic. They called his statues acts of patriotism. Indeed, the story of Mills's remarkable journey from restive runaway to national symbol does illustrate the spirit of nineteenth-century America. Of his generation, he was both exceptional and prototypical. Having achieved unprecedented feats, sculptor and nation alike strode the world stage with bravado.

Only one of Mills's "teachers" was to fight for the recognition—and remuneration—he considered his due. That was Carl Ludwig Richter. For years the immigrant foundryman, outraged and aggrieved by the way Mills had treated him, would employ official channels and the national press to assail his former employer. Richter's story, too, just as much as Mills's, reflects the spirit of nineteenth-century America, only in diametric contrast. Because the country encompassed diametric contradictions as stark as Black and White.

Standing at the long table, surveying the beribboned and bemedaled civic and military leaders who filled the hall, Mills said:

> "I wish merely to express my gratitude for the compliment you have just paid me. Words cannot express my feelings because of your approbation of my work. Unaccustomed to public speaking, I must allow the Hero and his charger to speak for me."

Then, amid applause, the guest of honor sat down and members of the Committee of Arrangements proceeded to offer 22 complimentary toasts to invited guests. Honorees were expected to respond and propose a toast of their own. Most honorees thanked their colleagues briefly with befitting courtesy. A few of them, though, could not refrain from intoning the florid and prolix accolades they had prepared.

When Senator Douglas was toasted, he protested, "You certainly do not expect a speech from me to-night." The speaker of the day, esteemed for his stirring rhetoric, had eulogized General Jackson for nearly an hour at the statue's dedication ceremony.[17] "I think I have performed my whole duty to-day in that respect." But the company shouted, "Go on! Go on!" and the "Little Giant" from Illinois mounted a chair to augment his five feet, four inches. His face was round and clean-shaven, his brow massive. The senator discoursed for 12 minutes. His voice filled the hall. Before stepping down, he concluded, "I give you . . . General Robert Armstrong."

> This toast was drunk with much enthusiasm, and three hearty and deafening cheers were given.

Armstrong, they all knew, had served on Jackson's staff at the Battle of New Orleans.[18] The general enjoyed an aura of reflected glory. He eulogized his erstwhile commander at length.

Colonel George W. Hughes, after he was toasted, stood up and thanked his colleagues. The topographical engineer's "gallant and meritorious conduct" in the late victorious war with Mexico had won him both national recognition and a promotion in rank. His fabulous wealth and vast plantations in Maryland were well known to his fellow Association members. Many of the Democrats gathered in the hall were owners of slaves, as their beloved "Hero of New Orleans" had been.[19] But the Colonel's Black workforce of more than 77 men, women and children far outnumbered those of his confederates.[20] Hughes had served as Chief Marshal of the day's pageantry. He continued:

> "To have to-day through the genius of an American artist the form of Andrew Jackson on his war horse as he appeared in the ever-memorable battle of New Orleans, given to the world in a shape as enduring as the everlasting hills, and presenting an appearance which can hardly be excelled by nature itself, is something of which we may well boast. . . . Of Clark Mills, therefore, gentlemen, we may well be proud. . . . No one else is entitled to the credit of it—he conceived it, he designed it, and he executed it—encountering opposition wherever he turned his face, scientific men telling him, You cannot do it; you cannot do it, sir; give it up.

He heeded them not; he overcame their opposition, and has to-day proved the fallacy of their prediction. Well done, Clark Mills!"

Then Thomas Ritchie—a venerable 74 years old now—was toasted. The Richmonder had been summoned to Washington many years earlier by President Polk to champion Democratic policies in the *Daily Union*. The powerful newspaperman acknowledged his colleagues' regard by recalling:

"the magnificent spectacle which we have this day witnessed—the sculptured horse and the rider, who had been raised as one of the highest triumphs of art, one of the noblest trophies of American genius, and one of the proudest productions of *Liberty* herself."[21]

Letters were read in response to four toasts, because, regrettably, pressing duties had prevented the honorees from attending. Notified in advance, though, they tendered their thanks and tributes to Jackson in writing. When a glass was raised to His Honor the Mayor of "the National Metropolis," John Walker Maury did not respond or offer his own toast because—the gentlemen just noticed—he had retired for the night. By this time, several of the men had lit cigars and the air was pungent-sweet with smoke. Mills would not have declined; he enjoyed a leisurely cigar.[22]

After the complimentary toasts, the advancing hour did not deter the long-enduring revelers—begging indulgence of their brethren—from declaring volunteer sentiments.

Colonel William M. Devoe, attending from Baltimore:

"Andrew Jackson: Mills, the accomplished artist, has this day given us a truthful casting of his majestic figure—Douglas, the gifted orator, has given us an equally exact delineation of his moral grandeur."[23]

R. J. H. Handy, a lieutenant in the U.S. Revenue Service, forerunner of the Coast Guard:

"The Statue and the Artist: Immortal Jackson! Triumphant Mills!"[24]

S. L. Lewis:

"Clark Mills: The greatest artist known to history. A monument more durable than brass or marble will perpetuate his fame; for he has successfully blended his name with the historical fame of Jackson, the 8th of January, and battle of New Orleans; has succeeded in rearing a self-poised equestrian statue, which genius of every age and clime has hitherto tried in vain to accomplish; and has thus demonstrated the fact that American genius and enterprise, like the American continent, rivers, lakes, and men, are superior to the balance of the world."[25]

James Owner:

"Clark Mills: He has achieved a triumph of art which will be forever inseparable from the triumph of Andrew Jackson over the Britons."[26]

William H. Minnix, a clerk in the House of Representatives:

"Clark Mills: Like the rivulet whose source is hidden in the shadows of the mountain-side, and glides on silent and unseen until it expands into the broad and majestic river—so the genius of Mills, nurtured in obscurity, has this day found vent in the execution of a work unrivaled in the productions of art, and challenges the admiration of the world."[27]

John N. Minnix, William's kinsman:

"Stephen A. Douglas and Clark Mills—the orator and the artist: They have both risen from mechanical pursuits to their present high and enviable positions."[28]

Douglas Howard:

"Clark Mills: The architect of the highest production of art extant, and which we have seen unveiled to-day. May our country long enjoy his genius and not forget to reward it."[29]

S. A. Jackson:

"Imperishable renown to the noble artist whose unrivaled genius has presented to his delighted and admiring countrymen the equestrian statue of Andrew Jackson!"[30]

And so on . . . until midnight. Then the exhausted brotherhood tottered down the long staircase, doffed their gloves and high hats, and dispersed up and down Pennsylvania Avenue. The air had taken on a seasonal chill. Washington City slumbered. The patch of brilliance on the Avenue went dark. The next morning's *Daily Union* would report that the stalwart Jacksonian Democrats were "evidently well pleased with the incidents of the evening." Mills headed back to the Willard.

This day had been the most gratifying of his life. But had he noticed the omen? Lying abed in his room, did the self-taught, self-promoting, runaway orphan relive the scene? Not one sculptor—other than himself—had sat at the four long rows of tables in the Jackson Hall banquet room that evening. Maybe that was not remarkable. After all, it was a political affair. Still, the event had been open to the public, announced in the *Daily Union*, and three dollars was not an unreasonable price. Yet the hall had not held a single artist or patron of the arts—other than Mayor John Maury, an ardent supporter of Mills from the start, who left early. At the close of this day-long fanfare of popular praise, did the guest of honor suspect that his defiant struggle was not over? No representative of the nation's cultural establishment would ever deem Mills's "ingenious contrivance" a work of art, or esteem its "deviser" an artist.

NOTES

1 Description of the banquet and all quotations, unless otherwise cited, are derived from: "Banquet of the Jackson Democratic Association," [Washington] *Daily Union*, Jan. 14, 1853, p. 2–3; and "Thirty-Eighth Anniversary of the Battle of New Orleans. Its Celebration in the Capital and Metropolis of the Union," [New York] *Herald*, Jan. 11, 1853, p. 8. Quotations throughout this book reproduce the quoted text exactly, including 19th-century punctuation, misspelled words and names, incorrect grammar, and terms and expressions that are offensive today. Only when essential for clarity is the editorial [sic] used. Quoted text that originally appeared in print is reproduced in standard font; quoted text that was originally handwritten is reproduced in a script font. Description of Jackson Hall is derived from: James M. Goode, *Capitol Losses, A Cultural History of Washington's Destroyed Buildings* (Washington, D.C.: Smithsonian Institution Press, 1979): 250–51.
2 "Tully" is an error; it should be "Sully."
3 "Eighth of January Banquet at Jackson Hall," [Washington] *Daily Union*, Jan. 4, 1853, p. 3. Philip Barton Key II (1818–59), see https://en.wikipedia.org/wiki/Philip_Barton_Key_II. In the 19th century, "Esq." or "Esqr." after a surname (abbreviations for Esquire) was a title of courtesy reserved for any man of notable social standing. It did not necessarily denote an attorney-at-law. By 1846 newspapermen were acknowledging Mills's achievement as a sculptor by calling him, "Clark Mills, Esq." (see Bk. 1, Ch. 13 et seq.).
4 "Eighth of January Banquet . . . ," *Daily Union*, Jan. 4, 1853, p. 3.
5 Donald B. Cole and John J. McDonough, eds., *Witness to the Young Republic, A Yankee's Journal, 1828–1870* (Hanover and London: University Press of New England, 1989): 228.
6 "The Celebration Yesterday," [Washington] *Daily Union*, Jan. 9, 1853, p. 2.
7 See Bk. 1, Epilogue.
8 Cole and Donough, *Witness to the Young Republic*, 228.
9 Alfred Hunter, comp. and pub., *The Washington and Georgetown Directory, Strangers' Guide-book for Washington, and Congressional and Clerks' Register* (Washington: printed by Kirkwood & McGill, 1853): 104. See also Absalom Shadd entry, 1850 U.S. Census, Ward 4, Washington City, D.C., p. 462 (handwritten), p. 231[b] (stamped); National Archives and Records Administration (hereafter NARA) Microfilm (hereafter M) 432, roll 56, viewed at www.ancestry.com. Throughout this book, all U.S. Census Population and Slave Schedules cited were viewed at www.ancestry.com.
10 The Hon. James M. Buchanan "of Maryland," is a mistake; it should be "of Pennsylvania."
11 Jonah D. Hoover (ca. 1822–70), see Jonah Hoover entry, 1850 U.S. Census, Ward 1, Washington City, D.C., p. 126 (handwritten), p. 63[b] (stamped);

NARA M432, roll 56; and William H. Boyd, pub., *Boyd's Washington and Georgetown Directory* (Washington, D.C.: William H. Boyd, 1858): 154.

12 Francis McNerhany, see Hunter, *Washington and Georgetown Directory* (1853), 69.

13 "History of the Jackson Statue," [Washington] *Daily Union*, Jan. 18, 1853, p. 2; reprinted in the *New York Daily Times*, Jan. 22, 1853, p. 3; abbreviated version in Hunter, *Washington and Georgetown Directory* (1853), 91–93.

14 "An Hour with Clark Mills," [Washington] *Evening Star*, Dec. 24, 1870, p. 2; and "Sketches of Washington. By Child Harold. Washington, March 29, 1853. An Hour with Clark Mills, the Sculptor," *Brooklyn Daily Eagle*, Mar. 30, 1853, p. 2.

15 "Clark Mills, The Sculptor, From a Daguerreotype by Whitehurst" (engraving), [N.Y.] *Illustrated News*, Jan. 29, 1853, p. 72.

16 Biographical information about Mills's patrons appearing in Bk. 1: (1) John Schnierle, Ch. 4; (2) Franklin Harper Elmore, Ch. 5; (3) Cave Johnson, Ch. 9; (4) John Walker Maury, Ch. 9; (5) Francis Preston Blair, Ch. 9; (6) John Cook Rives, Ch. 9; (7) Henry Workman Conner, Ch. 10; (8) A. G. Rose, Ch. 10; (9) John Smith Preston, Ch. 11; (10) William Campbell Preston, Ch. 11; (11) Isaac Edward Holmes, Ch. 12; (12) James Henry Hammond, Ch. 12; (13) Abraham Watkins Venable, Ch. 29; and (14) Benjamin Brown French, the lone northern patron, Ch. 9. For other supporters later in Mills's career, see Bk. 2.

17 Stephen A. Douglas (1813–61), see https://www.senate.gov/senators/FeaturedBios/Featured_Bio_Douglas_Stephen.htm; and Hunter, *Washington and Georgetown Directory* (1853), 30. For physical description, see https://www.essentialcivilwarcurriculum.com/stephen-a.-douglas.html.

18 Robert Armstrong (1792–1854), see https://en.wikipedia.org/wiki/Robert_Armstrong_(military officer).

19 Author's conclusion based on a search of 1850 U.S. Census Population and Slave Schedules.

20 George Wurtz Hughes (1806–70), see https://bioguideretro.congress.gov/Home/MemberDetails?memIndex=H000921; and Geo. [sic] W. Hughes entry, 1850 U.S. Census, First Dist., Anne Arundel Co., Md., p. 615 (handwritten), p. 308 (stamped); NARA M432, roll 278; and Geo. [sic] W. Hughes entry, 1850 U.S. Census Slave Schedule, First Dist., Anne Arundel Co., Md., p. 269, 271, 281 and 283; NARA M432, roll 300.

21 Thomas Ritchie (1778–1854), see https://en.wikipedia.org/wiki/Thomas_Ritchie_(journalist); and Thos [sic] Ritchie entry, 1850 U.S. Census, Ward 1, Washington City, Washington Co., D.C., p. 103 (handwritten), p. 52 (stamped); NARA M432, roll 56; and Thos [sic] Ritchie entry, 1850 U.S. Census Slave Schedule, Ward 1, Washington City, Washington Co., D.C., p. 651 (handwritten); NARA M432, roll 57; and Gaither & Addison, *Washington Directory, and National Register, for 1846* (Washington: John T. Towers, 1846), 72.

22 "Sketches of Washington . . . ," *Brooklyn Daily Eagle*, Mar. 30, 1853, p. 2.

23 William M. Devoe, author cannot identify.

24 Robert Jenkins Henry Handy (1826–59), see https://www.wikitree.com/wiki/Handy-585; and https://www.findagrave.com/memorial/99021020/robert-jenkins_henry-handy.
25 S. L. Lewis, author cannot identify.
26 James Owner, author cannot identify.
27 William H. Minnix (ca. 1819–?), see Wm [sic] H. Minnix entry, 1850 U.S. Census, Ward 1, Washington City, Washington Co., D.C., p. 32 (handwritten), p. 16[b] (stamped); NARA M432, roll 56; and Hunter, *Washington and Georgetown Directory* (1853), 38.
28 John N. Minnix, author cannot identify.
29 Douglas Howard, author cannot identify.
30 S. A. Jackson, author cannot identify.

CHAPTER 1
1815–Spring 1836

Unfortunately for the venerable Clark Mills, the sculptor, the old family Bible in which his birth was recorded was destroyed by the burning down of the humble home of his mother. So that important event is shrouded in mystery. The best guess has named December 1, 1815, as the auspicious day.

"Clark Mills at Home," *The Washington Post*, Feb. 7, 1880, p. 2.

Historical sources record Mills's birth variously between 1809 and 1821.[1] However, *The Washington Post* reporter's "best guess" is indeed the most probable. People took Mills to be older than he was. His hair grayed early.[2] One interviewer in 1870, when Mills was 55, referred to him as "the indomitable old man ... of 65 probably, white of hair and whiskers."[3] But Mills's son, Theophilus Fisk, knew better and clarified in a 1910 letter:

Clark Mills was born 1816 ... was not over 66 years of age at the time of his death, not 72 years of age as recorded.[4]

Biographical sketches of Mills abound.[5] Beginning in the 1850s, when the sculptor achieved celebrity, journalists seeking interviews came knocking at his door. Mills always took pleasure in obliging them. More than that, though, he frequently took the initiative, calling at the offices of newspapers or inviting members of the "reportorial corps" to his place. He reveled in living in the public eye. Observed one reporter:

Mr. Mills loves to talk of his art, his struggles, and himself.[6]

An interviewer writing in 1853 under the pseudonym, Childe Harold, opined:

[I] listened to a recital of his life, which I found interesting from the fact of the example which it sets, showing how an indomitable will and determined perseverance will triumph over all obstacles and difficulties.[7]

That judgment was shared by other writers:

> Like most of the successful men in all vocations of life, Mr. Mills is a self-made man. The story of his life is one of the most romantic and instructive among American biographies.[8]

Mills's eagerness to talk about himself notwithstanding—and the potfuls of printer's ink that that propensity emptied—everything that is known about his childhood and adolescence, in particular, derives from a handful of historical materials. Moreover, it appears that, early on, Mills settled on an "official narrative" of his origins, one that both gratified his self-image and appealed to popular sentiment, because the same few facts are reiterated, over and over, to the exclusion of all others. One letter, though, printed in the *Utica* [N.Y.] *Morning Herald* in 1863, contains the reminiscences of a long-time resident of Mills's neighborhood who knew the family. The author—who signed simply, "T"—wrote:

> Clark Mills was born in an obscure hovel, long since demolished, which stood near the boundary line between Fabius, Onondaga county, and Truxton, Cortland county; but whether in Fabius or Truxton I have now forgotten.[9]

That was a rugged country of sheer-walled plateaus separated by deep valleys where three counties adjoined: Onondaga, Madison and Cortland. Ancient hardwood and evergreen forests covered the hilltops. Streams of fresh water cascaded majestically from the heights into slow, meandering rivers far below. Widely dispersed settlers from New England cultivated the rich glacial soil of the valleys, their cabins tucked up against the steep hillsides for shelter from winter winds and spring floods. A couple of millers' wheels churned along the major rivers, but the irregularity of the terrain favored pasturage. The principal industry of both Fabius and Truxton was dairy farming. The open valleys afforded not only summer forage, but adequate excess to cut and store for the long, cold, gray months of heavy snow.[10]

Mills's mother, Julia, was born about 1781 in Connecticut; his father's name, birth year and birth place are all undiscovered.[11] It appears that the couple married in Connecticut and had a son there, Phineas Gurley, who was blind, before removing to central New York State, around 1810. Their "obscure hovel"—as "T" called it—would have been a log cabin, standing probably in the far southeastern corner of Onondaga County. How Mills's father provided for his family is not known, but chances are good he was a dairy farmer. That was the staple livelihood of the region, and Clark Mills himself, later in life, would engage in dairy farming, as would one of his sons.[12]

In 1817, two years after Mills's birth, a brother, Emory, was born over the line in Madison County. Emory would remain in the area his entire life, farming and raising a family.[13] "T" also named a fourth brother:

> John, who was a remarkably tall, lithe, athletic young man, became a notorious horse-thief, for which he was incarcerated in Sing Sing Prison from about 1844 to 1848, and since his release has not made his whereabouts known.[14]

Research has neither corroborated nor refuted this.

An article that appeared in *The Round Table, A Saturday Review of Politics, Finance, Literature, Society and Art*, in 1864 and one published many years later in *The Washington Post* reflect the "stock version" of Mills's youth. Both resulted from an in-person conversation with the subject himself and both contain almost verbatim prose.[15] *The Round Table* reporter wrote:

In consequence of the death of his father, he was put, at the early age of five years, with an uncle by marriage, whom he left between the ages of twelve and thirteen for imagined ill treatment.[16]

Mills's son, Theophilus Fisk, would put it this way in his 1910 letter:

[He] ran away as a boy from his aunt with whom he had been placed to live.[17]

Mills told many news writers that he ran away from home because his uncle mistreated him. But he never named the offender or particularized the offense. Being overworked on a farm, however, would not have been an uncommon fate for a poor boy "taken in."

The interview Mills gave to the pseudonymous author, Childe Harold, appeared in the *Brooklyn Daily Eagle* and included this classroom anecdote:

When [Mills] was about ten years old, he remembered that he used to make his slate a complete miniature gallery. Everything which came under his observation at that time, was immediately transferred to his slate.

[A pupil's "notebook" at that time was a sheet of slate, his writing implement, a piece of chalk.]

A friend's face, a hated chum, the trees from the windows, pictures in the books, everything that passed around him in movement was caricatured. When he was cyphering, one side of his slate was always devoted to drawing, and the moment the schoolmaster came in sight, he turned his slate over and commenced his mathematical figuring, without knowing whether it was division or multiplication.

One day the master had been punishing one of the boys in the usual mode, which was drawing him over his knee and then applying the rule to a very uncomfortable portion of his frame; the boy kicked and struggled, yelled and squalled, but to no avail. The blows came down upon the outward covering of his person with mathematical precision—one, two, three, four, &c., till he came to eighteen, when the boy brought his heel in juxtaposition with the schoolmaster's cranium, and the master dropped the rule, clapped his hand to the wounded part, while the boy stood trembling, holding his hands behind, with a half laugh of triumph at his victory. This was the moment seized upon by the artist for his second picture—"The Punishment and the School Boy's Revenge." In the meanwhile the boy received an extra 20 for his insubordination.

The boy artist had finished his drawing; the work was done, and he exhibited his picture to his chum; a laugh was its reception: the eagle eye of the school master was upon them; the slate torn from their hands, and the school master in rage dreadful to behold, stood like an angry God in the middle of the floor. His white hair stood on an end, his eyes dilated in anger, the slate was held aloft to exhibit to the boys. Such a breach of propriety had never occurred; how any boy could ridicule his sacred person and expect to live after, he could not imagine; he gave the poor artist a look, annihilating, dreadful, terrible; he quivered in his seat. One spring and the tiger in human form had clutched his prey; he held him aloft a few minutes, his feet dangling in the air, and then placed with greatest care his body across his knees, he gave him "the darndest licking he ever had."[18]

How much of what Mills related about himself was fact and how much was elaboration, no one can say. But it didn't matter to his listeners. Mills's yarns were always rousing good entertainment.

The Round Table's account of Mills's childhood continued:

The following spring he worked on a farm and drove a wagon.[19]

That was the spring of 1829, when a man of humble origins, General Andrew Jackson, entered the Executive Mansion in Washington, D.C. Jackson's vice president was John C. Calhoun. To the runaway farm boy in upstate New York, the national capital was a far-distant galaxy. Nevertheless, the youngster's self-reliance and ambition—not unlike Jackson's and Calhoun's—typified the spirit of their time. Mills's social, scientific and artistic achievements would mirror the America of his day.[20] Fittingly, therefore, his representations of Calhoun and Jackson would be the most consequential works of his life. A marble bust of Calhoun would launch his career as a sculptor, and a monumental statue of Jackson would catapult that career skyward.[21]

The biographical sketch in *The Round Table* moved on from 1829:

> He went to school that winter, working night and morning, before school hours, for his board. The next spring he went to Syracuse, N.Y., in search of work, and found employment at five dollars a month with board.[22]

Syracuse promised employment. The Erie Canal, which bisected the village from east to west, had opened locally in 1820 and statewide in 1825, and the Oswego Canal, running north to Lake Ontario, was operating by 1828. The astonishing success of these waterways was transforming Syracuse rapidly into an important commercial center. Situated amid rich farmland, salt springs, limestone deposits for making mortar, and low-lying marshes that provided timber, the village enjoyed a growing economy.

The *Troy* [N.Y.] *Weekly Times* noted in 1857:

> Clark Mills, the sculptor, in early life used to describe a circle behind a horse, in a brick-yard at Syracuse.[23]

A piece in the *Syracuse* [N.Y.] *Daily Standard* that same year ran:

> Many of our old citizens will recollect one Benton who formerly owned a brick yard in Syracuse. At that time Mills was a poor boy,

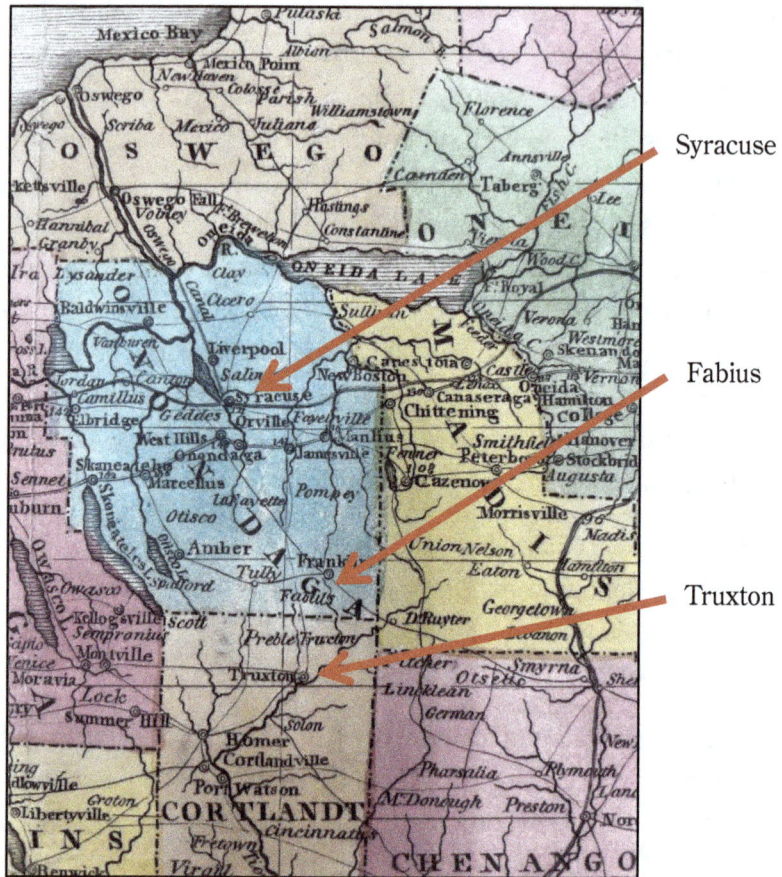

Detail of 1831 map showing the counties of central New York State where Mills was born and resided until he was 20. The Erie Canal, which passed through Syracuse, provided one of the runaway waif's many diverse jobs before he ventured South in 1836. (Library of Congress)

and worked on the yard of Mr. B., driving the horse that propelled the brick machine.[24]

Job opportunities in the boom town attracted not only 15-year-old Mills, but many other country boys just like him, as well as adventuresome entrepreneurs. In 1829 the rise of Syracuse was acknowledged and rewarded: it was made the seat of Onondaga County.[25] However, not everyone who hustled to the hub of prosperity succeeded.

The Round Table:

> [Mills] worked nine months, and received only five dollars. His employer failed in the fall, and [Mills] lost all that was due him.[26]

For nine months' work, Mills received one month's pay. And he was out of a job. It appears that his employer who "failed in the fall" was Mr. Benton.

The Round Table:

> [Mills] worked during the winter at a different employment, and in the spring he drove a wagon hauling lumber at Syracuse, where he remained one year at eight dollars a month and board. The horses were finally sold, and oxen substituted.[27]

Theophilus Fisk:

> *[He] hired as a driver of oxen hauling logs to a charcoal pit.*[28]

Massive chains were used to bind the logs in the ox-drawn wagon. At the "burn pit," the timber was released, cut into sticks, stacked into a mound, covered with earth, and set afire. The slow burn carbonized the wood into charcoal. In future years, when asked what inspired the design of his revolutionary furnace for making bronze, Mills would relate how once, "when a boy of 15," he had seen a log chain accidentally melted in a charcoal pit.[29] In reality, the furnace was the invention of the Prussian who built it for him, Carl Ludwig Richter.[30] Mills had a flair for storytelling. He delighted in embellishing personal anecdotes for maximum effect. His charcoal pit story would become commonplace in newspaper articles about him.

The Round Table:

> Finding an ox-team too slow for his "go ahead" disposition, he left his employer and went on the canal till the fall, and went to school that winter. In the spring he attended canal locks.[31]

Work on the Erie Canal was seasonal. When temperatures dipped below freezing and flurries of snow thickened to blizzards, the waterway was drained for the winter.[32] It was during the white months that Mills received his formal education. Come the thaws of March 1833, with the canal refilled and reopened to commerce, Mills returned to work. Seventeen years old now, he advanced to the post of lock tender. Due to the change in the canal's elevation, barges heading west needed to be "locked up" and barges heading east needed to be "locked down." All day long and even after dark, whenever Mills heard the blow of a captain's horn, he ran to operate the gates, flooding or draining the locks as required to keep water traffic flowing. It was an incessant responsibility. Come the winter of 1833–34, when work ended for the season, Mills did not return to the classroom. His days of schooling were over.

The Round Table:

> The following winter he worked in a swamp cutting cedar posts, and got his feet so badly frozen that he was unable to wear shoes for several months, which suffering determined him never to work again as a common laborer. He then secured a situation with a cabinet-maker, working first for instruction and then for board. He next learned the millwright's trade and worked at that about two years.[33]

Theophilus Fisk:

> *[He] served as an apprentis at building of mills.*[34]

Mills's haphazard schooling had come to an end, but not his thirst for learning. Unhappy with day labor, he resolved to acquire a trade. His mind was sharp and inquisitive. He mastered skills quickly—first making furniture, then building and operating mills. But, once mastered, these occupations did not hold his interest. Why was he never satisfied? Maybe he was not yet aware of his need for creative self-expression.

In his letter to the *Utica* [N.Y.] *Morning Herald*, "T" wrote:

> As nearly as I remember, about thirty years ago, perhaps longer, while yet in his boyhood, Clark left home and was not heard from for many years, till all his friends supposed him to be dead. Within the last fifteen years he has occasionally visited the place of his nativity."[35]

Mills did break free, that was true. But by no means did he abandon his mother or brothers. Julia and Phineas Gurley (who was led by a trained dog) were in later years—according to "T"—"dependant on Clark for support." As soon as success made it possible, Mills would bring the two of them, as well as a step-brother (Mills's mother had remarried and been widowed again by then) and Emory's daughter, Lovisa, to live with him in the District of Columbia.[36] It was this spring of 1836 when Mills, self-reliant, defiant and ambitious, turned to the world beyond the sheer-walled plateaus and deep valleys of Onondaga County for his destiny.

"T:"

> Before leaving home he had displayed considerable taste and skill in drawing, of which I have seen specimens; but he never enjoyed the advantages of a teacher in the art.[37]

Andrew Jackson was serving his second term as president. John C. Calhoun was representing South Carolina in the U.S. Senate. Though far removed from the sphere of 20-year-old Clark Mills, Jackson and Calhoun inspired young Americans like him. Their stories were legendary. Both men, by dint of forceful personalities, will power and ambition had overcome personal obstacles to achieve mythic stature.[38] In a country where a man born in a log cabin could get rich and become President of the United States, could not Mills, too, achieve his full potential? In a country where a man born on a farm, who lost his father as a boy, could acquire education and wealth and occupy a seat in Congress, could not Mills, too, aspire to distinction?

"T" concluded:

This brief and hasty sketch shows that Clark Mills presents another instance, of which we find so many in America, of that force of character and genius which, in the face of incredible circumstances, raise their possessor from the lowest obscurity to usefulness, honor and renown.[39]

Andrew Jackson and John C. Calhoun were both self-made slaveholding southerners. Clark Mills headed south.

NOTES

1   Sources for Mills's date of birth include, among others: (1) 1850 U.S. Census: "32" (i.e., 1817-18); (2) "Clark Mills, The Sculptor," *Illustrated* [N.Y.] *News*, Jan. 29, 1853, p. 72: "38" (1814–15); (3) "A Commencement of a New Era in the Arts. Jackson Statue," *The Washington and Georgetown Directory*, 1853, p. 92: "thirty-two" (ca. 1821); (4) "Clark Mills, The Sculptor," *Gleason's Pictorial Drawing-Room Companion*, vol. 6, no. 23 (June 10, 1854), p. 356: "about forty" (ca. 1814); (5) "Clark Mills, The Sculptor," *Frank Leslie's Illustrated Newspaper*, Mar. 3, 1860, p. 12: "born . . . some forty-seven years ago" (ca. 1813); (6) 1860 U.S. Census: "44" (1815-16); (7) "Mr. Clark Mills, The Sculptor," *The Round Table*, May 14, 1864, p. 340: "born Dec. 13, 1815;" (8) 1870 U.S. Census: "60" (1809-10); (9) 1880 U.S. Census: "70" (1809-10); (10) "Clark Mills at Home," *The Washington Post*, Feb. 7, 1880, p. 2: "December 1, 1815;" (11) [no title], *The Atlantic Constitution*, May 20, 1880, p. 2: "seventy" (ca. 1810); (12) "The Name of Clark Mills," *New York Times*, May 31, 1880, p. 4: "about 65" (ca. 1815); (13) Death record, D.C. Department of Health, Vital Records Division: "died Jan. 12, 1883, age 72" (1810-11); (14) "Death of Clark Mills," [Washington] *Evening Star*, Jan. 12, 1883, p. 8: "December 13th, 1810;" (15) "A Great Sculptor Gone," *The Washington Post*, Jan. 13, 1883, p. 4: "December 1, 1815;" (16) "Clark Mills, the Sculptor," [Baltimore] *Sun*, Jan. 13, 1883, p. 1: "Dec. 13, 1810;" and (17) Tombstone, Glenwood Cemetery, Washington, D.C.: "MDCCCXV-MDCCCLXXXIII" (1815).
2   See Bk. 1, Prologue.
3   "An hour with Clark Mills," [Washington] *Evening Star*, Dec. 24, 1870, p. 2.
4   Letter, T[heophilus] F[isk] Mills to Elliott Woods, Superintendent, U.S. Capitol and Grounds, July 29, 1910, contains a biographical sketch of his father; Archives, Office of the Architect of the Capitol, Washington, D.C.
5   All that is known about Mills derives from four types of historical sources that sometimes contain conflicting and often verifiably inaccurate information: (1) what Mills himself told reporters and wrote in a few business letters;

(2) what newspapers and business correspondents wrote about him; (3) Theophilus Fisk's 1910 letter; and (4) federal, state and local public records. The only biography of Mills to date has been: Rosemary Hopkins, *Clark Mills: The First Native American Sculptor* (M.A. thesis, University of Maryland, 1966). Adequate for an academic work of its time, Hopkins' biography is immature, sketchy, and contains errors of fact and speculation. The digitization of millions of historical materials since the 1960s—particularly old newspapers—allows today for a more complete and more accurate picture of Mills's life. No personal papers of Mills have been found. For this current narrative history, therefore, the author has relied on original sources and eschewed materials published after 1890 (except for select scholarly articles), because that literature reiterates from generation to generation the same handful of facts and the same persistent misinformation. The author thanks Skip Duett, a professional researcher in New York State, for his assistance locating Mills materials on the local level, 2017–18.

6   "Clark Mills at Home," *The Washington Post*, Aug. 7, 1879, p. 1.
7   "Sketches of Washington. By Childe Harold. Washington, March 29, 1853. An Hour with Clark Mills, the Sculptor" (hereafter "Sketches of Washington. By Childe Harold"), *Brooklyn Daily Eagle*, Mar. 30, 1853, p. 2.
8   "Clark Mills at Home," *The Washington Post*, Feb. 7, 1880, p. 2. See also "Clark Mills, the Sculptor," *Syracuse* [N.Y.] *Daily Standard*, Jan. 1857, p. 3.
9   "Clark Mills, the Sculptor," *Utica* [N.Y.] *Morning Herald*, Dec. 18, 1863; reprinted in the *Syracuse* [N.Y.] *Daily Journal*, Dec. 22, 1863, p. 2. This biographical sketch contains many errors, but sufficient accurate detail to suggest that the author was indeed familiar with the Mills family, if not with the sculptor-to-be himself.
10 J. H. French, *Gazetteer of the State of New York*, 10th ed. (Syracuse, N.Y.: R. P. Smith, 1861): 472, 482-83; and W. W. Clayton, *History of Onondaga County, New York* (Syracuse, N.Y.: D. Mason & Co., 1878): 54.
11 Julia's maiden name may have been Parker, as Mills had an uncle Noah Parker. See Bk. 1, Ch. 2.
12 See Bk. 2.
13 "Clark Mills . . . ," *Utica Morning Herald*, Dec. 18, 1863; U.S. Censuses of 1850, 1860, 1870 and 1880; N.Y. State Censuses of 1855, 1865 and 1875; Joyce C. Scott and Mary K. Meyer, eds., *Deaths – Births – Marriages From Newspapers Published in Madison County, NY, 1818–1886* (Mt. Airy, Md.: Libra/Pipe Creek Publications, 1996): 91; Herkimer Co., N.Y., Probate Records, Estate Papers, File 5266, Emory S. Mills, 1886.
14 "Clark Mills . . . ," *Utica Morning Herald*, Dec. 18, 1863.
15 "Mr. Clark Mills, the Sculptor," *The Round Table, A Saturday Review of Politics, Finance, Literature, Society and Art* (hereafter *The Round Table*), vol. 1, no. 22 (May 14, 1864): 340; and "Clark Mills . . . ," *The Washington Post*, Feb. 7, 1880, p. 2. See also "A Great Sculptor Gone. The Career of Clark Mills Closed by Death," *The Washington Post*, Jan. 13, 1883, p. 4.

16 "Mr. Clark Mills . . . ," *The Round Table*, vol. 1, no. 22 (May 14, 1864): 340. Also "Clark Mills . . . ," *The Washington Post*, Feb. 7, 1880, p. 2 (a personal interview with Mills): "Long before the features of his father had been impressed upon the tablets of his memory, his natural protector was removed by death, and our hero was turned over to the care of an uncle-in-law." However, "Clark Mills . . . ," *Utica Morning Herald*, Dec. 18, 1863, claims that Mills's father "deserted his family, who never afterwards heard from him."
17 Letter, T[heophilus] F[isk] Mills to Elliott Woods, July 29, 1910.
18 "Sketches of Washington. By Childe Harold," *Brooklyn Daily Eagle*, Mar. 30, 1853, p. 2.
19 "Mr. Clark Mills . . . ," *The Round Table*, vol. 1, no. 22 (May 14, 1864): 340.
20 Samuel Eliot Morison, Henry Steele Commager and William E. Leuchtenburg, *The Growth of the American Republic*, 7th ed. (New York: Oxford University Press, 1980), vol. 1: 419 et seq.
21 See Bk. 1, Ch. 8, and Bk. 2.
22 "Mr. Clark Mills . . . ," *The Round Table*, vol. 1, no. 22 (May 14, 1864): 340.
23 [no title], *Troy* [N.Y.] *Weekly Times*, Jan. 17, 1857, p. 3.
24 "Clark Mills . . . ," *Syracuse Daily Standard*, Jan. 6, 1857, p. 3.
25 French, *Gazetteer of the State of New York*, p. 488-89; and Clayton, *History of Onondaga County*, p. 140.
26 "Mr. Clark Mills . . . ," *The Round Table*, vol. 1, no. 22 (May 14, 1864): 340; and "Clark Mills . . . ," *The Washington Post*, Feb. 7, 1880, p. 2.
27 "Mr. Clark Mills . . . ," *The Round Table*, vol. 1, no. 22 (May 14, 1864): 340.
28 Letter, T[heophilus] F[isk] Mills to Elliott Woods, July 29, 1910.
29 A[loha] Vivarttas, "The Clark Mills Furnace—A Reminiscence," *The Railroad & Engineering Journal*, vol. 63 (July 1889): 327-28. See Bk. 1, Ch. 30.
30 See Bk. 1, Chs. 26 and 27.
31 "Mr. Clark Mills . . . ," *The Round Table*, vol. 1, no. 22 (May 14, 1864): 340; and "Clark Mills . . . ," *The Washington Post*, Feb. 7, 1880, p. 2.
32 Robert E. Shaw, *Erie Water West: A History of the Erie Canal, 1792–1854* (Lexington, Ky.: University Press of Kentucky, 1966).
33 "Mr. Clark Mills . . . ," *The Round Table*, vol. 1, no. 22 (May 14, 1864): 340; and "Clark Mills . . . ," *The Washington Post*, Feb. 7, 1880, p. 2.
34 Letter, T[heophilus] F[isk] Mills to Elliott Woods, July 29, 1910.
35 "Clark Mills . . . ," *Utica Morning Herald*, Dec. 18, 1863.
36 See Bk. 2.
37 "Clark Mills . . . ," *Utica Morning Herald*, Dec. 18, 1863.
38 Morison, Steele and Leuchtenburg, *The Growth of the American Republic*, vol. 1: 419 et seq.
39 Ibid.

CHAPTER 2
Spring–Summer 1836

"I am acquainted with a Mr. Clark Mills, who was in some way concerned in preparing a bust of the late Washington Whitaker. He was introduced to me in New Orleans, and represented himself to be from New York. He is a man about thirty-two years old, five feet eight or nine inches high, light brown hair, and has a sort of red spot on one of his upper eye lids, . . . I am particular in describing the man, because I want to put the saddle on the right horse, and don't wish that any honest gentleman should be taken for him."

John Rist, quoted in: "A Vindication of the Whitaker Family," [Washington] *Native American*, Aug. 18, 1838, p. 4.

Mills walked down the gangplank into an exhilarating maelstrom of foreign faces, a babble of southern drawl, French and Spanish, pale blue walls with wrought iron balconies, tropical trees and plants, and pungent aromas. This was *not* Syracuse. Mills was 20—not 32, as John Rist surmised—just one of myriad young, wide-eyed opportunity seekers thronging the streets of New Orleans. It was 1836 and the population of the unique French-Spanish-African-Creole-Anglo enclave would more than double during this decade, from 46,082 to 102,193 inhabitants.[1]

The importance of New Orleans as a seaport was on the rise. Imported goods were channeled up the Mississippi River to widespread northern markets, while agricultural products—mostly rice, sugar cane and cotton—were shipped out to Europe. New Orleans had the largest slave market in the country, yet a third of its residents were free people of color, mostly French speakers. The metropolis was well on its way to becoming the wealthiest and third most populous in the country. Mills was far from the only hopeful quester setting foot ashore here.

It was a grand and exhilarating adventure for northern lads to work their way down the Mississippi River on a riverboat. The easiest way for Mills to reach the Mississippi from Syracuse would have been to take the Erie Canal to Buffalo, descend the Allegheny River to Pittsburgh, then hire onto an Ohio paddle wheeler heading south. Chugging through mile after mile of untouched woodlands and pulling in at numerous muddy settlements along the way, Mills saw that there was a great deal more to America than Onondaga County. He could not have chosen any place in the country more distant from his home territory, or more unlike it, than New Orleans.

Never, though, did Mills divulge what drew him to the southernmost metropolis of the Deep South. The "official narrative" of his life, which he recited readily for the public, leapfrogged over the year

Mills at 37 years of age, when his "self-poised" equestrian statue of General Jackson brought him national renown. Seventeen years earlier, working for an uncle in New Orleans, Mills was dazzled by the sumptuous lifestyle of Louisiana's aristocracy and resolved to realize his ambition in the Deep South. ([N.Y.] *Illustrated News*, Jan. 29, 1853, p. 72)

CLARK MILLS, THE SCULPTOR.

1836—"His next move was for New Orleans, La., where he stayed about one year, and then went to Charleston, S.C."—and for good reason.[2] The only information that has come to light regarding the restive New Yorker's sojourn in the Bayou State derives from the bizarre episode of the "bust of the late Washington Whitaker." Newspaper coverage of the affair portrayed Mills as a scoundrel, a "tremendous liar."[3]

Ironically, though, it was Mills's fleeting experience in New Orleans that planted the seed that would sprout in Charleston and blossom in Washington. It was in Louisiana that Mills sensed the unknown something he had been seeking. The footloose orphan meandered to New Orleans, most likely, because he had an uncle residing there who could employ him. That uncle was a bust maker.

Noah Parker had migrated down from New York a few years ahead of his nephew.[4] His livelihood was making portrait busts for clients who possessed the requisite means and self-satisfaction to have their features memorialized for future generations. Parker practiced the conventional method of the day. First, he took a plaster cast of the subject's face and head, either while the sitter was still spry or promptly after death. That cast then served as a mold, into which he poured plaster paste. When the paste hardened, he broke the mold, exposing the bust. Finally, he retouched surface details—eyes, eyebrows, ears, hair, etc.—to "liven" the portrait.[5]

Busts were a rarity in the United States in the early nineteenth century. Those that existed were the work of sculptors from Italy who carved them in marble. They were expensive and commemorated, for the most part, public men of statewide or national prominence. American stonecutters at the time carved gravestones, mantelpieces, balustrades, and other architectural elements, but not busts. They lacked the training. Besides, the market for the costly commodity was small.

By the 1830s, however—first in New York, then New Orleans and other centers of burgeoning prosperity—an increasingly affluent clientele generated a demand for this symbol of status and refinement.

Crafting busts of plaster, rather than stone, made them accessible to more Americans. Plaster busts were relatively inexpensive and could be replicated fairly readily once a master was cast. Still, though, clients who could pay for them continued to commission busts of marble. The "sculptor" would pass the plaster bust along to the "carver," who replicated it in stone.

Given Mills's association with his uncle, he surely learned about two sculptors of New York City, John Frazee and John Henri Isaac Browere. Frazee and Browere had started creating plaster busts in the mid-1820s and their work was discussed in newspapers, art journals and popular "revues of culture and civilization," because the two New Yorkers were trailblazers.[6] Their technique was the one that Noah Parker used. But John Frazee had gone one step further. In 1827 he became the first American to sculpt a bust in marble.[7]

Also circulating in the popular press that would have come under Mills's eyes were articles about two sculptors who hailed from New England, Horatio Greenough and Hiram Powers. A generation younger than Frazee and Browere, these two Americans—both residing in Italy—started producing plaster busts in the 1830s. But they did not take life masks. They sculpted a clay original, then used that to make the molds for casting the bust in plaster. That alternate process for creating busts was more comfortable for the sitter, but more costly, too, and required several long sessions.[8] After creating the plaster bust, Greenough and Powers normally handed it over to an Italian stonecutter to reproduce in marble.

Mills had had two years of apprenticeship as a millwright in Syracuse.[9] Now he managed the plaster and cement mill that supplied the raw material of Parker's craft.[10] But his association with his uncle's profession was closer than that. One witness avowed that Mills identified himself as "an assistant of Mr. Parker."[11] Another account did not name Mills, but described his involvement as "a young man who accompanied" the bust maker.[12] Whatever his precise role, Mills would have become familiar with the procedure his uncle followed to create plaster busts. He would have had occasion to interact with his uncle's elite sitters.

In March of 1836, Noah Parker was approached by a new client, Colonel Warren C. Whitaker. A rich sugar cane planter in his thirties, Whitaker resided in East Feliciana Parish, Louisiana. From New Orleans, that was a day's journey by paddle wheel steamer up the Mississippi. With a score of enslaved house servants and field hands at his command, Colonel Whitaker enjoyed the status, prerogatives, and esteem of a local first family.[13] He engaged Mr. Parker to make a bust of his younger brother, his only brother, Washington, who had just died.

Two months earlier, Washington Whitaker had gotten into a barroom brawl in New Orleans. He had stabbed the bartender, killing the man, and stood trial for murder. The Whitaker family "used every exertion to effect his acquittal," but Washington was found guilty and sentenced to be hanged. His kinfolk appealed to the governor to commute the punishment, but in vain. "They even endeavored to effect his escape." But that, too, failed. Confined in the New Orleans prison awaiting execution, the condemned man despaired. Rather than disgrace his family with the ignominy of the gallows, Washington took his own life. He was 21 years old. The Whitakers were devastated.

Noah Parker took Washington's death mask in the prison cell "while the body was yet warm." Then the corpse was transported upriver, where Colonel Whitaker, the head of the family, buried his brother with military honors on their aged mother's plantation in West Feliciana Parish. By the end of March, Parker had retouched the surface details of the bust and delivered it to the client. So far, Mills had played his customary role in his uncle's business. But the "affair" was not over.

New Orleans press reports of the bartender's murder and the subsequent trial and suicide of Washington Whitaker mortified the already-traumatized family. Sensationalized accounts containing inaccuracies and untruths made their way into newspapers as far north as Boston.[14] Colonel Whitaker was outraged. One report, written by a "gentleman informant" in the *New-York Gazette* in August 1836 was particularly salacious. The stilted account of the family's ordeal concluded with a raucous episode. It described the "persecution" that Mills had suffered at the hands of Whitaker when Parker sent his nephew to collect payment from the Colonel for the bust. The article, Whitaker insisted, contained "gross exaggerations, and misrepresentations injurious to the character of persons of as great respectability and as of fair a reputation as any in Louisiana." And he inferred from the piece that the "gentleman informant" was none other than the bust maker's assistant, Clark Mills.

Raw with grief, Whitaker was roused by indignation and the obligation to defend the family's honor to respond. He solicited affidavits sworn before a Justice of the Peace from his overseer, John Collins, a neighbor named John Rist, and a house guest, Robert Ross, to refute what he took to be the mendacious words of Mills.

The price of the bust had come to $108.26, roughly $3,000.00 in today's currency, which was very high. A plaster bust would normally have sold for about $20.[15] It would appear, therefore, that Colonel Whitaker had authorized Parker to engage a carver to replicate the bust in marble. Regardless of why the bust was so expensive, Parker had not received the money by April. He sent Mills to collect it from Whitaker in person.

Mills took a steamboat up the Mississippi to Port Hudson, then leased a horse to reach the Colonel's residence. Making his way across country, he called at the place of John Rist, a sugar cane planter,[16] who later swore:

"As it was late in the day, and he [Mills] would have twelve miles still to ride before he could reach Col. W's, I invited him to put up his horse and stay the night with me. He did so. I treated him and his horse well, and as is the custom in this country, his night's entertainment cost him nothing. He might have indeed have made it profitable to *himself,* for I contracted with him to have the walks of my garden laid down in cement, and he promised to undertake the job as soon as he could get the materials from New Orleans. He has not however as yet fulfilled his part of the bargain. In the morning, after eating his breakfast, Mr. Mills started for Col. Whitaker's, I giving him directions for his way there."

What transpired that day in the Colonel's home was deposed by Robert Ross:[17]

"I was residing at the house of Col. Warren C. Whitaker . . . when a Mr. Clark Mills arrived there on business connected with the bust of Washington Whitaker. . . . Some trifling alterations in the finish of the bust being thought necessary, Mills undertook to make them. He had made but little progress in the work when his evident want of skill induced Col. W. to decline having the alterations made, for fear the bust would be spoiled."

Whitaker asked for the due-bill and handed Mills two notes of one hundred dollars. Mills could not make the change. He took one of the notes and agreed to receive the balance of $8.26 the next morning in Jackson, the closest town. Robert Ross avowed:

"I would add, that while Mr. Mills was at Col. Whitaker's house, which was several days, he was treated by the whole family with every mark of attention, politeness and hospitality. . . . [H]e left the house apparently in the very best humor."

Under oath, John Collins[18] concurred:

"[A]t the time a certain Mr. Mills visited Col. W. C. Whitaker in this parish, the deponent [Collins] was living with the latter in the capacity of overseer, and had every means of observing and knowing what kind of treatment Mills received during said visit; and that the same was courteous and friendly, such as ought to have been satisfactory to any person not remarkably fastidious. Deponent further says, that if any quarrel or difficulty had occurred between Col. Whitaker and the said Mr. Mills, the same would no doubt have come to the knowledge of deponent; but he has never had information of any difficulty occurring between them, nor does he believe there ever was any."

The next day, as promised, Whitaker rode into Jackson to meet with Mills and pay the outstanding $8.26. But the Colonel was unable to break his hundred-dollar bill. At last, though, he ran into his neighbor, John Rist, who obliged him by giving Mills eight dollars. The unpaid "two bits," Mills forgave so he could return to New Orleans without further delay. Rist later deposed:

"Between two and three o'clock next afternoon, he [Mills] rode up to my gate again, and I asked him to alight and walk in. He declined doing so, saying he was in a hurry for the five o'clock boat for New Orleans, and wished to get to Port Hudson as soon as possible. He put off, and I have never seen him since, although he promised at parting to come again in a short time, and fix my garden walks.... I would add that I never heard him make any complaint about his treatment at Col. Whitaker's, where I have every reason to believe he met with all that hospitality and kindness for which the Colonel is proverbial. As to his story about the fight, there is not one word of truth in it, as every body in this parish knows. The fact is, the man is a tremendous liar."

"His story about the fight:" that was the salacious report that appeared in the *New-York Gazette* and was copied in newspapers up and down the East Coast. "Some of the facts... are so monstrous," the editor of *The Schenectady Cabinet* forewarned his readers, "as almost to transcend belief." Headed "The Whitakers," the piece described Mills's visit to Whitaker's place to collect payment for the Washington bust this way:

The elder brother [Colonel Whitaker] bade him [Mills] be off, or he would kill him and drew his knife, but his purpose was prevented by the interposition of his mother.—The young man [Mills] mounted his horse, and was returning to New Orleans, but was intercepted the next evening on the road by two of the Whitakers, painted and disguised. They first insulted him by asking him who he was, whence he came, &c. but he knowing their object, drew a pistol and shot one of them dead on the spot. He fled soon after, abandoned his horse, and took to the woods, where he secreted himself during the day, and travelled by night. An hour after his arrival at New Orleans, he had been preceded by the remaining Whitaker and another person who inquired for him at his lodgings. His landlord kindly informed him of the fact, and placed him on board a ship for Mobile, at which place he arrived in safety.[19]

Either Mills related this narrative to his uncle, as Whitaker presumed, or Noah Parker made it up, because it was Parker who had submitted the piece—in writing—to the *New-York Gazette*. Parker, not Mills, was the "gentleman informant." Parker himself made that defiant revelation, insisting that his statements were "true in all essential points."[20]

Nevertheless, by early November the nation's newspapers were printing retractions.

The *New York Evening Post* took pains—"from a regard for truth"—to refute every assertion made in the story, one after the other.[21] Other dailies did likewise.[22] Even the *New-York Gazette*, "as an act of common justice," explained the regrettable circumstances that had allowed the article to go to press in the first place.[23] The editor of the newspaper had been attending the funeral of his predecessor, the apology went, when "a person who acted for a day or two only as his substitute" found the manuscript and "gave it a ready insertion."

The point-by-point refutation that the Colonel would eventually publish under the title, "A Vindication of the Whitaker Family," filled two pages with emotional newsprint. It included not only the sworn depositions of his overseer, neighbor, and house guest, but also letters of condolence that he had received from three of "the most estimable citizens of Feliciana." Whitaker himself remarked in his passionate "vindication:"

> "[W]hile at my house Mr. Mills behaved himself with politeness and propriety, and my treatment of him was precisely the same as if he *had* been a 'gentleman.' I can only account for his after conduct by supposing that having appropriated his uncle's money to his own use, he invented his heroic tale to account for its nonappearance, and to conceal the theft of which he was guilty."

Long before any retractions or rebuttals appeared, though, Mills was gone. And so was Noah Parker. The bust maker was back in New York, where he submitted his manuscript titled, "The Whitakers," to the *Gazette*. Parker was to insist "that he had lodged in the same house with the Whitakers, was in their confidence, and would vouch for the truth of his story."[24] He never backed down.

Did Mills hand the $108.00 over to his uncle? If he did, Parker's fabrication sullied his nephew's reputation and forced him to flee. But what motive Parker may have had for spinning such a yarn—and publicizing it in a newspaper—is hard to conjecture. If the story was indeed a lie, Mills was wronged by his uncle, just as he had been mistreated by another uncle in his boyhood.

On the other hand, if Mills pocketed the $108 and told his uncle the tale to conceal his treachery, then it was Noah Parker who was wronged and compelled to flee. Why Mills would have behaved in this manner, though, cannot be fathomed.

Either way, uncle and nephew both had a compelling incentive to leave New Orleans, which they did precipitously.

Mills's sojourn in the Crescent City lasted less than a year, but the experience influenced his future. The rustic orphan had seen a universe dazzlingly unlike the backcountry of upstate New York that had left him unsatisfied. Working with his uncle, he had participated in a livelihood that ingratiated the sculptor into the client's sphere of opulence and power. Mills had been received into the residence of an aristocratic planter and treated by the proprietor and his enslaved servants as a gentleman. The rough-and-tumble waif had learned how to behave "with politeness and propriety." Most life-changing of all, though, Mills had tasted the euphoria of personal creativity. The compulsive sketching on his schoolhouse slate had evidently denoted something deeper in the boy than whimsy.

Despite its pivotal importance for him, though, the year 1836 would never figure in the "official life story" Mills was always quick to tell. The sole trace of his time in New Orleans would remain buried in faded newsprint that impugned his name. No one would know, 20 years later, when Mills returned as an official guest of the city—when he was celebrated, feasted, and honored by the citizenry—that the famous sculptor had been there once before. Yet it was there, indeed, at the age of 20, that Mills resolved that he could do anything he put his mind to. His "want of skill" (as one observer put it) could be remedied—though not in Syracuse.

When he left New Orleans, Mills did not backtrack up the Mississippi and Ohio rivers to New York State. He ventured onward to Charleston.

NOTES

1   Description of New Orleans in 1836, unless otherwise cited, is derived from "New Orleans" at https://en.wikipedia.org/wiki/New_Orleans.
2   "Mr. Clark Mills, the Sculptor," *The Round Table*, vol. 1, no. 22 (May 14, 1864): 340. See also "Clark Mills at Home," *The Washington Post*, Feb. 7, 1880, p. 2; and "Clark Mills," *New-York Tribune*, Jan. 13, 1883, p. 5. No biographical sketch of Mills other than these three mentions his time in New Orleans.
3   Description of the Whitaker affair and all quotations, unless otherwise cited, are derived from: (1) "Depravity," *The Schenectady Cabinet*, Aug. 17, 1836, p. 2 (this is a reprint of "The Whitakers," *New-York Gazette*, about Aug. 11,

1836, which was copied in many newspapers); (2) "[From the New York Evening Post.]," *Albany* [N.Y.] *Evening Journal*, Aug. 13, 1836, p. 2; (3) "The Whitakers," [N.Y.] *Commercial Advertiser*, Nov. 4, 1836, p. 1 and 2; (4) "The Whitakers," [N.Y.] *Commercial Advertiser*, Nov. 5, 1836, p. 2; (5) "The Louisiana Whitakers," [Boston] *Columbian Centinel*, Nov. 9, 1836, p. 1; (6) [no title], [N.Y.] *Morning Herald*, May 4, 1838, p. 2; and (7) "A Vindication of the Whitaker Family," [Washington] *Native American*, Aug. 18, 1838, p. 1 and 4.

4   Efforts to identify Noah Parker in censuses, newspapers, city directories and published local history have been unsuccessful. Everything known about him derives from the sources listed in note 3. Particularly important for establishing the nephew/uncle relationship of Mills and Parker is a quotation of Robert Ross. He stated under oath, "This bust (a cast) as I understood from Mills, had been made by an uncle of his in the city [New Orleans]," quoted in "A Vindication...," *Native American*, Aug. 18, 1838, p. 4.

5   Regarding this process, see Bk. 1, Ch. 5.

6   John Frazee (1790–1852), see https://en.wikipedia.org/wiki/John_Frazee_(sculptor). John Henri Isaac Browere (1790–1834), see https://en.wikipedia.org/wiki/John_Henri_Isaac_Browere.

7   Catherine Hoover Voorsanger and John K. Howat, eds., *Art and the Empire City: New York, 1825–1861* (New Haven and London: Yale University Press, 2000): 137–41.

8   Horatio Greenough (1805–52), see https://en.wikipedia.org/wiki/Horatio_Greenough. Hiram Powers (1805–73), see https://en.wikipedia.org/wiki/Hiram_Powers.

9   See Bk. 1, Ch. 1.

10 "Clark Mills...," *The Round Table*, vol. 1, no. 22 (May 14, 1864): 340: "left the employment to take charge of a plaster and cement mill;" and "Clark Mills...," *The Washington Post*, Feb. 7, 1880, p. 2: "then he took charge of a plaster and cement mill. He remained in New Orleans about one year;" and "Clark Mills," *New-York Tribune*, Jan. 13, 1883, p. 5: "for one year he had charge of a plaster and cement mill in New-Orleans."

11 Warren C. Whitaker, quoted in "A Vindication...," *Native American*, Aug. 18, 1838, p. 1 and 4.

12 "Depravity," *Schenectady Cabinet*, Aug. 17, 1836, p. 2.

13 "W C [sic] Whitaker" entry, 1840 U.S. Census, East Feliciana Parish, La., p. 14 (handwritten), p. 262 (stamped); NARA M704, roll 130.

14 [Boston] *Columbian Centinel* (Aug. 13, 1836, p. 4), *Boston Courier* (Aug. 15, 1836, p. 4), and [Boston] *American Traveller* (Aug.16, 1836, p. 1) all reprinted "The Whitakers," *New-York Gazette*.

15 Ten years later Mills would be pricing his plaster busts at $25–$35. See Bk. 1, Ch. 13.

16 John Rist entry, 1840 U.S. Census, East Feliciana Parish, La., p. 12 (handwritten), p. 260 (stamped); NARA M704, roll 130.
17 Robert Ross was a portrait painter.
18 John Collins entry, 1840 U.S. Census, East Feliciana Parish, La., p. 11 (handwritten), p. 259 (stamped); NARA M704, roll 130.
19 "Depravity," *Schenectady Cabinet*, Aug. 17, 1836, p. 2.
20 "The Whitakers," *Commercial Advertiser*, Nov. 5, 1836, p. 2.
21 "[From the New York Evening Post.]," *Albany Evening Journal*, Aug. 13, 1836, p. 2.
22 See, for example, "[From the New York Evening Post.]," *Albany Evening Journal*, Aug. 13, 1836, p. 2.
23 "The Louisiana Whitakers," *Columbian Centinel*, Nov. 9, 1836, p. 1.
24 "The Whitakers," *Commercial Advertiser*, Nov. 4, 1836, p. 1 and 2; and "The Louisiana Whitakers," *Columbian Centinel*, Nov. 9, 1836, p. 1.

CHAPTER 3

Fall 1836–Fall 1838

When about nineteen, he commenced the business of plastering, in Charleston, without ever having served at the trade.

"Clark Mills and His Statue," *Camden* [S.C.] *Journal*, reprinted in "Clark Mills," [Charleston] *Courier*, May 8, 1850, p. 2.

To be precise, Mills was 20. And it is probable that he did in fact pick up "the business of plastering" easily. He was quick to catch onto things, and he had innate artistic talent. In addition, he had operated a "plaster and cement mill" in New Orleans for his uncle, a maker of portrait busts. Nevertheless, Mills must have served, at least for a while, as "an apprentice to a plasterer"—as a less partial *Brooklyn Daily Eagle* reporter would write.[1] The craft required particular tools and materials and skills that had to be mastered.

From New Orleans to Charleston, Mills may have sailed. Brigs ferried passengers between these two major seaports every "fortnight" in 1836—that is, every two weeks.[2] By this time, though, railroads connected Charleston to Mobile, Alabama. Mills could have sailed the short distance from New Orleans to Mobile, then taken "the cars"—as trains were called at that time—to Charleston. That trip, though, necessitated several transfers from the rails of one company to those of another, an arduous exercise. Traveling by sea took longer—navigating around Florida—but would have been a more pleasant journey.[3] Mills's choice of transport likely depended on his purse. However the questing New Yorker reached Charleston, that is where he would settle, at least, for a dozen years.[4]

No published source reveals why Mills chose to put down roots in Charleston. One possible attraction may have been the city's resemblance to New Orleans, only on a much-reduced scale. With a population of roughly 30,000 people, Charleston was about two-fifths the size of the Crescent City.[5] Prosperous, cultured, powerful and proud, the metropolis was built on the production of rice, indigo and cotton, shipping, retailing and the slave trade. About one-third Black—counting enslaved and free—Charleston was dominated socially and economically by a White gentry of lineage and land. Other traits that the flat, low-lying port shared with New Orleans were periodic hurricanes and visitations of yellow fever and cholera. When Mills entered Charleston, many of its residents were deathly ill. An outbreak of cholera was running its course between August and October of 1836. The epidemic took 380 lives, mostly people of color.

Mills worked sundry jobs to sustain himself. One was "sprinkler of dusty avenues."[6] None of Charleston's streets was paved. Riding a horse-drawn water cart, Mills doused the dirt roadways "to lay the dust" and wash away the horse dung. (City fathers tended to pay particular attention to adequate street cleaning after occurrences of disease.) But Mills would not remain a laborer for long. Early on, he "learned the stucco trade."[7]

Stucco is a fine white plaster used for architectural decoration, such as chandelier medallions, cornices, and wall and ceiling moldings, including coffers.[8] Much stucco work was "run in place," but some was cast in molds in a workshop, then assembled and installed in the intended place. Having tried and abandoned a half dozen livelihoods in his brief span of years, Mills stuck with this one. Apparently, it was the element of personal creativity that made the difference.

Mills already knew how to crush and heat shells to make lime and how to mix the lime with gypsum and water to make plaster paste. Learning to fine-tune the proportions of the ingredients to obtain different kinds of plaster, however, required diligent application. Stucco

Charleston, S.C., viewed from the harbor, 1837. The patronage of rich and powerful slaveholding men of South Carolina allowed Mills, a scarcely literate but headstrong, shrewd and hard-working house plasterer, to achieve his audacious goal of becoming a sculptor. (Print made ca. 1845 from an engraving in *The Family Magazine; or, Monthly Abstract of General Knowledge,*" 1837, p. 201, courtesy of the South Caroliniana Library, University of South Carolina, Columbia, S.C.)

was very fine and served well for indoor decorative detail. Plaster of Paris, coarser than stucco and quicker-setting, was also used on interior surfaces. Roman cement, on the other hand, was a sturdier compound that held up to weather. It was used to coat the exterior of buildings, often being scored to simulate stone. Mills also worked with scagliola, a composite that imitated marble. It was used for floors, columns, and other ornamental interior work.[9]

Mills appreciated the versatility of plaster: it could be modeled, cast, incised, colored, stamped, or stenciled. All of which required tools. He bought a chest full of trowels, chisels, brushes, rasps with teeth, rasps without teeth, miter rods, design templates, and molds for casting egg-and-dart molding, bead and reel units, floral swags, acanthus foliage, and other stock elements of decoration. He also purchased equipment—buckets, ladders, a hod, planks and rope to erect scaffolding, tarpaulins—as well as supplies—shells, gypsum, lattice strips, paints, glazes, maybe even gold leaf for gilding. He acquired everything he needed "on account," making payments when he was able.[10] His earnings were two dollars a day.[11]

The requisite skills, tools, equipment, and materials for plastering—as well as the soul of an artist—were all akin to those of a sculptor. Mills could not have suspected it at the time, but he surely would realize it later in life: as he "learned the stucco trade," he was in effect a sculptor-in-training.

Affluent Charlestonians supported a phalanx of plasterers—Caucasian, free Black and slave. The seaport's opulent architecture, both interior and exterior, was a point of civic pride. Mills's occupation took him into the city's public buildings and churches and the grand residences of its aristocracy. Even the dwellings of tradesmen contained plaster decoration, just plainer, with less surface decoration. It could have been his livelihood, therefore, that brought Mills face to face with Eliza Susanna Tucker Ballentine.[12] More likely, though, it was his love of horses.

"Well, I had always a passion for horses," Mills once told a reporter. "When I was a plasterer in Charleston, and with very little money to spare, I always owned the finest horses I could find."[13] Surely, then, Mills had dealings with hostlers, saddlers and harness makers. And Eliza's father, Alexander Ballentine, was a harness maker. He plied his trade at the intersection of Market and Beaufain Streets, the heart of the city's commercial district.[14] That's where he resided with his wife, five children—including daughter Eliza—and a free Black female domestic.[15]

Clark Mills and Eliza Ballentine could not have had a very long courtship. They were married less than a year after Mills arrived in Charleston. It was July 2, 1837, a Sunday evening.[16] Mills was "nearly 21," Eliza, 17.[17] Although the marriage notice appeared in the *Charleston Observer*, a Presbyterian weekly, the couple were wed in Trinity Church, the oldest Methodist parish in the city. It stood on the corner of Hasell Street and Maiden Lane, three blocks from the Ballentine home.[18] The Reverend Mr. James Sewell, pastor, officiated.[19]

Prior to the wedding, the bride, groom, and father of the bride had all signed a "marriage settlement." By the terms of this legal instrument—witnessed, but not recorded right away—Alexander Ballentine promised to provide a dowry of $700 for his daughter. It was a stunningly large amount for a tradesman with a numerous family, the equivalent of about $19,000 today.

> *The Said Marriage Portion or dowry . . . Should be retained and Kept in the hands and Custody of the Said Alexr. Ballentine untill Such time as a reasonable and Judicious investment thereof Could be Effected in such property as the Said Clark Mills might Elect.*[20]

However, a telling proviso followed. The property purchased with the dowry was:

> *Subject nevertheless in no manner or form to the Engagements, liabilities or Contracts of the Said Clark Mills.*

Obviously, Alexander Ballentine was wary of his son-in-law-to-be. Mills was in debt.

In November of 1837, four months after the wedding, the plasterer was the target of a disturbing incident that may have been perpetrated by a disgruntled creditor. Mills narrowly escaped injury. But he did not cower. Rather, he posted a defiant response in the Charleston *Courier*:

> The ropes that secured the scaffolding in front of a house in King-st. erected for the purpose of making some repairs to the building, were cut by some evil disposed person or persons, on Thursday night last, and the Subscriber is desirous of detecting whoever was concerned therein. He therefore offers a reward of $50, to any one who will discover those engaged in an offence which would if successful, not only injure him in a pecuniary view, but might also cause the destruction of human life. It is hoped and believed that every good citizen will aid in the detection of the offender.   CLARK MILLS.[21]

Candidates for the "evil disposed person or persons" were several:

C. &. J. Gibbes vs. Clark Mills[22]

In January 1838, C. & J. Gibbes, commission merchants, brought suit against Mills for $366.34. Mills had purchased "goods, wares and merchandise sold and delivered to him upon open account," but had refused to pay for them. After a series of legal actions by plaintiff and defendant, the Charleston County Court of Common Pleas ordered Mills to pay C. & J. Gibbes $175 plus costs, which brought the amount to $201.

George W. Olney vs. Clark Mills[23]

In September 1838, George W. Olney, a Charleston merchant, filed suit against Mills for loans amounting to $650 that Mills refused to repay, "altho often requested so to do." Summoned to the Court of Common Pleas, Mills confessed to a much smaller debt than Olney claimed. Ultimately, the court decreed that Olney recover from Mills $351.07.

R. R. Hunt vs. Clark Mills and Clark Mills vs. R. R. Hunt[24]
In November 1838, Reuben R. Hunt sued Mills for $400 for "nonperformance of certain promises and assumptions." Mills admitted buying a bay horse from Hunt on a promissory note, but told the Court of Common Pleas that he found the animal to be "unsound and valueless." After much haggling and a counter-suit by Mills, the court ordered him to pay Hunt $123.85.

Clearly, Mills's freewheeling financial dealings caused hard feelings among men who extended credit to him in good faith. However, there is no evidence that the vandals who severed the ropes of his scaffolding on King Street—and might have caused "the destruction of human life"—were peeved creditors. The "evil disposed person or persons" were never discovered.

At about nine o'clock on the evening of April 27, 1838, alarm bells throughout Charleston began to clamor. Two blocks from Alexander Ballentine's workshop and home, fire had broken out. The flames spread quickly from building to building. The city was in the grip of a long spell of dry weather. Block after block succumbed rapidly to the conflagration. Trinity Church, the historic wooden structure where Clark and Eliza were wed, was reduced to ashes.[25] Before drastic measures succeeded in containing it, the "Great Fire" had leveled a quarter of Charleston.[26] Ballentine very likely lost his home and workshop, together with his tools and leather supply, because the 1840 census taker would find him and his family residing in the less densely populated neighborhood north of the city called the "Charleston Neck."[27] Ironically, though, for Mills the disaster was likely a boon.

Rebuilding the "late beautiful and flourishing, but now fallen city" created plentiful work for tradesmen, including plasterers.[28] By the autumn of the catastrophic year, despite being enmeshed in multiple judicial disputes, Mills was positioned to acquire a prime piece of Charleston real estate. On September 1st he bought a lot 44 feet wide and roughly 130 feet deep at the southern tip of the city, several blocks below the burned-out borough.[29]

It was lot number 9 on the south side of Lamboll Street, just a block off the Ashley River. The seller was a prosperous planter, ship builder and merchant named James Poyas.[30] The price was $1,800. Mills handed Poyas three dollars cash and Poyas assumed a mortgage in the form of two "bonds and obligations:" one for $560, the other for $1,240.[31] If Mills paid them with interest, as agreed, number 9 Lamboll Street would be his. If he defaulted, the lot would revert to Poyas. There was no house on the property.[32] Mills probably intended to build one.

Five months after buying land, Mills turned his attention to another money matter. He decided on *"a reasonable and Judicious investment"* for Eliza's dowry: *"a certain Mulatto boy named Phillip."*[33]

NOTES

1 [no title], *Brooklyn Daily Eagle*, Feb. 27, 1860, p. 2.
2 Daniel J. Dowling, *The Charleston Directory; And Register, for 1835–36* (Charleston: Daniel J. Dowling, pub. and print., 1835): 159. The transcribed edition of this work by James W. Hagy, *Directories for the City of Charleston, South Carolina* (Baltimore: Clearfield, 1997), available online, is incomplete and does not include the "Packets" and other information of the original.
3 Samuel Augustus Mitchell, *Mitchell's map of the United States: showing the principal travelling turnpike and common roads, . . . also the courses of the canals & rail roads . . .* (Philadelphia: S. A. Mitchell, 1836), at https://www.loc.gov/item/87692342.
4 "Mr. Clark Mills, the Sculptor," *The Round Table*, vol. 1, no. 22 (May 14, 1864): 340.
5 Description of Charleston, unless otherwise cited, is derived from: (1) Walter J. Fraser, Jr., *Charleston! Charleston! The History of a Southern City* (Columbia, S.C.: University of South Carolina Press, 1989); and (2) W. Williams, *Charleston*; map published in 1849, at www.carolana.com.

6   "Clark Mills and His Equestrian Statue," *DeBow's Review*, vol. 16 (Jan. 1854): 39, 41.
7   "Mr. Clark Mills, the Sculptor," *The Round Table*, vol. 1, no. 22 (May 14, 1864): 340.
8   David Flaharty, *Preserving Historic Ornamental Plaster*, Technical Preservation Services Brief No. 23 (National Park Service, U.S. Department of the Interior, Oct. 1990), at https://www.nps.gov/orgs/1739/upload/preservation-brief-23-ornamental-plaster.pdf.
9   A[loha] Vivarttas, "The Clark Mills Furnace—A Reminiscence," *The Railroad and Engineering Journal*, vol. 63 (July 1889): 327.
10 C. & J. Gibbes vs. Clark Mills, Charleston County Court of Common Pleas, Judgment Rolls, L10018 (1839), no. 281A; South Carolina Department of Archives and History, Columbia.
11 "Sketches of Washington. By Childe Harold," *Brooklyn Daily Eagle*, Mar. 30, 1853, p. 2.
12 Unfortunately, no plasterwork of any kind in Charleston today can be identified as Mills's handiwork.
13 "An Hour with Clark Mills," [Washington] *Evening Star*, Dec. 24, 1870, p. 1. See also Bk. 1, Chs. 17 and 21.
14 Daniel J. Dowling, *The Charleston Directory; And Register, for 1837–38* (Charleston: Daniel J. Dowling, pub. and print., 1837); transcribed selectively in Hagy, *Directories for the City of Charleston*, 73.
15 Alexander Ballantine [sic] entry, 1830 U.S. Census, Ward 4, Charleston, S.C., p. 75; NARA M19, roll 170.
16 "Marriages," *Charleston Observer*, July 8, 1837, p. 3.
17 Letter, T[heophilus] F[isk] Mills to Elliott Woods, Superintendent, U.S. Capitol and Grounds, July 29, 1910; Archives, Office of the Architect of the Capitol, Washington, D.C. Also "Obituary," Eliza Susanna Tucker Mills, [Charleston] *Courier*, Aug. 30, 1855, p. 2.
18 Dowling, *Charleston Directory . . . for 1835-36*, 158. The transcribed edition of this work in Hagy, *Directories for the City of Charleston,* available online, is incomplete and does not include the "Churches and Ministers" and other information of the original. This parish is Trinity United Methodist Church today.
19 "Marriages," *Charleston Observer*, July 8, 1837, p. 3.
20 Trustee Bill of Sale in Trust, Mills Clark and Eliza his wife to Ballantine [sic] Alexander, Feb. 18, 1839, recorded May 14, 1839; South Carolina Department of Archives and History, Secretary of State, Miscellaneous Records, vol. 5-V: 282–84. The document states in quotation marks the terms that were "mutually understood and agreed upon by and between the Said Parties *Prior to* the intermarriage of the Said Eliza, and the Said Clark Mills." (emphasis added)
21 [no title], [Charleston] *Courier*, Nov. 11, 1837, p. 5.
22 C. & J. Gibbes vs. Clark Mills, Charleston County Court of Common Pleas, Judgment Rolls, L10018 (1839), no. 281A; South Carolina Department of Archives and History, Columbia.

23 George W. Olney vs. Clark Mills, Charleston County Court of Common Pleas, Judgment Rolls, L10018 (1839), no. 287; South Carolina Department of Archives and History, Columbia.
24 Clark Mills vs. R. R. Hunt, Charleston County Court of Common Pleas, Judgment Rolls, L10018 (1839), no. 257A; South Carolina Department of Archives and History, Columbia.
25 "Trinity Methodist Church Original Site," The Historical Marker Database, at https://www.hmdb.org/m.asp?m=31850.
26 "Charleston Fire of April 1838," at http://halseymap.com/flash/window.asp?HMID=48.
27 Alexander Ballentine entry, 1840 U.S. Census, Charleston Neck, Charleston, S.C., p. 112; NARA M704, roll 509.
28 "Mayor's Office," [Charleston] *Southern Patriot*, Apr. 30, 1838, p. 2.
29 Conveyance in Fee, Poyas James to Mills Clarke [sic], Sept. 1, 1838, recorded Sept. 8, 1838; RMC Book W10, p. 239–40; Charleston County Deeds, Charleston County Register of Deeds, Charleston, S.C. The author thanks Christina Rae Butler of Butler Preservation, L.C., Research Consulting and Renovation, Charleston, for the reports she prepared, 2018–24, on several Charleston properties.
30 Dowling, *Charleston Directory . . . for 1840–41,* transcribed selectively in Hagy, *Directories for the City of Charleston,* 122. For the launches of two of Poyas' ships, see [Charleston] *Courier,* Jan. 10, 1837, p. 2, and Jan. 18, 1839, p. 2.
31 Mortgage, Mills Clarke [sic] to Poyas James, Sept. 1, 1838, recorded Sept. 4, 1838; RMC Book W10, p. 234–36; Charleston County Deeds, Charleston County Register of Deeds, Charleston, S.C.
32 Four facts suggest that the lot was vacant when Mills bought it: (1) Charleston land records normally state "with the buildings thereon" when there is a structure on the property, but the 1838 "conveyance in fee" for the Lamboll Street lot does not contain this phrase; (2) If there had been a house on the lot, Mills would have lived there, but the 1840–41 directory of Charleston records Mills on Mary Street, not Lamboll. The directory lists 12 Lamboll Street residents, but none specifically at no. 9; (3) The 1840 U.S. Census does not list Clark Mills as a head of household, signifying that he did not reside in a house of his own, but rather someone else's; and (4) The 1852 tax-assessment values of neighboring houses on Lamboll Street, frame as well as brick, were all much higher than $1,800. These are the earliest tax records extant; it is possible that property values increased substantially between 1838 and 1852. Report of Christina Rae Butler of Butler Preservation, L.C., Research Consulting and Renovation, Charleston, 2018.
33 Trustee Bill of Sale in Trust, Mills Clark and Eliza his wife to Ballantine [sic] Alexander, Feb. 18, 1839, vol. 5-V: 282–84.

CHAPTER 4
February 1839–February 1844

Will be sold THIS DAY, the 4th May, before my office, north east corner of the Court House, by virtue of sundry writs of fieri facias to me directed, at half past 12 o'clock, . . . a Negro Boy, named Philip, about 20 years old, a first rate plasterer by trade. Levied on and to be sold as the property of Clark Mills, at the suit of George W. Olney.

"Sheriff's Sale," [Charleston] *Courier*, May 4, 1840, p. 3.

On February 18, 1839, Alexander Ballentine handed his son-in-law $700 cash. According to the "marriage settlement" that Mills had signed before marrying Ballentine's daughter, the money was "*the Marriage Portion or dowry of his wife, the said Eliza.*" Mills had elected to use the entire amount to purchase "*a certain Mulatto boy named Phillip, agreed to be sold to him by James Davidson of Charleston.*"[1] However, the two-page Trustee Bill of Sale in Trust, which was witnessed and recorded at the Charleston County Courthouse, included other, telling provisions. It recorded also that Ballentine paid Mills $5.00 cash for:

> *the household and Kitchen furniture now in the possession of the said Clark Mills, viz., Bedstead, Bed and Bed furniture, Chests of Drawers, Crockery, China, Chairs, Tables, Table Cloths, Glasses, Spoons, Knives, Forks, Pots, Kettles, and all other like articles.*

But that was not all. Ballentine would hold "*the boy Phillip*" and the household and kitchen furniture:

> *in Trust, to and for the Sole And Exclusive use, benefit, and behalf of the Said Eliza Mills for and during the term of her natural life and after her Death then in trust to and for the use, maintenance, benefit*

and behalf of the lawful issue of the Said Eliza, to be and remain clear and free now and forever of All and Singular the Debts, Contracts, liabilities and demands whatsoever of or from the Said Clark Mills or any other person or persons whatsoever.

Dowries and pre-nuptial agreements, called "marriage settlements," were not uncommon in South Carolina at this time.[2] However, the terms of this one were not only uncommon, but revealing, as well. Mills was to have no legal claim to any of the household goods or to the "*Mulatto boy named Phillip*" purchased with Eliza's dowry. Everything would be held in trust for Eliza's benefit. Even if she should predecease her husband, the property would not be inherited by him. It would continue to be held in trust "for the use of the Said Clark Mills, his Heirs and Assigns forever." Clearly, Ballentine's distrust of this son-in-law's financial habits had not changed. He was ensuring the future welfare of his daughter and expected grandchild. Eliza was seven months pregnant.[3]

The *Charleston City Directory for 1840 and 1841* records: "Mills, Clarke, Plasterer, Mary St."[4] That was in the neighborhood just north of Charleston called the "Northern Neck." It was less densely populated than the city, downright rural in parts, and would not be incorporated into Charleston until December 1849. Since Mills is not named in the 1840 U.S. census as a head of household, he and Eliza must have been counted as members of someone else's household.[5] After the "Great Fire," Alexander Ballentine had moved his family to the Northern Neck, where he managed to "get back on his feet." A kinsman of his, John Ballentine, a saddler, resided there, too, right on Mary Street.[6] Extended families helped one another through difficult times. Not only Charlestonians, but people across the country were enduring the depressed economy that followed the Panic of 1837.[7] Clark and Eliza were obviously renting lodgings close to her kin. Mary Street was four blocks long. The depot of the South Carolina

Railroad anchored its western end and the Cooper River lapped at its eastern end.

Although the Northern Neck was home to skilled workers, such as the Ballentines and Mills, its population was vastly diverse.[8] Residents included not only saddlers, harness makers and at least one house plasterer, but also a carpenter, distiller, rice merchant, ship captain, wood factor, broker, one affluent planter (during the winter social season), five grocers, a farmer, and the editor of the *Mercury* newspaper. A majority of them owned slaves; most, just one or two; others, as many as 14. Some of the tradesmen trained their slaves as apprentices, then worked with them, side-by-side, in their shops. Others derived income from "hiring out" their bondmen. Free families of color lived on every block of the Northern Neck. One free woman of color had a husband who was enslaved. Alexander and John Ballentine were in the minority; they did not own slaves. Alexander, however, now held in trust for his daughter Eliza Mills the *"Mulatto boy"* Philip Reid.

He was about 18 years old, some five years younger than Clark Mills.[9] Years later Mills would swear that he purchased Reid *"because of his evident talent for the business in which he [Mills] was engaged."*[10] The youth was "a first rate plasterer by trade."[11] That description suggests that Reid was an experienced craftsman, proficient in making various kinds of plasters, applying and sculpting them *in situ*, and casting plaster forms in a workshop. Mills had made an astute choice. He gained a seasoned assistant immediately, no lengthy and costly apprenticeship required.

The young Black tradesman was a native of South Carolina.[12] A Ledger of Depositors of the Freedmen's Bank in Charleston would one day record his father as "Caleb" (no surname) and his mother as "Fanny Reed." Philip Reid had evidently acquired his surname from his mother (the two spellings, Reed and Reid, were used interchangeably at that time).[13] He had three brothers and four sisters.[14]

A "Slave Sale" near the wharfs of Charleston's harbor, where slavers arriving from Baltimore, Md., Alexandria, Va., and other ports of the Upper South docked and unloaded their human cargo. Auctions of enslaved persons were also held regularly at Charleston's Slave Market on Chalmers Street. (*Illustrated London News*, Nov. 29, 1856, p. 555)

They were all bound to service for life. The 1840 U.S. census of South Carolina, as well as the 1840–41 directory of Charleston, enumerate several slave-owning heads of household named Reed and Reid. Any one of these individuals may have been Philip's original master.

By the time he was sold to Mills, however, Reid's owner was a man named James Davidson. Only one James Davidson is listed in Charleston directories, 1835 through 1841, a "Painter" residing at 42 Tradd Street."[15] The 1840 U.S. census records 10 slaves in his household, including seven males, 10 to 23 years of age.[16] This suggests that Davidson was the proprietor of a house painting business with an enslaved workforce. Painters worked closely with plasterers. Mills may have leased Reid from Davidson before buying him. He would have wanted to be sure that the young man's temperament was compatible with his own. Seven hundred dollars was a high price to pay, even for a "first-rate" tradesman.

A master plasterer now, with a more-than-competent helper, Mills could solicit more work and bid on more contracts. On the other hand, he had taken on additional financial obligation: another dependent to feed, clothe and shelter. Moreover, in April 1839 Eliza delivered her second child. But Mills's income had diminished. Following the Great Fire of 1838, "an immense influx" of tradesmen and laborers had flocked to Charleston. Re-erecting the city's commercial district—some 500 properties—had provided employment for all.[17] But as building after building rose from the ashes, jobs decreased, competition increased, and wages declined.[18] Depressing income further was the economic slump that came with the outbreak of yellow fever in the spring of 1839. It grew into the worst epidemic that Charleston had ever known and raged through the summer.[19]

Mills and his wife and infant survived. But he defaulted on the mortgage he held for no. 9 Lamboll Street. The property reverted to James Poyas. The lot was still vacant, as Poyas's subsequent resale price was much too low for a house.[20] So Mills's family would never reside on Lamboll Street. His status as a landowner had not lasted long.

Moreover, he had been unable to muster the court-ordered $351.07 he owed George W. Olney. By the spring of 1840, the irate merchant would be put off no longer. He complained to the Court of Common Pleas, which sent *fieri facias* to Alexander H. Brown, sheriff of Charleston County. The writ instructed the officer to seize upon and auction off property belonging to Clark Mills to satisfy the judgment against him. In spite of the explicit stipulation of the prenuptial agreement—that the property bought with Eliza's dowry would never belong to Clark Mills—Sheriff Brown seized upon "*the Mulatto boy Phillip.*"

The first notice of the "Sheriff's Sale" appeared in the *Courier* in April: "A Negro Boy, named Philip, about 20 years old, a first rate plasterer by trade," would be auctioned off at the Charleston County Courthouse on Monday, May 4, 1840.[21] The fourth and final notice was published that very morning. Yet the auction never took place. Mills—or, more likely, his father-in-law—must have made a last-minute settlement with George W. Olney. Mills got to keep his "first-rate" helper.

The following year, Philip Reid probably worked with Mills on an important job for the City of Charleston. Reported the *Southern Patriot* of August 11, 1841:

> Alderman Schnierle from the Committee on Contracts, who were requested to advertise for estimates for covering the west and south sides of the Guard House with Roman Cement, and coloring the building: Reported that the estimates enclosed were all that had been received, and recommended that the offer of Clark Mills be accepted for $450, the money to be paid when the Committee on Contracts shall be satisfied that the materials are of the best quality and the work executed in a workmanlike manner. Concurred in.[22]

This is the earliest known interaction between Mills and John Schnierle, a city alderman at the time, formerly a representative in the South Carolina legislature, and later to serve two non-consecutive terms as mayor of Charleston.[23] A strong friendship was to grow between the two men, though on what basis is unclear. Schnierle—pronounced and sometimes misspelled as "Schnerlie"—was a wealthy attorney of 33 with a wife, two children (six more would follow), and two slaves (18 more would follow).[24] He held the rank of Major General in the state militia.

Schnierle's father was a carpenter from Germany. Exercising industry and thrift, the immigrant had acquired property and the comforts of the middle class and sent his son to college. In the fashionable neighborhood of the Parishes of St. Philip's and St. Michael's, he had built a fine Greek Revival house.[25] When the well-off tradesman died in 1844, his son—by then the Mayor of Charleston—moved his growing family into that residence at 25 Pitt Street (no. 31 today). Maybe John Schnierle saw something of his carpenter father in Mills. Or maybe the Mayor, who "was always interested in the success of working men and mechanics," simply wanted to encourage Mills's initiative.[26]

Whatever its foundation, a bond grew between Mills and Schnierle. One year after securing the contract to cover and paint the Guard House, Mills named his fourth child, a son, John Schnierle. The Mayor of Charleston would be the first in a succession of wealthy, slave-owning, southern men of power and influence who were to befriend Mills and advance his ambitions.[27]

The Guard House, just recently completed, was a monumental addition to downtown Charleston. The Greek Revival building dominated the corner of Meeting and Broad Streets with two imposing façades. A colonnade ran along Meeting and a massive two-story Doric portico framed the entrance on Broad. It served the city's police force, traditionally known as the City Guard. Like many public buildings in South Carolina at this time, it was constructed of brick, but stuccoed and scored to resemble (more expensive) stone.[28] Mills's performance evidently satisfied the municipal officials, because three months later the City Council authorized his payment of $450.[29]

It is probable that all of Eliza's children came into the world on Mary Street, except her first and last:

(1) "*First child born, and died, 1838.*" So wrote Theophilus Fisk Mills in a sketch of his father's life.[30] Born most likely in or near the Ballentine home at Market and Beaufain Streets.

(2) Theodore Augustus, born April 24, 1839.[31]

(3) Theophilus Fisk, who would go by his middle name, born June 15, 1840.[32]

(4) John Schnierle, born Sept. 7, 1842, named for His Honor, the Mayor of Charleston, who may have acted as his godfather.[33]

(5) "*Other three children born after I was born,*"[34] wrote Fisk. Eliza must have had a child around April 1844 who died prior to August 1850.[35]

(6) Clark, Jr., born Nov. 20, 1845, probably at 49 Broad Street.[36]

Mills's children, though, would never be the principal focus of his attention. Indeed, over the following quarter century, he would spend more time in the company of his enslaved helper, Philip Reid, than with Eliza or any of their sons.[37] What quickened Mills's pulse was an urge to analyze, experiment and invent. To whatever skill he learned, he brought a critical eye: was there a better way of doing it? One *Camden Journal* reporter was to write:

> His genius soon induced him to introduce a new style of cornishing, as tasty as it was elegant.
>
> ["Cornishing" referred to the crafting of cornices; "tasty" meant stylish.]
>
> And soon his business was such as to enable him to hire his jobs done, and devote his talent to something of a higher nature.[38]

Relying on Reid and hirelings to fulfill his contracts, Mills spent his time experimenting and developing improved materials and methods for his trade. He may have reasoned that pursuing "something of a higher nature" would lead to a better future for his wife and children, as well as himself. In reality, though, Mills's self-absorption caused not only persistent financial instability, but rancor within his household. It eclipsed all practical matters. A writer for the *Camden Journal*, though, would express the perception of the public:

> There is, perhaps, no living man in whom South Carolina should feel more pride than Clark Mills, the native, self-taught, unequalled genius of the South. How many of the citizens of Charleston, who saw him when a boy, along the streets, ever thought his name would grace the proudest page of our history, and place us ahead of Italia, the land of arts and song?[39]

"Native . . . genius:" this reporter was not alone in mistakenly believing Mills to be a Charlestonian by birth. Though Mills would reside there only a dozen years—and never "when a boy"—he would talk of Charleston for the rest of his life as though it were his home town. The city made a deep and enduring impression on him. It provided the receptive ground in which the inchoate seed he had discovered in New Orleans was able to take root. Rich, cultured, powerful and proud Charleston enabled the "sprinkler of dusty avenues" to pursue his impulse to create. The *Richmond Enquirer* was to put it this way:

> It is true, Clark Mills is a native of New York—but, when a boy, he removed to Charleston, and while a common plasterer in that city his genius and his ambition were aroused by a Southern climate, his noble aspirations were fostered by Southern hearts and hands.[40]

How fitting, then, that two titans of the South—or, rather, the legendary renown of two titans of the South—Andrew Jackson (after his demise) and John C. Calhoun (while he lived)—would form the bedrock of Mills's career as a sculptor.

NOTES

1 Trustee Bill of Sale in Trust, Mills Clark and Eliza his wife to Ballantine [sic] Alexander, dated Feb. 18, 1839, recorded May 14, 1839; Secretary of State, Miscellaneous Records, vol. 5-V: 282–84; South Carolina Department of Archives and History, Columbia.
2 Reports of Brent Howard Holcomb, professional genealogist of Columbia, S.C., prepared for the author, 2015–18. The author thanks Brent in particular for finding this key record documenting Mills's purchase of Philip Reid.
3 The author thanks Judy Russell, J.D., "The Legal Genealogist," for her explication of this "marriage settlement."
4 T. C. Fay, *Charleston City Directory and Strangers' Guide for 1840 and 1841* (Charleston: T. C. Fay, 1840): 118. See also J. H. Bagget, *Directory of the City of Charleston, for the Year 1852* (Charleston: printed by Edward C. Councell, 1851): 88.
5 The 1840 census lists heads of household by name, followed by the members of the household in age and gender categories only, not by name. It is also possible that the census taker simply missed the Mills family, a failing that did sometimes occur.
6 Alexander Ballentine entry, 1840 U.S. Census, Charleston Neck, Charleston, S.C., p. 12 (handwritten), p. 112 (stamped); NARA M704, roll 509. He heads a household of 11 White persons, no persons of color, free or enslaved. Also Ballantine [sic], John, entry, Daniel J. Dowling, *The Charleston Directory; And Register, for 1840–41* (Charleston: Daniel J. Dowling, pub. and print., 1840); transcribed selectively in James W. Hagy, *Directories for the City of Charleston, South Carolina* (Baltimore: Clearfield, 1997): 96.
7 "Panic of 1837," at https://en.wikipedia.org/wiki/Panic_of_1837.
8 Description of the Northern Neck population is derived from: (1) 1840 U.S. Census of Charleston District, S.C.; NARA M704, roll 509; and (2) Dowling, *Charleston Directory . . . for 1840–41*, passim.
9 Eight sources provide various birth years for Reid ranging from 1817 to 1830: (1) "Sheriff's Sale," [Charleston] *Courier*, Apr. 20 and 30, May 1 and 4, 1840, p. 3: "about 20;" (2) District of Columbia tax assessment for Jan. and Feb. 1855: "30;" (3) 1860 U.S. Census Slave Schedule, taken in July: "30;" (4) Petition for Compensation for Slaves, June 18, 1862: "42;" (5) 1870 U.S. Census, taken in July: "50;" (6) 1880 U.S. Census, taken in June: "55;" (7) Washington, D.C., death certificate: died "Feb. 6, 1892, age 75;" (8) Civil War Draft Record, June–July 1863: "36." Considering the relative reliability of these sources, a birth

year of about 1820 appears most probable. One other source, the 1850 U.S. Census Slave Schedule, gives an age of nine, but this is obviously an error for 29. Perhaps the enumerator misunderstood the verbal reply to his query.

10 Petition for Compensation for Slaves, Claim 741, Clark Mills, June 18, 1862, filed June 20, 1862, Washington, D.C.; accessed at www.Fold3.com.
11 "Sheriff's Sale," [Charleston] *Courier*, Apr. 20 and 30, May 1 and 4, 1840, p. 3.
12 The 1870 U.S. Census lists Scotland as Reid's birthplace, but this obvious error is contradicted by the 1880 U.S. Census, Reid's Civil War Draft Registration record, and his death certificate, all of which list South Carolina as his place of birth.
13 Philip's surname appears in documents as both Reed and Reid, both before emancipation and afterwards. Likewise, his given name was written as Phillip and Philip, arbitrarily, throughout his lifetime.
14 Patsey Whiteman entry, Ledger of Depositors, 3 Feb. 1870, Freedmen's Bank, Charleston, S.C.; viewed at www.familysearch.org.
15 Daniel J. Dowling, *The Charleston Directory; And Register, for 1835–36, 1837–38* and *1840–41* (Charleston: Daniel J. Dowling, pub. and print., 1835, 1837 and 1840); transcribed selectively in Hagy, *Directories for the City of Charleston*, 38, 77 and 102.
16 James Davidson entry, 1840 U.S. Census, Ward 1, Charleston, Charleston Co., S.C., p. 14; NARA M704, roll 509.
17 "Charleston Fire of April 1838," at http://halseymap.com/flash/window.asp?HMID=48.
18 "Sketches of Washington. By Childe Harold," *Brooklyn Daily Eagle*, Mar. 30, 1853, p. 2.
19 Walter J. Fraser, Jr., *Charleston! Charleston! The History of a Southern City* (Columbia, S.C.: University of South Carolina Press, 1989): 217.
20 Title, James Poyas to Thomas O. Elliott, Trustee, Feb. 27, 1844; RMC Book Q11, p. 187–89; Charleston County Deeds, Charleston County Register of Deeds, Charleston, S.C. Today the address of the property is 23 Lamboll Street. Based on the style and construction of the house standing on the site—known as the "Poyas-Edwards House"—architectural historians believe it dates from about 1837–45. It was most likely the new owner in 1844 who built the house. The original 1840s dwelling comprises the front portion of the Poyas-Edwards House, which includes later additions. It was typical domestic Charleston architecture of the period: a two-story brick structure two bays wide with a gable roof of slate and two massive chimneys. Deep porches on both levels ran the width of the street façade and the entire length of one side (called the piazza). The wide lot allowed for a spacious yard beside the house, which today contains a garden. Report of Christina Rae Butler of Butler Preservation, L.C., Research Consulting and Renovation, Charleston, prepared for the author in 2018.
21 "Sheriff's Sale," *Courier*, Apr. 20 and 30, May 1 and 4, 1840, p. 3.

22 "Proceedings of the Council, Monday, August 9, 1841," [Charleston] *Southern Patriot*, August 11, 1841, p. 2.

23 John Schnierle (1808–69), see https://en.wikipedia.org/wiki/John_Schnierle. However, for correct date of death, see "Death of General John Schnierle," *Charleston Daily News*, Apr. 15, 1869, p. 3.

24 The Hon. John Schnirlie [sic] entry, 1850 U.S. Census, Parishes of St. Philip's and St. Michael's, Charleston, S.C., p. 515 (handwritten), p. 256 (stamped); NARA M432, roll 850; and John Schnerlie [sic] entry, 1850 U.S. Census Slave Schedule, Parishes of St. Philip's and St. Michael's, Charleston, S.C., p. 679 (handwritten); NARA M432, roll 862; and Jno Schnirlie [sic] entry, 1860 U.S. Census, Ward 4, Charleston, S.C., p. 114 (handwritten), p. 353[b] (stamped); NARA M653, roll 1216; and Jno Schnerlie [sic] entry, 1860 U.S. Census Slave Schedule, Ward 4, Charleston, S.C. p. 26 (handwritten), p. 451[b] (stamped); NARA M653, roll 1232; and Dowling, *Charleston Directory . . . for 1840 and 1841,* transcribed selectively in Hagy, *Directories for the City of Charleston,* 125; and J. H. Bagget, pub., *Directory of the City of Charleston, for the Year 1852* (Charleston: Edward C. Councell, printer, 1851): 113.

25 "John Schnierle House" at https://en.wikipedia.org/wiki/John_Schnierle_House.

26 "Death of General John Schnierle," *Charleston Daily News*, Apr. 15, 1869, 3. Schnierle's mother-in-law was a Reed, but no relationship between her and Philip Reid has been discovered.

27 See Bk. 1, Prologue.

28 "Alfred O. Halsey Map 1849," Preservation Society of Charleston, at http://www.halseymap.com/flash/window.asp?HMID=25. The Guard House was destroyed by an earthquake in 1886.

29 [no title], [Charleston] *Courier*, Nov. 3, 1841, p. 2.

30 Letter, T[heophilus] F[isk] Mills to Elliott Woods, Superintendent, U.S. Capitol and Grounds, July 29, 1910; Archives, Office of the Architect of the Capitol, Washington, D.C. No baptismal record has been found. Regarding this child's birthplace, see Bk. 1, Ch. 3.

31 Letter, T[heophilus] F[isk] Mills to Elliott Woods, July 29, 1910; and "Theodore A. Mills" entry in W. J. Holland, ed., *Annals of the Carnegie Museum*, Pittsburgh, Pa., vol. 11 (Nov. 1917): 9. No baptismal record has been found. Died in Pittsburgh, Dec. 11, 1916.

32 Letter, T[heophilus] F[isk] Mills to Elliott Woods, July 29, 1910. No baptismal record has been found. Died in Washington, D.C., Sept. 21, 1916.

33 "John S. Mills Dead, Son of Sculptor," [Washington] *Evening Star*, Aug. 16, 1928, p. 23. No baptismal record has been found. Died in Washington, D.C., Aug. 15, 1928.

34 Letter, T[heophilus] F[isk] Mills to Elliott Woods, July 29, 1910. No baptismal record has been found.

35 No child is enumerated between John and Clark in the Mills family entry of the U.S. Census taken Aug. 5, 1850. See also Bk. 1, Ch. 7.
36 Clarke [sic] Mills, jr., entry, Student Rosters, Columbian College, Washington, D.C., 1864 and 1866; and Clark Mills, Certificate of Death, Nov. 28, 1910, Philadelphia, Pa.; Pennsylvania Death Certificates, 1906–1963, Series 11.90, Records of the Pennsylvania Department of Health, R.G. 11, Certificate 115026; Pennsylvania Historic and Museum Commission, Philadelphia; both viewed at www.ancestry.com. Regarding Clark, Jr.'s, birthplace, see Bk. 1, Ch. 8.
37 See Bk. 2.
38 "Clark Mills and His Statue," *Camden* [S.C.] *Journal*, reprinted in "Clark Mills," [Charleston] *Courier*, May 8, 1850, p. 2.
39 Ibid.
40 "Clark Mills," [Baltimore] *Sun*, Jan. 24, 1853, p. 1, quoting the *Richmond Inquirer*.

CHAPTER 5
Ca. 1839/40–August 1844

In this poverty and obscurity in Charleston, whilst working at his trade of house plasterer, [Clark Mills] kept a bear and a dog, which he would make fight for fourpence. Between this exhibition of his dog and bear, and with the assistance of his trowel, he made his living in a sort of way, and would, in all probability, have died in these humble pursuits, but for the phrenologist.

"Genius and Phrenology," [Greenville, S.C.] *Southern Patriot,* Jan. 27, 1853.

Mills told Benjamin Franklin Perry, senior editor of the *Southern Patriot,* how he came to take up sculpting:

One morning as he was going to his work he passed by a door where a phrenologist had hung up his sign, with a notice that skeptics were not charged for the examination of their heads. This induced him to go in and have his bumps examined.

The Phrenologist said to him, "You have the organ of sculpture in a very eminent degree, and if you were to cultivate your talent you would undoubtedly be a very distinguished artist."

Mills replied to him, "You have confirmed me in my skepticism. I never had any confidence in your pretended science, but if I had, your account of my own head would utterly destroy it. I am, sir, a house plasterer, and know nothing about sculpture, whatever."

The phrenologist replied, "I don't care for that; you have the organ in a most wonderful degree, and should cultivate your talent."

Mr. Mills said the idea that he possessed a rare and valuable talent, that he was not conscious of, haunted him night and day.

But still, he never thought of trying his talent, for he did not know how to begin.

One day he saw an Italian going through the streets of Charleston, with a bust of Napoleon, in plaster, and he asked him how it was moulded. The Italian promised to show him, and did so. He caught the idea instantly, and was enraptured with it.[1]

This is the story that Mills told and retold. It was printed in many newspapers and magazines.[2] But—typical of the amiable raconteur—it was not the whole truth. In reality, Mills already had some familiarity with bust-making from working for his uncle, Noah Parker, in New Orleans. In addition, the journalist known as Childe Harold would attribute a more practical motive to Mills's newfound interest:

> Mills having lost a contract for which he had offered proposals, was perfectly idle for some time, and determining to be doing something, he set about moulding a cast of a saddler.[3]

Nevertheless, it was evidently the obdurate judgment of the phrenologist that prompted Mills to try his hand at sculpting, and the anecdote lent an aura of destiny to Mills's decision to do so. Moreover, as his bust-making evolved into the profession of an artist, Mills himself became convinced of the legitimacy of the pseudo-science. For the rest of his life, he would be a zealous advocate of it.

Phrenology is the study of the shape of the skull, founded on the belief that it is indicative of mental faculties and character traits. The concept was first articulated by Franz Joseph Gall in Vienna, Austria, around 1796:

(1) The brain is the organ of the mind;
(2) The mind is composed of multiple distinct, innate faculties;
(3) Because they are distinct, each faculty must have a separate seat or "organ" in the brain;
(4) The size of an organ, other things being equal, is a measure of its power;

(5) The shape of the brain is determined by the development of the various organs; and

(6) As the skull takes its shape from the brain, the surface of the skull can be read as an accurate index of psychological aptitudes and tendencies.[4]

Phrenology gained popularity in Scotland and England in the 1820s and from there spread to the United States. Numerous volumes on the subject appeared in English in the 1830s–1850s and they were all available in Charleston. Three examples, among many advertised by booksellers in the *Courier* were: *Christianity and Phrenology,* by John Epps, M.D.; *Phrenology Simplified,* by a member of the Phrenological Society of Edinburgh;

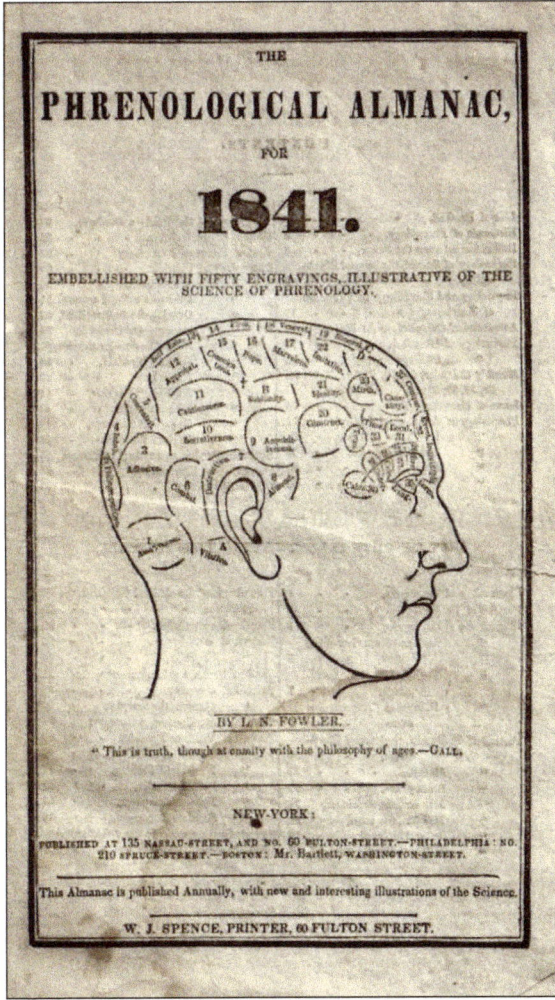

Fowler's *Phrenological Almanac*, published annually, was akin to publications available for sale in Charleston in the 1840s. Mills took up sculpting, he said, because a phrenologist who "read" his skull told him he had an extraordinary aptitude for it. His own success at making busts convinced Mills of the legitimacy of the pseudo-science and made him a lifelong believer. (Internet Archive)

and *Combe's Lectures on Phrenology*, by George Combe.[5] A periodical, *The American Phrenological Journal and Miscellany*, began publication in 1838.[6]

British proponents of the new discipline made speaking tours through the United States. As early as 1825, a Dr. Cameron gave a series of lectures on phrenology in Charleston.[7] In 1837, another advocate, Samuel Kirkham, publicized his talks in the *Courier*:

> **PHRENOLOGY. S. KIRKHAM**, author of "English Grammar in Lectures," and "Essay on Elocution," respectfully announces to the ladies and gentlemen of Charleston, that he will commence a course of Lectures on PHRENOLOGY, THIS EVENING, (Friday, Dec. 22,) in the Medical College in Broad-street, commencing at 7 o'clk. The Lectures will be continued for a few weeks, on every Tuesday and Friday evenings, at the same hour and place; and, as a practical test of the truth of the Science, each Lecture will be followed by an examination of the head, and a delineation of the character and talents of such individuals as may be selected by the audience. The Introductory Lecture this evening, will be free. After the first Lecture, tickets of admission will be 50 cents—to be had at Mr. Beile's book store, or at S. Kirkham's office, in King street.[8]

Kirkham's lectures were popular. Within a few years he opened a more commodious office at 56 Queen Street:

> [H]e is prepared to give correct descriptions of character and talent to all who wish to secure an examination of their heads. Examinations, $1, with a chart, 1.50, written description, 3 extra. Ladies and Gentlemen are invited to call, free of charge, and examine Mr. K's collection of casts, sculls, books, &c.[9]

The concept garnered ardent advocates and vehement detractors. In early 1838 the editor of the *Courier* called phrenology a "humbug," provoking a lengthy, point-by-point rejoinder from an incensed reader. The editor printed the believer's letter in its entirety, but held his ground:

> Although our cranium has been mapped out in a manner very agreeable to our self-love, we do not think it likely that we can ever be either flattered or *bumped* into a belief of the humbug.[10]

When Mills's curiosity prompted him to cross the phrenologist's threshold that fateful day—it must have been Kirkham's office, about 1839 or 1840—he professed his "skepticism." Even after the consultation, though the judgment of the phrenologist "haunted him night and day," Mills did not act on it. "He did not know how to begin." It was the subsequent encounter on the street with the Italian "image maker" that prompted Mills to start learning.

The Italian—whom Mills never named—would have instructed his eager apprentice in the two ways to produce a plaster bust. One was to sculpt the bust in clay, make a plaster mold from it ("mould" in 19th-century English), then pour liquid plaster into that mold to cast the bust. The other method was to begin with plaster casts of the subject's face—called a "life mask"—and head, join those two pieces to form the mold, then cast the plaster bust in that mold. That was the method that Mills had witnessed during his brief sojourn in New Orleans. His uncle, Noah Parker, had employed it. Now Mills mastered the multi-step process:[11]

TAKING A PLASTER CAST OF THE HEAD

(1) Shave the subject's whiskers and comb his hair flat against the scalp;
(2) Apply sweet oil liberally to the face, neck, ears and scalp to prevent the plaster from adhering;
(3) Using an iron spoon, mix plaster powder and water in an earthenware bowl to make a liquid plaster of paris;
(4) Heat the plaster of paris to 90 degrees;

(5) Pour half of it into an earthenware box, in one side of which a half-round opening has been cut to accommodate the subject's neck;

(6) Place the subject in a supine position on a long table, settling his head into the plaster in the box, as though onto a pillow;

(7) Draw a string over the head from ear to ear;

(8) Insert long quills into the nostrils to allow the subject to breathe;

(9) Pour the warm plaster of paris over the subject's head until his face, neck and ears are fully covered to a depth of at least one-half inch;

(10) Allow the plaster of paris to cool, dry and harden into a cast (at least five minutes);

(11) Pull on the string to separate the cast into two halves (life mask and skull);

(12) Remove the two halves and secure them together to make a mold of the head;

(13) Pour plaster of paris into the mold and swish it around to fill every surface to a thickness of about one-half inch; and

(14) Using a mallet and chisel, break the mold carefully (or peal it off) to release the cast of the head.[12]

Practicing these steps, most likely on members of his wife's family, it became obvious to Mills that the ordeal was not only uncomfortable for the sitter, but dangerous as well. He probably had trouble recruiting volunteers. Years later he would relate to the Washington correspondent of the *Boston Journal* how the New York sculptor, John Henri Isaac Browere, when he took the life mask of the elderly Thomas Jefferson, nearly suffocated the former president![13]

"The process was simply a torture," Mills was to tell a reporter of *The Washington Post*, illustrating the point with another horrific story:

> "[Mr. Custis, the stepson of Washington,] told me that when a boy he saw Houdon make the celebrated cast of Washington.

The sculptor had the Father of his country to lie down upon his back upon a table. He placed a tube in each nostril, so as to let him breathe. He poured plaster of Paris over the face, and it took several minutes for it to crystalize, the distinguished subject suffering at the time with quinsy, which made the operation unusually disagreeable to him. After he got up he said, 'That is the last time they will ever get my head in that fix.'"[14]

On yet another occasion Mills would explain:

"[With] the old process, when the casting was removed more or less of the eyebrows and beard were pulled out with it. . . . The process was so disagreeable that it gave a painful look to the casting."[15]

Furthermore, the subject's resemblance "was almost lost by the compression of the weight of the plaster on the softer portions of the face."[16]

So Mills analyzed the procedure and experimented—as he had done when he devised "a new style of cornishing"—and invented a better way of doing it. An early admirer described in a letter to the Charleston *Courier* how Mills simplified the process:

Instead of being placed on your back and having your head put into a box and running the risk of being suffocated, as has heretofore been the case, he places you in a chair as would a barber and by the time the barber could give you a clean countenance, the young artist will stamp your features upon his mixture and be ready to bid you good morning.[17]

Mills himself would explain it this way:

"I make the subject take a seat comfortably in a chair. I place an India rubber cap on the head and gather all the hair out of the way. I place a sheet in the lap, and with a brush I apply my preparation to the face. In a few minutes it is crystalized. The person leans forward and the matrix or mould drops on the cloth. I take that and pour the plaster of Paris in it, and when it crystalizes then I peel or pull the mould or matrix off—then I have a cast which I use instead of the living subject."[18]

Three modifications of Mills's devising made the seated position possible. One, he experimented with the plaster until he came up with a paste that dried in just three minutes.[19] Two, he encased the skull in a tight rubber cap and applied oil to the cap, rather than to the hair. Three, instead of pouring quantities of warm plaster over the subject's head, he applied a half-inch coat all around with a brush. These changes eliminated the need to immobilize the head in a box. When the plaster hardened, Mills simply asked the sitter to lean forward and flex the face muscles, and he caught the plaster fragments in a cloth placed on the sitter's lap.[20] Mills would eventually obtain a patent for his new "Mode of Taking Casts from the Faces of Living Persons."[21]

This was a remarkable beginning. But Mills had a lot yet to learn. Creating a bust from the plaster cast of a head required additional steps:[22]

CREATING A PLASTER BUST

(1) Make a plaster cast of the head;
(2) Build an armature of wire;
(3) Sculpt a chest and shoulders on the armature (or use a pre-cast chest and shoulders);
(4) Mount the head on the chest and shoulders;
(5) Mount the bust on a pedestal, either a short pillar (round) or herm (square);
(6) Meet with the subject a second time; and
(7) Complete the resemblance by opening the eyes and sculpting eyebrows, hair, etc.[23]

Reported Richard Yeadon, editor of the *Courier*, after undergoing the procedure:

The paste is inodorous and insipid, and produces no unpleasant sensation; but, on the contrary, with the thermometer at 90, is actually agreeable and refreshing. . . . The whole operation is over in fifteen minutes, and only a second sitting of less duration is necessary to complete the resemblance. The first mould, being taken from the face while the eyes are closed, represents the sleeping subject—and the second sitting becomes necessary to impart, by lifting the eyelids and also a muscle or two, the waking expression, and also to adjust the hair.[24]

That ability to turn a vacuous sleeping face into the expressioned countenance of a living person is what distinguished a sculptor from a tradesman. It called for artistic skill. Making a plaster head was craft; creating a portrait bust was art.

Once again, Mills turned to family members for practice. "First he commenced a likeness in plaster of his father-in-law, who had very prominent features. It was the wonder of all who saw it."[25] A later chronicler would relate it this way:

At that time there lived in Charleston a saddler and harness-maker, who was one of the characters of the place, and who, by a habit of drawing his mouth to one side as he stretched his stitches, had got a comical kink in one side of his face. Clark Mills got him for his first subject, and modeled his portrait in plaster. The likeness was universally recognized and approved.[26]

It could not have hurt Mills's situation to flatter **Alexander Ballentine**, whose respect for his son-in-law was dubious.[27] "He next tried his hand in modelling a ladies' bust, which was also pronounced excellent."[28] The female sitter was not identified, but Eliza would have been a likely subject for her husband's budding skills.

Certainly, perfecting his distinctive plaster and innovative technique through trial and error took Mills more than two family portraits, and producing a bust from a head cast required practice, patience and dedication. By 1844 though—maybe as much as a year earlier—Mills was approaching "distinguished fellow citizens," offering to make their busts. Eager to establish a name for himself, he may not yet have charged for the service. Among his earliest sitters were:

> The Honorable *Mitchell King*, Scottish-born teacher, lawyer and judge of Charleston City Court.[29]

> *Franklin Harper Elmore*, former U.S. Congressman, President of the Bank of the State of South Carolina, friend and ally of John C. Calhoun, whose U.S. Senate seat he would occupy after Calhoun died in office. Elmore's support would soon prove decisive in advancing Mills's career as a sculptor.[30]

Mills's plaster bust of one of his earliest sitters, U.S. Congressman and Senator from South Carolina, Franklin Harper Elmore, ca. 1844. Elmore's close friendship with the South's most powerful and popular spokesman, John C. Calhoun, proved decisive in advancing Mills's artistic aspiration. (South Caroliniana Library, University of South Carolina, Columbia, S.C.)

Given the social and economic realities of South Carolina in the 1840s, all of Mills's early patrons—such as King and Elmore—would be wealthy men of prominence whose households included enslaved domestics and whose fields were worked by enslaved laborers. When these proud owners vaunted their portraits by Mills, his safer, faster, less unpleasant way of taking a face mask became known to Charlestonians. The eminent status of his satisfied customers drove Mills's business. By 1844 his success warranted a visible, public presence.

Mills set up shop on Meeting Street between Broad and Tradd in a room that he rented (presumably from the city) in the rear of the Guard House, a municipal property.[31] His Honor the Mayor of Charleston, John Schnierle, may have been instrumental in securing this work space for the promising artist. It was Schnierle who, as city alderman in 1841, had contracted Mills to cover the Guard House with Roman Cement and paint it.[32] The following year, after Schnierle was elected mayor, Mills had named a son after him. Mills's workshop had an entrance off the grand colonnade that ran the length of the building along Meeting Street. A large window or two provided light and air. The room's strategic location in the heart of Charleston guaranteed the notice of many "distinguished fellow citizens," though its interior would have been a modest affair.

The occupation required no bulky or expensive equipment. Mills's shop would have contained a high work bench that he could stand at, sacks of dry plaster, water pitcher and basin, a cast-iron cook stove, wire, pliers, mallets, an assortment of files, rasps, chisels, deck scrapers, punches, knives, spoons, and his long smock. He would have kept paint on hand, too, for "bronzing." That was a finishing touch some clients ordered for their likeness: painting it to resemble bronze. One comfortable chair would have accommodated sitters who chose to undergo the procedure in the shop.

However, most of the time Mills took the head cast in the privacy of the client's home, boardinghouse, hotel room, or workplace. Almost all of his sitters so far were men. The materials he needed could easily be carried in a satchel or two: straight razor, shaving cream, comb, India rubber caps, sweet oil, sack of dry plaster, bowl, spoon, string, straws or quills, and towels. Philip Reid may have accompanied Mills to do the toting. After taking the head cast, Mills repaired to his workshop to rejoin the two halves into a mold, pour in the plaster, and affix the head on shoulders. Meeting with the sitter a second time, Mills "livened" the likeness, then took it back to his shop to mount on a pedestal. When the bust was finished, Mills either notified the patron "to send for it," or he had Reid carry it through the streets of Charleston to an address provided by the client.

Before relinquishing the finished bust, though, Mills always made a fresh mold from it and cast a copy for himself. Following this practice, he could replicate the bust as often as desired. In short order, the walls of his workshop were covered with shelves lined with plaster heads. They made an effective showcase of his wares for the inspection of potential customers. In August of 1844 the *Courier* printed a letter from a reader who rhapsodized about Mills's creations:

> Messrs. Editors: If you or the citizens of Charleston wish to see a man who can neither speak nor hear, take a stroll down Meeting street between Broad and Tradd, and step into the workshop of Mr. C. Mills, and you shall be introduced to several distinguished fellow-citizens, who will give you an earnest gaze, but they will neither speak nor heed your speaking. To divest the subject of every thing like enigma, Mr. Mills is a young artist, who has but recently commenced taking busts, and the specimens in his office at once demonstrate that he has attained a degree of correctness and perfection, that has not, and I will probably not go too far in saying, that never can be surpassed. The likeness is perfect, there is not a single expression of the countenance, not a single mole or wrinkle upon the face or lip that is not firmly impressed upon the solid substance. I have understood from modern rumor that the greatest difficulty the artist has to encounter, is to obtain the consent

of his customers to permit the perfection of his work to remain untouched. When men see themselves without any varnish or false coloring, not one in ten is half so handsome as he supposes.³³

This is the first known published piece about Mills as an artist. It fanned word of mouth among the landed families who comprised the elite of Charleston. The vocation of "Sculptor" was a novelty, his creations were wondrous. Heightening the excitement for Charlestonians, *this* sculptor was a young "fellow-townsman." One journalist would later reckon:

What an hour for the back-woods wheelwright boy, for the sweating plasterer, the exhibiter of the bear and the dog, and the unknown sprinkler of dusty avenues!³⁴

Mills was on his way. Convinced of the legitimacy of phrenology—Was he himself not living proof?—Mills would make a study of it, become masterful in its practice, and promote it unabashedly. Throughout his career, he would describe his portrait busts in terms of the pseudo-science. But phrenology would not be the only controversial concept to capture his imagination. His intellectual meandering was bold and boundless. Mills's focus at the moment, however, was on honing the skills of his new profession. A house plasterer no longer, he was about to put an original sculpture on public display.

NOTES

1 "Genius and Phrenology," [Greenville, S.C.] *Southern Patriot*, Jan. 27, 1853.
2 Examples include: (1) "Genius and Phrenology," *Brooklyn Daily Eagle*, Feb. 18, 1853, p. 4; (2) "Sketches of Washington. By Childe Harold," *Brooklyn Daily Eagle*, Mar. 30, 1853, p. 2; (3) "Clark Mills and the Equestrian Statue of General Jackson," *American Phrenological Journal*, vol. 17, no. 4 (April 1853): 77; and (4) "The Utility of Phrenology," *The Phrenological Journal and Science of Health*, vol. 80, no. 5 (May 1885): 311. See also "Choosing a Pursuit Scientifically," *Scientific American*, vol. LII, no. 25 (June 20, 1885): 385.
3 "Sketches of Washington," *Brooklyn Daily Eagle*, Mar. 30, 1853, p. 2.

4 "Phrenology," at https://en.wikipedia.org/wiki/Phrenology.
5 [Charleston] *Courier*, July 3, 1837, p. 1; Aug. 7, 1837, p. 1; and Nov. 14, 1840, p. 1.
6 *The American Phrenological Journal and Miscellany*, at https://catalog.hathitrust.org/Record/003987208. The journal was published in Philadelphia.
7 "Phrenology," [Charleston] *Courier*, Mar. 11, 1825, p. 1.
8 "Phrenology," [Charleston] *Courier*, Dec. 22, 1837, p. 3.
9 "Phrenology," [Charleston] *Courier*, Nov. 25, 1839, p. 2.
10 "Phrenology," [Charleston] *Courier*, Apr. 18, 1838, p. 2.
11 "Admirable Casts," [Charleston] *Courier*, June 30, 1845, p. 2; and "An Hour with Clark Mills," [Washington] *Evening Star*, Dec. 24, 1870, p. 2.
12 Mr. Butler, "Directions for Taking Plaster Casts," *Zoist*, no. V: 40; reprinted in *The Phrenological Journal*, no. LXXX (New Series—no. XXVII), (July 1844): 251–53, and "Hints as to the Making of Plaster Casts," *The Phrenological Journal and Magazine of Moral Science*, vol. XVIII (New Series vol. VIII), (1845): 98.
13 Charles Henry Hart, *Browere's Life Masks of Great Americans* (New York: Doubleday and McClure, 1899): 36.
14 "Clark Mills at Home," *The Washington Post*, Feb. 7, 1880, p. 2.
15 "An Hour with Clark Mills," *Evening Star*, Dec. 24, 1870, 2.
16 "How Marble Busts Are Made. The Inside of a Studio—Clark Mills at Work," *Chicago Tribune*, Apr. 10, 1863, p. 3.
17 "Messrs. Editors," [Charleston] *Courier*, Aug. 26, 1844, p. 2. See also "Mr. Clark Mills, the Sculptor," *The Round Table*, vol. 1, no. 22 (May 14, 1864): 340.
18 "Clark Mills at Home," *Washington Post*, Feb. 7, 1880, 2.
19 "Admirable Casts," *Courier*, June 30, 1845, 2.
20 "Clark Mills at Home," *Washington Post*, Feb. 7, 1880, 2.
21 Entry no. 47,121, "Mills, Clark," Apr. 4, 1865, "Mode of Taking Casts from the Faces of Living Persons," *Annual Report of the Commissioner of Patents for the year 1865*, vol. 1, 39th Cong., 1st Sess., House of Representatives Ex. Doc. No. 52 (Washington, D.C.: Govt. Print. Off., 1867): 251.
22 "Admirable Casts," *Courier*, June 30, 1845, 2.
23 "How Marble Busts Are Made," *Chicago Tribune*, Apr. 10, 1863, 3.
24 "Admirable Casts," *Courier*, June 30, 1845, 2.
25 "Genius and Phrenology," *Southern Patriot*, Jan. 27, 1853.
26 A[loha] Vivarttas, "The Clark Mills Furnace—A Reminiscence," *The Railroad and Engineering Journal*, vol. 63 (July 1889): 327; and "Sketches of Washington, *Brooklyn Daily Eagle*, Mar. 30, 1853, p. 2.
27 Throughout this book, all busts created by Mills are designated in ***bold italics***. If a bust is known to be extant, its current (2025) location is given.
28 "Sketches of Washington," *Brooklyn Daily Eagle*, Mar. 30, 1853, 2.
29 Mitchell King (1783–1862), see Mitchell King entry, 1840 U.S. Census, 4th Ward, Charleston, S.C., p. 21[b] (handwritten), p. 82[b] stamped; NARA M704,

roll 509 (household includes 22 enslaved members); and The Hon. M. King entry, 1850 U.S. Census, Parishes of St. Philip's and St. Michael's, Charleston, S.C., p. 507 (handwritten), p. 252 (stamped); NARA M432, roll 850; and Mitchel [sic] King entry, 1850 U.S. Census Slave Schedule, Parishes of St. Philip's and St. Michael's, Charleston, S.C., p. 687 and 877, (handwritten); NARA M432, roll 850.

30 Franklin Harper Elmore (1799–1850), see https://scencyclopedia.org/sce/entries/elmore-franklin-harper. Today copies of this bust are in the South Caroliniana Library, University of South Carolina, Columbia, S.C., and Charleston Library Society, Charleston, S.C.

31 "Messrs. Editors," *Courier,* Aug. 26, 1844, 2; and "Clark Mills and His Equestrian Statue," *DeBow's Review,* vol. 16 (Jan. 1854): 38.

32 See Bk. 1, Ch. 4.

33 "Messrs. Editors," *Courier,* Aug. 26, 1844, 2.

34 "Clark Mills . . . ," *DeBow's Review,* vol. 16 (Jan. 1854): 39.

CHAPTER 6
December 9, 1844

State of South Carolina

To the Honorable the Senate and House of Representatives of the State of South Carolina

The undersigned petitioners residents of the Parishes of St Phillip and St Micheal City of Charleston Shew unto your honorable body that they have asociated themselves under the Style and name of the Charleston Friendly Botanic Thomsonian Society having for their object the advancement of knolledge and the mutual asistance of of each other, the aleviating the distresses and infermatties of those who believe in the eficacies of the Thomsonian Medicines the supplying to the indigent and helpless the means of procuring the aid and services of such practitioners as are skilfull in administering them.

They therefore pray your honorable body to grant them an act of incorporation. So as to enable them to cary out the above objects stated with the usual privelige and immunities granted to other Charitable institutions and your petitioners as in duty bound will ever pray &c

December 9, 1844

1844-104-03

Geo M Keils Pres.dt
J F Alderson Vice Pres.dt
Samuel S. Miller Treasurer
John Symons   Sec.ty
Henry Brown   John DeBow
Thos. K. Chew   Clark Mills
John M Lunquest   Joseph Ballard
J L Pelmoins   S. Finagin
Wm F Barton   Jno Smith
John E. Michel   Edwin C Prince
C. G. Erichson   Wm S. Wallace
D. Truesdell   G. H. Rumph
Henry Regnall   William Murdock
Charles Mathey

Petition to the Senate and House of Representatives of the State of South Carolina, Dec. 9, 1844; Petitions to the General Assembly (S165015), 1844-104, South Carolina Department of Archives and History, Columbia; viewed at https://scdah.sc.gov.

CHAPTER 7
December 1844–June 1845

We have observed in the Exchange Reading Room a very admirable piece of modelling, which would do credit to artists of long study and mature age, executed by our townsman, Mr. Mills, who has only within a few months undertaken the making of likenesses in casts.

An Admirer of the Arts "[Communicated],"
[Charleston] *Courier*, Dec. 20, 1844, p. 2.

Winter of 1844 was nigh when someone stepped from the colonnade of the Guard House into Mills's workshop and made a disconcerting request. The caller may have been Mrs. Simons herself or a friend of her husband's, perhaps a member of the Medical Society. Whoever it was, the person asked Mills to make a bust of **Benjamin Bonneau Simons, M.D.**[1] Dr. B. B. Simons was a surgeon of celebrated South Carolinian lineage and international reputation. But he had died in his house on East Gay Street on September 27th and been interred in St. Michael's churchyard two days later.[2] Obviously, Mills could not take a cast of the illustrious surgeon's head. But the visitor promised to provide two oil portraits of the doctor, as well as his death mask. Mills accepted the challenge.

Remarkably, he succeeded. The bust he sculpted was put on display in the Exchange Reading Room, which was part of "the *Courier* establishment in the Post Office building" on East Bay Street at the foot of Broad.[3] The portrayal of Dr. Simons so impressed "An Admirer of the Arts," that he dispatched a letter to the *Courier*:

> The bust we now allude to, which is one of our late distinguished citizen, Dr. B. B. Simons, was modeled from two likenesses, neither of which was accurate, and the proportions obtained from a

cast after death, but which was of no use, but as giving the proportions, having nothing of the character of Dr. S. With these aids and the suggestions of a friend of Dr. S. of the defects of the portraits, the artist who did not know the original has produced a striking and characteristic likeness, an elegant specimen of art.[4]

How did Mills do it? Two reporters would later write that Mills, early in his career, "began modelling busts in clay."[5] If that is so, he abandoned that medium very early on in favor of working directly in plaster. This bust of Simons is the only known work that Mills may have sculpted first in clay, then cast in plaster. "An Admirer of the Arts" was evidently familiar with Mills's usual practice of working from a head cast, because he opined, "[T]hat method was somewhat mechanical, although requiring much cleverness."[6] This bust, by contrast, was not "mechanical," observed the critic, but rather "an elegant specimen of art." Ironically, this anomaly of Mills's career was his first work to be exhibited in a public venue.

The exposition of the Simons bust, the published encomium of "An Admirer of the Arts," and word of mouth among influential Charlestonians (planters had brought their families to town for the social season) generated commissions for Mills, including:

Richard Yeadon, lawyer, South Carolina state representative, editor of the Charleston *Courier* and *City Gazette*.[7] Yeadon would describe his positive reaction to undergoing the procedure in the June 30, 1845, issue of the *Courier*.

James Louis Petigru, former Attorney General of South Carolina and state representative, renowned lawyer and future codifier of the laws of South Carolina. The bust was commissioned by "young men of the bar, who have ordered a number of copies."[8]

George McDuffie, South Carolina state representative, U.S. Congressman, governor of South Carolina, and U.S. Senator.[9]

John Blake White, lawyer, painter, author, dramatist; four historical paintings of his hang in the U.S. Capitol.[10]

Rev. Samuel Foster Gilman, pastor of the Archdale Street Unitarian Church, Charleston; author.[11]

Rev. John Bachman, longtime pastor of St. John's Lutheran Church in Charleston, author and eminent naturalist.[12]

William Alston Hayne, son of Robert and Rebecca Hayne, future South Carolina state representative and Confederate Army officer.[13] A soirée given by William's mother while Mills's bust of Dr. Simons was on display illustrates how the novice sculptor's reputation spread.[14]

On the evening of Monday, December 16, 1844, Rebecca Brewton Alston Hayne entertained three close friends from Columbia in her palatial, in-town residence on Ladson's Court.[15] She was the widow of Robert Young Hayne, a planter who had been mayor of Charleston, a member of the South Carolina House of Representatives, Attorney General of South Carolina, then Governor, and a U.S. Senator.[16] A more influential family in Charleston would have been hard to find.

One of Mrs. Hayne's guests was the Honorable Langdon Cheves. Judge Cheves was the elderly owner of several rice and cotton plantations and a political power broker, thanks to his considerable experience in Washington, D.C. He had served multiple terms as a U.S. Congressman, as well as Judge of the Court of Appeals and President of the United States Bank.[17] The other two guests were the Judge's daughter, Louisa Susannah, and her husband, David James McCord. McCord was a very wealthy planter, lawyer, editor, and one-time mayor of Columbia.[18] Louisa Susannah was an accomplished poet and essayist of ultra-conservative views and independent means. She had inherited 50 slaves from an aunt and managed the McCord plantation, Lang Syne, which she owned—a wedding gift from her father, the Judge.[19]

Mrs. Hayne showed her guests the bust of her son, William—then about 23 years old—that Mills had fashioned. The plaster cast was "*well executed*," McCord later penned in his diary, "*and we all united to solicit Judge Cheves to have his taken for his children.*"[20] The Judge consented.

The very next day, at noon, Mills called on the **Honorable Langdon Cheves** and took a cast of the magistrate's head. This probably transpired in the home of his hostess, Mrs. Hayne, given the time frame and the fact that the judge's son-in-law was present and noted in his diary, "*The model was taken in the course of half an hour or so.*" Judge Cheves ordered one bust for each of his children and one for Mrs. Hayne. It was a lucrative commission—the jurist had ten children.[21]

About this same time, Mills also made a bust of the Judge's literary daughter, **Louisa Susannah McCord**. Her father and husband both praised the likeness. The outspoken celebrity, on the contrary, would turn out to be one sitter whom Mills failed to please.[22]

When the three Columbians returned home, they carried their busts—and the name of Clark Mills—north to the state capital. Given the patrician circle in which the Cheves and McCord families socialized, Mills could not have wished for a more powerful endorsement. He "was given job after job, until the new artist was the theme of conversation in every circle of society in Charleston."[23]

One reason for Mills's success was that, when he began to charge for his busts, he priced them very reasonably. His method, wrote one reporter, "enabled him to make portrait busts so cheaply that he soon had as much work as he could do."[24] In addition, Mills's business benefited from his "kindly bearing." He put sitters at ease.[25]

In the early weeks of 1845, a member of the Board of Trustees of the Apprentices' Library Society stepped into Mills's shop. The Society wanted a bust of its benefactor, Dr. Joseph Johnson.[26] A physician by training, **Joseph Johnson** was president of the Charleston branch of the Second Bank of the United States and served two terms as mayor of Charleston.[27] Mills accepted the charge, took the doctor's face and head casts, and made the bust. The *Courier* called it "a very striking likeness."[28]

A year later, another bust by Mills was donated to the Apprentices' Library Society. It was commissioned by James Louis Petigru—who himself had sat for Mills—to honor **Henry Schultz**. Schultz was a flamboyant entrepreneur and founder, proprietor and promoter of the town of Hamburg, South Carolina.[29] Petigru informed the Society that the German immigrant, being "in large measure self-taught," served as an example to emulate. The donor likened Mills to Schultz: "the artist has owed his distinction more to the energies of his own will, than to the favor of fortune or friends."[30] The Society's Board of Trustees accepted Petigru's gift and thanked Mills profusely at their meeting in February 1846.

Business was brisk for Clark Mills, the bust maker. But not brisk enough. His family was growing, and with it, his financial obligations, which included—events suggest—bills from doctors. Eliza's fifth child, born around April 1844, may have been sickly.

Later that year Mills joined with neighbors of his Guard House workplace to found the Charleston Friendly Botanic Thomsonian Society and petition the General Assembly of South Carolina for its incorporation.[31] Samuel Thomson, a self-taught New Hampshire farmer who had just died the previous year—1843—had devised a system of health care using herbs and plants.[32] His book, *New Guide to Health; or, Botanic Family Physician*, published in 1822, decried conventional medicine and prescribed remedies prepared at home from natural products. The *New Guide*'s treatments gained wide popularity throughout the United States in the 1830s and '40s, especially in remote frontier areas. Thomson's ideas were debated in Charleston newsprint.[33]

It is not hard to imagine Mills, faced with an ill infant, exploring alternative remedies. The couple had lost their first-born. They would have been frantic to save this one. The General Assembly granted the Society's petition for incorporation.[34] But the fifth child of Clark and Eliza Mills would not reach the age of six.[35]

What the up-and-coming sculptor needed to pay the bills was a best seller. He needed a bust of an admired public figure that he could reproduce in multiple copies to meet the public demand for it. Moreover, a powerful incentive other than financial need was pressuring Mills to succeed: his pride.

The issue raised by "An Admirer of the Arts"—whether busts derived from face masks were truly art or simply mechanical—rankled Mills. A few months after Admirer's letter appeared in the *Courier*, the newspaper's editor, Richard Yeadon, aired his own observations on the subject, concluding, "The art of Mr. Mills is partly mechanical and partly that of statuary."[36] Being deemed a clever mechanic, rather than an artist, motivated Mills more than any importunate creditor.

How did artists manage to support themselves and their families? Mills surely considered a variety of ways.

One option was the American Art-Union in New York City. This membership organization fostered American painters by commissioning works from them. For five dollars a year, each member received an engraving of a famous painting and was entered into a Christmas lottery for one of the paintings the Art-Union purchased that year. Membership was growing rapidly and the concept had spread to Philadelphia. But the American Art-Union was not yet commissioning sculpture.[37]

Another way that artists gained income was by hiring an impresario to take their works—statues as well as paintings—on tour throughout the United States. Exhibitions were advertised in local newspapers and the public paid an admittance fee to view the artwork.[38] But only artists who had already earned a name for themselves could go this route. The name of Clark Mills did not resonate—not yet—beyond Charleston and Columbia.

Unknown painters and sculptors on the threshold of their careers, such as Mills, needed a patron to support them. They lived on the largesse of a wealthy lover of art who believed in their potential and wanted to see it realized. Although Mills had benefitted from the kindness of John Schnierle, financial underwriting from the mayor—and other patrons—still lay in his future.

But there was yet another way to finance a career in art: enlist subscribers. An artist would propose a work and subscribers would pledge in advance to purchase a copy of it. This option suited Mills's entrepreneurial instincts. Besides, the business venture was almost imposed upon him by the well-connected South Carolinians who were enthralled with his busts. It was they who urged him to offer by subscription a bust of a friend of theirs, a man whom they admired greatly. Mills acceded wholeheartedly.

While his "very admirable" bust of Dr. Simons was being displayed in the Exchange Reading Room, Mills was enlisting subscribers for a bust of the most famous and beloved South Carolinian of them all, a man who happened to be one of the most powerful personages in Washington, D.C. Mills was promising subscribers a bust of the "Cast-Iron Man."

NOTES

1 Benjamin Bonneau Simons (1776–1844), see Howard Atwood Kelly, M.D., ed., *A Cyclopedia of American Medical Biography, Comprising the Lives of Eminent Deceased Physicians and Surgeons, 1610 to 1910* (Philadelphia and London: W. B. Saunders Co., 1912), vol. II: 377–78.
2 [no title], [Charleston] *Southern Patriot*, Sept. 28, 1844, p. 3.
3 "[Communicated]," [Charleston] *Courier*, Dec. 20, 1844, p. 2. A report of Sept. 12, 2018, prepared by Christina Rae Butler of Butler Preservation, L.C., Research Consulting and Renovation, Charleston, confirms the historic address.
4 "[Communicated]," *Courier*, Dec. 20, 1844, 2.
5 "Clark Mills at Home," *The Washington Post*, Feb. 7, 1880, p. 2; and "Mr. Clark Mills, the Sculptor," *The Round Table*, vol. 1, no. 22 (May 14, 1864): 340.
6 "[Communicated]," *Courier*, Dec. 20, 1844, 2.
7 Richard Yeadon (1802–70), see Jan Onofrio, ed., *South Carolina Biographical Dictionary*, 2nd ed. (St. Clair Shores, Mich.: Somerset Publisher, Inc., 2000), vol. I: 399.

8 James Louis Petigru (1789–1863), see http://www.scencyclopedia.org/sce
/entries/petigru-james-louis. Rosemary Hopkins, *Clark Mills: The First Native American Sculptor* (M.A. thesis, University of Maryland, 1966): 156–57, quotes a letter of July 5, 1845, sent from Petigru in Charleston to his wife at their plantation, Badwell, which implies that this bust was executed before, or around the same time as, those of Calhoun and McDuffie, i.e., spring 1845. Today a copy of this bust is in the Charleston Library Society, Charleston, S.C.
9 George McDuffie (1790–1851), see http://www.scencyclopedia.org/sce
/entries/mcduffie-george. Today copies of this bust are in the Smithsonian American Art Museum, Washington, D.C.; South Caroliniana Library, University of South Carolina, Columbia, S.C.; and Charleston Library Society, Charleston, S.C.
10 John Blake White (1781–1859), see http://www.scencyclopedia.org/sce
/entries/white-john-blake. See also Charles E. Fairman, *Art and Artists of the Capitol of the United States of America* (Washington, D.C.: U.S. Govt. Print. Off., 1927): 315–16.
11 Samuel Foster Gilman (1791–1858), see http://www.scencyclopedia.org/sce
/entries/gilman-samuel-foster.
12 John Bachman (1790–1874), see http://www.scencyclopedia.org/sce/entries
/bachman-john. Today a copy of this bust is in the Charleston Library Society, Charleston, S.C.
13 William Alston Hayne (1821–1901), see www.findagrave.com/
memorial/13905000/william-alston-hayne.
14 Richard C. Lounsbury, ed., *Louisa A. McCord, Poems, Drama, Biography, Letters* (Charlottesville, Va.: University Press of Virginia, 1996): 351.
15 Daniel J. Dowling, *The Charleston Directory; And Register, for 1840–41* (Charleston: Daniel J. Dowling, pub. and print., 1840); transcribed selectively in James W. Hagy, *Directories for the City of Charleston, South Carolina* (Baltimore: Clearfield, 1997): 109. The address of the house today is 30 King St. It is a bed-and-breakfast known as the "Hayne House."
16 Robert Young Hayne (1791–1839), see http://www.scencyclopedia.org/sce
/entries/hayne-robert-young.
17 Langdon Cheves (1776–1857), see http://www.scencyclopedia.org/sce
/entries/cheves-langdon. Today a copy of this bust is in the South Caroliniana Library, University of South Carolina, Columbia, S.C.
18 David James McCord (1797–1855), see James Grant Wilson, John Fiske and Stanley L. Klos, eds., *Appleton's Cyclopaedia of American Biography* (New York: D. Appleton & Co., 1887–89), vol. 4: 94; at https://babel.hathitrust.org/cgi
/pt?id=mdp.39076005094219&view=1up&seq=118.
19 Louisa Susannah Cheves McCord (1810–79), see "Louisa Susanna [sic] Cheves McCord" at http://www.scencyclopedia.org/sce/entries/mccord
-louisa-susanna-cheves.
20 Lounsbury, *Louisa A. McCord,* 351.

21 Today a copy of this bust is in the South Caroliniana Library, University of South Carolina, Columbia, S.C.
22 This bust was later willfully destroyed. See Lounsbury, *Louisa A. McCord,* "Chronology," 9.
23 "Clark Mills and His Statue," *Camden* [S.C.] *Journal*; reprinted in "Mr. Mills," [Washington] *Daily Union,* May 1, 1850, p. 3; and "Clark Mills," [Charleston] *Courier,* May 8, 1850, p. 2.
24 "Mr. Clark Mills, the Sculptor," *The Round Table,* vol. 1, no. 22 (May 14, 1864): 340.
25 "Clark Mills at Home," *The Washington Post,* Aug. 7, 1879, p. 1.
26 "Tribute of Respect to Dr. Joseph Johnson," [Charleston] *Courier,* Feb. 26, 1845, p. 2.
27 Joseph Johnson (1776–1862), see https://en.wikipedia.org/wiki/Joseph_Johnson_(South_Carolina).
28 "Tribute of Respect . . . ," *Courier,* Feb. 26, 1845, 2.
29 Henry Schultz (1776–1851), see http://www.scencyclopedia.org/sce/entries/hamburg.
30 "Apprentices' Library Society," [Charleston] *Courier,* Feb. 10, 1846, p. 2.
31 Petition to the Senate and House of Representatives of the State of South Carolina, Dec. 9, 1844; Petitions to the General Assembly (S165015), 1844-104, South Carolina Department of Archives and History, Columbia; at https://scdah.sc.gov.
32 Samuel Thomson (1769–1843), see https://en.wikipedia.org/wiki/Samuel_Thomson.
33 See, among others, (1) "Thompson's [sic] Patent," *Charleston Mercury,* June 18, 1831, p. 1; (2) "Messrs. Editors," [Charleston] *Courier,* Aug. 18, 1835, p. 2; and (3) "Messrs. Editors," [Charleston] *Courier,* Sept. 29, 1835, p. 2.
34 "South Carolina – Acts & Joint Resolutions on Education During the 1800s; Dec. 15, 1845, Act to Authorize Practice of Medicine Under the Botanic or Thomsonian System to Receive Compensation" at https://www.carolania.com/SC/Education/acts_on_education_in_sc_1800s.html.
35 See Bk. 1, Ch. 4.
36 "Admirable Casts," *Courier,* June 30, 1845, 2.
37 Catherine Hoover Voorsanger and John K. Howat, eds., *Art and the Empire City: New York, 1825–1861* (New Haven and London: Yale University Press, 2000): 59 and passim.
38 See, for examples, Bk. 1, Ch. 19 (Powers' exhibition of his *Greek Slave*) and Bk. 2 (Mills's exhibition of his rampant horse model).

CHAPTER 8
April 1845–January 1846

Charleston Apl 8th 1845

Honored Sir:

When in Charleston on your way to take charge of the State Department at Washington, you were kind enough to give your consent to have your bust taken by me, at some future day, as you could not make it convenient to delay your departure at the time. Having obtained a list of one hundred of our most respectable citizens who are desirous of having it taken, I had made arrangements to proceed to Washington for that purpose, when the news was received of your illness. In this taking the liberty of addressing you my object is, most respectfully to solicit that you would allow me the opportunity as early as your convenience may admit, to gratify the wishes of those of your fellow citizens who have honored me with their names.

With great respect & Consideration,
Yr. Obt. Servt.
Clark Mills

Letter, Clark Mills to John C. Calhoun;
John C. Calhoun Papers, Clemson University, Clemson, S.C.

The "*Honored Sir*" was John C. Calhoun. One year earlier—March of 1844—he had been a private citizen living on his estate, Fort Hill, in Clemson, South Carolina, when President Tyler asked him to serve as Secretary of State. One of the most powerful political figures in the country by that time, Calhoun had already served as a U.S. Congressman, Secretary of War, Vice President under James Madison and Andrew Jackson, and U.S. Senator. His was the stentorian voice of the ascendency of state government over the federal government, the institution of slavery, and Southern solidarity. Calhoun accepted Tyler's invitation to head the Department of State.[1]

Making his way to the nation's capital, Calhoun passed through Charleston precisely when Mills was winning his first clients there. One of them was a friend and political ally of Calhoun's: Franklin Harper Elmore.[2] Elmore told his colleague about the city's talented plasterer-turned-sculptor. "Many of your friends here," Elmore informed Calhoun, wanted a bust of him and—at the insistence of those friends and the sculptor himself—he asked Calhoun to sit for Mills. Calhoun deferred. He could not delay getting to Washington. But he consented to have his bust "taken" by Mills "at some future day."[3]

Mills immediately started soliciting subscribers. By early 1845, he had reached his goal of 100 and planned to make a trip to Washington to take a cast of Calhoun's head.[4] At that moment, though, ill health forced the Secretary of State to resign. In March, he returned to Fort Hill.[5]

Mills was eager to remind Calhoun of his promise. But he hesitated to impose on the convalescent 63-year-old. On April 7, 1845, he called on Elmore to intercede on his behalf. Elmore promptly wrote to Calhoun:

> *Mr. Mills is now anxious to procure your sitting, & in this he is but the exponent of very many here who wish to have copies.*[6]

Mills rushed to press the matter the very next day, sending his own respectful appeal to Calhoun. He closed his letter with this reassurance:

> *I beg permission to state that the process I have adopted for taking busts is altogether different from the usual mode, & inflicts scarcely any inconvenience, and does not occupy more than fifteen minutes.*[7]

Calhoun consented.

That April of 1845, therefore, Mills traveled to Fort Hill and was conducted into the presence of the formidable statesman. Age and declining health had sharpened the traits that made Calhoun's face arresting and unforgettable: broad forehead, jutting brows and cheek bones, clean-shaven sunken cheeks and chin, firm mouth, and deep-set, ferocious eyes.[8] His hair, mostly gray now, was abundant and long. Brushed back and covering his ears and neck, it conjured the mane of a lion. One author had dubbed the serious intellectual the "Cast-Iron Man." The descriptive was spot-on and stuck.[9]

Many years later a writer would relate a story Mills told him:

> In one of his sittings, Mr. Calhoun relieved the weariness of the hour by discoursing to Mills upon his specialty in art, and, with great precision, went minutely through all the details, from the finding of the facial angle to the completion of the bust. Mills was astonished; but his astonishment was greater yet when Mr. Calhoun laughingly confessed that the whole thing was a mere narration on his part, a simple effort of memory in recollecting the detailed information once given him by Hiram Powers, when sitting to him in Washington as to his method of modeling a bust.[10]

Mills took plaster casts of Calhoun's face and head. From these he made molds which, when filled with plaster paste, yielded a head. Mills fixed the head on half-shoulders and mounted the bust on a short, round pedestal inscribed simply: **CALHOUN**. Then he met with the legendary sitter a second time to open the eyes and sculpt the eyebrows and hair. The portrait was striking. Rather than draping the bust in classical garb—as Hiram Powers had done with his bust of the Cast-Iron Man—Mills left the statesman's throat unadorned. Nothing softened the severity of Calhoun's angular features and fixed gaze.

Delighted subscribers stared, spellbound, at the mighty head. It elicited exuberant acclaim. In the *Courier* of June 30, 1845, Richard Yeadon announced:

> The skill and taste of Mr. Mills have already attracted a large and increasing custom, and his gallery of heads of busts (exhibiting Messrs. Calhoun, McDuffie, Petigru, King, and numerous others,) is continually challenging admiration, by a fidelity and accuracy of delineation and expression which betray the originals at a glance.[11]

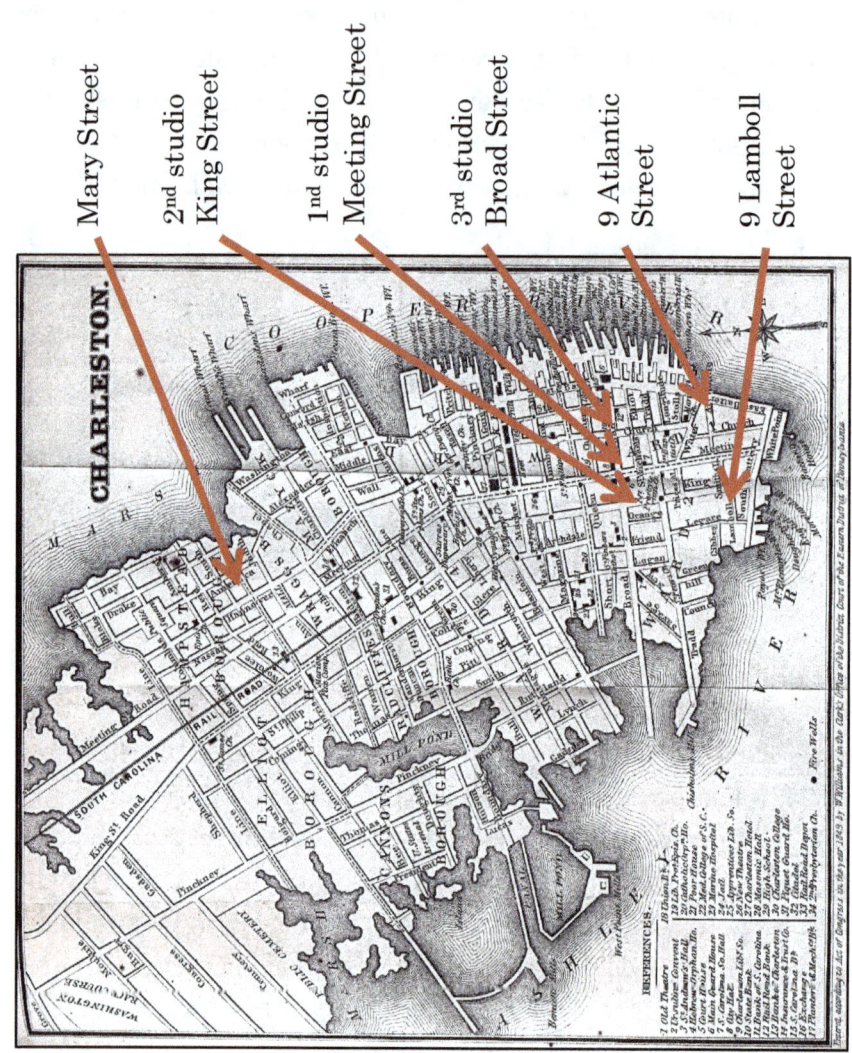

Mills first resided with his wife Eliza most likely near Market and Beaufain Streets in Charleston (1837-38), then with their children on Mary Street in the Northern Neck (1838-45), then at 49 Broad Street (1845-46), while his three consecutive studios were all located in the heart of downtown Charleston. He purchased the house at 9 Lamboll Street in 1838, but defaulted on the mortgage. In 1847 Eliza's father bought the house at 9 Atlantic Street for her and her four sons, where they lived until 1854. (W. Williams, *Charleston*, map published in 1849, at www.carolana.com)

The increased volume of Mills's distinguished patronage warranted a larger, more suitable shop where he could showcase his handiwork. He moved from the room in the rear of the Guard House to "the Eastern side of King Street, a few doors South of Broad-street."[12] That was just one block away. "Several small busts, the work of his own hands, adorned his window."[13]—Faces all Charlestonians recognized as they walked by Mills's shop.

Making more plaster busts, though, did not satisfy Mills. His every achievement seemed to demand of him another, surpassing achievement. Yeadon had closed his laudatory editorial with a phrase that nettled the would-be sculptor:

> Mr. Mills displays great skill and taste in design, and exquisite dexterity and delicacy in execution; and we augur for him success and reputation in the higher branches of his art.[14]

"In the higher branches of his art:" that was the same sentiment that "An Admirer of the Arts" had expressed in the *Courier* six months earlier. Creating busts from life masks, while commendable, was a mechanical process. The public expected more of Mills; they expected "Art." But that was nothing more than what Mills himself aspired to. "The plaster bust of Mr. Calhoun was so successful," one chronicler would relate, "that his friends desired it might be preserved in marble."[15] Straightaway, Mills undertook the challenge. A journalist for *The Round Table* was to put it succinctly: "He then resolved to try cutting in marble."[16]

Mills was familiar with the careers of New York sculptors John Frazee and John Henri Isaac Browere. Both had started out in the 1820s by creating plaster busts from life masks, just as Mills was doing. But by the 1830s, Frazee had advanced to carving busts in marble and gained the reputation of "artist," while Browere, who continued to work in plaster, never shed the status of "artisan."[17] Mills aimed to emulate Frazee. The goal was ambitious. To succeed, Mills would have to acquire skills that normally took long apprenticeship to master:

CREATING A MARBLE BUST

(1) Make a plaster bust, either from a clay original or from plaster casts of face and head;
(2) Build a wooden box around the bust that duplicates the dimensions of the block of marble to be used to carve it;
(3) Insert metal rods, "guide points," into numerous places all over the plaster bust; these rods extend out as far as the walls of the box;
(4) Using these fixed points as guides to measure how far to cut into the stone, carve the bust out of the block of marble; and
(5) Finish the surface of the bust, sculpting hair, eyes, lips, etc.[18]

Mills was already adept at step one. Now he needed to learn how to build the box, affix guide points, and carve stone. The unnamed Italian "image maker" whom he had encountered on the street, and who had shown him how plaster busts were made, may have taught Mills how to enliven the sleeping face: open the eyes, chisel eyebrows and hair, retouch the ears, etc. But those finishing details were all carved in plaster, not stone. Although Mills never acknowledged any teacher, someone must have shown him what tools to use and how to wield them to carve marble. That was Mills's *modus operandi*. First, he would commit wholeheartedly to a formidable goal, then he would seek out the expert who could teach him how to achieve it. His self-confidence was absolute. But who was "expert" at carving marble in Charleston in 1845?

Prominent among the city's stonecutters were the four sons of Thomas Walker. Their sister's son, John White, was another respected stonecutter.[19] One or more of the Walker brothers, or possibly John White, may have introduced Mills to the tools and techniques of working in stone—though certainly *not* how to sculpt a bust. What these master carvers fabricated were cemetery headstones. Marble busts, statues, mantelpieces, balustrades, table tops, and other embellishments of the city's fine houses and public buildings were imported from Italy. Deming, Bulkley & Co., whose home office was in New York City, was Charleston's major importer of such goods.[20] The firm's local agent, Erastus Bulkley, kept an office at 49 Broad Street and a marble yard next-door.[21]

In addition to Bulkley's, marble yards at 141 and 123 Meeting Street might have served as Mills's "school of carving." One belonged to James E. Walker & Brothers, the other to John White.[22] All three were within a few blocks of Mills's workshop on King Street. Remarkable as it may seem, therefore, Mills may indeed have "picked up" sculpting simply by observing stonecutters at work.[23]

A journalist of *The Round Table* would write:

> [A]fter procuring a block of native Carolina stone, he commenced the bust of John C. Calhoun. At that time he was not familiar with the rules for carving a bust, and was compelled to adopt a rule of his own, which was a very tedious process, requiring extraordinary care.[24]

Whatever "rule" the autodidact may have adopted, within a span of about five months—May through September—Mills succeeded in reproducing his plaster bust of Calhoun in marble. To the portrait in stone he added one subtle feature: a narrow diagonal band across the statesman's chest simulated the hem of a garment. The achievement beggars understanding. From never having held a chisel and mallet in his hands, Mills fashioned out of stone a strikingly truthful portrait of a man whose face was well-known throughout the country, all in five months' time!

As soon as it was done, Mills made sure the public was aware of his accomplishment. The response was tremendous. The bust "was then considered the best likeness ever taken of Calhoun."[25] "There was but one word spoken of it: 'inimitable.'"[26]

Interestingly, it was at this pivotal moment in his career when Mills made what appears to be a strategic move. He notified the public of it in the *Courier* of September 19, 1845:

> **REMOVAL.**—The subscriber has removed from King-street and has taken rooms in Broad-street, south side, one door west

of Church-street, where he is prepared to execute BUSTS; either by cast or modelling, and would invite inspection to a number of specimens now on hand.   CLARKE MILLS.[27]

The "removal" was only a matter of two blocks. What is noteworthy is that the "rooms" that Mills had taken were the very house where the marble agent, Erastus Bulkley, once had his office, and the large open space next door to it was a marble yard with a stonecutting shed.[28] Did Mills envision for himself a future of carving busts in marble?

The building on Broad Street, number 49 in Mills's time, number 51 today, has been extensively changed over the years. It is listed on the National Register of Historic Places and a bronze plaque on the façade announces, "Clark Mills Studio."[29] When Mills took possession of the house, it comprised two stories with a livable attic and back porch. It stood between an alley on one side and the marble yard on the other.[30] It had "good out buildings," too, meaning at least a kitchen and privy.[31] Mills's landlady was Mrs. Caroline P. Huard, a 50-year-old widow who had inherited the property from her late husband. She advertised it in the *Courier*:

> TO RENT, the HOUSE, No. 49 Broad-street, it has a good Store, four upright rooms and two garrets, a piazza, and every convenience for a genteel family. The store and upper part will be rented, together or separate. It is a good stand for any kind of business, or for a lawyer's or doctor's office.[32]

Or for a sculptor's atelier and living quarters. When Mills was plying his fledgling trade in the rear of the Guard House, then on King Street, he rented only a workroom. Chances are he continued to reside with his wife and sons and bound assistant, Philip Reid, on Mary Street—perhaps in the home of Eliza's father, Alexander Ballentine. This move, however, was different. Mills leased the whole two-and-a-half-story house with outbuildings. It seems evident, then,

Mills's last studio in Charleston, 51 Broad Street (no. 49 then), stood next to a marble yard with a stone-cutting shed. The building is totally transformed from the two-and-a-half-story house Mills rented from September 1845 to November 1846. His wife and sons probably lived with him during that time. (South Carolina Department of Archives and History)

that he brought his family and Reid to live with him at 49 Broad Street. If so, Eliza was seven months pregnant at the time and delivered her last child, Clark, Jr., in their new abode. Mills would rent from Mrs. Huard for a total of 14 months.[33] Never, though—despite his strategic location—would he ever carve marble, or any other stone, again.

Although the address of Mills's shop changed three times, it always fell within one block of Charleston's beating heart: the intersection of Meeting and Broad Streets. There stood St. Michael's Episcopal Church, the Guard House, city hall, and the county courthouse. Foot traffic was heavy. "His humble shop became the centre of attraction to many admirers of art."[34] Reported the *Evening News* of October 4, 1845:

> We invite the attention of our readers to a bust of J. C. Calhoun,
> in stone, the production of our ingenious townsman, Mr. Clarke

Mills. Mr. Mills is a self-taught artist, and this is his first effort in the noble art of sculpture. The material is a block of free-stone, obtained from the vicinity of Columbia; and thus on a native mineral of Carolina, our artist, has succeeded in correctly stamping the features of Carolina's favorite son.[35]

Four days later, Richard Yeadon told his *Courier* readers:

Mr. Clark Mills, a native artist, whose busts in plaster, actually mounted on the human head and face, have excited such general admiration, by their truth to life, has recently, as we predicted on a former occasion, made a successful attempt in a higher branch of art. From a block of native white free stone, procured near Columbia in this State, he has sculptured, with hammer and chisel, a stone bust of the great Southern Statesman, (his first attempt in this line,) in a manner that speaks well for the skill and taste of the artist.[36]

Immediately, Mills secured a design patent for his "Bust of Calhoun."[37] Luckily for him, the following month—November 1845—the voters of South Carolina returned Calhoun to the U.S. Senate. That enhanced the value of the popular statesman's bust and boded well for its continued demand. Orders poured in.[38] Mills filled them:

The subscribers for the BUSTS of the Hon. John C. Calhoun and the Rev. Dr. Bachman, are respectfully requested to send for them.   CLARK MILLS.[39]

From the inception of Mills's career as a sculptor, the quasi-political or patriotic resonance of his work transcended its artistic merit. The subject—"Carolina's favorite son"—and medium—"a native mineral of Carolina"—and the fact that the creator was "a native artist" and "self-taught"—all of these factors conferred a cultural importance on the work, regardless of its quality as art. Moreover, Mills's busts were readily accessible to the masses. No resident of Charleston had any trouble naming every one of them "at a glance." The social and historical significance of his creations roused interest in their creator. One journalist was to put it this way:

> [E]very one was in exstacies; a common plasterer, laying down the trowel and taking up the chisel, had produced a most admirable head and bust of Calhoun. Calhoun was their idol, the representative of South Carolina; any one who could cut his facsimile in marble must necessarily be a great man.[40]

None of this was lost on Mills. One reporter would comment on the sculptor's business savvy:

> He has an ardent mind and temperament, controlled by a sound judgment, and a thorough practical knowledge of men and business. This, with a well-balanced mind, so uncommon in artists, he has acquired in the school of poverty and in the struggle of everyday life.[41]

Mills started a practice he was to follow throughout his career: making gifts of his works. He knew the gesture would be publicized, spreading his name, garnering public esteem, and generating referrals. In January 1846 he gave copies of his busts of George McDuffie and John C. Calhoun to the Apprentices' Library Society.[42] The following year, he would present a copy of his bust of Daniel Webster to Richard Yeadon, editor of the Charleston *Courier*.[43] Yeadon had sat for Mills, had described the experience to his readers, and was to publish many more articles praising the sculptor's efforts.[44] Nevertheless, the *Camden Journal* would insist:

> But the old opinion, even in the face of these evidences against it, revived, that an artist, to be an artist, must study under Italian masters, and beneath Italian skies.[45]

Building on the success of the trailblazers, John Frazee and John Henri Isaac Browere, a new generation of American sculptors was seeking to learn from the world's master carvers, and the world's master carvers—as everyone knew—were Italian. The Boston sculptor, Horatio Greenough, had headed to Rome. Hiram Powers, Greenough's contemporary and fellow New Englander, had done likewise. If society were ever to concede Mills's advancement from "mechanic" to "artist," he knew what his next move had to be: study in Italy. But he had no money, and a family to support. He needed a patron.

Horatio Greenough had been able to study in Rome thanks to the largesse of Dr. George Parkman, the eminent physician and philanthropist of Boston. After that, Robert Gilmore, Jr., a Baltimore merchant, organized a group of businessmen to present Greenough with a purse of one thousand dollars so the sculptor could return to Italy and establish his home and studio in Florence.[46]

The young Hiram Powers had had Nicholas Longworth, a winemaker of Cincinnati, to finance his emerging career. While sojourning in Washington, D.C., making portrait busts to establish a reputation, Powers used a letter of introduction from Longworth to meet Senator William Campbell Preston of South Carolina. Preston and his wife, Louise Penelope Davis, both "sat to Powers" for portrait busts. In October 1836, Preston introduced Powers to his younger brother, John Smith Preston, a planter and attorney of Columbia.

The Preston brothers were not only immensely rich and well-connected, they had both studied the fine arts, traveled widely in Europe, cultivated discriminating taste, and avidly supported the artistic endeavors of fellow Americans. It was a series of generous, yearly drafts from John Preston that allowed Hiram Powers to study in Rome, then reside permanently with his family in Florence.[47] In just a few years, William and John Preston would both champion another aspiring American sculptor: Clark Mills. But that was still in the future. Mills needed a patron now.

Three showed up.

NOTES

1. John Caldwell Calhoun (1782-1850), see http://www.scencyclopedia.org/sce/entries/calhoun-john-caldwell. See also John C. Calhoun entry, 1840 U.S. Census, Pickens District, Pickens Co., S.C., p. 23 (handwritten), p. 353[b] (stamped); NARA M704, roll 514 (household includes 69 enslaved members).
2. See Bk. 1, Ch.5.
3. Letter, Elmore to Calhoun, Apr. 7, 1845; John C. Calhoun Papers, Clemson University, Clemson, S.C.; published in Clyde N. Wilson, ed., *The Papers of John C. Calhoun* (Columbia, S.C.: University of South Carolina Press, 1993), vol. XXI, 1845: 474–75.
4. "[Communicated]," [Charleston] *Courier*, Dec. 20, 1844, p. 2.
5. Calhoun, at http://www.scencyclopedia.org/sce/entries/calhoun-john-caldwell.
6. Letter, Elmore to Calhoun, Apr. 7, 1845; in Wilson, *Papers of John C. Calhoun*, vol. XXI, 1845: 474–75.
7. Letter, Mills to Calhoun, Apr. 8, 1845; in Wilson, *Papers of John C. Calhoun*, vol. XXI, 1845: 481–82.
8. Photograph of John C. Calhoun taken of a ca. 1845 daguerreotype, National Portrait Gallery, Washington, D.C.; at https://npg.si.edu/object/npg_NPG.77.258.
9. Harriet Martineau was the first to call Calhoun the "cast-iron man" in her *Retrospect of Western Travel* (London: Saunders and Otley, 1838), vol. 1: 147.
10. "Clark Mills," *Lippincott's Magazine*, vol. XXXI (Old Series), vol. 5 (New Series) (Mar. 1883): 315–16. Today, a plaster bust of Calhoun by Powers, dated 1835, is in the Smithsonian American Art Museum, Washington, D.C.
11. "Admirable Casts," [Charleston] *Courier*, June 30, 1845, p. 2.
12. Ibid.
13. "Clark Mills and His Statue," *Camden* [S.C.] *Journal*; reprinted in "Mr. Mills," [Washington] *Daily Union*, May 1, 1850, p. 3; and "Clark Mills," [Charleston] *Courier*, May 8, 1850, p. 2, quoting the *Camden* [S.C.] *Journal*.
14. "Admirable Casts," *Courier*, Jun. 30, 1845, 2.
15. "Clark Mills and His Equestrian Statue," *DeBow's Review*, vol. 16 (Jan. 1854): 39.
16. "Mr. Clark Mills, The Sculptor," *The Round Table*, vol.1, no. 22 (May 14, 1864): 340.
17. Catherine Hoover Voorsanger and John K. Howat, eds., *Art and the Empire City: New York, 1825–1861* (New Haven and London: Yale University Press, 2000): 137–41.
18. In Massachusetts, stonecutter Benjamin Harris Kinney, five years Mills's junior, would create his first clay bust in 1849 and first marble bust in 1853. Kinney's career would follow the "artisan-to-artist" evolution of Frazee's and Mills's, only some years later. See William D. Wallace, *B. H. Kinney,*

       1821–1888, Gravestone Carver and Sculptor (Worcester, Mass.: Worcester Historical Museum, 1985): 26.
19 "Long Cane Cemetery," *The Historical Marker Database* [of South Carolina], at www.hmdb.org/m.asp?m=50740. The Walker brothers are listed in the Charleston City Directory of 1840–41 as "Stone Cutters" (141 Meeting St.) and 1852 as "marble cutters" (4 anson st.). John White is listed in 1840–41 as "Stone Cutter" (123 Meeting St.) and 1852 as "marble yard" (117 queen st.). The Walkers and John White are enumerated in the 1840 and 1850 U.S. Censuses and Slave Schedules of Charleston.
20 Email correspondence and telephone discussions between the author and Valerie Perry, Assistant Museums Director, Historic Charleston Foundation, Dec. 2024–Jan. 2025.
21 Bulkley, Erastus, Firm of Deming, Bulkley & Co. entry, and Bulkley, Erastus, entry, in T. C. Fay, *Charleston Directory and Strangers' Guide for 1840 and 1841* (Charleston: T.C. Fay, 1840): 99.
22 See n. 19–21 above.
23 Mills was evidently not the only "amateur sculptor" in Charleston at this time. Joseph Daniel Aiken, a wealthy planter who practiced law, became proficient at sculpting marble as an avocation. His bust of his wife, Ellen Martin, is on display in the Joseph Aiken House today. How much formal instruction Aiken may have received, however, is unknown. See n. 20 above.
24 "Mr. Clark Mills, The Sculptor," *The Round Table*, vol. 1, no. 22 (May 14, 1864): 340.
25 Ibid.
26 "Clark Mills . . . ," *Camden Journal*.
27 "REMOVAL," [Charleston] *Courier*, Sept. 19, 1845, p. 3.
28 See n. 21 above and n. 29 below.
29 "Clark Mills Studio," National Register of Historic Places, at http://www.nationalregister.sc.gov/charleston/S10817710008/S10817710008.pdf. Also Report by Christina Rae Butler, Butler Preservation, L.C., Research Consulting and Renovation, Charleston, prepared for the author in 2018: "The information about Mills in the NRHP report is drawn exclusively from a handful of derivative sources and contains numerous errors." Butler used city directories, maps, and land and tax records to research 51 Broad Street. Subsequent research by the author in newspapers online confirms Butler's assessment of the NRHP report.
30 Report of Christina Rae Butler. See also n. 19–21 above and n. 32 below.
31 "TO RENT," [Charleston] *Courier*, Dec. 6, 1850, p. 3.
32 "TO RENT," [Charleston] *Courier*, June 14, 1843, p. 3, and July 11, 1845, p. 3.
33 "TO LET, the HOUSE," [Charleston] *Courier*, Nov. 12, 1846, p. 3: "49 Broad-street, now occupied by Mr. Clark Mills."
34 "Clark Mills and His Equestrian Statue," *DeBow's Review*, vol. 16 (Jan. 1854): 40.
35 "Bust of J. C. Calhoun," [Charleston] *Evening News*, Oct. 4, 1845, p. 2.

April 1845–January 1846

36 "Bust of Mr. Calhoun," [Charleston] *Courier*, Oct. 8, 1845, p. 2; reprinted in the *Edgefield* [S.C.] *Advertiser*, Oct. 15, 1845, p. 2.
37 "Bust of Calhoun," Oct. 7, 1845; Patent Drawings, 1791–1877; Records of the Patent and Trademark Office, RG 241; NARA microfilm T1239, roll 7, no. 38; and "Clark Mills," Entry no. 38, *Report of the Commissioner of Patents, for the year 1845*, 29th Cong., 1st Sess., House of Representatives Doc. No. 140 (Washington, D.C.: Govt. Print. Off., Feb. 24, 1846): 1376.
38 "Clark Mills . . . ," *DeBow's Review*, vol. 16 (Jan. 1854): 40.
39 [no title], [Charleston] *Courier*, Jan. 3, 1846, p. 3.
40 "Sketches of Washington. By Childe Harold," *Brooklyn Daily Eagle*, Mar. 30, 1853, p. 2.
41 "History of the Jackson Statue," [Washington] *Daily Union*, Jan. 18, 1853, p. 3.
42 "Apprentices' Library Society," [Charleston] *Courier*, Feb. 10, 1846, p. 2; and Rosemary Hopkins, *Clark Mills: The First Native American Sculptor* (M.A. thesis, University of Maryland, 1966): 157–58.
43 "Bust of Daniel Webster," [Charleston] *Courier*, Aug. 2, 1847, p. 2.
44 See Bk. 1, Chs. 5 and 17.
45 "Clark Mills," *Courier*, May 8, 1850, 2.
46 Richard P. Wunder, *Hiram Powers, Vermont Sculptor, 1805–1873* (Newark, Del.: University of Delaware Press, 1991), vol. I, *Life*: 97.
47 Ibid., 96.

CHAPTER 9
June–October 1845

MONUMENT TO JACKSON.
Pursuant to public notice, a numerous and highly respectable meeting of the citizens of Washington, favorable to the erection in that city of a colossal equestrian statue in honor of the memory of Andrew Jackson, assembled at the Apollo Hall in that city, on Monday evening, the 15th September, 1845.

"Monument to Jackson," [Charleston] *Courier*, Sept. 23, 1845, p. 2.

When Mills was cutting his bust of Calhoun in stone in his shop on King Street, Andrew Jackson died at the Hermitage, his plantation outside of Nashville. "The Hero of our two wars of independence; one of the most popular of Presidents and of men that our country has ever known," announced the *Courier* on a page framed in mourning, "is no more."[1] Across the nation, "Old Hickory" was mourned, and immediately the idea circulated that he should be memorialized with a statue, but not just any statue.

Within days of Jackson's demise, the editor of the *Nashville Union*, Jeremiah G. Harris, wrote a letter to the American sculptor, Hiram Powers, in Florence, Italy. Harris asked Powers what a "monumental bronze equestrian statue" of the general would cost.[2] Meanwhile, an editor in New York City, John L. O'Sullivan of the *United States Magazine and Democratic Review*, wrote that "a grand, colossal *Equestrian Statue in bronze*, at Washington, to be erected by a voluntary national subscription, is the proper monument for Jackson."[3] From the inception of the idea, Jackson's memorial was to be "a colossal equestrian statue in imperishable bronze."[4] That modifier, "imperishable," was used repeatedly.

O'Sullivan acted on his conviction. He traveled to Washington and initiated a flurry of consultations among the bereaved compatriots of Jackson. The comrades in arms and associates in civil service rallied to the proposal.[5] On September 10, 1845, accompanied by Secretary of State, James Buchanan, O'Sullivan took his cause to President Polk himself in the Executive Mansion.[6]

James Knox Polk, during his tenures as governor of Tennessee and U.S. senator and congressman, had been a staunch friend, advisor and supporter of fellow Tennessean, Andrew Jackson. Jackson, in turn, had acted as Polk's mentor and ally. During much of his political career, Polk was called "Young Hickory."[7] The president supported O'Sullivan's undertaking wholeheartedly, but declined his invitation to head a committee to raise the necessary funds. The gesture, Polk feared, would appear politically motivated: the president, Buchanan, O'Sullivan—everyone associated with the proposal—was an unabashed "Jacksonian Democrat." However, Polk did agree to placing his name at the top of the subscription list.[8] He contributed, "most cheerfully . . . as a private citizen," $100.[9]

Having mustered the sponsorship of some of the most prominent residents of the national capital, as well as the blessing of the president himself, O'Sullivan published a notice to the public in that city's *Daily Union* newspaper on September 12 and 13, 1845:

MONUMENT TO JACKSON.

It is proposed to take the requisite measures for the erection of a *colossal equestrian statue* in honor of the memory of General Jackson, in the city of Washington, by voluntary national subscription, to be collected under the direction of a suitable central committee. The citizens of Washington, favorable to such an object, are requested to meet on Monday evening, at half-past seven o'clock, at the Apollo Hall.[10]

That Monday evening, September 15th, many Washingtonians made their way to the south side of E Street between 13th and 13½ Streets and entered Apollo Hall. They assembled in the second-floor meeting room, shook hands convivially, and at seven-thirty sharp—as the notice had specified—James Hoban Jr. called the meeting to order.[11] Hoban was in his mid-thirties, a well-known local attorney who had held several public offices. Old timers said he was "the spitting image" of his father, the architect of the President's House.[12] The *Daily Union* would report:

> On motion of James Hoban, Esq., General J. P. Van Ness was called to the chair, who, on taking his seat, made a short but feeling address, in which he referred to the civil and military virtues distinguishing the life of the hero, patriot, and statesman, to whose memory it was the purpose of the meeting to do justice.[13]

General John Peter Van Ness, a 76-year-old veteran of the War of 1812, had shared a life-long friendship with Andrew Jackson.[14] After Van Ness's florid accolade of his erstwhile commanding officer, James Hoban read a series of resolutions drafted by John L. O'Sullivan. They spelled out the purpose stated in the published notice and named the 13 men who, acting as the "Jackson Monument Committee," would be responsible for carrying the plan into effect:[15]

> John Peter Van Ness, officer in the War of 1812; U.S. Congressman from New York; alderman and mayor of Washington; officer of the D.C. Militia; officer of the Washington National Monument Society; elected President of the Committee;
>
> Amos Kendall, lawyer and newspaper editor in Kentucky; then U.S. Postmaster General under President Jackson; member of Jackson's "Kitchen Cabinet;" elected First Vice President of the Committee;[16]

James Hoban Jr., U.S. District Attorney for the District of Columbia; Washington City alderman and councilman; elected a Secretary of the Committee;

Charles Kitchell Gardner, Army officer during the War of 1812; First Assistant U.S. Postmaster General under President Jackson; Auditor of the U.S. Treasury under President Van Buren; D.C. Postmaster General under President Polk;[17]

Charles P. Sengstack, grocer on D Street; petitioned President Polk for the office of U.S. Commissioner of Public Buildings (declined);[18]

Thomas Ritchie, editor of the Richmond *Enquirer* for 41 years, then editor of the Washington *Daily Union*;[19]

Jesse Erskine Dow, Doorkeeper of the U.S. House of Representatives for the 28th Congress (1843–45); reporter for the *United States Journal* and the *Congressional Globe*;[20]

William Alexander Harris, lawyer; U.S. Congressman from Virginia; publisher of the *Daily Union*, *Spectator* and *Constitution*.[21]

Over time, some members were to become particularly critical in enabling Clark Mills to achieve the Jackson equestrian:

John Walker Maury, prominent attorney of Washington; city councilman, then alderman, soon to be mayor; elected a Secretary of the Committee; later a member of the Committee of Arrangements for the dedication ceremony of the Jackson equestrian; Maury would be a steadfast and generous patron of Mills;[22]

Francis Preston Blair, came to Washington by invitation of President Jackson to assume the editorship of the *Washington Globe*; co-founder with John Cook Rives and editor of the *Congressional*

Globe; "General Jackson's own most trusted and beloved friend, and the selected inheritor of his papers and guardian of his fame;" elected Treasurer of the Committee; Blair would assist Mills financially;[23]

John Cook Rives, co-founder with Francis Preston Blair and editor of the *Congressional Globe;* President of the Democratic Association of Washington; later a member of the Committee of Arrangements for the dedication of the statue; Rives would assist Mills financially;[24]

Benjamin Brown French, prominent attorney and successful businessman; Clerk of the U.S. House of Representatives; later a member of the Committee of Arrangements for the dedication of the statue; would be U.S. Commissioner of Public Buildings under Presidents Pierce and Lincoln; French would be a major benefactor of Mills, monetarily and professionally;[25]

Cave Johnson, U.S. Congressman from Tennessee; U.S. Postmaster General under President Polk; his chance introduction to Mills would be the fateful encounter that changed the course of Mills's life;[26]

Most of these men cherished memories of close ties to the deceased general and president. Several of them had served with "the Hero of New Orleans" in the 1812–14 war against England, America's "second War of Independence." Others fought at his side against Spanish troops in Florida, or in Indian campaigns. Some of them had collaborated with Jackson while holding elected or appointed federal posts. The three younger members of the Committee, who were in their thirties, had not known their Hero personally, but were inspired by his legacy. Of the 13 founding members, eight had been born south of the Mason and Dixon Line, nine owned enslaved servants or laborers, as Jackson had.[27] All were resolute Democrats still heady at having recently snatched the presidency away from the Whigs.[28] All enjoyed privileged access throughout Washington society.

Addressing the gathering in Apollo Hall, Secretary Hoban orated on the admirable qualities of Jackson and the appropriateness of "erecting, at the seat of the federal government . . . a colossal equestrian statue, in imperishable bronze . . . to the memory of the Hero, Patriot, and Sage."[29] Then "a discussion arose (in which many citizens took part) as to the proper time and manner of organization; which eventually resulted in the unanimous passage of the resolutions" penned by O'Sullivan.[30] The New Yorker himself, however, relinquished his leadership to the more-than-capable Washingtonians, who now formally assumed the cause that the editor had roused to action.[31]

Before the convocation adjourned and attendees dispersed into the darkened streets of the capital, Hoban handed his handwritten notes to Thomas Ritchie of the *Daily Union*. The resolutions would appear in the morning edition.[32] A great work had been set afoot.

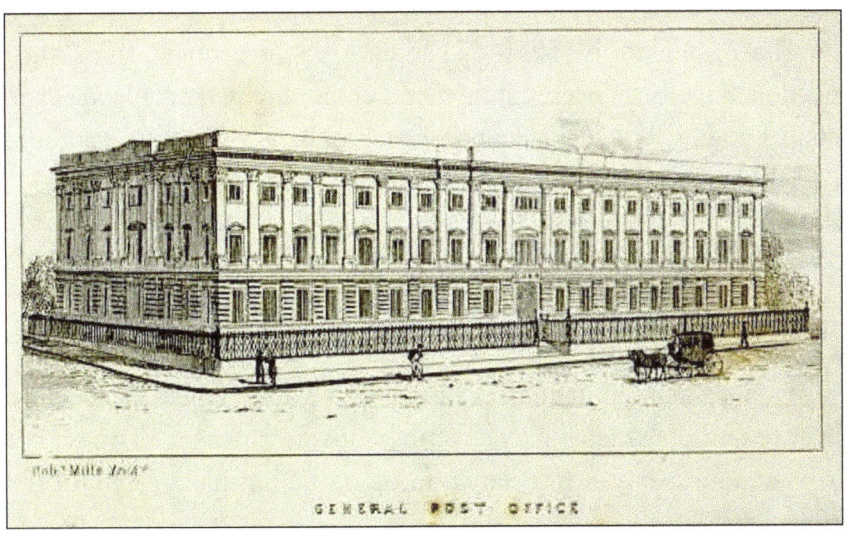

Newly completed Post Office Building in Washington, D.C., 1842. President Polk's Postmaster General, Cave Johnson, convened the first meeting of the 13-member Jackson Monument Committee in his office here on September 19, 1845. At that time, monumental sculpture of bronze was unknown in the United States. (*Morrison's Stranger's Guide to the City of Washington*, 1842, p. 38)

The Jackson Monument Committee convened that Friday, September 19, 1845, at noon, in the office of Postmaster General Cave Johnson.[33] The pristine halls of the new General Post Office building provided an impressive setting for their work: initiating the subscription drive to raise the funds for their statue. When John O'Sullivan met with President Polk, he had suggested a goal of "$100,000 or more."[34] That was a wild overstatement. But the astronomical sum betrayed how uninformed the nobly intentioned layman was about the enterprise he was promoting. In this morning's *Daily Union*, Jeremiah Harris had published Hiram Powers's reply to the letter he had sent 12 weeks earlier:

> [G]iving an estimate of the probable cost of a bronze equestrian statue of Gen. Jackson, sixteen to eighteen feet from the base to the head of the rider. [Powers] thinks that the casting alone would amount to between 12,000 and 15,000 dollars, and that 30,000 dollars in all would not be too much for the total expense of the work.[35]

Having this more informed estimate of "the requisite sum" they needed to raise, the Committee members authorized agents to solicit contributions "in every section of the country."[36] It was paramount that the undertaking be national in scope:

> The smallest contribution will be received, even "the widow's mite;" for the country will feel more pride in the multitude of hearts engaged in this work, than in the amount of money.[37]

Donors of $100 or more would receive a miniature facsimile in bronze of the statue, while subscribers giving at least $10 would get a "steel engraving of the statue, to be framed in hickory cut at the Hermitage."[38]

Committee members who were editors printed appeals in their respective papers.[39] The Democratic Association of Washington published a series of resolutions endorsing the project, made an initial pledge of $393.00, and challenged fellow Democratic organizations to follow suit.[40] Forthwith, $700 came into the Committee's coffer.

> It is the intention of the committee to invest in some secure funds the sums received in the progress of the subscription; ... No compensation will be received by any of the committee—not even by the treasurer or secretary—for their services. ... [However,] agents authorized to obtain subscriptions and make collections will be allowed a reasonable per centage.[41]

What did Clark Mills, working in Charleston on his marble bust of Calhoun, know of all this? Chances are, a great deal. The *Southern Patriot* and the *Courier* both printed several articles reporting that citizens of Washington had formed a committee to commission a monumental bronze equestrian statue of Jackson and that Hiram Powers estimated its likely cost at $30,000.[42] More than that, though, during the years when Mills was establishing himself as a bust maker, Charleston newspapers carried no fewer than 11 articles about statues of revered Americans planned for U.S. cities, among them:

> A marble statue of Henry Clay, to be carved by Thomas Crawford, was intended for New York;[43]

> The U.S. Senate passed a resolution authorizing an equestrian statue in bronze of George Washington by Luigi Persico for the national capital;[44]

> Citizens of New Orleans initiated a subscription to hire Powers to carve a statue in stone of Benjamin Franklin;[45]

> Edward Augustus Brackett completed the model for his full-length statue of the South Carolina painter and poet, Washington Allston;[46]

> The statue of French-born American philanthropist, Stephen Girard, sculpted in Paris, arrived in Philadelphia;[47]

A joint resolution of Congress authorized contracting Powers to execute a series of marble busts of U.S. presidents;[48]

The city of Boston hired Francisco Cichi to make a bronze replica of Houdon's famous statue of Washington.[49]

In 1840s America, monumental public sculpture was a topic of popular interest and bronze was considered the most appropriate material to perpetuate the physical appearance of a national hero. It was superior to marble, because it was "imperishable" and it had a centuries-long history as the most appropriate medium for memorials of great leaders. Deliberations of U.S. senators and representatives about commissioning an equestrian statue in bronze of George Washington were printed verbatim in "Proceedings of Congress" columns throughout the country. (Consideration passed swiftly from hiring Luigi Persico—an Italian working in Washington—to Thomas Crawford—an up-and-coming American sculptor—to Powers—the American master; but nothing came of the initiative.)[50] Newspapers reported not only on projects to memorialize eminent citizens of the United States, but the latest statues being made in Europe, too, as well as the popular sensation that Powers's *Greek Slave* was making in London.[51]

An aspiring sculptor hoping one day to study in Italy, Mills surely kept abreast of developments in his field. He would have known that a "colossal equestrian statue" of General Jackson "in imperishable bronze" was anticipated in Washington, D.C.

NOTES

1 "Death of Andrew Jackson," [Charleston] *Courier*, June 17, 1845, p. 2. See also https://thehermitage.com/learn/andrew-jackson/.
2 [no title], [Washington] *Daily Union*, Sept. 19, 1845, p. 3, citing the *Nashville Union*. The original article has not been found, but it was also reported in the

[Boston] *Daily Evening Transcript*, Sept. 15, 1845, p. 2, and [Charleston] *Southern Patriot*, Sept. 17, 1845, p. 2. Therefore, it probably appeared in the *Nashville Union* about Sept. 13th. Allowing six weeks for a letter from Nashville to reach Florence and six weeks for the reply, Harris must have written to Powers within days of Jackson's death.

3 "Statue to Jackson," *United States Magazine and Democratic Review*, vol. XVII, no. LXXXV (July and Aug., 1845): 3–4. Italics in original.

4 See, for example, "Baltimore Correspondence of the U.S. Gaz.—July 9," *Alexandria* [Va.] *Gazette*, July 12, 1845, p. 2. See also [no title], *Daily Union*, Sept. 19, 1845, 3.

5 When O'Sullivan met with President Polk on Sept. 10, 1845, he already had a list of "certain citizens who were named, numbering in all fifteen" who would be members of the committee. See Milo Milton Quaife, ed., *The Diary of James K. Polk During His Presidency, 1845 to 1849* (Chicago: A. C. McClurg, 1910), vol. I: 23–25. See also Donald B. Cole and John J. McDonough, eds., *Benjamin Brown French, Witness to the Young Republic; A Yankee Journal, 1828–1870* (Hanover and London: University of New England, 1989): 179–80.

6 Quaife, *Diary of James K. Polk*, vol. I: 23–25.

7 James Knox Polk (1795–1849), see https://www.whitehouse.gov/about-the-white-house/presidents/james-k-polk/.

8 Letter, James K. Polk to John L. O'Sullivan, Sept. 15, 1845; James K. Polk Papers, Microfilm 13,072-67N-67P, Series 2, Reel 41, Manuscript Division, Library of Congress, Washington, D.C.

9 Quaife, *Diary of James K. Polk*, vol. I: 25.

10 "Monument to Jackson," [Washington] *Daily Union*, Sept. 12, 1845, p. 2. Italics in original. Reprinted Sept. 13, 1845, p. 3.

11 "Monument to Gen. Jackson," [Washington] *Daily Union*, Sept. 16, 1845, p. 3. Also Anthony Reintzel, comp., *The Washington Directory, and Governmental Register, for 1843* (Washington, D.C.: Jno. T. Towers, 1843): 22; viewed at www.Fold3.com.

12 James Hoban Jr. (1808–46), see William B. Bushong, "Honoring James Hoban, Architect of the White House," *CRM: The Journal of Heritage Stewardship*, vol. 5, no. 2 (summer 2008), at https://www.nps.gov/crps/CRMJournal/Summer2008/research1.html; and Jas [sic] Hoban entry, 1840 U.S. Census, Washington City, Washington Co., D.C., p. 28 (handwritten), p. 32 (stamped); NARA M704, roll 35 (household includes two free people of color and two enslaved). See also Tim Kerr, *The History of the Equestrian Statue of General Andrew Jackson, Lafayette Park, Washington, D.C.* Typescript report prepared for the National Park Service, White House Liaison, August 1999, p. 81.

13 "Monument . . . ," *Daily Union*, Sept. 16, 1845, 3.

14 John Peter Van Ness (1769–1846) see https://en.wikipedia.org/wiki/John_Peter_Van_Ness; and J P VanNess [sic] entry, 1840 U.S. Census, Washington City, Washington Co., D.C., p. 19 (handwritten), p. 22[b] (stamped); NARA

M704, roll 35 (household includes four slaves); and Gaither & Addison, *Washington Directory, and National Register, for 1846* (Washington: John T. Towers, 1846): 82.

15 "Monument...," *Daily Union*, Sept. 16, 1845, 3. Also "History of the Jackson Statue," [Washington] *Daily Union*, Jan. 18, 1853, p. 2; reprinted in the *New York Daily Times*, Jan. 22, 1853, p. 3. Kerr, *History of the Equestrian Statue*, 81, includes a fourteenth member, John Boyle. Although Boyle served as Second Vice President during the meeting of Sept. 15, 1845, he was never named to the Jackson Monument Committee. See B. B. French, "The Jackson Statue—Its Origin, &c," [Baltimore] *Sun*, Jan. 11, 1853, p. 4.

16 Amos Kendall (1789–1869), see https://en.wikipedia.org/wiki/Amos_Kendall; and Amos Kendall entry, 1850 U.S. Census, Washington, D.C., p. 515 (handwritten), p. 258 (stamped); NARA M432, roll 56: "61, Treasurer F.G. Co., no real estate;" and Gaither & Addison, *Washington Directory... for 1846*, 53.

17 Charles Kitchell Gardner (1787–1869), see James Grant Wilson and John Fiske, eds., *Appleton's Cyclopaedia of American Biography* (New York, N.Y.: D. Appleton & Co., 1887), vol. II: 597; and Charles K. Gardner entry, 1850 U.S. Census, Washington Co., Washington City, D.C., p. 53 (handwritten), p. 27 (stamped); NARA M432, roll 56: "60, no occupation, no real estate."

18 "Chas. P. Sengstack" entry, 1850 U.S. Census, Ward 2, Washington Co., Washington City, D.C., p. 180 (handwritten), p. 90[b] (stamped); NARA M432, roll 56: "58, Grocer, no real estate;" and Gaither & Addison, *Washington Directory... for 1846*, 75. See also Kerr, *History of the Equestrian Statue*, 82.

19 Thomas Ritchie (1778–1854), see Bk. 1, Prologue, n. 21.

20 Jesse Erskine Dow (1809–50), see "Dow, Jesse E." at https://history.house.gov/People/Listing/D/DOW,-Jesse-E-/; and Jake E. [sic] Dow entry, 1850 U.S. Census, Ward 2, Washington City, Washington Co., D.C., p. 138 (handwritten), p. 69[b] (stamped); NARA M432, roll 56: "42, Agent for Claimants, $3,000;" and J. E. [sic] Dow entry, 1850 U.S. Census Slave Schedule, Ward 2, Washington City, Washington Co., D.C., p. 655 (handwritten); NARA M432, roll 57; and Gaither & Addison, *Washington Directory... for 1846*, 38.

21 William A. Harris (1805–64), see "Harris, William Alexander," *Biographical Directory of the United States Congress*; at https://bioguide.congress.gov/search/bio/H000257; and Gaither & Addison, *Washington Directory... for 1846*, 47.

22 John Walker Maury (1809–55), see https://en.wikipedia.org/wiki/John_Walker_Maury; and John W. Maury entry, 1850 U.S. Census, 4th Ward, Washington City, Washington Co., D.C., p. 453 (handwritten), p. 227 (stamped); NARA M432, roll 56: "40, Exchange Broker, $57,000;" and John W. Maury entry, 1850 U.S. Census Slave Schedule, 4th Ward, Washington City, Washington Co., D.C., p. 685 (handwritten); NARA M432, roll 57; and Gaither & Addison, *Washington Directory... for 1846*, 61. See also Bk. 1, Ch. 34.

23 Francis Preston Blair (1791–1876), see https://en.wikipedia.org/wiki/Francis_Preston_Blair; and Francis P. Blair entry, 1850 U.S. Census, 5th or Berry's District, Montgomery Co., Md., p. 716; NARA M432, roll 295: "59, farmer, $30,000;" and Francis P. Blair entry, 1850 U.S. Census Slave Schedule, 5th or Berry's District, Montgomery Co., Md., p. 427 (handwritten); NARA M432, roll 301. See also Bk. 1, Ch. 34.
24 John Cook Rives (1795–1864), see Wilson and Fiske, eds., *Appleton's Cyclopaedia of American Biography*, vol. 5: 267; and John C. Rives entry, 1850 U.S. Census, Bladensburgh [sic] District, Prince George's Co., Md., p. 27 (handwritten), p. 14 (stamped); NARA M432, roll 295: "55, Printer, $24,000;" and John C. Rives entry, 1850 U.S. Census Slave Schedule, Bladensburgh [sic] District, Prince George's Co., Md., p. 721 (handwritten); NARA M432, roll 301; and Gaither & Addison, *Washington Directory . . . for 1846*, 52. See also Bk. 1, Ch. 34.
25 Benjamin B. French (1800–70), see https://en.wikipedia.org/wiki/Benjamin_Brown_French; and B. B. French [sic] entry, 1850 U.S. Census, Ward 5, Washington City, Washington Co., D.C., p. 42 (handwritten), p. 21[b] (stamped); NARA M432, roll 56: "49, Lawyer, $15,000;" and Gaither & Addison, *Washington Directory . . . for 1846*, 95. See also Donald B. Cole and John J. McDonough, eds., *Witness to the Young Republic, A Yankee's Journal, 1828–1870, Benjamin Brown French* (Hanover and London: University Press of New England, 1989): passim. See also Bk. 1, Ch. 34.
26 Cave Johnson (1793–1866), see https://en.wikipedia.org/wiki/Cave_Johnson; and Cave Johnson entry, U.S. 1850 Census, Montgomery Co., Tenn., p. 286 (handwritten), p. 143[b] (stamped); NARA 432, roll 891: "57, Attorney at Law, $20,000;" and Cave Johnson entry, 1850 U.S. Census Slave Schedule, Montgomery Co., Tenn., p. 781 (handwritten); NARA M432, roll 905; and Gaither & Addison, *Washington Directory . . . for 1846*, 52.
27 See the biographical notes of the individual members.
28 Samuel Eliot Morison, Henry Steele Commager and William E. Leuchtenburg, *The Growth of the American Republic*, 7th ed. (New York: Oxford University Press, 1980), vol. 1: 519–20, 546.
29 "Monument . . . ," *Daily Union*, Sept. 16, 1845, 3.
30 Ibid.
31 Ibid.
32 "Monument . . . ," *Daily Union*, Sept. 12, 1845, 3.
33 [no title], [Washington] *Daily Union*, Sept. 16, 1845, p. 3.
34 Allan Nevins, ed., *Polk, The Diary of a President, 1845–1849* (New York: Longmans, Green & Co., 1952): 7.
35 [no title], *Daily Union*, Sept. 19, 1845, p. 3. The original article has not been found, but it was reported in the [Boston] *Daily Evening Transcript*, Sept. 15, 1845, p. 2; [Charleston] *Southern Patriot*, Sept. 17, 1845, p. 2; as well as the

[Washington] *Daily Union*. Therefore, it probably appeared in the *Nashville Union* about Sept. 13th. Allowing six weeks for a letter from Nashville to reach Florence and six weeks for the reply, Harris must have written to Powers within days of Jackson's death. In 2025 currency, $12,000–$15,000 is equivalent to about $420,000–$524,000; $30,000 is equivalent to about $1,048,000.

36 "The Monument to Jackson," [Washington] *Daily Union*, Oct. 6, 1845, p. 3. See also "Jackson Monument," *Alexandria* [Va.] *Gazette*, Nov. 12, 1845, p. 2; and "The Jackson Monument," *Abbeville* [S.C.] *Banner*, Apr. 28, 1847, p. 4.
37 "The Monument to Jackson," *Daily Union*, Oct. 6, 1845, 3.
38 "The Jackson Statue," [Charleston] *Southern Patriot*, Sept. 23, 1845, p. 2. These early intentions were never fulfilled.
39 See, for example, "The Monument to Jackson," *Daily Union*, Oct. 6, 1845, 2. The *Daily Union* had espoused the concept even before the meeting; see "Statue to Jackson," Sept. 12, 1845, 2.
40 "Monument to Jackson," [Washington] *Daily Union*, Nov. 8, 1845, p. 2.
41 "The Monument to Jackson," *Daily Union*, Oct. 6, 1845, 3.
42 "Monument to Jackson," [Charleston] *Courier*, Sept. 23, 1845, p. 2; "The Jackson Statue," *Southern Patriot*, Sept. 23, 1845, p. 2; "Monument to Jackson," [Charleston] *Southern Patriot*, Oct. 9, 1845, p. 2; and [no title], [Charleston] *Southern Patriot*, Oct. 17, 1845, p. 2.
43 "Mr. Clay," [Charleston] *Southern Patriot*, Jan. 6, 1845, p. 2.
44 "Congressional Intelligence. Washington, Feb. 14," [Charleston] *Southern Patriot*, Feb. 17, 1845, p. 2.
45 "New-Orleans, May 8, 1845," [Charleston] *Courier*, May 26, 1845, p. 2.
46 "Washington Allston," [Charleston] *Southern Patriot*, Nov. 7, 1845, p. 2.
47 "Stephen Girard," [Charleston] *Southern Patriot*, Mar. 2, 1846, p. 2.
48 "From our Correspondent. Washington, April 27," [Charleston] *Southern Patriot*, Apr. 30, 1846, p. 2. Also 28th Cong., 1st Sess., Joint Resolution S. 13, "Directing the purchase of certain marble busts," Mar. 21, 1844; and "Marble Busts of Presidents," [Washington] *Whig Standard*, Mar. 30, 1844; and "House of Representatives," *Alexandria* [Va.] *Gazette*, Feb. 13, 1846, p. 3.
49 "Houdon's Statue of Washington," [Charleston] *Southern Patriot*, May 6, 1846, p. 2.
50 See, for example, "Proceedings in Congress" and "New York Correspondence," [Washington] *Weekly National Intelligencer*, Feb. 15, 1845, p. 2 and 3. See also *Journal of the Senate*, Jan. 20, 1845, p. 96; Feb. 14, 1845, p. 170; Feb. 25, 1845, p. 165; Feb. 26, 1845, p. 168; May 11, 1846, p. 784; and Jan. 21, 1851, p. 97.
51 For example, in the [Washington] *Daily Union*: [no title], June 23, 1845, p. 2; and "Fine Arts," July 14, 1845, p. 2; and "The American Review," Aug. 8, 1845, p. 3; and "Miscellaneous from the Columbus (Ohio) Statesman, Oct. 31," Nov. 14, 1845, p. 2. See also Bk. 1, Ch. 19.

CHAPTER 10
January–June 1846

We delight to record any instance of the due encouragement of genius. And hence we have pleasure in stating that three gentlemen of this city, who with disinterested liberality, will not permit us to make known their names, have subscribed the sum of one thousand dollars, for the purpose of affording our fellow-townsman, Mr. Clarke Mills, an opportunity of visiting Italy there to improve in the art of sculpture.

"Liberality," [Charleston] *Courier*, Jan. 6, 1846, p. 2.

Years later *DeBow's Review* would print an imaginative recreation of the moment when Mills learned of his good fortune:

While busy at his work, one day, his sleeves rolled up to the elbows, and the materials of his toil scattered around him, a gentleman dropped in, and accosted him thus:

"Mills! how would you like to go to Italy?"

"Go to Italy! What do you mean?"

"I mean—would you be willing to go abroad, and study the old masters, if you could?"

"Willing? Ah! my dear sir! don't ask such a question of a man situated as I am."

"Why not?"

"Why, because of all things in this world, I should love to go to Italy; but how can I go, when I have no money?"

"If that is all," added the friendly visitor, "make yourself easy. The means will be provided, and you can go to Italy."

The delight of poor Mills at this announcement can be better imagined than described. He turned from his work, and sprang to the side of the gentleman, looking intently in his face for a further explanation.

"Yes, Mills," resumed his gratified friend, "it is all fixed that you are to go abroad."

Without waiting to put on his coat, he rushed into the street, hailing each acquaintance that he met.

"Have you heard the news? I'm going to Italy; going to study the old masters!"

"Going where?" said one, not exactly comprehending the coatless and bare-headed genius.

"Going to Italy, I tell you! Going to study the old masters of art! Do you hear that? I'm going to the land of sculpture, and painting, and song!"

"Wa'll, go along, then'" muttered a social passer-by, who doubtless thought of Mills as he had seen him on his water-cart, "Go along, who cares?"[1]

Only later would the identities of Mills's three benefactors be revealed. The surprise visitor was Henry Workman Conner, member of a leading mercantile firm, president of the Bank of Charleston and president of the South Carolina Rail Road Company.[2] Conner was joined by his colleague, A. G. Rose, a director and cashier of the Bank of Charleston.[3] The third sponsor was none other than His Honor the Mayor of Charleston, John Schnierle—who had earlier hired Mills to stucco the Guard House and for whom Mills had named one of his sons.[4] All three men, having not only professional rank but fortunes, families and enslaved servants, were pillars of Charleston society. Reported the *Courier* of January 6, 1846:

> Mr. Mills will leave here in April, and is determined to remain in Italy, until as he himself says, "he has learned all that he can learn in that birth-place of the fine arts." Mr. Mills carries with him an order from Col. Alston of Waccamaw, for the busts of Mr. Calhoun

and Mr. Petigru, which works will engage his chisel as soon as he has acquired some of those advantages in the arts, the obtaining of which, is the object of his visit.[5]

Mills started accepting orders for marble replicas of his plaster busts. Colonel Alston's was among the first. This is what Greenough and Powers had done: they sailed for Europe only after amassing a sufficient number of clients to make the trip worthwhile. Once established in Italy, they more often than not assigned the carving to master stonecutters, while they themselves sculpted new works in clay and cast plaster models of them. Mills was following precedent.

But when April came, Mills did not sail for Italy. He had decided to make the grandest public gesture he could to promote his career and attract more orders for busts:

Charleston, S.C., April 13, 1846

To the Hon. the Mayor and Aldermen of Charleston:—

Gentlemen—I have with some labor, executed a Bust of the Hon. John C. Calhoun—it is from the native stone of this State found near Columbia, and is my first effort in sculpture.

I do not feel myself a competent or proper judge of the merit of this work, if it has any—some of my friends, more in kindly feelings towards me perhaps than in their better judgment, have encouraged me to hope, that it is not without some small claim that way, at least as a first essay; and as it is intended to represent the lineaments of Carolina's greatest and most gifted son, I trust it may not be without some recommendation, on that account if no other, to the favorable notice of the Council.

I, therefore, respectfully ask permission to present the Bust to your Honorable body. If considered worthy of acceptance, you will make such disposition of it as you may deem proper. Respectfully,

Clark Mills[6]

The City Council not only accepted the gift, it passed resolutions congratulating and encouraging "our meritorious fellow townsman:"

> Resolved, That we regard this first essay of our artist as indicative of the highest promise of future and increasing excellence in the noble study of sculpture, to which he has devoted himself—and while we admire the genius, the decided taste and elaborate skill he has thus practically exhibited, we feel a just pride in congratulating Charleston in possessing the most accurate and approved delineation of the expression and features of Carolina's greatest and most gifted son.

> Resolved, That Council, in common with this community, entertain a lively interest in the untiring exertion and future success of Mr. Mills in the arduous and very difficult profession he has selected, and anticipate for him that eminence which his undoubted talent, his unpretending merit and preserving purpose of character must ultimately attain.[7]

Mills's bust of John C. Calhoun, U.S. Congressman from South Carolina, then Secretary of War, then Vice President, then Senator, 1845. This was the only work Mills ever carved in marble. Because of Calhoun's prominence in national affairs and tremendous esteem among Southerners—and Mills's unabashed self-promotion—this bust launched the sculptor's career in a spectacular way. (photo courtesy of J. Douglas Walker)

Mayor Schnierle—always a champion of tradesmen—and the aldermen enshrined Mills's bust of Calhoun in Charleston's City Hall "in a prominent place in Council Chamber."[8] But that was not all. They also voted to give the sculptor an award for his achievement. They commissioned a local artist, Mr. Keenan, to design a gold medal. By June it was struck. Reporting on the "Tribute to a Native Artist," the *Courier* and the *Southern Patriot* both described the medallion:

> On one side of the medal is a very beautiful devise, representing the artist in the act of crowning the bust of Mr. Calhoun with a wreath, just presented him by a female figure, emblematic of the City of Charleston, while the City and Harbour are most tastefully delineated in the back ground. Encircling the devise is the motto "Aedes, Mores, Juraque Curat;" and at the foot are the words "Ingenii praemium virtutis calcar, Id Apr. MDCCCXLVI."[9]

The official seal of Charleston depicts the Greek goddess Athena as the protector of the city, whose motto is *Aedes Mores Juraque Curat*: "She guards her buildings, customs and laws." *Ingenii praemium virtutis calcar* may be translated, "Award for Excellence and Talent in Sculpting." The Latin date is the ides of April (13), 1846.

On the other side of the medal is the following inscription—

> Clark Mills,
> as a mark of respect
> for his genius for sculpture,
> exhibited in his Bust
> of the favorite son of Carolina
> JOHN C. CALHOUN;
> And as an incentive to further exertions,
> This medal is presented
> by the
> City Council
> of Charleston.[10]

The medal was enclosed in an elegant gold case.[11] There was no presentation ceremony, though, because Mills was out of town. The city council engaged a former client and zealous supporter of his to deliver the award. Mills conveyed his thanks in writing:

Columbia, June 9, 1846

To the Hon. the Mayor and Aldermen of the City of Charleston:

Gentlemen—I have received, by the hands of Col. Franklin H. Elmore, the beautiful Medal with which you have been pleased to signify your appreciation of my effort to delineate, in stone, the features of "Carolina's favorite son." This distinguished expression of your regard fills me with gratitude and embarrassment. In whatever spirit of enthusiastic devotion I may pursue the difficult art in which I would engage, I feel fully that the future may not disclose a degree of success adequate of your expectations. At no period of the most successful career could I have proposed to myself a more gratifying or triumphant reward than to be thus honored by the representatives of my city.

Your gift, gentlemen, shall be my strong incentive to exertion now, and I trust, will prove the source of just pride here after.

That your kindness towards me, the humble recipient in this instance may excite emulation in others, and bring out, from among her citizens, artists worthy to decorate and adorn the city of Charleston, and perpetuate, in monuments of artistic skill and beauty, the memory of those of her sons who may excel in moral and intellectual attainments, is the heartfelt wish of

Your fellow citizen and servant,
Clark Mills[12]

The neophyte sculptor was writing from the state capital because he had received a letter of invitation from one of the city's most esteemed residents, John Smith Preston.[13] It was tantamount to a royal summons. Italy could wait.

NOTES

1 "Clark Mills and His Equestrian Statue," *DeBow's Review*, vol. 16 (Jan. 1854): 40.
2 Henry Workman Conner (1797-1861), see https://www.scencyclopedia.org/sce/entries/conner-henry-workman; and H. W. Conner entry, 1850 U.S. Census, Parishes of St. Philip's and St. Michael's, Charleston, S.C., p. 309 (handwritten), p. 153 (stamped); NARA M432, roll 850; and H. W. Conner entry, 1850 U.S. Census Slave Schedule, Parishes of St. Philip's and St. Michael's, Charleston, S.C., p. 129 (handwritten); NARA M432, roll 862.
3 A. G. Rose (1793-1852+), see A. G. Rose entry, 1850 U.S. Census, Parishes of St. Philip's and St. Michael's, Charleston, S.C., p. 713 (handwritten), p. 355 (stamped); NARA M432, roll 850; and A. G. Rose entry, 1850 U.S. Census Slave Schedule, Parishes of St. Philip's and St. Michael's, Charleston, S.C., p. 723 (handwritten); NARA M432, roll 862; and J. H. Bagget, pub., *Directory of the City of Charleston, for the Year 1852* (Charleston: Edward C. Councell, printer, 1851): 110; and "Business Directory," [Charleston] *Courier*, Mar. 30, 1847, p. 1. The author has not been able to discover Rose's two given names.
4 See Bk. 1, Ch. 4. Curiously, no evidence has been found that Mills ever made a bust of Conner, Rose or Schnierle.
5 "Liberality," [Charleston] *Courier*, Jan. 6, 1846, p. 2.
6 "Proceedings of Council, Monday, April 13, 1846," [Charleston] *Courier*, Apr. 15, 1846, p. 2.
7 Ibid.
8 This bust is still displayed in Charleston City Hall today.
9 "Tribute to a Native Artist," [Charleston] *Courier*, July 15, 1846, p. 2; reprinted in the *Southern Patriot*, July 15, 1846, p. 2.
10 Ibid.
11 [no title], [Washington] *American Telegraph*, Apr. 15, 1851, p. 3.
12 "Proceedings of Council, Monday, July 20, 1846," [Charleston] *Courier*, July 22, 1846, p. 2.
13 "Mr. Clark Mills, the Sculptor," *The Round Table*, vol. 1, no. 22 (May 14, 1864): 340.

CHAPTER 11
June–July 1846

Mr. Mills is, we understand, temporarily sojourning in Columbia, and is busily engaged in executing busts for the citizens of that place.

"Tribute to a Native Artist,"
[Charleston] *Courier*, July 15, 1846, p. 2.

Winding northwesterly from Charleston toward the state capital, Mills traversed South Carolina's "Low Country." First came the sprawling rice fields of Moncks Corner. The dense profusion of slender yellowish-green leaves resembled tall grass, acre upon acre of tall grass. Still immature, the plants had not yet sprouted their seed heads. Farther along, Mills surveyed the cotton plantations of the Orangeburg District. Long rows of dark-green foliage, waist high, were sprinkled with white, pink and purple blossoms that would mature into bolls. Throughout the striped landscape, from horizon to horizon, brown-faced men, women, boys and girls bent over hoes, chopping, stepping, chopping, stepping, turning pokeweed into the earth. White overseers sitting tall mounts supervised.[1]

Even if Mills did keep his own horse—"the finest" he could find, as he boasted—he would not have made this trip in the saddle, because he was toting a satchel containing the tools of his trade and a carpetbag stuffed with clothes.[2] He would most likely have taken "the cars"—that is, a train—or traveled by water. The South Carolina Rail Road Company ran cars from Charleston to Columbia at nine o'clock every morning.[3] This service had displaced the stagecoaches that used to run between the two cities.[4] And steamers made scheduled trips upriver to the capital.[5] However, Mills may have rented a buggy and taken the State Road (Highway 176 today). The distance by straight line was only about 112 miles, but no mode of conveyance, public or private, made a straight line.

Newspaper accounts of Mills's bust of the "Cast-Iron Man," the honor the Charleston City fathers had conferred on him, and his plan to study in Italy had reached Columbia.[6] In May, John Smith Preston, "the gentleman who sent Hiram Powers to Italy," had invited Mills to make busts of several members of his extended family, which Mills might cut in marble "when he had farther advanced in the art."[7] The aspiring sculptor could not have wished for a more propitious invitation. Besides the invaluable endorsement of Preston's quasi-royal patronage, additional orders for marble replicas presaged a profitable sojourn in Italy. Study abroad could wait.

Mills wasted no time. By June he had packed his tools and headed to Columbia, most likely leaving Philip Reid behind to support Eliza and the boys. Whether traveling by "the cars," river, or State Road, he would have been en route for about ten hours.[8] At length, high on a bluff above the Congaree River, amidst towering cedars and lanky palmettoes, a hodgepodge of dwellings edged into view.

Columbia was surprisingly small—roughly one-sixth the size of Charleston—and bucolic.[9] The state capitol, an old federal-style wooden structure of two stories on a stuccoed brick basement, looked badly weather-worn. Designed by James Hoban, it was built a few years before George Washington hired the Irish-born architect to erect a President's House in Washington.[10] By contrast, the new Trinity Episcopal Church, though still under construction, promised to be a breathtaking landmark of the latest architectural style, Gothic Revival. It was huge. Already the massiveness of the brick walls and twin towers was evident.

Moving through Columbia's streets, Mills saw the opulent homes of the town's leading families. Architectural gems with broad covered porches, they were shaded year-round by ancient oaks, magnolias and junipers. Enslaved servants' quarters and other dependencies stood primly in back yards. The capital's thoroughfares were wider than Charleston's—though alike unpaved—and shaded by numerous trees, most prominently the "Pride of India," a giant crape myrtle bearing large, feathery, reddish blossoms at the tip of every branch at this time of year.

The residences of John Smith Preston and his elder brother, William Campbell Preston, were among the finest of the fine houses of Columbia. The Preston brothers were two of the best-educated and most widely traveled connoisseurs of art in the South and both men delighted in the aristocratic prerogatives of "collector" and "benefactor." With family fortunes amplified by advantageous marriages, they were among the richest men in the state and by dint of their political involvement, two of South Carolina's most powerful leaders.[11] With which of the brothers did Mills lodge during his sojourn in Columbia?

The home of John Smith Preston on Walnut Street (now Blanding Street) stood in its own city square of four acres surrounded by formal

This 1872 depiction of the Hampton-Preston Mansion shows the famed gardens surrounding it that Mills would have seen during his sojourns in Columbia in 1846. Also obvious is the rear addition—constructed 1848-51—that doubled the size of the house to accommodate John Smith Preston's extended family. (Library of Congress)

gardens. Called the Hampton-Preston Mansion today, the house by the 1840s had become too small for the family. Preston's household included not only his wife, Caroline, and their six children, but his mother-in-law and perhaps the children of his recently deceased sister-in-law, Susan Manning, as well. For this reason the family resided primarily at The Houmas, a sugar cane plantation on the Mississippi River in Ascension Parish, Louisiana. Comprising thousands of acres worked by several hundred enslaved men, women and children, The Houmas belonged to John's wife, Caroline, who had received it from her half-brother, Colonel Wade Hampton II. The main house there was palatial in size.[12] However, Preston's numerous household may have crowded into his in-town residence for the social season each winter.

John had a plantation of his own, too, in Richland County, not far from Columbia. While hardly modest, the place was substantially smaller than The Houmas, having a population of about three dozen Black workers. It never served as a residence for his family.[13]

When Preston invited Mills to Columbia, he was planning a massive addition to his Walnut Street house. He would double its size and his extended family would live there year-round. But that would not happen for another couple of years. In sum, it is impossible to know whether Mills stayed in the Hampton-Preston Mansion or not. It could be that John Preston, a lawyer and businessman, was working in town this June and July of 1846 while his family remained in Louisiana.[14] Equally possible, though, is that Mills stayed with John's older brother, William.

William Campbell Preston resided with his wife, Louise, in a capacious house on Sumter Street. It backed up to the horseshoe campus of the College of South Carolina.[15] Preston was serving as the head of that institution and his residence would remain the college's official "President's House" until it was demolished in 1959. William had no surviving children and was renowned for his liberal hospitality. Louise set the capital city's standard for beauty, grace and lavish entertaining. A large staff of highly skilled enslaved Black servants made it possible. In light of the patron/protégé relationship that was to blossom between William Preston and Mills, it may be that the sculptor stayed in the "President's House" during his time in Columbia.

Wherever Mills lodged, John Preston must have provided a workplace for him. He would also have paid for the sacks of dry plaster, bottles of sweet oil, coils of wire and other supplies his guest needed to fulfill the commission. For every bust, Mills had to meet with the sitter, take casts of the face and head, assemble the casts into a mold, pour plaster into the mold to obtain a head, mount the head on shoulders fixed on a wire armature, meet a second time with the client to "liven" the portrait, and fashion a pedestal. During the time he spent in the state capital this year—he would make more than one trip—Mills executed this process for at least 20 sitters, probably more, including:[16]

> ***John Smith Preston***, planter, lawyer, businessman, leader in civic and political affairs of South Carolina, known as a liberal spender. Later this summer he was to sail for Italy and spend several months in Florence and Rome with his protégé, American sculptor Hiram Powers.[17]

> ***Mrs. John Smith Preston***, née Caroline Martha Hampton, daughter of Colonel Wade Hampton I and co-owner with her brother-in-law, John Laurence Manning, of The Houmas.[18]

> ***William Campbell Preston***, former mayor of Columbia, South Carolina state representative, and U.S. Senator. Widely traveled and cultivated, he had served as chairman of the Senate Committee on the Library, the arbiter of all matters artistic submitted to Congress. In January of this year, 1846, he had begun his duties as President of the College of South Carolina, where he taught belles lettres.[19] In May he was elected to the vestry of Trinity Episcopal Church, which was already, though unfinished, a landmark of the city.[20] In August the U.S. Congress would appoint him to the initial Board of Regents of the Smithsonian Institution.[21] William Campbell Preston was about to play a decisive role in furthering Mills's career.

Mrs. William Campbell Preston,[22] née Louise Penelope Davis, an acclaimed belle and doyenne of Columbia society.[23]

Col. Wade Hampton II, immensely wealthy son of Colonel Wade Hampton I, planter, politician, commander of Light Dragoons (mounted infantry) in the War of 1812, famed for being an avid hunter, outdoorsman, breeder of thoroughbreds, and horse-racing enthusiast.[24]

Years later Mills would tell a reporter:

"I spent a good deal of time about Wade Hampton's stables, studying the points of his horses. He had a large stable of race-horses, . . . and imported the famous Argyle, that beat everything in those days."[25]

The superlative quality of Colonel Hampton's fleet thoroughbreds, which he stabled at Millwood, his plantation just outside of Columbia, was legendary.[26] Race week, which Columbians celebrated every February, brought special excitement to the Hampton household, and often sterling silver trophies, as well. It was most likely during this sojourn in Columbia that Mills, a lifelong lover of horses, first saw the renowned steeds for himself. Curiously, it seems to have been their mutual passion for horses that engendered a rapport between these two men of vastly disparate stations in society. Within a couple of years, Colonel Hampton would give Mills "a race-horse no longer fit for the turf" to study equine anatomy for his Jackson equestrian statue.[27]

The colonel had five daughters. None of them married. Mills made *busts of all five*, but only one survives: **Catharine P. Hampton**, called Kate.[28]

Even if Mills did not stay in the Hampton-Preston Mansion, it is hard to imagine that his host did not invite the aspiring artist into his home at least once to show him his outstanding collection of oil paintings and sculpture. As Preston discoursed on art, he may have lingered with particular pride at the marble mantel that Hiram Powers had carved for him. Mills, having studied, mastered and practiced the craft of stuccoing, likely complimented Preston on the ornamentation of the high-ceilinged rooms. The cornices, chandelier medallions, and wall moldings were all extraordinarily elaborate and exquisitely painted and gilded.

A member of the Preston household—if not the master himself— would have escorted their guest along the paths of the famed gardens that surrounded the house. Boxwood, laurel, holly, hawthorn and yew provided a variety of luxurious leafy-dense greenery. Tall canna lilies were aflame and the loquat plants bore yellow-orange fruit. The azalea bushes were lofty billows of green, as their springtime cloaks of color had already disappeared. Robins swooped down to gobble the hard berries of the dogwoods as soon as the fruit turned red. The lithe limbs of the crape myrtles held bulbous, feathery flowers. Enormous creamy blossoms spotted the waxy leaves of gigantic magnolia trees. As evening breezes ruffled the tops of the spruce and pine trees and rocked the palmettoes, the Hampton-Preston house and grounds flickered softly in mottled shade.

One day Mills's host took him into the grand sanctuary of Trinity Episcopal Church. Like his brother William, John Preston was a parishioner there, a friend of Pastor Peter J. Shand, and a generous donor of the breathtaking new Gothic edifice. The cornerstone had been laid on November 26, 1845. In the seven months since then, the thick brick walls had risen, the massive hammerbeams had been raised into place, and the roof was being covered with slate. The walls and massive twin towers flanking the principal entrance were not yet stuccoed and scored to resemble stone, but they soon would be. The interior was still a work in progress. Preston had already commissioned Powers to design the baptismal font. Now the connoisseur of the arts pointed out to Mills the places where the timber roof trusses met the side walls: a decorative sculptural element, called a corbel, was needed to "finish" each one. He asked, would Mills carve them?

It would be an honor![29]

The unexpected offer was a tremendous boon and decidedly warranted putting off plans to study in Italy. Where, however, Mills fulfilled the commission is unknown. By this time, mid-July, he had sojourned in Columbia for at least five weeks, and his host was about to sail for Europe.[30] Mills may have returned to his workshop in Charleston, or he may have arranged to stay on in Columbia to create the corbels there.

He designed each one to represent the bust of an angel emerging from a floral motif. Almost certainly, he cast the corbels in plaster. His casts might have gone to the shop of a stonecutter to replicate, but this is unlikely. The church's exterior was stucco scored to simulate stone, and its decorative beams and ceiling were painted to resemble English oak. Clearly, Reverend Shand was exercising fiscal restraint. Most probably, therefore, Mills's plaster angels were installed in place and then simply painted to look like stone.

Before departing Columbia, Mills "called to take leave of Wm. C. Preston." During the senator's tenure in Congress, he had observed with more than casual interest the unprecedented activity of sculptors, mostly Italians, busily decorating the Capitol. As chairman of the Senate Committee on the Library, he had received Hiram Powers and afterwards encouraged his brother to foster the ambition of the promising young sculptor. That was when John Preston's role as art patron began. Now, William C. Preston was about to take on a protégé of his own. He remarked to Mills:

> [T]hat he should see the statuary at Washington before visiting Europe.
>
> [Mills] replied that "if he should spend his means in traveling about, he would not be able to accomplish his main object."

Mills's plaster bust of William Campbell Preston, U.S. Senator from South Carolina and ardent patron of the neophyte sculptor, ca. 1846. Preston financed Mills's 1847 trip to Richmond, Va., and Washington, D.C., where the political power broker's reputation as a learned connoisseur of the fine arts ensured Mills's legitimacy as a sculptor-in-the-making. (Smithsonian American Art Museum)

"As for the expense," said Mr. P., "if you will go to Washington and take the busts of my friends Webster and Crittenden, I will pay your expenses there and back, and pay you for the busts also."

[Mills] readily accepted the offer.[31]

Once again, a Preston had given Mills good reason to delay studying abroad. If Mills did not return to Charleston that July, he certainly did by November, if only to "close up shop."[32]

NOTES

1. Unless cited otherwise, description of Columbia and Richland County in 1846 is derived from: (1) Helen Kohn Hennig, ed., *Columbia, Capital City of South Carolina*, 1786–1936 (Columbia: The Columbia Sesqui-Centennial Commission, 1936): passim; (2) John Hammond Moore, *Columbia and Richland County, A South Carolina Community, 1740–1990* (Columbia: University of South Carolina Press, 1993): Part II, 77–180; and (3) Alexander MacKay, *The Western World; Travels in the United States in 1846–47*, 2nd ed. (Philadelphia: Lea & Blanchard, 1849), vol. 2: 23–27; at www.loc.gov/resource/lhbtn.2679b/?sp=gallery.
2. "An Hour with Clark Mills," [Washington] *Evening Star*, Dec. 24, 1870, p. 1.
3. See, for example, "RAIL ROAD," [Charleston] *Courier*, Dec. 15, 1845, p. 4, and Jan. 5, 1847, p. 1: "Passage to Columbia, $6.50." This ad ran daily. See also B. F.

Perry, *Letters of Gov. Benjamin Franklin Perry to His Wife*, Second Series (Greenville, S.C.: Shannon & Co., Printers, 1890): 91 (July 6, 1846) and 118 (Nov. 24, 1846).
4   See, for example, "Principal Stage Routes," [Charleston] *Southern Patriot*, Nov. 3, 1846, p. 4.
5   See, for example, "FOR COLUMBIA, S.C.," [Charleston] *Courier*, May 4, 1840, p. 2; and "FOR COLUMBIA AND ALL THE INTERMEDIATE LANDINGS ON THE RIVER," [Charleston] *Courier*, Feb. 22, 1847, p. 2.
6   "Clark Mills at Home," *The Washington Post*, Feb. 7, 1880, p. 2.
7   "Mr. Clark Mills, the Sculptor," *The Round Table*, vol. 1, no. 22 (May 14, 1864): 340.
8   Author's calculation.
9   Population estimate derived from the 1840 (4,340) and 1850 (6,060) U.S. censuses; quoted in Moore, *Columbia and Richland County*, 481.
10 See "State House" at http://www.scencyclopedia.org/sce/entries/state-house
11 John Smith Preston (1809–81), see https://en.wikipedia.org/wiki/John_S._Preston; William Campbell Preston (1794–1860), see http://www.scencyclopedia.org/sce/entries/preston-william-campbell.
12 "Houmas House History," at https://houmashouse.com/history/.
13 John S. Preston entry, 1850 U.S. Census, District of Richland Co., S.C., p. 168 (handwritten), p. 84[b] (stamped); NARA M432, roll 858; and John S. Preston entry, 1850 U.S. Census Slave Schedule, District of Richland Co., S.C., p. 359 (handwritten); NARA 432, roll 867.
14 "Hampton-Preston Mansion and Gardens" at https://www.historiccolumbia.org/tours/house-tours/hampton-preston-mansion-and-gardens. The author thanks Katharine Allen and Keith Mearns of Historic Columbia for their assistance with this period description of the house and gardens.
15 William C. Preston entry, 1850 U.S. Census, Columbia, Richland Co., S.C., p. 77 (handwritten), p. 39 (stamped); NARA M432, roll 858; and William C. Preston entry, 1850 U.S. Census Slave Schedule, Columbia, Richland Co., S.C., p. 153 (handwritten); NARA 432, roll 867.
16 "Mr. Clark Mills, the Sculptor," *The Round Table*, vol. 1, no. 22 (May 14, 1864): 340. The historical record does not allow for establishing a definitive chronology of Mills's trips to Columbia in 1846. It appears most probable that he made two, but he may have made more. This chapter and the next enumerate the busts Mills made in Columbia that year, but which ones were made on which trip is impossible to say. The order provided here is speculative, based on available evidence.
17 Richard P. Wunder, *Hiram Powers, Vermont Sculptor, 1805–1873* (Newark, Del.: University of Delaware Press, 1991), vol. I, *Life*: 97.
18 Caroline Martha Hampton Preston (1807–83), see https://en.wikipedia.org/wiki/The_Houmas.
19 "[no title]," *Georgetown* [D.C.] *Advocate*, Jan. 15, 1846, p. 2.

20 "Easter Monday—Episcopal Elections," [Charleston] *Southern Patriot,* May 6, 1846, p. 2.
21 "Twenty-Ninth Congress, First Session, Monday, August 10, 1846. IN SENATE," [Washington] *Daily Union,* Aug. 11, 1846, p. 3.
22 Today a copy of Mills's bust of William Preston is in the Smithsonian American Art Museum, Washington, D.C.
23 Louise Penelope Davis Preston (1807–53), see https://www.findagrave.com/memorial/141787686/louisa-penelope-preston.
24 Wade Hampton II (1791–1858), see http://www.scencyclopedia.org/sce/entries/hampton-wade-ii.
25 "How John Robinson Helped Sculptor Mills," *Turf, Field, and Farm,* vol. 12, no. 5 (Feb. 3, 1871): 74; reprinted from the *Cincinnati Enquirer.* Mills is quoted as saying, "When a boy, I spent a good deal of time about Wade Hampton's stables." However, Mills was never "a boy" in South Carolina; he moved to Charleston when he was 20 years old.
26 "Halsey Map," *Preservation Society of Charleston,* no. 79, "Washington Race Track 1792–1900," at http://halseymap.com/flash/window.asp?HMID=29.
27 "Clark Mills," *Lippincott's Magazine,* New Series, vol. 5 (Mar. 1883): 315–16. See Bk. 1, Ch. 17.
28 Catharine P. Hampton (1824–1916), see https://en.wikipedia.org/wiki/Wade_Hampton_II. Today a copy of this bust is in the Smithsonian American Art Museum, Washington, D.C.
29 Walter Edgar, "Chapters in Trinity's History" at https://www.trinitysc.org/about/explore-trinity.
30 Wunder, *Hiram Powers,* vol. I, *Life*: 97.
31 "Mr. Clark Mills . . . ," *The Round Table,* vol. 1, no. 22 (May 14, 1864): 340.
32 Precisely how long Mills sojourned in Columbia on his first trip there is vague. He wrote to the mayor of Charleston from Columbia on June 9, 1846, and on July 15, 1846, the *Courier* noted that he was "sojourning in Columbia." By late November 1846 he was back in Columbia (see Bk. 1, Ch. 12). Therefore, he must have returned to Charleston from his first trip between late July and mid-November 1846, depending on whether he made the corbels for Trinity Episcopal Church in Columbia or Charleston.

CHAPTER 12
November 1846–January 1847

Columbia, November 26, 1846

My Dear Wife,

There is one thing which I wish you to do for me—and you must do it. As you pass through Columbia you must let Clark Mills take your bust. It will look handsome and be much better than a portrait. I have had mine taken. He came to my room, took a brush and put on my face a sort of paste which dried in a few minutes and fell off a complete mould for a likeness. The operation is not disagreeable.

B. F. Perry

B. F. Perry, *Letters of Gov. Benjamin Franklin Perry to His Wife*, Second Series (Greenville, S.C.: Shannon & Co, Printers, 1890): 120.

In mid-November 1846, Mills vacated the house at 49 Broad Street in Charleston.[1] Apparently, he was arranging his affairs before setting out on his grand adventure. His plan, evidence suggests, was this: return to Columbia for a few weeks to make busts and take orders for marble copies; stop one last time at home; travel to Washington for a few days to fulfill his commitment to William Campbell Preston; then continue on to New York and embark for Europe.[2]

Heading up to Columbia, Mills observed a countryside much changed since making the trip in June. In Moncks Corner the extensive fields of rice plants were withered and brown. The seed heads had matured in July and been harvested, threshed and winnowed. Farther along Mills's route, the endless rows of cotton plants that marked the Orangeburg District were also transformed. Their deep green foliage and colorful blossoms had given way to ungainly branches speckled with thousands of bolls hung with white fluff. Black families with heads wrapped in bandannas and heads covered with broad-brimmed hats moved above the plants. As the pickers inched along, they threw the precious harvest into long burlap sacks hanging from their shoulders and dragging behind them. Distant clanging and wheezing of cotton gins pervaded the vast expanses.

On the Congaree River, traffic was visibly heavier than in June. Steamboats piled high with sacks of rice and bales of cotton destined for Europe were paddling downriver toward the Santee and the factors in Charleston.

Arriving in Columbia, Mills found the city as transformed as the countryside. The state legislature was in session. Members of the General Assembly and scores of South Carolinians having business with the government packed the capital's hotels and boardinghouses. Planters were returning from their agricultural domains with their families and servants to reanimate their in-town residences for the winter. The social season was under way.

In the cool evenings, fireplaces blazed and elegant gatherings lit up Columbia's windows. At dinner parties and gala balls, word spread that the brilliant young artist from Charleston was back in town. Portrait busts by Mills, recently acquired, commanded places of prominence in parlors and drawing rooms. Senator Benjamin Franklin Perry wrote to his wife in Greenville:

> *I saw Mrs. David F. McCord's. It is very fine and looks well.... His busts of Judge Johnson and Elmore are admirable. Also of Pettigru, Preston, Judge Cheves, and Hampton.*[3]

John Smith Preston was just back from Italy.[4] He had spent the summer in Florence and the entire month of October exploring Rome in the company of his protégé, Hiram Powers.[5] Sculpture, therefore, and the promising prospects of the self-taught bust maker from Charleston, figured prominently in the season's conversation. A thornier topic of discussion was the war in Mexico. South Carolina's "Palmetto Regiment" had just been called up for immediate service.

The border between Mexico and the United States was in dispute. Mexico held to its claim to Texas, which the United States had just annexed as its 28th state. In addition, Mexico declined to sell Upper California and New Mexico to the United States. In May, after President Polk announced that Mexicans had killed Americans on American soil, Congress had passed a declaration of war. Since then, General Zachary Taylor had marched his troops into Mexico and taken the city of Monterrey. The victory was swift, but cost many lives. To replenish Taylor's ranks, the War Department had just activated the Palmetto Regiment.[6]

Prestons, Hamptons, Wades—they all knew young men serving in the untested outfit. They also held substantial financial interests in Texas. Colonel Wade Hampton II, for one, owned 8,000 acres there.[7] However, Senator John C. Calhoun, wary of American ambition for expansion, had abstained from voting for the war. Consequently, South Carolinians were conflicted. Guarded exchanges troubled Columbia's soirées. Portrait busts by Mills was the safer topic.

During his sojourns in the capital this year, Mills made busts of many South Carolinian men of social, professional and political eminence, including:[8]

> *John Laurence Manning*, planter, South Carolina state representative, then senator, later governor.[9] His late wife, Susan Hampton, daughter of Wade Hampton I and co-owner of The Houmas, had died in 1845. Their children now resided more with John Smith Preston's family than with their father.
>
> *Benjamin Franklin Taylor*, scientific agriculturist, owner of four large plantations and a Columbia residence; South Carolina state representative.[10]
>
> *Andrew Pickens Butler*, South Carolina state representative, then senator, then judge, then U.S. Senator.[11]

Francis Kinloch Huger, physician, South Carolina state senator and representative; colonel in the War of 1812.[12]

Maximilian LaBorde, physician, author, professor at the College of South Carolina, later chairman of its faculty.[13]

David Johnson, South Carolina state representative, judge of several state-level courts, governor of South Carolina during the war with Mexico.[14]

Reverend George Howe, Presbyterian minister, author, professor at the Theological Seminary, Columbia.[15]

Benjamin Franklin Perry, lawyer and senior editor of three newspapers, including the *Southern Patriot* and *Greenville Mountaineer*, resided in Greenville, South Carolina. He was in Columbia this November of 1846 serving as a senator in the state legislature when he "sat" for Mills and wrote his wife about "the operation."[16]

Several years later—after Perry had been elected governor—he would publish his recollection of the much-talked-about plasterer-turned-sculptor:

> The history of Clark Mills is a most extraordinary one. He gave it to the senior editor himself, some six or seven years ago. He was at that time taking casts and executing busts in Columbia. We went to him to make an engagement for ourself, and the next day he called at our room in the hotel, prepared to take a mould of our head and face and shoulders. Whilst performing this operation, he commenced his narrative in regard to his own life and talents.[17]

That's when Mills told Perry how he came to begin sculpting, the anecdote about his whimsical step into the phrenologist's shop and his subsequent chance encounter with the Italian bust maker.[18] The Greenvillian would declare to his readers:

So we say in regard to phrenology, that if this science had never done any good to the world than that of developing the genius of Clark Mills, it would be quite enough to endear it to the world.[19]

After having his bust "taken" by Mills, Perry exhorted his wife to do the same.[20] Whether or not Mrs. Perry ever fulfilled her husband's wish, though, is not known.

Among Mills's sitters in Columbia were two men who would become powerful forces in Washington, D.C., and play particularly important roles in furthering Mills's career:

Isaac Edward Holmes, planter, lawyer, author, South Carolina state representative, then U.S. Congressman.[21] Holmes would soon initiate the meeting that was to change the course of Mills's life.[22]

James Henry Hammond, planter of Beech Island, Aiken County, South Carolina, U.S. Representative, then governor of South Carolina, then U.S. Senator. The outspoken defender of slavery and states' rights would later proclaim, "Cotton is King!" In time, Hammond would help Mills secure the most prestigious commission imaginable for a bronze founder in the nation's capital.[23]

Since Mills met with his subjects in the comfort and privacy of their own lodgings—their home or room in a boarding house or hotel—he was admitted into some of the grandest residences of Columbia. Although the houses varied in style, all were swaddled in meticulously cultivated parterres. The colorful gardens and trees reflected the weather this fall, which one reporter described as "glorious:"

[W]e have been favored with the blandest winds which emanate from Heaven.—We have had spells of cold weather it is true, but they have not been of any long duration;—the temperature generally being even and bland, and the air of that exhilarating and healthful quality which infuses vigor and energy into the whole animal frame.[24]

Profusions of camellias ranged from white to pink, jasmine everywhere was yellow, and the hard fruit hanging on the thorny branches of the Japanese quince bushes was a mustard green. Forsythia and honeysuckle were all green foliage now, having dropped their fragrant blossoms. The "blandest winds" of autumn rustled the cones in the cedars, spruce and cypress trees. Cushions of pine needles carpeted the garden paths that Mills trod.

Once again, as in June, Mills must have set up shop somewhere to perform the work of turning plaster casts into finished busts. But the location of his workshop in Columbia has not been discovered.

By now, though, his corbels had been installed in the sanctuary of Trinity Episcopal Church. It may have been in the company of John Smith Preston that Mills went to inspect them. The Charleston *Courier* described the state capital's new Gothic wonder:

> The Roof of the Church rests on ornamental supporters, which, as is likewise the ceiling, is painted in imitation of English oak. At the foot of each support is a miniature angel or corbel with the lower part enveloped in fig, or other leaves, executed by Mr. Clark Mills.[25]

But his little angels would not last long. Oral tradition claims that the corbels "were destroyed by General Sherman on his march through Columbia in 1865."[26] Powers' font of Carrara marble, on the other hand, graces the baptistry of Trinity Episcopal Church to this day.

Mills's sojourns in Columbia had been phenomenally successful. They had brought him state-wide exposure. Word of the "native Artist" had even reached the town of Edgefield in South Carolina's far west. "It is the intention of Mr. Mills," the *Edgefield Advertiser* had informed its citizens in August, "to finish his studies in Rome."[27] Mills had gained many new sitters—Holmes and Hammond, most auspiciously—and taken orders for 12 busts to be cut in stone once he reached Italy.[28] In addition, John Smith Preston's commission for Trinity Episcopal Church had been a totally unexpected boon.

More valuable than anything, though, for the self-trained sculptor, was winning the patronage of one of the country's most respected connoisseurs of the arts, the man for whom Hiram Powers had named his fifth child: William Campbell Preston. The former senator's gift of a trip to Washington, D.C., augured breathtaking prospects, national in scope. Was this not the very path that Powers' career had taken?

It appears that Mills may not have spent Christmas that year with his wife and sons. He may not have returned to Charleston until mid-January 1847. That's when he picked up his mail, which had been accumulating at the post office.[29] Nor, once home, was he to stay with his family for long. He only needed to put his household affairs in order—he would be gone for a year, perhaps longer—then embark on his dream-come-true pilgrimage. His wife and four sons were to remain in Charleston. Eliza did not share her husband's high spirits regarding this unexpected upheaval of their domestic life. Fortunately, she had numerous family connections in Charleston and a father who was about to intervene on her behalf.

NOTES

1. "To Let," [Charleston] *Courier*, Nov. 12, 1846, p. 3: "TO LET, the HOUSE 49 Broad-street, now occupied by Mr. Clark Mills. Possession can be had on the 16th inst.;" reprinted Nov. 16, 17, 18, 21 and 23, 1846.
2. "Clark Mills and His Equestrian Statue," *DeBow's Review*, vol. 16 (Jan. 1854): 41. See also Bk. 1, Ch. 17, n. 2.
3. B. F. Perry, *Letters of Gov. Benjamin Franklin Perry to His Wife*, Second Series (Greenville, S.C.: Shannon & Co, Printers, 1890): 120–21. "Mrs. David F. McCord" is an error for "Mrs. David J. McCord." This was evidently the bust that Louisa Susannah Cheves McCord detested. See Bk. 1, Ch. 7, and Bk. 2.
4. John S. Preston entry, passenger list of the ship *Great Western*, arrived New York, Nov. 17, 1846; Passenger Lists of Vessels Arriving at New York, N.Y., 1820–1897, NARA 237, roll 64; viewed at www.ancestry.com.

5 Richard P. Wunder, *Hiram Powers, Vermont Sculptor, 1805–1873* (Newark: University of Delaware Press, 1991), vol. I, *Life*: 97.
6 Samuel Eliot Morison, Henry Steele Commager and William E. Leuchtenburg, *The Growth of the American Republic*, 7th ed. (New York and Oxford: Oxford University Press, 1980), vol. 1: 551–52; and "Palmetto Regiment" at http://www.scencyclopedia.org/sce/entries/palmetto-regiment.
7 "Wade Hampton II" at https://www.scencyclopedia.org/sce/entries/hampton-wade-ii/.
8 See Bk. 1, Ch. 11, n. 16.
9 John Laurence Manning (1816–89), see http://www.scencyclopedia.org/sce/entries/manning-john-laurence. Today a copy of this bust is in the South Caroliniana Library, University of South Carolina, Columbia.
10 Benjamin Franklin Taylor (1791–1852), see https://www.wikitree.com/wiki/Taylor-63640.
11 Andrew Pickens Butler (1796–1857), see http://www.scencyclopedia.org/sce/entries/butler-andrew-pickens.
12 Francis Kinloch Huger (1773–1855), see https://en.wikipedia.org/wiki/Francis_Kinloch_Huger. Today a copy of this bust is in the South Caroliniana Library, University of South Carolina, Columbia.
13 Maximilian LaBorde (1804–73), see biographical sketch in M. LaBorde, M.D., *History of the South Carolina College* (Charleston, S.C.: Walker, Evans & Cogswell, Printers, 1874): v–xxxiv. Today a copy of this bust is in the South Caroliniana Library, University of South Carolina, Columbia.
14 David Johnson (1782–1855), see http://www.scencyclopedia.org/sce/entries/johnson-david. This bust is listed in an old inventory of the South Caroliniana Library, University of South Carolina, Columbia, but its current disposition is unknown.
15 George Howe (1802–83), see https://www.presbyteriansofthepast.com/2014/12/11/george-howe.
16 Benjamin Franklin Perry (1805–86), see http://www.scencyclopedia.org/sce/entries/perry-benjamin-franklin/.
17 "Genius and Phrenology," [Greenville] *Southern Patriot*, Jan. 27, 1853; reprinted in *Brooklyn Daily Eagle*, Feb. 18, 1853, p. 4.
18 See Bk. 1, Ch. 5.
19 "Genius and Phrenology," *Southern Patriot*, Jan. 27, 1853.
20 Perry, *Letters*, 122.
21 Isaac Edward Holmes (1796–1867), see https://en.wikipedia.org/wiki/Isaac_E._Holmes. Today a copy of this bust is in the Charleston Library Society, Charleston, S.C.
22 See Bk. 1, Ch. 16.
23 James Henry Hammond (1807–64), see http://www.scencyclopedia.org/sce/entries/hammond-james-henry. See also Bk. 2.
24 "The Weather," [Charleston] *Southern Patriot*, Dec. 17, 1846, p. 2.

25 [Charleston] *Courier*, July 17, 1847; quoted in Rosemary Hopkins, *Clark Mills: The First Native American Sculptor* (M.A. thesis, University of Maryland, 1966): 210. The author has not been able to find this article.
26 Hopkins, *Clark Mills,* 210.
27 "Mr. Clarke [sic] Mills, a native Artist," *Edgefield* [S.C.] *Advertiser*, Aug. 5, 1846, p. 3.
28 "Sketches of Washington. By Childe Harold," *Brooklyn Daily Eagle*, Mar. 30, 1853, p. 2.
29 "List of Letters Remaining at the Post Office at Charleston, So. Ca.," [Charleston] *Courier*, Dec. 31, 1846–Jan. 13, 1847, p. 3.

CHAPTER 13
February 1847

Know all men by these presents that I, George Kinloch of the City of Charleston in the State of South Carolina in consideration of the sum of nine hundred Dollars to me paid by Alexander Ballantine, Trustee of Mrs. Eliza Mills of the City of Charleston in the state aforesaid have granted, bargained, sold and released unto the said Alexander Ballantine, All that Lot, piece or parcel of Land and the Buildings thereon now occupied, by and situate lying and being on the south side of Atlantic Street in the said City of Charleston.

Charleston County Deeds, vol. Y11: 393–95, Feb. 5, 1847.

The word "*Mrs.*" is the only indication that Eliza had a husband. Nowhere in the deed is Mills referenced, let alone named. Their marriage was strained.

For nine years, the couple had lived in rented lodgings: first most likely in or near the home of Eliza's father, Alexander Ballantine, at Market and Beaufain Streets; then on Mary Street in the Northern Neck; then in Mrs. Huard's house at 49 Broad Street. Since Mills had defaulted on the Lamboll Street lot, he owned no property. Eliza had given birth to six children. Two had died young, leaving four healthy sons.[1] Mills had just spent a number of months in Columbia, now he was on his way—via Washington—to Italy. How long he would remain there, no one knew. On February 5, 1847, Mills's father-in-law acted—not for the first time—to safeguard the welfare of his daughter and grandchildren. As "Trustee of Mrs. Eliza Mills," he bought them a house.[2]

It was small. The lot at No. 9 Atlantic Street was only 23 feet wide and 35 feet deep. Nonetheless, it provided stability for Eliza and her sons. Of the seven years that they were to live there, Mills would spend only one.[3]

In contrast to his thorny domestic situation, Mills's professional posture was rosy. While basking in the imprimatur of the illustrious Preston brothers, he had arranged to have two of his busts exhibited in Boston. The *Boston Evening Transcript* carried the news on August 14, 1846:

> The friends of Hon. John C. Calhoun will be glad to learn that there is an excellent bust of that distinguished gentleman, now at the Athenaeum Gallery. It is by Clark Mills, Esq., an artist residing in Charleston, S.C. There is also one of governor McDuffie, by the same artist; they are both said to be excellent likenesses, as well as fine works of art.[4]

The two busts may have been on view at no cost or, possibly, Mills had tapped into one of the ways in which artists financed their careers: hiring an impresario to exhibit his work and charge the public an admittance fee. Even if the event brought Mills no remuneration, though, the publicity it generated was likely to bring him more orders for busts. The *Evening Transcript* notice was copied verbatim in newspapers of Philadelphia, New York, Newport (Mass.), Portsmouth (N.H.) and perhaps other cities, as well. The name of Clark Mills, linked to the name of John C. Calhoun, was reverberating in the country's major art centers as far north as New England.

Just as Mills had hoped, the legendary renown of the "Cast-Iron Man" had launched his own celebrity. His bust of the famous titan of South Carolina was the best seller he needed. Mills would make at least five copies of Calhoun's life mask and nine of his bust—very likely, many more than that.[5] So popular was the sculpture that forgeries began to surface. Mills would run a "CAUTION" in two Charleston newspapers, informing the public that he had patented the bust and that "the law will be rigidly enforced."[6]

Within the short span of three years, Mills had created a pantheon of portrait busts of eminent South Carolinians. In a 1966 M.A.

thesis, *Clark Mills: The First Native American Sculptor*, Rosemary Hopkins writes:

> From 1844, when Mills began his career, until 1847, when he journeyed to Washington, at least sixty works have been catalogued . . . and many have probably been destroyed or lost. . . . Almost every prominent South Carolinian had his bust made by the now illustrious artist.[7]

Some of Mills's sitters—they included women now—already owned a portrait bust by Hiram Powers.[8] As the preeminent American bust maker, Powers reigned unchallenged. Not only his fellow countrymen, but also European nobility called at his studio in Florence.[9] Acquiring "a Powers," though, entailed traveling to Italy, sitting through multiple long sessions (he worked in clay), and paying top dollar. The primary reason for Mills's popularity was the fact that he needed only two brief sittings at virtually any location the client desired, and a bust by him could be finished within a matter of days at a small fraction of the cost of a Powers. Benjamin Franklin Perry wrote to his wife in 1846, "The price is $25 and $35. You may have copies for $5 and 7.50."[10] Mills advertised in the Columbia *Telegraph* that busts could be "had at very moderate prices if applied for soon."[11]

In addition, Mills delivered what his clients expected: a portrait bust that was neoclassical in style. That was the standard for the genre. In the beginning, his busts consisted of the head and neck and a scant amount of bare chest mounted on a squat round base. As the neophyte sculptor grew in confidence and skill, he added shoulders, then shoulders draped with the requisite classical garb: a toga for a man, a simple gown for a woman. The price differential that Perry noted probably depended on whether Mills added shoulders or shoulders with drapery to the head and neck. Many of his busts were bronzed or polychromed, which enhancement would have cost extra, too.

This was exactly how the trailblazing bust makers of New York City, John Frazee and John Henri Isaac Browere, as well as the New England master, Hiram Powers, depicted their sitters. Mills was emulating his predecessors. But his allegiance to the neoclassical esthetic was about to change. Mills's own concept of naturalistic representation in sculpture would soon inform his portraits.

Mills's faster and more comfortable method for taking life masks would serve him well for the rest of his life. Even when engaged on monumental sculptures of national significance, he would fulfill orders for life masks, death masks, and busts. Casting multiple copies of his images of famous Americans, particularly popular politicians, would provide continual, albeit modest, income. A few of the busts he would cast in bronze. But only one, Calhoun's, did he carve in stone.

When Alexander Ballentine bought the little house at No. 9 Atlantic Street for Mills's wife and sons, it was occupied. However, the residents soon moved out and Eliza and the boys—aged 7, 6, 4, and a few months—moved in. By that time, Mills may already have left for Washington.

There is no evidence that Eliza or anyone else condemned Mills for "abandoning" his family—not at this time, at least. It was not uncommon for respectable heads of households, men of commerce, the courts, and government, to spend extended periods of time away from their families, particularly those whose vocations took them overseas—such as aspiring sculptors. Indeed, being a responsible provider sometimes demanded long separations from family. Mills was laying the foundation for a career that, hopefully, would provide a decent living for his wife and sons. Besides, he left his enslaved assistant, Philip Reid, a master plasterer, to serve as breadwinner in his stead. Reid was about 26 years old now and a bachelor. Whether he resided with Eliza and the boys or elsewhere—possibly a boardinghouse for Black tradesmen—is not known. He had family residing in Charleston, whom he may have been allowed to visit on occasion.[12]

Heading north to the nation's capital, Mills carried one particularly precious possession. It was the only "credential" the self-trained sculptor could produce when interviewed by reporters: the gold medal he had been awarded by the Honorable Mayor and Aldermen of the City of Charleston.[13]

NOTES

1. See Bk. 1, Ch. 4.
2. Title, Geo. Kinloch to Alex. Ballantine [sic], Trustee, Mrs. E. Mills, Feb. 5, 1847; Charleston County Deeds, vol. Y11: 393–95; Charleston County Register of Deeds, Charleston, S.C.
3. Charleston directories for 1849 and 1852, as well as the 1850 U.S. Census, record Mills and his family at 9 Atlantic Street. See James William Hagy, *Directories for the City of Charleston, South Carolina: For the Years 1849, 1852 and 1855* (Baltimore: Clearfield Press, 1998), 30 and 87; and J. H. Bagget, pub., *Directory of the City of Charleston, for the Year 1852* (Charleston: Edward C. Councell, printer, 1851): 88. See also Clark Mills entry, 1850 U.S. Census, Parishes of St. Philip's and St. Michael's, Charleston, S.C., p. 182 (handwritten), p. 91[b] (stamped); NARA M432, roll 850. In reality, however, Mills was residing in Washington, D.C., during those years, while his wife and sons were residing in Charleston.
4. [no title], *Boston Evening Transcript,* Aug. 14, 1846, p. 4.
5. Today copies of this bust are in the Smithsonian Museum of American Art, Washington, D.C.; South Caroliniana Library, University of South Carolina, Columbia, S.C.; and Charleston Library Society, Charleston, S.C.
6. "CAUTION," [Charleston] *Southern Patriot,* Feb. 23, 1848, p. 3; and "CAUTION," [Charleston] *Courier,* Feb. 24, 1848, p. 3. Sculptural works today are protected under Copyright Law, not Patent Law.
7. Rosemary Hopkins, *Clark Mills: The First Native American Sculptor* (M.A. thesis, University of Maryland, 1966): 40–41. Hopkins' tally includes copies Mills made from his originals. Several busts by Mills not included in Hopkins' tally have been located by the author and cataloged in this present work.
8. For example, George McDuffie and John C. Calhoun, as well as John Smith Preston and William Campbell Preston and their wives, all owned busts by Powers. Others of Mills's clients would commission a bust from Powers after having sat for Mills—Louisa Susannah Cheves McCord, for example, who detested Mills's likeness of her. See Richard P. Wunder, *Hiram Powers, Vermont Sculptor, 1805–1873* (Newark, Del.: University of Delaware Press, 1991), vol. II, *Catalogue*: 26, 70, 85–88.

9 Wunder, *Hiram Powers,* vol. I, *Life*: passim.
10 B. F. Perry, *Letters of Gov. Benjamin Franklin Perry to His Wife*, Second Series (Greenville, S.C.: Shannon & Co., Printers, 1890): 120.
11 [Columbia] *Telegraph*, Nov. 30, 1847, quoted in Hopkins, *Clark Mills,* 41–42.
12 See Bk. 1, Ch. 4.
13 "An Honored Sculptor," [Washington] *Saturday Evening News*, Mar. 6, 1847, p. 3.

CHAPTER 14
February 1847

On his way to the National Capital he stopped at Richmond, Va., where he saw the statue of Washington by Houdon. This was the first one he ever saw.

"Clark Mills at Home," *The Washington Post*, Feb. 7, 1880, p. 2.

As soon as Mills walked into the rotunda of the Virginia capitol, he stopped short. There before him, life-size, ivory-white in the luminescence wafting down from the skylight overhead, stood George Washington. Looking trim in his Revolutionary War uniform, but jacket open and head uncoverd, the General in flawless Carrara marble posed assertively atop a square pedestal of like stone. His right hand rested on a walking stick, his left on fasces draped with a cape and sword. Behind him lay a plow. The classical allusion was unmistakable: here stood Cincinnatus, the Roman general who, after conquering in war, returned to his farm. In awe, Mills studied "the finest statue in America."[1]

The foremost French sculptor of the age, Jean-Antoine Houdon, had been commissioned by the Virginia General Assembly to create it. Houdon came to the United States in 1785 and stayed at Mount Vernon as the guest of Washington for several weeks. He took the bodily measurements of his illustrious subject as well as the General's face mask, used the mask to make a plaster bust, and sculpted a clay bust as well. Leaving the plaster bust at Mount Vernon as a gift to his host, Houdon took the mask and clay bust back to Paris, where he used them to carve the statue in his studio. It was shipped to the United States and installed in 1796 precisely where Mills was viewing it this winter day in February 1847.[2]

Jean-Antoine Houdon's *Washington*, Virginia capitol, Richmond, considered America's finest statue and most accurate portrait of the General when Mills viewed it in 1847. Washington hosted Houdon at Mount Vernon and posed for him in 1785. The figure's stance and the sculpture's allusion to the Roman General Cincinnatus reflect ideals of neoclassicism, but Washington's face and attire are meticulously naturalistic. (Library of Virginia, Richmond)

He had accepted the generous offer of former U.S. Senator William Campbell Preston to view the sculpture in the nation's capital on his way to Italy. En route, however, Preston considered it *de rigueur* for Mills to stop in Richmond to see Houdon's *Washington*. The revered masterpiece was the object of pilgrimage for all serious artists, as well as gentlemen and ladies having the means to travel at leisure. For Mills, the detour was worth the prolonged ordeal of travel.

Benjamin Franklin Perry had made the same Charleston-to-Richmond trip the previous summer, shortly before Mills took the state senator's face mask and fashioned his bust in Columbia. Perry described "the excessive fatigue of the journey" in a letter to his wife. The trip took two and a half days and two nights:

The boat [from Charleston] started at 4 o'clock [Saturday afternoon]. We had a crowd on board.... Sunday morning we landed in Wilmington [North Carolina] and took the cars for Weldon, where we arrived at night—160 miles. Travelled all night; came to Petersburg [Virginia] about sunrise [Monday], ate breakfast at Richmond.[3]

Approaching the capital of Virginia, the Richmond & Petersburg cars rattled across a long wooden bridge on high stone piers that spanned the James River.[4] The water below was white with rapids that roiled around several islands. Seafaring ships had to dock at piers some distance below the city. Their masts were scarcely visible far to the right. But passengers could clearly see the barges plying the Kanawha Canal, which hugged the northern shore of the James. The barges carried cargo from the ocean-going vessels westward into Virginia's hinterland and delivered products of the Old Dominion back to the ships for export. Groggy but excited, Mills would have surveyed a metropolis a century younger than Charleston, and much smaller, too: roughly 24,500 people, compared to Charleston's 32,500. Yet the vibrancy of the commercial district was striking.

Visible left of the railroad bridge, lining the north bank of the river, spread an industrial complex that drew its power from the rushing water. A brawny red brick cube four stories high with attic and dormers was the Crenshaw Flour Mill. The tall chimneys spewing smoke and ash into the sky belonged to the Tredegar Iron Works, celebrated as the largest foundry in the South. Nearer the bridge, just ahead, stood the massive Virginia Manufactory of Arms with its rolling mill, iron works and machine shops. Along the streets of the commercial district on the right—called Shockoe—stretched immense tobacco factories and warehouses. The aroma of the precious commodity scented the air. Red-brick houses of business with second-story lodgings, banks, offices of shipping firms and insurance companies, hotels and boardinghouses crowded the neighborhood. The city's two largest flour mills, Gallego and Haxall, stood near the

Kanawha Canal's turning basin, a man-made body of water several blocks long. The Richmond & Petersburg depot, toward which Mills was hurtling at 35 miles an hour, sat on the northern bank of the James at 8th and Byrd Streets, amid paper, flooring, corn and saw mills. For passengers wishing to continue north, the Richmond, Fredericksburg & Potomac Railroad had its depot across town on Broad Street.

But newcomers did not focus on the waterfront or Shockoe for long. Their eyes were drawn upwards. Richmond was built on hills. Church steeples and neoclassical public buildings punctuated the skyline. The great white mass of the State Penitentiary, though situated at the far western edge of the city, sat high enough to be seen from the railway bridge. City Hall stood out on the horizon because of its dome. Close to City Hall, the governor's elegant mansion was also visible. Most striking of all, though, claiming the majestic summit of the highest eminence, like an ancient Greek temple, reigned the Virginia capitol. Richmond flaunted itself to the arriving visitor as the preeminent industrial powerhouse and de facto cultural capital of the American South.

Mills would have found no shortage of lodging possibilities around the depot; however, it is unlikely that Senator Preston had sent him off without letters of introduction. The traveler may have stayed with a friend or colleague of Preston's, who would have been honored to show off his city to the senator's highly regarded protégé.[5] Richmonders were proud of their buildings designed by the country's preeminent architects. The State Penitentiary was the creation of Benjamin Henry Latrobe, the "Father of American Architecture," who had served as Architect of the Capitol in Washington. City Hall was the creation of Robert Mills. A generation older than Clark—and no relation—Robert Mills also hailed—coincidentally—from Charleston. Early works of his would have been familiar to Clark, including the Charleston County Records Building and the Marine Hospital on Franklin Street.[6] The architect's forte of designing neoclassical edifices that were fireproof had landed him in Washington, where Clark Mills would soon see his grandest structures under construction. Virginia's capitol, that, of course, was the well-known masterwork of Thomas Jefferson himself. Mills could not have doubted that he had arrived in a very important and very prosperous place.

Like Charleston, Richmond owed its wealth to a thriving slave trade. Close to half of the city's residents were Blacks—roughly 9,927 bound and 2,369 free. They and their scattered rural kin, along with numerous lawyer/planter families who divided their time between city residences and tobacco plantations, connected the urban economy intimately to the surrounding countryside. Richmond breathed tobacco.

Standing in the rotunda of the Virginia capitol, Mills turned from the world-famous *Washington* to examine a bust occupying a niche just steps away. Representing the Marquis de Lafayette, it, too, had been executed by Jean-Antoine Houdon in Carrara marble at the behest of the Virginia General Assembly.[7] To create an exact portrait, the sculptor had begun, as he had with Washington, by taking a plaster cast of Lafayette's face. He portrayed the Marquis in his American military uniform, his chest decorated with the cross of the Order of Saint Louis and the badge of the Society of the Cincinnati. This was unlike the "standard" neoclassical portrait busts of Frazee, Browere and Powers that Mills had been emulating.

Houdon's statues, praised as masterpieces, presented the subjects, not in idealized fashion, but as realistically rendered individuals. They wore, not togas and sandals, but the attire of their own day, down to the telling detail of the pocket watch fob dangling beneath Washington's too-tight doublet and the two medals pinned to Lafayette's left lapel. Both generals were readily identifiable as themselves. For his *Washington*, Houdon had invoked the classical world through peripheral symbols—the Roman fasces, the plow of Cincinnatus—not the portrayal of the man. And for *Lafayette*, the French master's sole nod to Greek antiquity had been to swathe his countryman's shoulders in elaborate drapery—an emblem of everlasting fame—that cascaded down to enfold the base of the bust.

Mills took it all in with eager eyes. His practical instruction in "Sculpture" had begun with the best examples the United States had to offer. In three years, he would be back in the Virginia capitol, a member of an official delegation from Washington. In just three years' time, he would see Houdon's masterpieces with an educated eye and an informed appreciation, although not from having studied in Italy. Mills's artistic journey was to take him down an uncharted path.

Leaving Richmond for Washington City, Mills faced another bout of fatiguing travel. No railroad bridge spanned the Potomac River in 1847.[8] The Richmond, Fredericksburg & Potomac Railroad provided service (via Fredericksburg) to Aquia Creek, Virginia, a port on the Potomac. There, travelers transferred to a Washington & Fredericksburg Steamboat Company packet heading upriver.[9] Mills's initial view of the nation's capital, therefore, was from the south.

NOTES

1 "Clark Mills at Home," *The Washington Post*, Feb. 7, 1880, p. 2. See also "Mr. Clark Mills, The Sculptor," *The Round Table*, vol. 1, no. 22 (May 14, 1864): 340. Throughout Mills's life and afterwards, it was often repeated in print that Houdon's *Washington* was the first statue he ever saw. However, a larger-than-life-size marble statue of William Pitt stood on a pedestal in the front yard of the Orphan House in Charleston from 1808 to 1880. Mills could not have missed seeing it. Dating from 1770, the statue was neoclassical in style. See D. E. Huger Smith, "Wilton's Statue of Pitt," *The South Carolina Historical and Genealogical Magazine*, vol. 15, no. 1 (Jan. 1914): 34–35.

2 See "Statue of George Washington (Houdon)" at https://en.wikipedia.org/wiki/Statue_of_George_Washington_(Houdon).

3 B. F. Perry, *Letters of Gov. Benjamin Franklin Perry to His Wife*, Second Series (Greenville, S.C.: Shannon & Co., 1890): 91.

4 Unless cited otherwise, description of Richmond in 1847 is derived from: (1) Gregg D. Kimball, *American City, Southern Place: A Cultural History of Antebellum Richmond* (Athens, Ga.: University of Georgia Press, 2000): passim;

(2) Charles S. Morgan, *Plan of Richmond (Henrico County), Manchester & Springhill, Virginia, 1848*; Library of Virginia, Richmond, at http://rosetta.virginiamemory.com:1801/delivery/DeliveryManagerServlet?dps_pid=IE3526829; (3) Alexander MacKay, *The Western World; or, Travels in the United States in 1846–47,* 2nd ed. (Philadelphia: Lea & Blanchard, 1849), vol. 1: 247–55, at www.loc.gov/resource/lhbtn.2679a/?sp=gallery; and (4) 1850 U.S. Census statistics.

5   Mills's name does not appear in the lists of "Hotel Arrivals" published regularly in the *Richmond Enquirer.*

6   Robert Mills (1781–1855), see https://en.wikipedia.org/wiki/Robert_Mills_(architect); and Rhodri Windsor Liscombe, *Altogether American: Robert Mills, Architect and Engineer, 1781–1855* (New York: Oxford University Press, 1994).

7   See "Houdon's Lafayette" at http://rodama1789.blogspot.com/2015/12/houdons-lafayette.html.

8   "Richmond, Fredericksburg and Potomac Railroad" at https://en.wikipedia.org/wiki/Richmond,_Fredericksburg_and_Potomac_Railroad.

9   Lloyd Van Derveer, *Map of the City of Washington, D.C., 1850*; Library of Congress, at https://www.loc.gov/resource/g3850.ct004378/?r=0.593,0.095,0.317,0.192,0.

CHAPTER 15
February–March 1847

We noticed a few days ago, in the Rotundo of the Capitol, four handsome busts, which appeared to be very admirable likenesses of the Hon. John C. Calhoun, W.C. Preston, G. McDuffie and A.P. Butler, distinguished sons of South Carolina. Mr. Clark Mills, the sculptor, and exhibitor, of these striking busts has been lately presented with a large and beautiful gold medal, which we had the pleasure of examining.

"An Honored Sculptor," [Washington]
Saturday Evening News, Mar. 6, 1847, p. 3.

The steamer was approaching Greenleaf's Point, the southern-most tip of the District of Columbia, where the Eastern Branch flowed into the Potomac. Onboard, Mills could see the hilly cityscape of Washington dominated by four stately neoclassical buildings and a fifth in the works.[1] Crowning the highest point, the U.S. Capitol, painted milk white to preserve the sandstone, with its famous Bulfinch dome, was unmistakable. Directly ahead of Mills's packet, the Executive Mansion came into view. Sitting much lower than the Capitol and much smaller in size, it was still discernible from a distance, because its sandstone walls, too, had been covered with an oil-based white paint to preserve them. Washingtonians early on had taken to calling it the "White House."[2]

Midway between the President's House and the Capitol, prominent atop its own hill, stood the dark brick silhouette of City Hall. After 27 years of sporadic construction, the building was finally nearing completion. Still lacking, though, were its coat of stucco and its stately portico of six two-story columns and broad pediment.[3]

Beyond City Hall stood two masterworks of Robert Mills's: the Patent Office and the Post Office Department. Both were Greek revival and fireproof—hallmarks of the South Carolinian's designs—as was his new east wing for the Treasury Department. All three buildings, though unfinished, were in use while additional wings remained under construction. Recently, Robert Mills had won the competition for the city's Washington Monument, but the cornerstone would not be laid for another year.

As Clark Mills's steamer veered toward the wharves at the foot of 6th and 7th Streets, passengers on deck heard the sounds and observed the bustle of Washington's waterfront. Fishing craft bobbed in the water. Boardinghouses, taverns, warehouses and commercial buildings skirted the coast. Draymen, most of them Black, maneuvered their carts along the piers, trading calls with deck hands and captains onboard sailing vessels and steamers. But this was clearly not a harbor anywhere near the size of Charleston's, or even Richmond's.

Though home to roughly 44,500 people—substantially more populous than both Charleston and Richmond—Washington was no hub of commerce and trade, as those port cities were. Rather, it was a "city of grand distances," an ambition striving for realization. Eyeing the urban panorama from the Capitol southward to the swampy shores of the Potomac and Eastern Branch revealed the city's spotty development. Unkempt squares of weeds and brush and roving milk cows, hogs and chickens alternated with squares containing a house or two or a short cluster of rowhouses. Mills may have caught sight of the enormous shed and forest of masts in the distance; they marked the site of the Navy Yard. *That* was Washington's major industry. There, on the shore of the Eastern Branch, ships were built and arms and ammunition were manufactured.

That February of 1847, Mills viewed all of the public sculpture in the nation's capital. It did not take long. There were only 15 works.[4] Other than those—and the rare portrait bust or ornamental piece brought from Europe and displayed in a private residence—the only

Casimir Bohn's lithographic print, "View of Washington City and Georgetown," 1849, shows the Washington Monument and Jackson equestrian statue (both still in progress) as they were intended to look when finished. Visiting the capital in 1847, Mills found a southern city more populous than Charleston, but much younger and less refined. (Library of Congress)

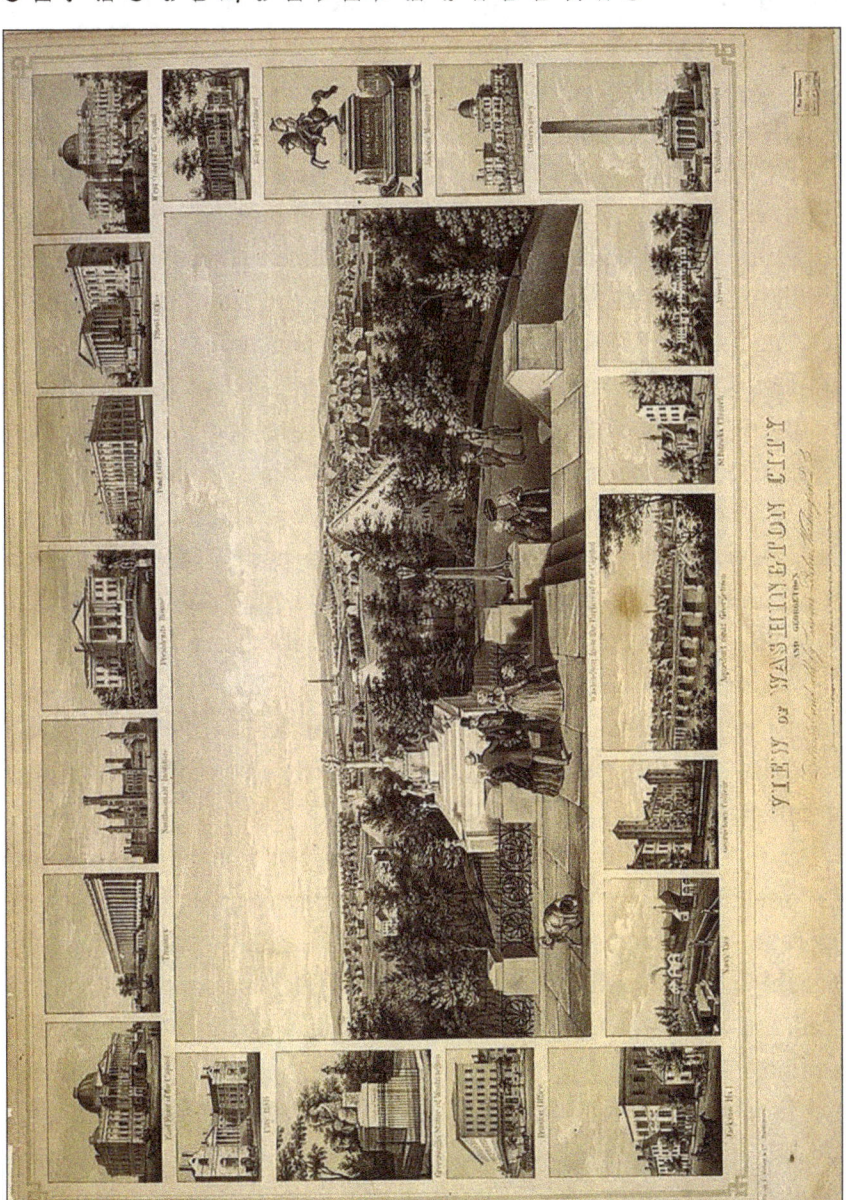

sculpture a Washingtonian might see, occasionally and by paying an admittance fee, was a famous statue touring the country on exhibition. Occasionally, too, a member of Congress would vaunt his home state by displaying the work of a promising young constituent in the rotunda of the Capitol or some other federal building. Those exhibitions were free to the public.

The city had one bronze statue. It stood on the north lawn of the President's House. Created by the French sculptor, Pierre-Jean David d'Angers, it was a life-size *Thomas Jefferson* cast in Paris.[5] David d'Angers was a generation younger than Houdon and never ventured to America. He had been commissioned to make the statue by Uriah Phillips Levy, a lieutenant in the U.S. Navy, who gifted it to the American people in 1834. David d'Angers's *Jefferson* stood in dynamic contraposto, a quill in one hand and the Declaration of Independence unfurling from the other. This was likely the first statue of bronze that Mills ever "experienced," rather than seen in an engraving or print.

Similar to Houdon's *Washington* and *Lafayette* in the Virginia capitol, David d'Angers's figure bore accurate period detail. Jefferson was attired in a cutaway, waistcoat, breeches and big-buckled shoes. Moreover, Mills could read every word of the sacred document in Jefferson's hand, so clear was the script. Other than the statue's pose, therefore, there was no inference of the classical world—no toga, no sandals—about this statesman: he was clearly an eighteenth-century gentleman.

This contrasted starkly with the only work of public sculpture in Washington created by an American: *Washington Enthroned* by Horatio Greenough. A contemporary of Hiram Powers, and equally accomplished, Greenough also resided in Florence and revered the classical prototypes he found in Italy.[6] He was the first American sculptor to receive a contract from Congress, and all of his major works would be larger-than-life-size marble statues commissioned for the Capitol. Greenough's colossal, twenty-ton *Washington Enthroned* had reached the city in 1841 and—with considerable travail—been ensconced in the rotunda. Two years later, however, because its tremendous weight was causing structural damage to the building, it was moved outside to the east lawn of the Capitol. Mounted on a tall square pedestal and enclosed in an iron fence, the statue faced the building's imposing facade. Mills probably stepped slowly around the enormous sculpture to examine every facet of its masterful carving.

When the American public saw the "Father of Their Country" enthroned like a Roman god, naked to the waist, wrapped in a toga, and shod with sandals, they sniggered. Years later Mills was to tell an *Evening Star* reporter:

> "When I first came to Washington I went to see Greenough's statue of Washington, east of the Capitol. It seemed to me a wonderful work of art; but while I was looking at it others came up. Said one: 'I never heard that Washington wore a blanket like an Indian.' Another inquired: 'What are those things on his feet?' 'Oh,' said a third party, 'they must be moccasins—Indians wear moccasins.' Then others came up of more cultivation; 'There,' said

Stereoview of Horatio Greenough's *Washington Enthroned*, 1860s. The 20-ton statue—the first commission Congress ever awarded an American sculptor—arrived in Washington from Greenough's s studio in Florence, Italy, in 1841. Americans, including Mills, admired their fellow countryman's virtuosity as a carver of marble, but deplored his depiction of the Father of His Country in the neoclassical style. (courtesy of Peter R. Penczer)

one, 'is a work of art pronounced the most perfect that has been turned out of Italy for many years; but it proves an utter failure here, because it idealizes the Washington of the people out of all sympathy or recognition. The fact is, the American people will never stand having their Washingtons, Jeffersons and Jacksons put out bare-legged in togas and sandals.' . . . I determined, from that moment, that I would have nothing to do with the toga business; and that whatever else might be said of my works, they should at least be true to nature and to American ideas."[7]

Mills thought the anatomy perfect. But he could not see the flesh-and-blood general of the eighteenth century in this stern deity in pagan guise. He contrasted the allegorical sculpture with the literal portrayals of *Washington* and *Lafayette* by Houdon and the *Jefferson* by David d'Angers. Experiencing sculpture for the first time in his life was stimulating Mills's conception of naturalistic, rather than classical, depiction in art. "Should he ever have an order for a statue," Mills would later tell a journalist of *The Round Table*, "the world should find fault for his giving too much truth, and not for the want of it."[8]

Other than Greenough's hieratic *Washington*, all of the sculpture examined by Mills at the Capitol building was the handiwork of Italians, except for one relief panel by a Frenchman.

On the west grounds, Mills scrutinized the *Tripoli Monument* by Giovanni Carlo Micali.[9] Carved of white marble in Italy and brought to America in 1806, it commemorated six U.S. Naval officers who had perished in the first Barbary War. A rostral column crowned with an American eagle soared 30 feet up from a massive square base adorned with figures representing Glory, History, America and Commerce. Micali's sculpture stood in the center of a reflecting pool. The Tuscan sculptor never traveled to the United States.

On the principal façade of the Capitol, a majestic flight of stairs led up to a deep Corinthian portico. "Here," declared a mid-nineteenth-century guidebook, "is to be seen the grandest collection of statuary in this country."[10] Four works were by Luigi Persico.[11] His *Genius of America* adorned the pediment: three female figures sculpted in high relief symbolized, in the middle, the United States, and to either side, Justice and Hope. Niches flanking the central door contained Persico's two oversized allegorical statues, *Peace* (in the guise of the goddess Ceres) and *War* (the god Mars). His freestanding masterwork, *Discovery of America*, dominated the south cheek block of the grand staircase. The sculptural ensemble, larger than life-size, depicted a triumphant Christopher Columbus clad in Spanish armor holding aloft a globe, while an American Indian woman cowered at his side. After spending three decades in the United States, Persico returned to Europe.

Daguerreotype of the east front of the U.S. Capitol, ca. 1846, the year prior to Mills's visit. Visible to the left of the central staircase is Luigi Persico's *Discovery of America*, depicting a heroic Columbus with a Native American woman crouching at his feet. Washington offered Mills something no other American city could: 13 large works in stone contracted by Congress for the Capitol, all executed by master sculptors from Italy and France. (Library of Congress)

Standing in the portico, Mills could study close-up the broad rectangular relief panel over the central door. Sculpted by Antonio Capellano, it depicted *Fame and Peace Crowning George Washington*.[12] Stepping inside the Capitol rotunda, Mills viewed another creation of Capellano's: *Preservation of Captain John Smith by Pocahontas*. It was one of four relief panels carved into the circular sandstone wall of the rotunda, one above each door. They portrayed scenes of early encounters between European settlers and American Indians. *Landing of the Pilgrims on Plymouth Rock* and *Conflict between Daniel Boone and the Indians* were sculpted by Enrico Causici.[13] The fourth scene, *William Penn's Treaty with the Indians*, was the one work by a sculptor of French birth, Nicholas Gevelot.[14] Capellano remained in the United States; Causici and Gevelot did not.

Walking into the chamber of the House of Representatives and looking up to the gallery, Mills found the famous *Car of History* by Carlo Franzoni.[15] Clio, the muse of history, stood in a winged chariot of time, ledger in hand, recording human events. The wheel of the chariot bore the face of a clock with Roman numerals. Also in this hall, high above the Speaker's chair, stood a heroic-size plaster *Liberty* by Causici. Venturing into the Supreme Court chamber, Mills saw Franzoni's bas-relief, *Justice and Young America*, in the lunette of the west wall. Franzoni never returned to his native Carrara; he raised a family in Washington.

Mills would later relate his impressions to a journalist, who wrote:

> He saw much to admire, and much which, even to his unpracticed eye, appeared imperfect. The drapery on the "Statue of Peace" seemed to surpass human skill, and the "Muse of History," recording the events of time, he thought was the grandest and most sublime idea ever conceived.[16]

Actually, the Muse of History was an ancient motif known as the "chariot of time." But Mills's eye was indeed "unpracticed." It was all new to him.

Strolling through the high-ceilinged rooms and broad corridors of the Capitol, Mills would also have scrutinized decorative carvings, such as entablatures that depicted eagles and serpents, fireplace mantels, and the capitals of columns. These were the handiwork of Giuseppe Valaperti, Giuseppe Franzoni (Carlo's brother), Giovanni Andrei, and other Italians. The foreign carvers had to be shown what an American bald eagle looked like so they could reproduce one in stone. At the behest of their employers—principally the president of the United States, who suggested themes and subjects and approved all designs for the Capitol—the Italians also carved uniquely American capitals depicting ears of corn and tobacco leaves (designed by Benjamin Henry Latrobe). All of this stone decoration was considered to be the handiwork of "artisans." By contrast, the 15 public sculptures that Mills examined were deemed significant works by "Artists."

No wonder Senator Preston had sent him to Washington. Nowhere else in America was there a comparable colony of European sculptors. Boston, New York and Philadelphia had their portrait painters and, of late, were enraptured by gargantuan canvases depicting the "sublime" nature of the Hudson River Valley and American West.[17] But Washington had sculptors, real Italian sculptors. In New York City, American-born John Frazee had been sculpting busts in marble for two decades.[18] But Frazee was a carver of gravestones and mantelpieces who had taught himself how to take a face mask, turn it into a plaster bust, then replicate the bust in stone. He had no classical training. He had never been to Italy. Frazee was akin to Mills, only one step ahead of him.

By contrast, the foreign sculptors working in Washington had centuries of tradition in their veins. They had learned from masters and served long apprenticeships. The works that Mills saw in the Capitol, executed between 1817 and 1844, and the *Tripoli Monument*, created in 1806, were all neoclassical and allegorical. Even where the subject was specific to America, its representation conformed to Old

World conventions. Capellano's Pocahontas, one art historian was to write, "resembled a Greek goddess clad in native American garb."[19] Now Mills had an inkling of what he would find in Italy. Now he realized what constituted "Sculpture." It was admirable. It was enthralling. But it was not American.

In time, "the Honored Sculptor"—as the *Saturday Evening News* was to dub Mills—came upon his own busts of four "distinguished sons of South Carolina" on display in the rotunda. Unbelievable! The work of Clark Mills, here, amid the masterpieces of Greenough, Micali, Persico, Capellano, Causici and Franzoni! The physical proximity alone—not to mention the hallowed setting—conferred status and legitimacy on the sculpture of a man who had not spent a single day of formal training in art—on either side of the Atlantic.

It was most likely Mills's patron, William Campbell Preston, who had arranged the exhibition of his handiwork. The former senator was himself in Washington at this time to appear at the U.S. Circuit Court for the District of Columbia. Preston was defending a niece of his, Susanna Smith Preston McDowell, in a sensational trial. She was the wife of a former governor of Virginia and her honor had been impugned. Curious spectators crowded the courtroom on March 8, 1847, only to learn that the case had just that day been settled without trial. Preston's niece was vindicated.[20]

For Mills, the timing was perfect: Congress was in session.[21] An Englishman who had visited Washington the previous year wrote of the city:

> When Congress is not sitting, it is dull and insipid to a degree, its periodical excitements disappearing with the bulk of its population.... From this state of torpidity it is annually roused about the beginning of December, the first Monday of which is the day fixed by the constitution for the assemblage of Congress. For some weeks previously to this, the note of preparation is sounded; the hotels are re-opened, whole streets of boarding-houses are put

in order for the winter, shopkeepers replenish their stocks, and the deserted village once more assumes the aspect of a tolerably bustling town.[22]

The national capital was awhirl in social activity. As the protégé of former Senator Preston, Mills was hardly an anonymous sightseer. He enjoyed not only exposure for his work, but entrée into Washington society, as well. Preston introduced the novice sculptor to highly placed associates, men of influence in the nation's affairs. Members of the congressional delegation of South Carolina showed off his busts to their colleagues. The display, noted the *Daily Union*, "excited great interest."[23] And so did its creator.

Mills benefitted from a trait that came naturally to him. He was "utterly without affectation," one reporter would write.[24] Another would observe:

> [Mr. Mills is] plain in his manners and dress, and exceedingly modest; never advancing in conversation, but retiring, except with familiar friends and on the subject of the statue and of arts; then he would be free, communicative, and instructive.[25]

Mills kept his commitment to his benefactor, who was paying the bills. He executed busts of two Whig legislators whom Preston admired:

John Jordan Crittenden, governor of Kentucky; U.S. Attorney General; U.S. Senator and then Congressman.[26]

Daniel Webster, U.S. Congressman from New Hampshire; U.S. Secretary of State; U.S. Congressman and then Senator from Massachusetts.[27]

Mills made the bust of Crittenden during his stay in Washington. He probably met with the senator in Mr. Stettinius's Boarding House near Judiciary Square, where Crittenden lodged.[28] Webster, on the other hand, did not sit for Mills before the 29th Congress adjourned on March 3rd. Two months later, though, while making a "Southern Tour," the celebrated New Englander would spend three days in Charleston. Mills took his face and head casts there on the morning of May 10th.[29] Later that day, Senator Webster and his family traveled on to Columbia, where they were the guests of William Campbell Preston in the President's House at the College of South Carolina.[30]

Despite Mills's new-found passion for the literal and naturalistic portrayal of Americans in sculpture, he did not break with the convention of his day right away. His portraits of John Jordan Crittenden and Daniel Webster are both neoclassical in style. Both men are depicted wearing togas. The process as well as the finished products of the neophyte sculptor continued to parallel those of his predecessors, John Frazee, John Henri Isaac Browere, and Hiram Powers. Nevertheless, the masterworks of sculpture that dazzled Mills in Richmond and Washington—those by Houdon and David d'Angers, in particular—roiled his imagination and stoked his creative fire. He was on the verge of finding his own expression.

Among the influential men of the Federal City who viewed Mills's busts in the Capitol rotunda were members of the Jackson Monument Committee. Their interest was especially keen, because they were still—one and a half years after uniting in their cause—searching for a sculptor to create a memorial of the deceased friend whom they admired. One day Mills was introduced to the Honorable Cave Johnson, Postmaster General of the United States and President of the Jackson Monument Committee. It would be a fateful encounter. And it explains why Mills was back in Charleston on May 10, 1847, coating Daniel Webster's face and head with warm plaster paste, rather than studying sculpture in Italy.

NOTES

1 Unless cited otherwise, description of Washington in 1847 is derived from: (1) Wilhelmus Bogart Bryan, *A History of the National Capital* (New York: The Macmillan Co., 1916), vol. II; at https://babel.hathitrust.org/cgi/pt?id=hvd.32044055003685&view=1up&seq=19; (2) James Keily, *Map of the City of Washington, D.C.* (Camden, N.J.: Lloyd Van Derveer, 1850); at https://www.loc.gov/resource/g3850.ct004378/; (3) Alexander MacKay, *The Western World; Travels in the United States in 1846–47*, 2nd ed. (Philadelphia: Lea & Blanchard, 1849), vol. I: 108–24; at www.loc.gov/resource/lhbtn.2679a/?sp=gallery; and (4) 1850 U.S. Census.
2 Pamela Scott and Antoinette J. Lee, *Buildings of the District of Columbia* (New York: Oxford University Press, 1993): 152.
3 National Register of Historic Places, District of Columbia Courthouse, Nomination Form; at https://npgallery.nps.gov/pdfhost/docs/NRHP/Text/74002174.pdf; and "District of Columbia City Hall;" at https://en.wikipedia.org/wiki/District_of_Columbia_City_Hall.
4 Description of sculptors and sculpture in Washington in 1847, unless cited otherwise, is derived from: (1) James M. Goode, "Four Salutes to the Nation: The Equestrian Statues of General Jackson," *White House History*, Journal of the White House Historical Association, no. 27 (spring 2010); (2) Bryan, *A History of the National Capital*, vol. II; (3) Charles E. Fairman, *Art and Artists of the Capitol of the United States of America* (Washington, D.C.: U.S. Govt. Print. Off., 1927); (4) William C. Allen, *History of the United States Capitol, A Chronicle of Design, Construction, and Politics* (Washington, D.C.: U.S. Govt. Print. Off., 2001); (5) Richard P. Wunder, *Hiram Powers, Vermont Sculptor, 1805–1873* (Newark, Del.: University of Delaware Press, 1991), 2 vols.; and (6) Anita Jacobsen, ed., *Biographical Index of American Artists. Artists native to the United States or working in the United States from 1606 to 2002* (Carrollton, Tex.: A. J. Publications, 2002), 4 vols.
5 Bryan, *History of the National Capital*, vol. II: 329, writes that the statue was moved from the Capitol and "placed in front of the White House" in 1845. See also "Thomas Jefferson Statue" at https://www.aoc.gov/art/other-statues/thomas-jefferson-statue: "Beginning in the mid to late 1840s, it was displayed on the grounds of the White House." See also Fairman, *Art and Artists*, 66. James M. Goode, *Outdoor Sculpture of Washington, D.C.* (Washington, D.C.: Smithsonian Institution Press, 1974): 521, writes mistakenly that it was moved to the White House in 1847.
6 Horatio Greenough (1805–52), see https://en.wikipedia.org/wiki/Horatio_Greenough.
7 "An Hour with Clark Mills," [Washington] *Daily Evening Star*, Dec. 24, 1870, p. 2.
8 "Mr. Clark Mills, the Sculptor," *The Round Table*, vol. 1, no. 22 (May 14, 1864): 340.

9   Giovanni Carlo Micali (before 1794–1821), see Captain C. Q. Wright, Ch-C, U.S. Navy, ret., "The Tripoli Monument," *United States Naval Institute, Proceedings*, vol. 48, no. 237 (Nov. 1922); at https://www.usni.org/magazines/proceedings/1922/november/tripoli-monument. The monument was removed to the Naval Academy in Annapolis in 1860.
10 A Citizen of Washington, *Etiquette at Washington: together with the customs adopted by polite society in the other cities of the United States*, 3rd ed. (Baltimore: Murphy & Co., 1860): 141.
11 Luigi Persico (1791–1860), see https://en.wikipedia.org/wiki/Luigi_Persico.
12 Antonio Capellano (1780–1840), see Jacobsen, *Biographical Index*, vol. I: 537.
13 Enrico Causici (1790–1833), see https://fr.wikipedia.org/wiki/Enrico_Causici.
14 Nicholas Gevelot (before 1820–after 1850), see Jacobsen, *Biographical Index*, vol. II: 1212.
15 Carlo Franzoni (1789–1819), see https://www.senate.gov/art-artifacts/fine-art/sculpture.shtml.
16 "Mr. Clark Mills, the Sculptor," *The Round Table*, vol. 1, no. 22 (May 14, 1864): 340.
17 See Barbara Novak, *American Painting of the Nineteenth Century: Realism, Idealism and the American Experience*, 3rd ed. (New York: Oxford University Press, 2007).
18 See Bk. 1, Ch. 8.
19 "Circuit Court," [Washington] *Daily National Intelligencer*, Mar. 2, 1847, p. 3, and "United States vs. Francis Thomas—Indictment for Libel," [Washington] *Daily Union*, Mar. 11, 1847, p. 2.
20 "Letters from Washington. Correspondence of the Whig. Washington, Feb. 27, 1847," *Richmond Daily Whig*, Mar. 1, 1847, p. 2. Also "Correspondence of the Courier. Washington, Mar. 4, 1847," [Charleston] *Courier*, Mar. 8, 1847, p. 2. Also "United States vs. Francis Thomas," *Edgefield* [S.C.] *Advertiser*, Mar. 31, 1847, p. 2.
21 For sessions of the 29th Congress, see https://en.wikipedia.org/wiki/List_of_United_States_Congresses
22 MacKay, *The Western World*, 2nd ed., vol. I: 115–16.
23 "The Jackson Monument," [Washington] *Daily Union*, Mar. 23, 1848, p. 3.
24 "Clark Mills at Home," *The Washington Post*, Aug. 7, 1879, p. 1.
25 "History of the Jackson Statue," [Washington] *Daily Union*, Jan. 18, 1853, p. 3.
26 John Jordan Crittenden (1787–1863), see https://en.wikipedia.org/wiki/John_J._Crittenden; and John J. Crittenden entry, 1850 U.S. Census, District No. 1, Franklin Co., Ky., p. 72 (handwritten), p. 36[b] (stamped); NARA M432, roll 200: "63, Governor of Ky., $10,000."
27 Daniel Webster (1782–1852), see https://en.wikipedia.org/wiki/Daniel_Webster; and Daniel Webster entry, 1850 U.S. Census, Marshfield, Plymouth Co., Mass., p. 303 (handwritten), p. 153 (stamped); NARA M432, roll 332: "68, U.S. Senator, $125,000;" and Edward Waite, comp. and pub., *The Washington*

Directory, and Congressional, and Executive Register, for 1850 (Washington, D.C.; Columbus Alexander, Printer, 1850): 92 and 102. Today this bust is in the Smithsonian American Art Museum, Washington, D.C.

28   Gaither & Addison, comps. and pubs., *The Washington Directory, and National Register, for 1846* (Washington, D.C.: John T. Towers, Printer, 1846), Part II, *Congressional Directory*: 6.

29   Daniel Webster, *The Works of Daniel Webster*, 15th ed. (Boston: Little, Brown and Co., 1869), vol. II: 369–98. See also "A Bust of Mr. Webster," [Charleston] *Courier*, May 11, 1847, p. 2; and "The Reward of Merit," [Charleston] *Courier*, May 12, 1847, p. 2.

30   "Bust of Daniel Webster," [Charleston] *Courier*, Aug. 2, 1847, p. 2. Also Webster, *Works*, vol. II: 395.

CHAPTER 16
March 1846–March 1847

It was in the year [1847], whilst the Jackson-statue committee were looking for an artist, that Mr. Mills chanced to be passing through Washington city on his way to Italy.

"History of the Jackson Statue," [Washington] *Daily Union*, Jan. 18, 1853, p. 2.[1]

While Mills was making his tour of Washington's sculpture, the members of the Jackson Monument Committee were stymied. They had found no one to make their statue. It had to be of bronze, they insisted, and the sculptor must be an American. Three names had surfaced most prominently: Horatio Greenough, Hiram Powers and Thomas Crawford.

Greenough was a virtuoso, but his twenty-ton *Washington Enthroned* had failed to show "that Washington was an *American—*an American *general—*an American *statesman.*"[2] The Committee members did not want the "Hero of New Orleans" depicted bare-chested in a toga and sandals. Not to worry, though: Greenough did not work in bronze.[3] Powers was as masterful a sculptor as Greenough; however, the Committee learned that he also did not work in bronze. Crawford—a generation younger than Greenough and Powers, but their equal at carving marble—had just been named in a Senate bill proposing the commissioning of a bronze equestrian of Washington for the U.S. capital.[4] To date, though, Crawford, whose studio was in Rome, had not yet ventured into the realm of bronze casting.[5]

The name of one other American sculptor may have entered into the Committee's deliberations: Henry Kirke Brown. But Brown, although promising, was young—Crawford's peer, exactly—and still studying art in Italy. Besides—similar to Crawford—Brown's interest in making bronze statues had not yet matured.[6]

The United States in the mid-nineteenth century turned out very little bronze work, and most of it was utilitarian—bells for churches, schools and firehouses, pump parts, valves, steam fittings, and limited small arms and light field artillery. Bronze is an alloy composed mostly of copper (90 percent) with a small amount of tin (8 percent) and trace amount of zinc or lead (2 percent). The process of mixing bronze and casting the metal is complex, exacting, time-consuming, and exceedingly expensive. Moreover, the larger the cast, the more difficult and costly it is.

The business of making fine art in bronze had not developed in the United States because there was no market for it. Consequently, the country lacked the requisite expertise and facility—in short, a founder and a foundry capable of casting bronze statues. Creating colossal memorial sculpture of bronze was a uniquely European enterprise, centered principally in five world-famous foundries: Munich, Paris, Florence, Rome and Berlin.[7]

The Committee studied the celebrated equestrian statues of Europe.[8] *Peter the Great* in St. Petersburg had been famous worldwide for three generations. Depictions of it proliferated in prints and engravings. The *Duke of Wellington* had just been unveiled in London in 1844 to international acclaim. The stupendous equestrian of *Frederick the Great*, currently being cast in Berlin and larger than any bronze sculpture ever made, was already being heralded around the globe. All of these memorials were inspired by the ancient *Marcus Aurelius* in Rome and its Italian Renaissance descendants: *Colleoni* by Verrocchio in Venice and the *Gattamelata* by Donatello in Padua. These tributes to military leaders represented what the Jackson Monument Committee wanted for their own hero in their own national capital.[9] Although the work would have to be cast in a European foundry, the 13 Washingtonians never considered engaging a foreign sculptor. Theirs was to be a totally American creation.

But they had learned a hard fact: there were very few people in the world who could make a colossal bronze statue. Among Americans, not one.

Besides having no sculptor, the Committee had collected only a few thousand dollars. The members had been overly sanguine about Americans' eagerness to contribute. Even reducing by half the size of the statue that Powers had hypothesized in his 1845 letter to Jeremiah Harris—and, hence, its cost—$15,000 was still a greater sum than the Committee might ever collect. There was, however, one way to save many thousands of dollars: make the statue out of cannons seized in battle by Jackson himself. Through their research, the members had discovered:

> [T]hat the column of Napoleon [in Paris], formed after the model of that of the Emperor Trajan, is made of the cannon taken by Napoleon at the battle of Austerlitz—that the equestrian statue to Wellington, now in the course of completion [for London], is to be made of the brass pieces captured by that general at Waterloo.[10]

"Brass pieces:" that's what military personnel, members of Congress, newspaper reporters, even founders and metalworkers, called guns of bronze. Today, a distinction is made: "brass" is an alloy of copper and zinc, "bronze" is copper and tin. Prior to the middle of the nineteenth century, however, "brass" (a word of older usage than "bronze") signified all alloys of copper and tin. "In other words," writes art historian Michael Edward Shapiro in *Bronze Casting and American Sculpture, 1850–1900*, "before 'brass' received its modern connotation, it was applied to all objects that are known today as 'bronzes.'"[11] Furthermore, long after the term, "bronze statue," had become common, "brass gun" persisted in military jargon.

Casting the Jackson statue from cannons the general himself had seized from the enemy appealed to the Committee members. Besides saving them the cost of the metal, it would make the memorial an expression of patriotism, almost a national shrine, deserving of pilgrimage. But where could such trophies of war be found? In the spring of 1846, the Committee turned to Colonel George Bomford, Chief of the Army's Ordnance Department.[12] Bomford assigned the quest to his second-in-command, Lieutenant Colonel George Talcott. Talcott was a distinguished 60-year-old officer who knew more than anyone about the country's arsenals and armories.[13]

Talcott located several guns at Watervliet Arsenal in New York State that Jackson had seized from the Spanish at Pensacola, Florida, in 1818: four brass cannons and two brass mortars. The Lieutenant Colonel informed the Committee on April 14, 1846, that the artillery pieces "are not of the caliber used in service, and are reported unserviceable."[14] Hence, he had no objection to melting them down for a memorial to Jackson.

Before asking Congress for the Spanish guns, though, the Committee wanted to have "the fullest assurance, in the amount of voluntary contributions received, that adequate means [were] attainable to erect the monument."[15] Only after ten more months of fund raising, therefore, did the Committee enlist a staunch Jacksonian Democrat from Illinois to plead their cause to Congress: John Alexander McClernand.[16]

On February 19, 1847—while Mills examined sculpture and Preston prepared the defense of his niece—the Honorable McClernand rose from his desk in the crowded semicircular House of Representatives chamber. Facing the Speaker enthroned beneath Enrico Causici's heroic *Liberty*, he read the "memorial of the Jackson Monument Committee, praying that four brass cannon and two brass mortars, weighing in all 4,930 pounds," captured by Jackson at Pensacola, may be delivered to said committee "to be used as material in constructing a monument to the memory of the illustrious hero and statesman, Andrew Jackson." The congressman quoted the report that Lieutenant Colonel Talcott had written the previous year, verifying that the guns were "unserviceable."[17] He informed his colleagues:

> "Too much praise cannot be bestowed upon the members of this committee for their zeal and public spirit in so noble an enterprise, or upon the country for the promptness and liberality with which they have responded to it. . . . The name of Jackson—the indomitable, the strong-willed, the honest, the unflinching, the man of iron—has become a household word to his countrymen—an invocation of patriotism and duty to all lands."[18]

His appeal, McClernand assured the House, was not partisan. "There are many in this hall" who opposed Jackson when he "wielded, with boldness and energy, the sword of State. . . . But this arose from honest difference of opinion. . . . All that fierce denunciation, generated and sustained by party zeal, has passed with its cause."[19]

Then the legislator introduced Joint Resolution No. 58, granting the Committee's request. It passed the House and was forwarded to the Senate for concurrence.[20] The resolution was read in the Senate the same day, read a second time the following day, then referred to the Committee on the District of Columbia for consideration.[21] The chairman of that committee, Senator Simon Cameron of Pennsylvania, reported Joint Resolution No. 58 back to the Senate without amendment on March 1, 1847. But it was "laid on the table" and not taken up for a vote before the 29th Congress adjourned two days later.[22]

Free metal from the Army notwithstanding—and that was by no means assured at this point—the Committee still had insufficient funds. Treasurer Francis Preston Blair reported to his fellows that the national subscription had stalled at $12,500.[23]

In future years, newspapers would report that the Committee asked Congress to allocate public monies for their project and that the legislators denied the request.²⁴ But that was not so. Certainly, the 13 members had many highly placed and influential friends—senators, congressmen, military officers of the highest echelons. And, no doubt, the Jackson memorial was a topic of discussion at dinner parties and other gatherings, both casual and official. However, one of the Committee's resolutions stipulated that the money would be raised by means of a voluntary national subscription. This was a key component of the undertaking. In addition, some years later, Benjamin B. French, a founding member, was to write: "The committee have never yet received a single dollar from Congress."²⁵ Indeed, no public record of a petition to Congress seeking funds for the monument has been found.²⁶

In March of 1847, one and a half years into the grandiose venture, having no sculptor, an insufficient purse, and its request for metal from the Army tabled, the Committee turned to Washington's preeminent architect and engineer, Robert Mills.²⁷ The South Carolinian's career had been advanced by Jackson, who brought him to Washington in 1829 to build fireproof buildings for federal agencies. Since then Mills had designed the U.S. Patent Office, Treasury Department and General Post Office. He had won the competition for a Washington monument in Baltimore—an immense column topped with a huge marble statue of Washington by Enrico Causici—patterned after the ancient Column of Trajan in Rome. In addition, his was the winning design for the Washington monument projected for the nation's capital—a quasi-Egyptian obelisk rising out of a Greek peristyle surmounted by a colossal quadriga driven by Washington.²⁸ Robert Mills was steeped in classicism.

The Committee asked him "to submit designs in conjunction with" Hiram Powers for the Jackson memorial. In response, Robert Mills proposed a gigantic triumphal arch of marble similar to those of ancient Rome. He drew three pencil sketches. The memorial would be 130 feet high and 50 feet wide, topped by a larger-than-life-size marble statue of Jackson—sculpted by Powers—standing on a plinth.²⁹

The design was a disappointment. First of all, it was not the equestrian statue mandated by the Committee. Second, it was not made of "imperishable bronze." And third, the anticipated cost was prohibitive. Frustrated Committee members recommended reducing their vision to something more modest. "It was seriously debated whether or not a pedestrian statue should be erected and the work given to Mr. Powers."[30] The project stalled.

By this time, the Committee's composition had changed. Founding members Van Ness and Hoban had died, and Harris had resigned. One other original member, Jesse Erskine Dow, would not live to see the project to completion. New members were chosen to take their places:[31]

John Moore McCalla, attorney and U.S. Marshall of Lexington, Kentucky; Brigadier General during the War of 1812; appointed Second Auditor in the Treasury Department by President Polk; member of the American Colonization Society;[32]

George Wurtz Hughes, Captain, U.S. Army Topographical Engineers; served in the Mexican War making maps; surveyor of Washington, D.C.; Colonel of Maryland and District of Columbia Volunteers; future President of the Northern Central Railway, U.S. Representative from Maryland, and planter of Anne Arundel County, Maryland; would be chosen Chief Marshall of the dedication ceremony of the Jackson equestrian;[33]

Andrew Jackson Donelson, nephew and foster son of Jackson; aide-de-camp and personal secretary to Jackson; lawyer and planter of Davidson County, Tennessee; future Chargé d'Affaires to the Republic of Texas, Minister to Prussia, and vice presidential candidate;[34]

George Parker, prosperous grocer with his brother and business partner, Thomas, at Center Market on Pennsylvania Avenue.[35]

These later members, like their predecessors, were Democrats who had been ardent supporters of Andrew Jackson. All were originally slaveholders, although McCalla freed his bondspeople to Liberia, Africa.

The Committee's efforts had come to naught when "four handsome busts" of "distinguished sons of South Carolina" appeared in the Capitol rotunda. For the first time, the name of a neophyte sculptor from Charleston was resounding in Washington: Clark Mills. And he was in town, along with his patron, William Campbell Preston. The senators and representatives of the Palmetto State were delighted to present the talented protégé of their erstwhile colleague to their friends and associates. Members of the Jackson Monument Committee trod up Capitol Hill to view Mills's work. They were impressed.

Then came the fateful encounter. It must have been early March of 1847. Congressman Isaac Edward Holmes, a native Charlestonian, brought it about.

Holmes had known Mills before the plasterer-turned-sculptor appeared in Washington. The previous year, when Mills was in Columbia, the Congressman had sat for him.[36] By then, Holmes had already served in the South Carolina legislature, had represented his state in the 28th U.S. Congress, and had been reelected to the House of Representatives for the 29th.[37] He was a seasoned veteran of the nation's capital who enjoyed extensive social connections. One day, Holmes introduced the much-talked-about bust maker from Charleston to a fellow Southern Democrat, the Honorable Cave Johnson.[38]

Mr. Johnson, Holmes informed Mills, was a staunch Jacksonian who had served his home state of Tennessee in the U.S. House of Representatives for seven terms.[39] He was now President Polk's Postmaster General and—since the death of Van Ness—President of the Jackson Monument Committee. The Cabinet Member's appearance was imposing. He was in his mid-fifties, tall and spare, and bald on top, though a fringe of long, graying hair brushed his ears and the collar of his coat. His face was noble and kind. He described to Mills the grand memorial his Committee sought to erect:

> "A colossal equestrian statue in imperishable bronze, presenting to the eyes of all future generations the Hero and Patriot as he lived, exhibiting the features, the person, the apparel, the attitude, and almost the action, which belonged to him at the moment of rendering the highest service to his country."[40]

Johnson explained that his Committee had collected only $12,500, but he was confident that Congress would agree in due time to provide the metal. Then he uttered the words that would come to drive Mills's life and define it: Would he submit a design?[41]

Shock. Mills was speechless. He had never seen an equestrian statue. There weren't any in the United States to be seen. Only

Cave Johnson, a staunch Jacksonian Democrat from Tennessee who served in the U.S. House of Representatives and then as President Polk's Postmaster General, was President of the Jackson Monument Committee. Jackson and Polk were also Tennesseeans. In 1847 Johnson invited Mills to submit a design for a memorial to the "Hero of New Orleans." Mills's acceptance resulted in the fulfillment of his dreams and the transformation of American sculpture. (Tennessee State Museum and Dawn Majors/ TN Photographic Services)

recently, for the first time in his life, had he laid eyes on a statue of bronze. That was David d'Angers's *Thomas Jefferson* standing on the lawn of the President's House, the only life-size bronze statue in the country. Mills knew nothing about monumental public sculpture. He knew nothing about commemorative art. Besides, he was on his way to Italy.

Thanking the Postmaster General profusely for the honor of the invitation, Mills declined.[42] Years later, though, he would tell a journalist:

> "But that night, turning the thing over in my mind, it seemed to me that I need not go all the way to Italy to learn how to make an equestrian statue. They could not teach me anything I did not know about the horse, and I was sure that I could make a correct representation of Jackson."[43]

It was too extraordinary an opportunity to turn down out of hand. Before departing Washington, Mills told Johnson he would consider the offer. Then, rather than continuing on to Italy, as planned, he headed back to Charleston. All the way home, the idea "haunted his imagination."[44]

NOTES

1 Text erroneously reads "1848."
2 "Greenough's Statue of Washington," [Charleston] *Southern Patriot*, Sept. 2, 1845, p. 2. Italics in original.
3 "Greenough, the Sculptor," *Putnam's Monthly Magazine of American Literature, Science, and Art*, vol. I (Jan.–June 1853): 317–20.
4 "Proceedings in Congress. In Senate," [Washington] *Weekly National Intelligencer*, Feb. 15, 1845, p. 2.
5 "Thomas Crawford (sculptor)" at https://en.wikipedia.org/wiki/Thomas_Crawford_(sculptor).
6 Michael Edward Shapiro, *Bronze Casting and American Sculpture, 1850–1900* (Newark, Del.: University of Delaware Press, 1985): 44–45.
7 Ibid., 15, 24–29.

8   Rep. McClernand's remarks when presenting the Committee's memorial to Congress. See *Congressional Globe*, 29th Cong., 2nd Sess., Feb. 19, 1847, p. 461.
9   Rosemary Hopkins, *Clark Mills: The First Native American Sculptor* (M.A. thesis, University of Maryland, 1966): 51–54.
10 *Congressional Globe*, 29th Cong., 2nd, Sess., Feb. 19, 1847, p. 461.
11 Shapiro, *Bronze Casting*, 16.
12 George Bomford (1780/82–1848), see https://goordnance.army.mil/history/chiefs/bomford.html.
13 George Talcott (1786–1862), see https://goordnance.army.mil/history/chiefs/talcott.html.
14 Report of Lt. Col. George Talcott, Apr. 14, 1846, quoted in the memorial of the Jackson Monument Committee (*Congressional Globe*, 29th Cong., 2nd Sess., Feb. 19, 1847, p. 461) and referenced in Joint Resolution No. 25 (U.S. Statutes at Large, vol. 9 (30th Cong., 1st Sess., Res. 25, Aug. 11, 1848), p. 340). Rep. McClernand said, "[T]he pieces asked for are the same which were captured by General Jackson in a gallant and brilliant affair at Pensacola in 1814 [sic]." Jackson fought against the Spanish in Florida in 1814 and 1818. All references to these same four cannons and two mortars—other than McClernand's—state that Jackson seized them from the Spanish in 1818, not 1814. A commemorative inscription on one of the cannons confirms the year was 1818. Nevertheless, several newspapers would report mistakenly that the field artillery had been seized by Jackson from the British in the Battle of New Orleans in 1814. The error would be oft repeated in secondary literature about the Jackson statue.
15 Rep. McClernand's remarks. See *Congressional Globe*, 29th Cong., 2nd Sess., Feb. 19, 1847, p. 461.
16 John Alexander McClernand (1812–1900), see http://bioguide.congress.gov/scripts/biodisplay.pl?index=M000337.
17 *Congressional Globe*, 29th Cong., 2nd Sess., Feb. 19, 1847, p. 461. Also *House Journal*, Feb. 19, 1847, p. 378 80.
18 *Congressional Globe*, 29th Cong., 2nd Sess., Feb. 19, 1847, p. 461.
19 Ibid.
20 Ibid. Also *House Journal*, Feb. 19, 1847, p. 378–80.
21 *Congressional Globe*, 29th Cong., 2nd Sess., Feb. 20, 1847, p. 463. Also *Senate Journal*, Feb. 19, 1847, p. 211, and Feb. 20, 1847, p. 216.
22 *Congressional Globe*, 29th Cong., 2nd Sess., Mar. 1, 1847, p. 540. Also *Senate Journal*, Mar. 1, 1847, p. 246. For sessions of the 29th Congress, see https://en.wikipedia.org/wiki/List_of_United_States_Congresses.
23 "To the People of the United States," [Washington] *Daily Union*, Nov. 27, 1851, p. 2.
24 "The Jackson Statue—Its Origins, &c.," [Baltimore] *Sun*, Jan. 11, 1853, p. 4; and "History of the Jackson Statue," [Washington] *Daily Union*, Jan. 18, 1853, p. 2.

25 "The Jackson Statue...," *Sun*, Jan. 11, 1853, 4.
26 A search was made of the *Congressional Globe, House Journal* and *Senate Journal*, 1847–54.
27 Tim Kerr, *The History of the Equestrian Statue of General Andrew Jackson, Lafayette Park, Washington, D.C.* Typescript report prepared for the National Park Service, White House Liaison, Aug. 1999, p. 14. Also Rhodri Windsor Liscombe, *Altogether American: Robert Mills, Architect and Engineer, 1781–1855* (New York: Oxford University Press, 1994): 258–59.
28 Liscombe, *Altogether American*, 260–62.
29 "Robert Mills Papers," Microfilm 19,254-1P, Manuscript Division, Library of Congress, Washington, D.C.
30 "History of the Jackson Statue," *Daily Union*, Jan. 18, 1853, 2. Also "Correspondence of the Baltimore Sun. Washington, March 1, 1848," [Baltimore] *Sun*, Mar. 2, 1848, p. 4.
31 "History of the Jackson Statue," *New York Daily Times*, Jan. 22, 1853, p. 3. See also "The Jackson Statue...," *Sun*, Jan. 11, 1853, 4.
32 John Moore McCalla (1793–1873), see "McCalla, John M.," at https://papersofabrahamlincoln.org/persons/MC47458; and John M. McCalla entry, 1840 U.S. Census, Lexington, Fayette Co., Ky., p. 94 (handwritten): NARA M704, roll 109: 6 slaves; and John M. McCalla entry, 1850 U.S. Census, Ward 4, Washington City, Washington Co., D.C., p. 437 (handwritten), p. 219 (stamped); NARA M432, roll 56: "55, Attorney;" and Gaither & Addison, *Washington Directory, and National Register, for 1846* (Washington: John T. Towers, 1846): 58. See also Kerr, *History of the Equestrian Statue*, 83.
33 George Wurtz Hughes (1806–70), see https://en.wikipedia.org/wiki/George_Wurtz_Hughes; and Geo. W. Hughes entry, 1850 U.S. Census, First District, Anne Arundel Co., Md., p. 615 (handwritten), p. 308 (stamped); NARA M432, roll 278: "43, Farmer;" and Geo. W. Hughes entry, 1850 U.S. Census Slave Schedule, First District, Anne Arundel Co., Md., p. 269, 271, 281 and 283 (handwritten); NARA M432, roll 300.
34 Andrew Jackson Donelson (1799–1871), see https://en.wikipedia.org/wiki/Andrew_Jackson_Donelson; and A. J. Donelson entry, 1850 U.S. Census, Civil District No. 4, Davidson Co., Tenn., p. 411 (handwritten), p. 295 (stamped); NARA M432, roll 875: "50, Farmer:" and J. Donelson entry, 1850 U.S. Census Slave Schedule, Civil District No. 4, Davidson Co., Tenn., p. [517]; NARA M432, roll 902.
35 George Parker (ca. 1800–76), see George Parker entry, 1850 U.S. Census, 4th Ward, Washington City, Washington Co., D.C., p. 449 (handwritten), p. 225 (stamped); NARA M432, roll 56: "50, Grocer, $35,000;" and Geo. Parker entry, 1850 U.S. Census Slave Schedule, 4th Ward, Washington City, Washington Co., D.C., p. 685 (handwritten); NARA M432, roll 57; and Gaither & Addison, *Washington Directory...for 1846*, 67. See also Kerr, *History of the Equestrian Statue*, 83.

36 See Bk. 1, Ch. 12.
37 "Holmes, Isaac Edward" at https://bioguideretro.congress.gov/Home/MemberDetails?memIndex=H000738.
38 "Mr. Clark Mills, the Sculptor," *The Round Table*, vol. 1, no. 22 (May 14, 1864): 340; and "An Hour with Clark Mills," [Washington] *Evening Star*, Dec. 24, 1870, p. 1.
39 "Cave Johnson" at https://tennesseeencyclopedia.net/entries/cave-johnson.
40 "Jackson Monument," [Washington] *Daily Union*, Oct. 6, 1845, p. 3.
41 "An Hour with Clark Mills," *Evening Star*, Dec. 24, 1870, 1; and "Mr. Clark Mills, the Sculptor," *The Round Table*, vol. 1, no. 22 (May 14, 1864): 340.
42 "History of the Jackson Statue," *Daily Union*, Jan. 18, 1853, 2; and "Mr. Clark Mills, the Sculptor," *The Round Table*, vol. 1, no. 22 (May 14, 1864): 340; and "An Hour with Clark Mills," *Evening Star*, Dec. 24, 1870, 1.
43 "An Hour with Clark Mills," *Evening Star*, Dec. 24, 1870, 1. Also "History of the Jackson Statue," *Daily Union*, Jan. 18, 1853, 2.
44 "History of the Jackson Statue," *Daily Union*, Jan. 18, 1853, 2.

CHAPTER 17
March 1847–March 1848

This statue was given to my uncle, who was my mother's brother-in-law, by Clark Mills, who was a close friend of Uncle Charlie. My mother gave me what information I know, and it was said to be the original model & has been in my family for years.

Note, Clara Marie Balderston Hughes
to the Maryland Historical Society, 1945[1]

It measures 18½ inches long—from the rearing horse's forehooves pawing the air to its rump—and stands 19 inches high—from the base to the cocked hat the rider is waving above his head. The charger's ears and tail are missing, as are some of the reins. The rider's limbs are broken and his saber is gone. The bulk of the statuette is plaster applied to a wire armature, but the finer parts—arms and legs—are clay and the vestige of rein is leather. The base simulates a rocky mound. The whole is painted dark gray-green to look like bronze.

This miniature of the Andrew Jackson equestrian statue that stands in Washington's Lafayette Square is stored at the Maryland Center for History and Culture in Baltimore. According to Clara Hughes's handwritten note that came with the gift in 1945, it is Mills's *"original model."* But it was not his original concept, or his first maquette.

In March of 1847, when Mills returned to Charleston from Washington and walked into the house at no. 9 Atlantic Street, it must have shocked Eliza. He was supposed to be in Italy.[2] But he was home. And for how long, he could not say.

Right away, he met with John Schnierle, Henry Workman Conner and A. G. Rose to make "honorable arrangements with his kind

Mills's final maquette for the Jackson equestrian statue, which he made in Charleston and transported to Washington to submit to the Jackson Monument Committee in March of 1848. Scientists and sculptors insisted that the statue, enlarged to monumental size and cast in bronze, could not remain standing without a support of some kind. (photo courtesy of Maryland Center for History and Culture, Baltimore)

patrons."[3] It was over a year since they had offered their "fellow townsman" one thousand dollars to visit Italy, "there to improve in the art of sculpture."[4] Now Mills was set on accepting Cave Johnson's invitation to submit a design for the Jackson memorial. Moreover, he was questioning the value of study in Italy altogether. Would his three admirers support him at home for one year, rather than abroad? They said yes. Mills had one year to come up with a design.

He threw himself into a rigorous regimen of self-education.[5] He had to familiarize himself with monumental bronze equestrian memorials from ancient Rome, through the Renaissance, to contemporary Europe. He also needed to learn about Jackson, the man, his life, his physical appearance. Fortunately, he found himself in the heart of a city of outstanding research institutions.

Two *public* libraries were located a brisk 20-minute walk from 9 Atlantic Street. The Charleston Library Society leased rooms upstairs of the Bank of Charleston, which stood directly across from Mills's former studio at 49 Broad Street.[6] The Apprentices' Library Society (for whom Mills had made a bust of benefactor and president, Doctor Joseph Johnson) rented space a couple of blocks farther up Meeting Street near Horlbeck Alley.[7] Both collections were open to members who paid an annual subscription fee. But guests could also be admitted by recommendation of a subscriber, many of whom knew Mills: he had captured their physiognomies in plaster.

That same connection—local bust maker to the well-to-do—may also have opened to Mills the doors of Charleston's two *private* libraries: the College of Charleston and the Medical College of the State of South Carolina. Both repositories stood an easy stroll from 9 Atlantic Street.[8]

To learn about Jackson, Mills was able to exploit more than books, prints and paintings. He interviewed old comrades-in-arms of the General: Colonels Arthur Perroneau Hayne, James Gadsden and Wade Hampton II, and Major Jacint Laval.[9] All four were South Carolinians. Mills had made a bust of Hampton.[10] He called upon the elderly veterans to hear their personal reminiscences of "Old Hickory."

How Eliza felt about her husband's abrupt change of plan is not recorded; however, later events would suggest that she considered his behavior irresponsible. She had four boys to raise. Her household budget was tight. Chances are it was Philip Reid, the bound "first-rate plasterer," who supported the family while the head of the household indulged in intellectual pursuits. Neither Eliza nor friends, though, could dissuade Mills from satisfying his creative drive . . . and his craving for recognition. Washington's *Daily Union* would later report:

[Mills's] friends ... were offended with him. Some hardly noticed him. They reproached him with presumption and folly; said, "he was going to throw himself away," and "that he could never do such a work."[11]

Meanwhile, Mills learned that making a colossal bronze statue entailed a number of steps executed in sequence, analogous to the process for taking a life mask or making a plaster bust. Those skills he had mastered in short order. These skills, now, he set about acquiring with equal zeal and confidence:

CREATING A BRONZE STATUE

(1) Settle on a concept and make sketches;
(2) Make a miniature model (called a maquette);
(3) Revise and perfect the concept and maquette;
(4) Make a full-scale model;
(5) Cut the model into pieces and make molds from them;
(6) Weigh out, melt down and mix the metals;
(7) Pour molten bronze into the molds;
(8) Extract the rough bronze casts from the molds;
(9) Finish the surface of the casts;
(10) Assemble the bronze pieces into a whole; and
(11) Patinate the statue.

It all sounded straightforward enough. Besides, Mills knew that he, as the sculptor, was only responsible for steps one through four. The rest were technical operations performed by a founder in Europe. Mills had no idea yet, of course, that he himself would end up being the founder as well as the sculptor.

Step 1: Settle on a concept and make sketches
To hit upon the concept for his *Jackson*, Mills must have toyed with a variety of ideas and sketched a variety of possibilities. None of these

survives. In fact, no preliminary drawing for any of Mills's statues survives. But at the end of about five weeks, he settled on the sculpture he wanted to create. It would be an historically accurate representation of the General astride his steed at the most celebrated victory of his military career: the Battle of New Orleans. Every detail of Jackson's person—face, body, uniform, sword, boots—and his mount—saddle, holsters, bridle, stirrups, buckles—everything—would be rendered as it appeared on the battlefield at Chalmette on January 8, 1815. The idea was revolutionary.

Mills was a forerunner and lifelong advocate of realistic sculpture, but he was not its sole originator, as the press of his day proclaimed. His compatriot and coeval, Henry Kirke Brown, had returned from studying in Italy the previous year dedicated to the same concept: a true-to-life, identifiably American sculpture.[12] Mills would insist repeatedly that his method from the beginning was simply to follow "Nature." However, the neophyte artist was also eager to give the members of the Jackson Monument Committee exactly what they wanted: a recognizable Jackson.[13]

Mills wrote to Cave Johnson that he would be pleased to submit a model.[14] When the Committee reconvened in early May, Johnson moved that Mills's proposal be accepted. However, "some of the Committee, doubting [Mills's] capacity, were disposed to have a pedestrian statue by Powers."[15] Debate ensued. At length, the 13 men decided that they would judge Mills's ability on the merits of his model.[16] As soon as their decision reached him, Mills shared it with the editor of the Charleston *Courier*. Richard Yeadon informed his readers on May 12, 1847:

> We learn and record with great satisfaction, that, at the last Meeting of the "Jackson Monument Committee" at Washington, D.C., it was unanimously ordered "That the proposition of Mr. Clark Mills, of Charleston, S.C., to make a model of the

proposed monument to Andrew Jackson, to be submitted to this Committee, be agreed to."[17]

Step 2: Make a miniature model (called a maquette)

To fashion an equestrian statue, Mills had to know equine anatomy. The subject was not new to him. "Well, I had always a passion for horses," he would later declare. "When I was a plasterer, in Charleston, and with very little money to spare, I always owned the finest horses I could find."[18] One account would report:

> He dissected horses. He studied the breed and character of different kinds of horses. He selected the various points of beauty and strength from them all, to produce the splendid bronze one he has made.[19]

A few years later, after visiting Mills in his studio, Henry Kirke Brown would write to his wife:

> *I saw hanging upon the walls casts from dissections of various parts of horses like beef to dry.*[20]

One article reprinted in multiple South Carolina newspapers claimed:

> He took casts of the limbs of a horse in the positions he has chosen, that he might not be mistaken in the anatomy of the animal.[21]

By the end of July 1847, Mills had made a miniature model of the horse in plaster, the finer parts of clay. Evidently, the steed was in a trotting, not rampant, position, because Yeadon wrote in the *Courier*:

> We have had the pleasure . . . of examining Mr. Mills' miniature model of the warhorse of Jackson, so true to life, that as you gaze, the feet seem to be in play, the horse in motion![22]

Next, Mills turned to making the rider. His quest for authenticity bordered on fanaticism. At one point the *Courier* reported:

> [O]n ascertaining by measurement that the General was not a well proportioned man, he wrote to the Committee for instructions on the subject, and their reply was "they wanted Jackson and nothing but Jackson."[23]

Within a month, Mills had added the rider to the mount:

> The artist has obeyed orders with military precision, and has therefore succeeded in producing the "counterfeit presentment" of the original.[24]

Contemplating his handiwork, though, Mills was not satisfied. It was too static.

Step 3: Revise and perfect the concept and maquette

"I tell you what the people want in statuary as well as in oratory," he would later declaim, "is action! action! action!"[25] He made a new maquette, this one with a horse rampant—that is, a horse rearing up on its hind legs. Achieving the balanced pose took repeated attempts. He would explain:

> "The conventional horse on three legs, or four, or with a prop under the belly, or with its tail fastened to a rock, won't suit. I have aimed to represent the horse in a spirited, natural attitude, unsustained by any external support, as in nature."[26]

On many occasions, Mills's gaze would have landed on just such a rearing horse and rider. It was a small image printed in the *Courier* to call attention to notices of "the regular monthly meetings" of the Charleston Light Dragoons. The icon depicted identically the statue that Mills would ultimately create, except for one tiny detail:

the horseman's raised right hand is waving a saber rather than his hat.[27] However, reproducing a comparable figure in bronze without an external support had never been achieved in the history of sculpture. Without a brace of some kind, the weight of the statue would cause it to topple.

What inspired Mills to challenge the greatest sculptors of all time? Years later, when asked, he never mentioned any newspaper image. Rather, he would recite this anecdote:

> "[W]hen I first commenced the Jackson statue my idea was to put a prop under the horse's breast after the manner of every equestrian statue then in the world, but while watching a restive horse, which was being exercised in front of my door the animal reared with his rider, and in an instant stood poised upon his hind feet. My position was such that the perpendicular jamb of the door drew a line from the horse's feet through the body to the crest of the neck, the front half of the body and the legs of the rider appearing to view, while the hind parts and body of the rider were behind the doorpost. As he stood for an instant, I caught the position of a horse balanced for a jump, and saw that he simply shifted his weight so as to bring the centre of gravity upon the hind feet. This idea I worked out upon my model."[28]

Mills used at least two horses for his study of equine anatomy, musculature and movement. The name of one is unknown:

> The steed [Mills used] was not an ideal but a real one—Colonel Wade Hampton, of South Carolina, having given to Mills for his model a race-horse no longer fit for the turf. It was a beautiful animal, which at the word of command would throw himself in a position and "sit for his picture" with an intelligent patience worthy of all praise.
> "Clark Mills," *Lippincott's Magazine*, vol. XXXI (Old Series), vol. 5 (New Series), Mar. 1883: 315–16.

The name of the other horse was Champion:

Uncle John Robinson was an intimate friend of Clark Mills, . . .
"Well, I met him in Charleston, South Carolina, about twenty-four years ago. I had my circus there, and Mr. Mills was introduced to me by my attorney. . . . He told me that he had decided to become a competitor for the [Jackson] statue now standing in front of the White House. . . . He stated that his idea was to have a figure of the great general riding a horse to be standing erect on his hind feet. I informed him that my performing horse Champion was an expert at the business, and that if it would be any assistance to him he might come to the tent and I would make the horse go through his tricks. . . . He came at least twenty times and sketched Champion in that position."
"The Dead Sculptor. An Incident in the Life of the Late Clark Mills," *The Washington Post*, Jan. 18, 1883, p. 2.[29]

Mills himself would later say:

"When a boy, I spent a good deal of time about Wade Hampton's stables, studying the points of his horses. He had a large stable of race-horses, and imported the famous Argyle, that beat everything in those days. Afterwards I studied horse anatomy and action with John Robinson, the old circus man. He had an excellent idea of a horse and its muscular action."[30]

In reality, Mills never came near Hampton's stables "when a boy." But he certainly did so when he was taking life masks in Columbia in 1846. Also, though Robinson's recollection of when he met Mills was off by a decade—it was not "about 24 years ago," but rather *thirty-four* years ago—the encounter did in fact take place. By his own testimony, therefore, Mills used at least two horses as live models. Later he would boast:

"I can claim to know as much about the anatomy and muscular action of the horse as any man living. I gave months of study to the muscular action of the rampant horse, with a model trained to rear at a look. Visitors who saw him rise on his hind legs whenever I turned towards him, thought him a most sagacious animal, but he had been trained to do it."[31]

It took Mills a total of eight or nine months to complete his maquette of Jackson astride a *rearing* warhorse.[32] The finishing touch was painting it to look like a bronze statuette.[33] He showed it to the editor of the *Courier*, who rhapsodized:

The universal testimony, as well of artists as others, is that Mr. Mills' performance is an exquisite achievement of art. The old hero is represented on his war horse, in the military costume of our own times, in the act of reviewing his troops on the morning of the 8th January, 1815, just before the commencement of the battle of that day, which covered him with laurels and his country with glory.... The truth of the delineation is admirably aided by the adoption of the modern instead of the Roman costume.... The figure of the horse, too, is the subject of universal approbation and applause. All the best judges among us, of the points and proportions of that noble animal, have pronounced Mr. Mills' success complete. They all agree that he has thrown more life, vigor and fire into his steed than they have before seen imparted to inanimate matter; and that the poise of the statue is a triumph of genius and skill![34]

The battered statuette of plaster, clay and leather in storage at the Maryland Center for History and Culture in Baltimore appears to be the precious cargo that Mills packed carefully for transport to Washington. The family lore related by Clara Hughes in her note accompanying the gift in 1945—that Mills gave it to her "*Uncle Charlie*"—may well be true. "Uncle Charlie" was Charles W. Buckingham, with whom Mills could have been a "close friend."[35] The sculptor had many associations in Baltimore, both business and personal.[36]

However, there is an alternate tradition.

It maintains that Mills gave his "original model" to "his friend, Daniel Ravenel of Charleston," and that it was destroyed in Ravenel's house "in the chaos of the Civil War and Reconstruction."[37] President of the Planters' and Mechanics' Bank and Vice President of The College of Charleston—owning a fine library that Mills probably used—Ravenel was a familiar of the many aristocrats whose busts Mills had sculpted.[38] The two men were certainly acquainted. When John C. Calhoun died in Washington in 1850, Ravenel invited Mills to join the official delegation returning the senator's remains to Charleston.[39] However, no evidence has been found that Mills gave Ravenel his maquette of the *rampant* Jackson equestrian. More probably, Mills presented "his friend" with his "original model," that is, the one depicting Jackson astride a *trotting* mount. That statuette has, indeed, long since disappeared.

In the afternoon of Tuesday, March 7, 1848, Mills bade his family farewell once again and embarked from Charleston harbor on the steamer to Wilmington, North Carolina. From there he was to proceed northward by rail, cross the Potomac to the nation's capital on a steamer, and present his maquette to the Jackson Monument Committee.[40] All the way up to Washington, Mills felt buoyed and hopeful.

NOTES

1 Object and donor files, acquisition A2580, 45.30.1, Maryland Center for History and Culture, Baltimore.
2 All accounts agree that Mills did not intend to return to South Carolina before continuing on to Italy. See, for example: (1) "The Equestrian Statue of Jackson, at Washington," *Merry's Museum and Parley's Magazine*, Jan. 1, 1853, p. 152: "[H]e left his home with the intention of travelling to perfect himself in the art. Passing through Washington on his way, . . .;" (2) "History of the Jackson Statue," *New York Daily Times*, Jan. 22, 1853, p. 3: "[He was] passing through

Washington city on his way to Italy;" (3) "Clark Mills and His Equestrian Statue," *DeBow's Review*, vol. 16 (Jan. 1854): 41: "[H]e was on his way to New-York, with a view of embarking thence for ... Rome. Passing through Washington, ... ;" (4) "An Hour with Clark Mills," [Washington] *Evening Star*, Dec. 24, 1870, p. 2: "Some of the citizens raised the money to send me to Europe, but on my way I stopped in Washington;" and (5) "Death of Clark Mills," [Washington] *Evening Star*, Jan. 12, 1883, p. 4: "He ... was about to start for Italy to pursue his art studies, when, in 1848 [sic; actually 1847], he was invited to submit a design for an equestrian statue of General Jackson."

3 "Clark Mills ... ," *DeBow's*, vol. 16 (Jan. 1854): 42.
4 See Bk. 1, Ch. 10.
5 "Clark Mills at Home," *The Washington Post*, Feb. 7, 1880, p. 2.
6 Charles C. Jewett, *Appendix to The Report of the Board of Regents of The Smithsonian Institution, containing A Report of the Public Libraries of The United States of America, January 1, 1850* (31st Cong., 1st Sess., Misc. Doc. No. 120), (Washington, D.C.: Printed for the Senate, 1850): 149–50.
7 Ibid., 154. Regarding Dr. Johnson, see Bk. 1, Ch. 7.
8 Jewett, *Appendix to The Report of the Board of Regents of The Smithsonian Institution*, 154–55.
9 "The Equestrian Statue of General Jackson," [Charleston] *Courier*, Mar. 8, 1848, p. 2.
10 See Bk. 1, Ch. 11.
11 "History of the Jackson Statue," [Washington] *Daily Union*, Jan. 18, 1853, p. 2.
12 Michael Edward Shapiro, *Bronze Casting and American Sculpture, 1850–1900* (Newark, Del.: University of Delaware Press, 1985): 44–45; and Wayne Craven, "Henry Kirke Brown in Italy, 1842–1846," *The American Art Journal*, vol. 1, no. 1 (spring 1969): 65–77.
13 Nineteenth-century newspaper accounts of the Jackson equestrian credit Mills with originating the idea of depicting Americans in a realistic, rather than classical, style. However, scholars today accord to Henry Kirke Brown the title of "Father of American Sculpture."
14 "History of the Jackson Statue," *Daily Union*, Jan. 18, 1853, 2; and "Mr. Clark Mills, the Sculptor," *The Round Table*, vol. 1, no. 22 (May 14, 1864): 340.
15 "History of the Jackson Statue," *Daily Union*, Jan. 18, 1853, 2.
16 Ibid.
17 "The Reward of Merit," [Charleston] *Courier*, May 12, 1847, p. 2.
18 "An Hour with Clark Mills," *Evening Star*, Dec. 24, 1870, 2.
19 "History of the Jackson Statue," *Daily Union*, Jan. 18, 1853, 2.
20 Letter, Henry Kirke Brown to Lydia Brown, Washington, D.C., May 18, 1849; Papers of Henry Kirke Bush-Brown, vol. 3: 567–75; Manuscript Division, Library of Congress, Washington, D.C. See Bk. 1, Ch. 23.
21 See, for example, "Statue of Jackson," *The Sumter* [Sumterville, S.C.] *Banner*, Mar. 22, 1848, p. 1; and *The Camden* [S.C.] *Journal*, Mar. 29, 1848, p. 1.

22 "Bust of Daniel Webster," [Charleston] *Courier*, Aug. 2, 1847, p. 2.
23 "The Equestrian Statue of General Jackson," *Courier*, Mar. 8, 1848, 2.
24 Ibid.
25 "An Hour with Clark Mills," *Evening Star*, Dec. 24, 1870, 2.
26 Ibid.
27 See, for example, "Charleston Light Dragoons," [Charleston] *Courier*, Feb. 8, 1847, p. 3.
28 "Clark Mills at Home," *The Washington Post*, Aug. 7, 1879, p. 1.
29 This article was summarized in "Notes on Art and Artists," *New York Times*, Jan. 28, 1883, p. 4.
30 "How John Robinson Helped Sculptor Mills," *Turf, Field, and Farm*, vol. 12, no. 5 (Feb. 3, 1871): 74 (reprinted from the *Cincinnati Enquirer*).
31 "An Hour with Clark Mills," *Evening Star*, Dec. 24, 1870, 2.
32 "History of the Jackson Statue," *Daily Union*, Jan. 18, 1853, 2 (eight months); and "Mr. Clark Mills, the Sculptor," *The Round Table*, vol. 1, no. 22 (May 14, 1864): 340 (nine months); and [no title], *New York Times*, May 31, 1880, p. 4 (eight months).
33 "The Jackson Monument," [Washington] *Daily Union*, Mar. 23, 1848, p. 3, states that the statue "is coated with bronze, so as to resemble a bronze statuette." This, however, is highly unlikely, as there would have been no way for Mills to accomplish this. Rather, the practice was to paint plaster statuettes to look like bronzes.
34 "The Equestrian Statue . . . ," *Courier*, Mar. 8, 1848, 2.
35 Clara Marie Balderston Hughes was "Mrs. Raymond Hughes," niece of "Charles W. Buckingham of Baltimore." Author's attempts at further identification have not been successful.
36 See, for example, Bk. 1, Chs. 33 and 35, and Bk. 2.
37 *Maryland History Notes* (Baltimore: Maryland Historical Society, 1945), vol. 3, no. 1 (May 1945): 34.
38 Daniel Ravenel (1790–1873): see Daniel Ravenel entry, 1850 U.S. Census, Parishes of St. Philip's and St. Michael's, Charleston, S.C., p. 173 (handwritten), p. 87 (stamped); NARA M432, roll 850; and Danl. Ravenel entry, 1860 U.S Census Slave Schedule, Ward 1, Charleston, S.C., p. 9 (handwritten), p. 408 (stamped); NARA M653, roll 1232; and J. H. Bagget, pub., *Directory of the City of Charleston, for the Year 1852* (Charleston: Edward C. Councell, printer, 1851): 105, 189 and 158; and "Daniel Ravenel III" at https://www.findagrave.com/memorial/41757966/daniel-ravenel.
39 See Bk. 1, Ch. 28.
40 Ibid.

CHAPTER 18
February 23, 1848

CAUTION.

THE subscriber having with much labor and great expense, succeeded in producing from life, a fac simile model of the Bust of the Hon. John C. Calhoun, obtained in October, 1845, a patent securing to him "the full and exclusive right and liberty of making, constructing, using, and vending to others to be used the said design."

Notwithstanding this fact the rights thus secured to him by the law of the land have been attempted to be violated by other persons, who having obtained one of his copies have in some measure disguised his original plan by a slight alteration of the hair and the addition of drapery. This is an evident infringement of the subscriber's rights under the Patent Law, and he hereby cautions all persons engaged either in the construction or sale of these impositions that the law will be rigidly enforced against them.

Feb 22   CLARK MILLS

"CAUTION," [Charleston] *Southern Patriot*, Feb. 23, 1848, p. 3, and [Charleston] *Courier*, Feb. 24 and 25, 1848, p. 3.

CHAPTER 19
March–April 1848

Why, then, should Clark Mills go to Italy, or Germany, or France, or England, or anywhere else, since the birth-place and home of his genius, since the incentives to his art and the monuments of his skill, are in America?

"Clark Mills and His Equestrian Statue,"
DeBow's Review, vol. 16 (Jan. 1854): 41.

Promptly upon arriving in the national capital in early March of 1848, Mills presented to the Jackson Monument Committee his maquette for a rampant equestrian statue of "Old Hickory." Postmaster Cave Johnson was delighted. He put the faux bronze statuette on display in one of the grand rooms of the new General Post Office building.[1] The timing—yet again—was ideal for the aspiring artist. On exhibit in the grand salon of the Odeon at the corner of Pennsylvania Avenue and 4½ Street was the latest masterwork of Hiram Powers, the *Greek Slave*.[2]

Touring the country ("Admittance 25 cts."), the *Greek Slave* was inciting both rapturous acclaim and vituperative condemnation, because it depicted—in lustrous, satiny white marble—a life-size female nude. The maiden's wrists were manacled, her head turned in modesty, and a cross showed among her cast-aside clothing.[3] Connoisseurs insisted that the sculpture's vague historical allusion redeemed its immodesty: the youthful figure was a devout Christian taken into slavery by a Turkish invader of Greece. While blushing at the nudity, Americans were transfixed by the work's sublime—and unabashedly sensuous—beauty. The *Greek Slave* was heralded throughout Europe and the United States as the apex of Powers's virtuosity. Mills surely paid his two bits to see the audacious and breathtaking creation of the modern-day Praxiteles.

In Washington City, the controversial statue had edged out of conversation two events of surpassing historic significance for the country. In January gold had been discovered in California, enticing young men in growing numbers to rush to San Francisco.[4] And in February the United States had won the war with Mexico, bringing the victor millions of acres of mineral-rich western land and the anticipation of war reparations.[5] But in March, when members of the Jackson Monument Committee stopped by the General Post Office to examine Mills's maquette, it was sculpture that Washingtonians were discussing.

Engraving of the *Greek Slave*, 1858. The masterwork in marble by the eminent American sculptor, Hiram Powers, was exhibited in Washington in March of 1848. Mills very likely viewed it. The life-size female's nudity and overt sensuousness incited a furor of both praise and condemnation. The statue could only be redeemed by Powers' breathtaking virtuosity and its vague historical allusion: the maiden was the Christian captive of a Turkish invader of Greece. (courtesy of Prof. Eugene Ham)

For two and a half years, the 13 admirers of Andrew Jackson had been frustrated in their efforts to commemorate their hero. They had no sculptor, no design, insufficient funds, and Congress had yet to respond to their request for cannons captured by the General for the metal. But here, now, before their eyes, was Mills's rearing steed, dynamic and glistening, with "the Hero of New Orleans"—not just sitting in the saddle—but gesturing exuberantly. It was more than they had asked for. It was more than they expected. It was without precedent. It was thrilling.

But that was not all.

Mills told the Committee that he could do the job for the $12,500 already collected, because he himself would cast the statue in Washington "at a cost not one-half the amount required for a statue to be made in Italy."[6]

The proposition was preposterous. No foundry in America had ever cast a monumental bronze statue. The Committee members—everybody—knew that. Nor did Washington have a facility capable of the task. The city had two commercial foundries, one iron, one brass, but neither was equipped to cast anything as large and complex as an equestrian statue.[7] Mills could only have had one place in mind: the Washington Navy Yard. Its foundry alone was of industrial proportion.

The untested sculptor's proposal was brazen and presumptuous and irresistible to the patriotic men of the Committee. It conjured a statue more totally American than even they had conceived. Mills must have convinced them that using the Navy Yard foundry, a military installation, might come cost-free, similar to free metal from the Army. By unanimous vote, the Committee adopted Mills's submission. On March 22, 1848, he signed the contract.[8]

Mills's dream of an American art for Americans had matured: not only was he rejecting Europe's classical tradition, now he was even rejecting Europe's foundries. "Mr. Mills," reported the *Daily Union*, "is animated by the spirit of an enthusiast."[9] Some years later, the Committee's secretary, John Maury, would write:

In justice to Mr. Mills, I ought to say that the work is a labor of love with him, and that when he undertook to execute the statue for twelve thousand five hundred dollars, he estimated that as the actual cost of the work—the only profit he expected being the reputation he would gain by its successful accomplishment.[10]

Immediately, news that Mills had won the commission appeared in the *Daily Union*:[11]

We always hail these refined productions of American enterprise and genius with pleasure, not only on account of their own beauty, but of the testimony which they bear to the ingenuity of the free people of this rising republic.[12]

The Charleston *Southern Patriot* picked up the story on the 27th and the Richmond *Enquirer* on the 28th.[13] From the outset, journalists across the country assigned a significance to this undertaking that transcended art. Similar to his bust of Calhoun, Mills's daring representation of Jackson was evidence of the greatness of a free republic. Its self-taught creator was the embodiment of the innate powers of the American people. The *Southern Patriot* proclaimed, "It will do high credit to American genius and patriotism."[14]

Mills himself appreciated the historic import of his venture. The United States had come of age. Victorious over Mexico, the country now stretched from the Atlantic to the Pacific. Its millions of pristine acres included incalculably rich land and minerals, California gold not the least of them. Unmistakably, America was a "rising republic." The nation no longer needed to look to Europe for standards—of art or anything else. The works of Clark Mills sprang naturally from the greatness of America. All of his fellow countrymen could take pride in them. It was a sentiment that Mills himself embraced. He believed it, deeply.

Even the wording of the contract rang with national ambition. Mills was to create an equestrian statue one-third larger than life-size depicting General Jackson that was: (1) cast in bronze from cannons donated by the U.S. government; (2) cast in Washington, D.C.; (3) the horse of which was self-poised on its hind legs; and (4) finished and delivered in two years.[15] For this, the Committee would pay Mills $12,500.

Mills had no inkling of the ordeal that lay ahead. How could he? He had no experience. The sheer physical labor of the undertaking, the many practical obstacles he would encounter, the mental anguish it would cost him . . . over—not two—but five years . . . it was all unimaginable to the naïve rookie. But neither were the nobly intentioned members of the Committee any better educated than Mills in the esoteric business of creating colossal public sculpture . . . of bronze!

On the other hand, though, these men of the world were eminently educated in matters of law and finance. They required surety. Mills rushed back to Charleston to make "honorable arrangements with his kind patrons."[16] The *Daily Union* would report:

> Ten gentlemen were the bondsmen for the due performance of the work. We give the names of these gentlemen, as it is highly honorable to them for this act of confidence and kindness. They are all men of property of the City of Charleston, and in the State of South Carolina.[17]

The roster was impressive. Most of the names resonated far beyond the boundaries of the Palmetto State. Half of them appeared in the Business Directory section of the Charleston *Courier* as bank and railroad officers.[18] All ten of the "men of property" listed enslaved people among their considerable financial assets.

Two of the backers were already benefactors. They had supported Mills while he devised the Jackson maquette: John Schnierle, former and future mayor of Charleston and namesake of Mills's son;[19] and A. G. Rose, director, cashier, then president of the Bank of Charleston.[20] They were joined by:

James Gadsden, U.S. Army engineer who served under General Jackson, President of the South Carolina Rail Road Company, Director of the Bank of South Carolina, cotton factor, future minister to Mexico who in 1854 would negotiate the Gadsden Purchase, which fixed the southern border of the United States;[21]

Henry Gourdin, a founding member and Director of the Bank of Charleston, commercial merchant, shipowner, art patron, correspondent of Hiram Powers;[22]

Franklin Harper Elmore, former U.S. Representative, President of the Bank of the State of South Carolina, Director of the South Carolina Rail Road Company, friend of John C. Calhoun, future U.S. Senator; one of Mills's earliest sitters and most helpful supporters;[23]

C. B. Northrop, attorney;[24]

Charles D. Carr, merchant draper and tailor;[25]

Edward Frost, former U.S. District Attorney, South Carolina state legislator and judge, President of the Blue Ridge Railroad;[26]

N. M. Porter, grocer;[27] and

George Kinloch, merchant grain dealer; his relative, **Francis Kinloch Huger**, had sat for Mills.[28]

These ten princes of South Carolina's social, financial, commercial and political empire stood foursquare behind their city's gifted son. For them, even if Mills failed to keep his contract, a forfeiture of $1,250 apiece would not be too great a price to pay for the prestige of being enshrined alongside the likes of the Hamptons, Prestons and Blairs as "Patron of the Arts."

Thus, the year financed by Conner, Schnierle and Rose came to a gratifying end. Mills had vindicated their faith in him. All thought of study in Italy was abandoned. Mills put his domestic affairs in order and packed what he would need for a prolonged residency in Washington. He must have made some kind of financial arrangement with Eliza for the family's upkeep, because this time, when he left, he most likely took Philip Reid with him. To make a full-scale plaster model of a statue nine feet tall and 12 feet long, the sculptor would need as many workers as he could afford. Reid was an experienced plasterer, and his skills came free of charge.[29] For the first time in his life, probably, the 28-year-old Black man, who was still single, would be separated from his blood kin in Charleston. Whether Reid viewed this trip as a personal hardship, though, or an exhilarating adventure, no one can say.

This domestic arrangement, everyone assumed, would only last two years. That was the stipulation in Mills's contract for the statue: "finished and delivered in two years." No one imagined that it would be three times that duration before the family was reunited. Or that neither Mills nor Reid would ever live in Charleston again.

Traveling back to Washington, the rough-and-tumble dreamer from the backcountry of New York State knew he had taken on a daunting responsibility. He knew he had a lot to prove. At this point, neither the metal he would need, nor the foundry, was assured. His maquette alone was a certainty, or so he thought. He could not have imagined the firestorm of controversy the little bronzed statue displayed in the new Post Office building was about to ignite.

NOTES

1 "The Jackson Monument," [Washington] *Daily Union*, Mar. 23, 1848, p. 3.
2 "Powers's Statue of the Greek Slave," [Washington] *Daily Union*, Jan. 24–Mar. 23, 1848, p. 2.
3 "The Greek Slave" at https://en.wikipedia.org/wiki/The_Greek_Slave.
4 Samuel Eliot Morison, Henry Steele Commager and William E. Leuchtenburg, *The Growth of the American Republic*, 7th ed. (New York and Oxford: Oxford University Press, 1980), vol. 1: 562.
5 Ibid., 553–56.

6   "The Jackson Monument," *Daily Union*, Mar. 23, 1848, 3; and [no title], [Richmond] *Enquirer*, Mar. 28, 1848, p. 1.
7   For the two foundries, see Edward Waite, comp. and pub., *The Washington Directory, and Congressional, and Executive Register, for 1850* (Washington, D.C.: Columbus Alexander, Printer, 1850): 213 and 221.
8   "The Jackson Monument," *Daily Union*, Mar. 23, 1848, 3.
9   Ibid.
10 "To the People of the United States," [Washington] *Daily Union*, Nov. 27, 1851, p. 3. Maury would recollect that "the agreement [was] entered into in June, 1848." However, that conflicts with the March date reported in the *Daily Union* article, which was contemporaneous with the event.
11 "The Jackson Monument," *Daily Union*, Mar. 23, 1848, 3.
12 Ibid.
13 "Clarke [sic] Mills," [Charleston] *Southern Patriot*, Mar. 27, 1848, p. 2; and [no title], *Enquirer*, Mar. 28, 1848, 1.
14 Ibid.
15 [no title], *Enquirer*, Mar. 28, 1848, 1.
16 "Clark Mills and His Equestrian Statue," *DeBow's Review*, vol. 16 (Jan. 1854): 42.
17 "History of the Jackson Statue," [Washington] *Daily Union*, Jan. 18, 1853, p. 2.
18 See, for example, "Business Directory" and "Rail Road," [Charleston] *Courier*, Mar. 30, 1847, p. 1.
19 See Bk. 1, Ch. 4.
20 See Bk. 1, Ch. 10.
21 James Gadsden (1788–1858), see www.scencyclopedia.org; and J. H. Bagget, pub., *Directory of the City of Charleston, for the Year 1852* (Charleston: Edward C. Councell, printer, 1851): 45. The 1850 U.S. Census Slave Schedule, Parishes of St. Philip's and St. Michael's, Charleston, S.C., enumerates eight slaveholders named James Gadsden.
22 Henry Gourdin (1804–79), see Henry Gourdin entry, 1850 U.S. Census, Parishes of St. Philip's and St. Michael's, Charleston, S.C., p. 173 (handwritten), p. 87 (stamped); NARA M432, roll 850; and Henry Gourdin entry, 1850 U.S. Census Slave Schedule, Parishes of St. Philip's and St. Michael's, Charleston, S.C., p. 11 (handwritten); NARA M432, roll 862; and Bagget, *Directory . . . for the Year 1852*, 49.
23 See Bk. 1, Chs. 5 and 8.
24 C. B. Northrop (1812–65), see C. B. Northrop entry, 1850 U.S. Census, Parishes of St. Philip's and St. Michael's, Charleston, S.C., p. 68 (handwritten), p. 152[B] (stamped); NARA M432, roll 850; and C. B. Northrop entry, 1850 U.S. Census Slave Schedule, Parishes of St. Philip's and St. Michael's, Charleston, S.C., p. 129 (handwritten); NARA M432, roll 862; and Bagget, *Directory . . . for the Year 1852*, 95.

25 C. D. Carr (ca. 1810–52+), see C. D. Carr entry, 1850 U.S. Census, Parishes of St. Philip's and St. Michael's, Charleston, S.C., p. 67 (handwritten), p. 152 (stamped); NARA M432, roll 850; and C. D. Carr entry, 1850 U.S. Census Slave Schedule, Parishes of St. Philip's and St. Michael's, Charleston, S.C., p. 127 (handwritten); NARA M432, roll 862; and Bagget, *Directory . . . for the Year 1852*, 21.

26 Edward Frost (1801–68), see https://en.wikipedia.org; and The Hon. Ed Frost [sic] entry, 1850 U.S. Census, Parishes of St. Philip's and St. Michael's, Charleston, S.C., p. 308; NARA M432, roll 850; and The Hon. Ed Frost [sic] entry, 1850 U.S. Census Slave Schedule, Parishes of St. Philip's and St. Michael's, Charleston, S.C., p. 91 and 93 (handwritten); NARA M432, roll 862; and Bagget, *Directory . . . for the Year 1852*, 44.

27 N. M. Porter (ca. 1812–76), see N. M. Porter entry, 1850 U.S. Census, Parishes of St. Philip's and St. Michael's, Charleston, S.C., p. 561 (handwritten), p. 279 (stamped); NARA M432, roll 850; and N. M. Porter entry, 1850 U.S. Census Slave Schedule, Parishes of St. Philip's and St. Michael's, Charleston, S.C., p. 921 (handwritten); NARA M432, roll 862; and Bagget, *Directory . . . for the Year 1852*, 102.

28 George Kinloch (1785–1867), see George Kinloch entry, 1850 U.S. Census, Parishes of St. Philip's and St. Michael's, Charleston, S.C., p. 335 (handwritten), p. 166 (stamped); NARA M432, roll 850; and George Kinloch entry, 1850 U.S. Census Slave Schedule, Parishes of St. Philip's and St. Michael's, Charleston, S.C., p. 739 (handwritten); NARA M432, roll 862; and Bagget, *Directory . . . for the Year 1852*, 69. See also Bk. 1, Ch. 12.

29 After visiting Mills in his Washington studio in May 1849, Henry Kirke Brown wrote to his wife: "There I saw the boots of the old Hero Jackson. These were partly chopped out in plaster, but the hewing out he [Mills] informed me was the rough part, that he kept a nigger for that." The Negro was likely Philip Reid. See Letter, Henry Kirke Brown to Lydia Brown, Washington, D.C., May 18, 1849; Papers of Henry Kirke Bush-Brown, vol. 3: 567; Manuscript Division, Library of Congress, Washington, D.C. See also John Philip Colletta, "Clark Mills and His Enslaved Assistant, Philip Reed: The Collaboration that Culminated in *Freedom*," *The Capitol Dome, Journal of the U.S. Capitol Historical Society*, vol. 57 (spring–summer 2020): 15–31.

CHAPTER 20
April–July 1848

"The schoolmen, scientists and philosophers of that day put me down as a fool—a lunatic. Finally, one of them, a Prof. Page, a man of great knowledge and influence, so far worked upon the committee as to convince them that if they wished to throw away any money to keep on with the lunatic."

Clark Mills, quoted in "Clark Mills at Home,"
The Washington Post, Feb. 7, 1880, p. 2.

Standing in President's Park, peering southward across the muddy mouth of Tiber Creek, Mills could see timber scaffolding and tall derricks. Workers, wagons, horses and oxen were maneuvering in a field strewn with massive blocks of granite. Construction of the long-planned memorial to George Washington was under way. Designed by the city's preeminent architect, Robert Mills (whose fireproof buildings Clark Mills had seen in Charleston and Richmond, as well as Washington), the obelisk ringed with a colonnade had been approved years ago, but private funding had lagged. Finally, this spring of 1848, was the ground being broken and the foundation laid.[1]

Clark Mills had re-entered the capital in April, most likely with his Black assistant, Philip Reid.[2] By that time, Congress had granted the Jackson Monument Committee the use of a small corner of U.S. Government land for its project. South of the President's House lay a swath of open terrain that descended all the way to Tiber Creek, which emptied into the Potomac. Designated "President's Park," the area would later be known colloquially as the "White Lot" (a wooden fence painted white enclosed it). Today it is called the Ellipse.[3] Where Pennsylvania Avenue dead-ended at 15th Street, just south of the

Treasury Building, a gate led into the park, and from there a carriage way wound up to the White House.[4] The parcel of land loaned to the Committee for Mills's studio was situated just south of this carriage way.[5] It was rumored that the site had been used formerly by a "celebrated artist" whose workshop "was burned."[6] But this inauspicious omen has not been verified.

The Committee, having been assured of adequate surety from Mills and a place for him to work, started making periodic cash payments to their unproven sculptor. Mills, in turn, hired workmen, purchased supplies, and commenced building a studio and living quarters.

During construction, Mills may have resided across the street in Owen House. The modest, two-story hotel "on the European style" at 212 Pennsylvania Avenue was owned by Edward Owen, a Welshman in his fifties. He and his son, Samuel, ran a thriving military tailoring business at the same address.[7] At a future date, Mills would take the face mask of **Edward Owen** and present him with a plaster bust "as a token of gratitude to his patron when he first came to Washington."[8]

The edifice that Mills raised for his workplace and lodging was Spartan. One reporter would later write:

> He put up his little shanty buildings of scantling and unplained boards, mingled with rough brick walls and coverings of canvass.[9]

But it was not "little" at all.

The main level consisted of three unplastered rooms.[10] The front door opened into an office about ten feet square, which led into the studio proper. That workspace was large enough to accommodate a model nine feet tall and 12 feet long, plus tools, materials, a few pieces of furniture, and a stall for Olympus, the horse Mills was to use as a model. Back of the studio, a small room, or "kitchen," had a cook stove. This rear room, or perhaps the office, would have held a cot for Philip Reid. Upstairs of the "kitchen" was another small room, this one plastered, containing a bed for Mills. There was a dirt cellar, windowless, under at least a portion of the building. Next to his studio/abode, Mills constructed a paddock for Olympus, and—at some distance—he located a privy. The sculptor enclosed his compound within a picket fence and hung a padlock on the gate.

Looking southward from his studio—beyond Tiber Creek and the construction activity of the Washington Monument—Mills enjoyed the same grand river vista as the President of the United States. Tiber Creek, a sluggish channel that arced through Washington City from the Eastern Branch to the Potomac, had been made into a canal that ended at 15th Street, so its brackish water still emptied into the mouth of the creek and flowed into the Potomac. Mills could easily make out swooping herons, clouds of levitating geese, and the billowing sails and belching smokestacks of vessels plying the river. Washington City was low-lying, its climate subtropical, not unlike Charleston's. It was common for newcomers to develop "ague."[11] Mills, too, before long, would begin suffering bouts of fever and achy muscles.[12]

North of his studio and dwelling, Mills looked upon a stark brick wall three stories high that terminated the southern end of the new east wing of the U.S. Treasury. A massive enlargement of the old building—a federal-style edifice erected between 1814 and 1818 to replace the one burned by the British during the War of 1812—was in progress. Robert Mills's Greek Revival design was being implemented and his spectacular 350-foot-long Ionic colonnade along 15th Street had been completed in 1842. But work on the southern wing would not start for another few years, after Mills had vacated President's Park.[13]

The precise orientation of Mills's studio is not recorded, but it could not have required many steps from his padlocked gate to behold the long eastward sweep of Pennsylvania Avenue up to the elevation crowned with the U.S. Capitol. The fledgling artist had landed, literally, in the heart of the Federal City, one of the closest neighbors of the President, James Knox Polk, and his wife, Sarah.

Suddenly the cash payments from the Committee stopped.

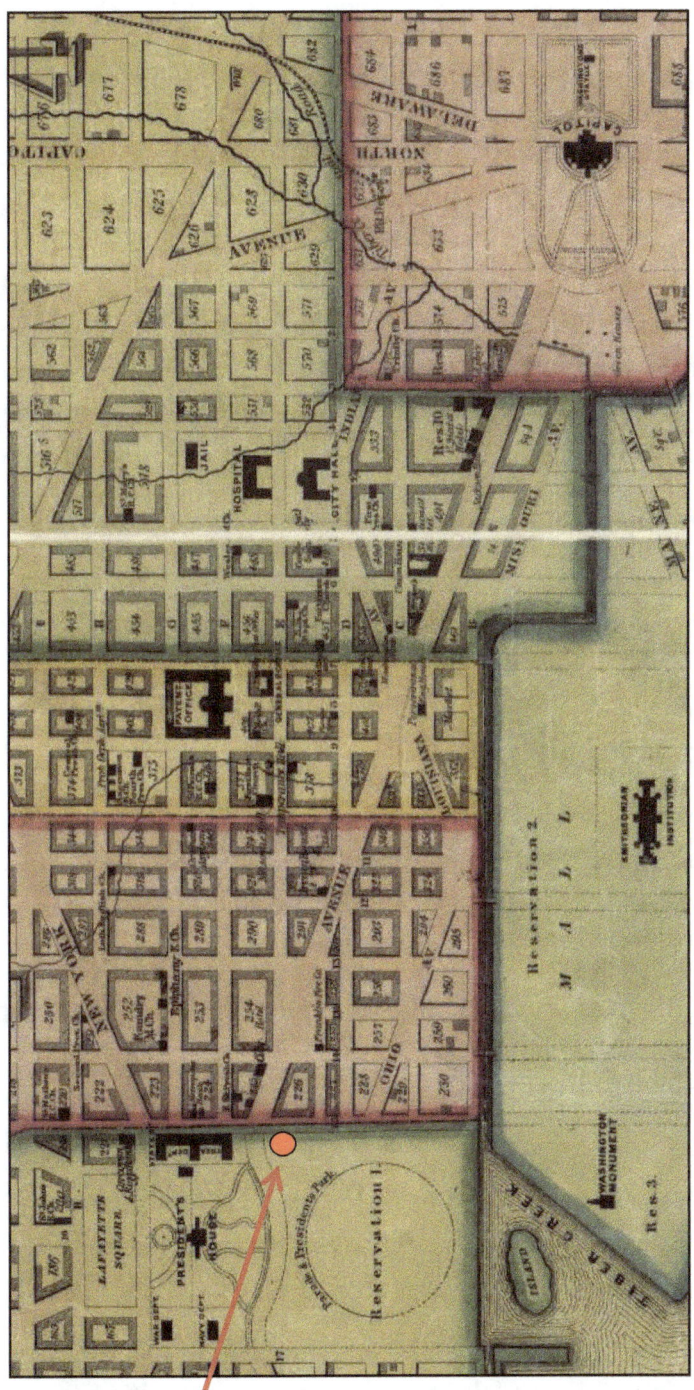

Map of Washington, 1851. The location of Mills's studio/abode and foundry in President's Park (Reservation 1, called the "White Lot" then, the "Ellipse" today) is indicated. His fenced-in compound lay across the carriage way from the unfinished southern wing of the Treasury Building. (Library of Congress)

Descriptions of Mills's maquette had reached the art centers of the North—Philadelphia, New York and Boston—and traveled from there to the workshops of Horatio Greenough, Hiram Powers and Thomas Crawford in Italy. A tempest of criticism erupted. The nation's most celebrated sculptors were unanimous in their agreement that Mills's multi-ton prancing horse was folly: the figure could not remain upright without some external support. Vocal among the detractors was Henry Kirke Brown, who was making rapid progress establishing his career in New York City.[14] Men of science, too—including the Secretary of the Smithsonian Institution, Joseph Henry, and eminent Professor Charles Grafton Page—insisted that the statue as proposed by Mills was a physical impossibility.[15]

Page was a well-to-do physician, patent attorney, inventor, scientist and professor. A graduate of Harvard, he was already—in his mid-thirties—impressively accomplished. His opinions commanded attention.[16] His arguments against the statue induced several members of the Jackson Monument Committee to reconsider their decision to hire Mills:

> There were complaints strong and loud, and speculations of failure. The committee was getting dissatisfied; they did not believe the horse could remain self-poised; that it would tumble forward, &c.[17]

In future years, though, Mills would delight in recounting the story of his vindication:

> "They stopped my money.
>
> "I knew that Page could only be reached by ocular demonstration of my principle, and that the committee could only be reached through him; so I went to his office so absorbed in my mission that I forgot the amenities of social life. I rushed into his room."
>
> [Page leased an office on the south side of F Street between 7th and 8th Streets, facing the magnificent

Greek Revival portico of the U.S. Patent Office—yet another of Robert Mills's triumphs.[18]]

"He was not in. I went out and paced up and down the street, awaiting his arrival.

"After a little a gentleman got out of his buggy and went in. I followed.

"'If you are Prof. Page,' said I, 'I wish to get some information. I want to know if the size will change the principle of it.'

"He thought a moment and said, 'No, if the proportions are preserved; because,' said he, 'a lever five feet long or twenty feet long is the same thing, provided you increase the size of the lever in proportion to the length, but if you increase the length of the lever without increasing the size, your lever will become so flexible that you could not raise as much with it as with a shorter lever, for it would be more like a whip-stock.'

"'Then, sir,' said I, placing my model on the table before him, which I had in my vest pocket, 'If the hind legs of this miniature horse will sustain a solid body, why will not the hind legs of my colossal horse sustain a hollow body?'

"At this he turned around and said, 'You are Mr. Mills, I presume?'

"He figured a little and said, 'Yes, you have it; but I never would have believed it if I had not seen it.'

"'I then went and saw John W. Maury, and he had the committee called together. Old man Francis P. Blair made the motion that I should go on. It was carried.'"[19]

Payments from the Committee resumed.[20] Mills got to "go on."

On the fourth of July 1848, 20,000 Washingtonians and out-of-town visitors congregated on the grounds of the Washington Monument.[21] Robert Mills was there. Also standing in the throng, very likely, was the city's new resident sculptor—"a fool, a lunatic?" No matter. Mills believed in himself. President Polk arrived and laid the cornerstone amid grandiloquent speeches and military fanfare. That night, fireworks outlined patriotic images on frameworks erected just south of Mills's recently finished studio/abode.²²

NOTES

1 National Park Service, "Washington Monument, History and Culture," at https://www.nps.gov/wamo/learn/historyculture/index.htm.
2 See Bk. 1, Ch. 19, n. 29.
3 Peter R. Penczer, "The Ellipse: The Nineteenth-Century Evolution of the White Lot," *White House History*, a journal published by the White House Historical Association, no. 38 (summer 2015): 12–21.
4 Susan Calafate Boyle, *The White House & President's Park, Washington, D.C.*, Cultural Landscape Report, Site History and Evaluation, 1791–1994 (Washington, D.C.: U. S. Department of the Interior, National Park Service, 2001): https://www.nps.gov/parkhistory/online_books/prpa/prpa_clr.pdf. On early city plats, the U.S. Government land appears as "Reservation 1."
5 [no title], [Charleston] *Courier*, June 12, 1848, p. 2; "Clark Mills," [Charleston] *Courier* (quoting the *Camden* [S.C.] *Journal*), May 8, 1850, p. 2; and "Correspondence of the Baltimore Sun. Washington, Feb. 13, 1851. Principle Places of Attraction," [Baltimore] *Sun*, Feb. 14, 1851, p. 4. No record has been found of Congress's grant to the Jackson Monument Committee; it appears that the arrangement was informal. The site of Mills's studio/abode today is occupied by the monumental equestrian statue of General Sherman.
6 "Clark Mills," *Courier*, May 8, 1850, 2.
7 Edward Owen (1793–1878), see Edward Owen entry, 1850 U.S. Census, Ward 2, Washington, D.C., p. 132 (handwritten), p. 66[b] (stamped); NARA M432, roll 56; and Edward Waite, comp., *The Washington Directory, and Congressional, and Executive Register, for 1850* (Washington, D.C.: Columbus Alexander, Printer, 1850): 67 and 208; and "Owen House," 1865 pencil sketch, Prints and Photographs Division, Library of Congress, Washington, D.C.
8 Rosemary Hopkins, *Clark Mills: The First Native American Sculptor* (M.A. thesis, University of Maryland, 1966): 187.
9 "Clark Mills and His Equestrian Statue," *DeBow's Review*, vol. 16 (Jan. 1854): 42.
10 Description of Mills's studio is derived from the writings of two men who visited it: (1) letter, Henry Kirke Brown to Lydia Brown, May 18, 1849; Papers of Henry Kirke Bush-Brown, vol. 3: 567–75; Manuscript Division, Library of Congress, Washington, D.C.; and (2) "Sketches of Washington. By Childe Harold. Washington, March 29, 1853. An Hour with Clark Mills, the Sculptor," *Brooklyn Eagle*, Mar. 30, 1853, p. 2.

11 Ernest B. Furgurson, *Freedom Rising, Washington in the Civil War* (New York: Alfred A. Knopf, 2004): 14; and Margaret Leech, *Reveille in Washington, 1860–1865* (New York: Harper & Bros., 1941): 6–7.
12 Letter, Henry Kirke Brown to Lydia Brown, May 18, 1849; Papers of Henry Kirke Bush-Brown, vol. 3: 567–71.
13 National Park Service, National Register of Historic Places Inventory, "United States Department of the Treasury," https://npgallery.nps.gov/NRHP/GetAsset/NHLS/71001007_text.
14 Michael Edward Shapiro, *Bronze Casting and American Sculpture, 1850–1900* (Newark, Del.: University of Delaware Press, 1985): 45; and Wayne Craven, "Henry Kirke Brown in Italy, 1842–1846," *The American Art Journal*, vol. 1, no. 1 (spring 1969): 65–77.
15 "Clark Mills at Home," *The Washington Post*, Feb. 7, 1880, p. 2; and A[loha] Vivarttas, "The Clark Mills Furnace—A Remembrance," *The Railroad & Engineering Journal*, vol. 63 (July 1889): 328.
16 Charles Grafton Page (1812–68), see https://en.wikipedia.org/wiki/Charles_Grafton_Page; and Chas [sic] Page entry, 1850 U.S. Census, Washington, D.C., p. 509 (handwritten), p. 255 (stamped); NARA M432, roll 56; and Waite, *Washington Directory . . . for 1850*, 159.
17 "Sketches of Washington . . . ," *Brooklyn Eagle*, Mar. 30, 1853, 2.
18 Alfred Hunter, comp., *The Washington and Georgetown Directory, Strangers' Guide-book for Washington, and Congressional and Clerks' Register* (Washington: Kirkwood & McGill, 1853): 77.
19 "Clark Mills . . . ," *Washington Post*, Feb. 7, 1880, 2.
20 "To the People of the United States," [Washington] *Daily Union*, Nov. 27, 1851, p. 3.
21 Allan B. Slauson, ed., *A History of the City of Washington, Its Men and Institutions* (Washington, D.C.: The Washington Post, 1903): 110.
22 "The Anniversary. Laying the Cornerstone of the Monument to Washington," [Washington] *Daily Union*, July 7, 1848, p. 2.

CHAPTER 21
June–December 1848

The horse is rearing—standing upon its hind legs, which are so placed as to form the centre of gravity. It is ten feet high. The statue of Peter the Great, of Russia, is considered as the greatest work of art extant, but Mr. Mills' will excel it, from the fact that his horse stands alone, unsupported, excepting by its hind legs—whereas that of Peter the Great is fastened by its tail, in addition to its two legs.

"Ahead of the Mail, Washington, Nov. 22,"
[Charleston] *Courier*, Nov. 28, 1848, p. 2.

Mills had welcomed the Washington correspondent of the Charleston *Courier* into his studio.[1] The full-scale model of the rampant horse, one-third larger than life, was nearly done. Mills was eager for his supporters—and detractors—to be aware of his progress. He told the reporter that, after putting Jackson in the saddle, he would cast the enormous statue in bronze from cannons captured by the General himself.

Two weeks later, Mills admitted another visitor to view the huge charger. This one was a friend of an editor at Washington's *National Intelligencer*. The editor's subsequent write-up would focus on the same aspect of the sculpture that the *Courier* reporter had stressed:

> The attitude of the animal is . . . uncommonly spirited, and the balance is managed with taste and skill. The line of balance extends from the toes of the hindermost hoofs to the back or top of the neck; and, as the figure now stands, a weight of two hundred pounds can be attached to the fore feet without threatening a fall. When the horse shall have been surmounted by the rider, the firmness of the whole statue will be greatly increased. In modeling his

work the artist has paid particular attention to the action of the animal, and, by way of ascertaining the precise play of the muscles, he has studied the life with particular attention.[2]

A Boston periodical for young readers, *Merry's Museum and Parley's Magazine*, would assert of the Jackson equestrian:

> The principal merit, and that which attracts the admiration of the critic, is not merely its beautifully symmetrical proportions, but its wonderful *balancing power*, an attainment which for centuries has defied the united talent of the most skillful of foreign artists.[3]

The fact that the artificial horse was rearing on its hind legs with no external support, exactly as a live horse would do, would forever eclipse every other observation ever made about the statue.

CREATING A BRONZE STATUE

Step 4: Make a full-scale model

Mills had been working on the model for five months. Back in June, having built a workplace for himself, he had equipped it with the requisite tools and materials and undertaken "his duties immediately."[4] First, examining his maquette, Mills had decided how he would break the horse down into manageable pieces. Next, he had calculated how much larger he would have to duplicate those pieces to make a full-scale model.

His method was unorthodox. Mills did not begin with a quarter-size or half-size model in clay, then enlarge it and cast it in plaster. That was the customary procedure. Rather, he started with plaster. An *Evening Star* reporter would explain:

> Dispensing with clay, Mills, by the aid of a quick hand and accurate eye, models directly in plaster for sculpture, dispensing with the tedious process of modeling in clay and then moulding from clay to plaster and cutting the plaster cast in sections for the use

of the founder. The other advantage gained over the clay process is that the plaster model neither shrinks or swells, and does not require wetting and covering with cloths to keep it in condition. But plaster sets so quick that only a skillful hand can deal with it.[5]

After mixing a batch of plaster, Mills would pour it into a cubical mold to form a large, solid block. When the paste dried and hardened, he would use sundry tools to sculpt a portion of the horse out of the block. In *Bronze Casting and American Sculpture, 1850–1900*, art historian Michael Edward Shapiro writes:

> While saving a step, Mills chose a rigid material that had to be carved like marble rather than modeled. . . . Sections of the sculpture were carved out of individual blocks of plaster and, when finished, were fitted together. With this method, changes and overall adjustments of scale were difficult.[6]

The process was laborious and time-consuming. Pieces that did not turn out right had to be discarded and remade from scratch. However, the *Evening Star* reporter wrote that Mills "models directly in plaster," as though it were clay. Possibly, therefore, when a piece required only minor reworking, Mills may have applied fresh wet plaster to it, then sculpted as necessary to remedy the flaw. He was perfecting the technique as he went along. Many skills that Mills mastered in the course of his career, he learned by repeated trial and error. Henry Kirke Brown, the virtuoso sculptor, admitted in a letter to his wife that Mills's method mystified him:

> *The tools with which he works, you must know he models in plaster, not clay, they consisted of two deck scrapers, one with and one without teeth, a hatchet and hand saw, masons hods and trowels. The manner in which he uses these I am yet ignorant of.*[7]

Periodically, as Mills progressed, one piece of the horse after the other, he would step out to the paddock beside his studio, sketchbook in hand. Coaxing a live model to rear, he would observe the animal's musculature, draw quickly, then return to his sculpting. Noted one reporter:

> The horse employed as a model is a handsome blooded animal, of a rich sorrel color, and so thoroughly trained that he throws himself into the very attitude which his master desires to study.[8]

To make the maquette in Charleston, Mills had used at least two models: a retired racehorse that Colonel Wade Hampton gave him and a circus horse belonging to "Uncle John" Robinson.[9] In Washington, Mills exercised and studied two, possibly three, others:

Arabian Pompey

The sire of this horse [of Washington County, Maryland] was a horse of the same name, which was purchased and used as a model for the equestrian statue of Jackson by Clark Mills. Mr. Mills paid $800 for him and sold him for $1,200 to a company, who took him West.

The American Farmer, a Monthly Magazine of Agriculture and Horticulture, vol. 1, no. 6 (Dec. 1859): 176.

[Name unknown]

According to lore of Arlington County, Virginia, Mills used a horse belonging to Gilbert Vanderwerken.[10] Vanderwerken, who resided in Georgetown, founded Washington's first omnibus in 1851.[11] The coach sat 12 passengers. Initially, it ran from the Aqueduct Bridge in Georgetown, along M Street and Pennsylvania Avenue, down to the Navy Yard. But the line was soon extended to Congressional Cemetery. Vanderwerken pastured his coach horses and a handful of prized thoroughbreds on his extensive acreage in Arlington, called "Falls Grove."

Eleanor Lee Templeman, *Arlington Heritage: Vignettes of a Virginia County* (Arlington, Va.: self-published, 1959): 126–27.

Olympus

Olympus was left upon the place [in Clarke County, Virginia], and, I think, presented to Scott Tidball. . . . Scott sold him for a few hundred dollars to Clark Mills, the sculptor, who purchased him to be used as a model for the horse in the casting of the equestrian statue of Old Hickory.

"Olympus," Turf, Field and Farm, vol. 16, no. 17
(Apr. 25, 1873): 264.

Although Mills may have used multiple horses when sculpting Jackson's charger, the "sorrel gelding, Olympus," is the only one identified by name in accounts of the statue's creation."[12]

After carving each part of the steed to his satisfaction, Mills bolted the solid piece of sculpture to an iron armature. The armature was sufficiently strong and stable to support hundreds of pounds of plaster on the horse's two flexed hind legs. To devise it, Mills must have consulted ironmongers—likely German-Americans—who would have cast or wrought the skeleton for him.[13] Throughout the summer and into the autumn of 1848, as Mills emptied barrel after barrel of plaster, the colossal rampant warhorse took shape.

Meanwhile, the 30th Congress was seated and members of the Jackson Monument Committee used their influence and connections to revive their request for metal.[14] It was over a year since Joint Resolution No. 58, providing guns captured by Jackson to cast the statue, had been tabled.[15] Now the Committee had a stronger argument to make: they had hired a sculptor and the project was underway. In addition, thanks to Mills's settling for $12,500, "There was now no doubt but that an ample sum would be received for the construction of the statue."[16] By this time, too, though, the Committee realized that the four cannons and two mortars won by Jackson from the Spanish would not suffice to cast a statue nine feet tall and 12 feet long. Altogether, the guns weighed 4,930 pounds. The job called for about six times that amount of bronze.

The savvy members called upon Senator John Adam Dix of New York to champion their cause. Dix was not only a Democrat, he was also a former Army officer and chairman of the Committee on Military Affairs.[17] On July 31, 1848, he rose from his desk in the Senate chamber and re-introduced the Committee's memorial as Senate Resolution No. 37. It was referred to the senator's own committee.[18] The following day, Dix reported S.R. 37 back to the Senate, unamended, for a vote. It passed without debate and went to the House of Representatives for concurrence.[19] There, however, debate did ensue.

Thomas Butler King of Georgia protested that it was a misuse of the "venerable and precious trophies of the valor of our ancestors" to melt them down for a memorial to a single individual:

"They belonged to the country; they should descend from generation to generation; they were so many heirlooms, which ought to descend to posterity, to show what their ancestors had done."[20]

On the contrary, responded John Alexander McClernand—who had introduced the original memorial the previous year—the practice was time-honored. He cited two examples:

"In France, where the column of Napoleon had been made of the cannon captured at Austerlitz, and in England, where an equestrian statue to Wellington had been made, or was being made, of the brass pieces taken at Waterloo."[21]

Other congressmen objected to a particular provision in S.R. 37. Senator Dix, having learned from the Jackson Monument Committee that Mills would need much more bronze than their original memorial requested, had inserted this phrase into the new one:

[T]ogether with such other pieces of brass ordnance, reported "unserviceable," as the chief of the ordnance office may designate as sufficient for the purposes of the said committee.[22]

Some congressmen feared that this open-ended provision might be applied to cannons taken from the British in the Revolutionary War, which were "cherished by the American people."

McClernand conceded the point. He agreed to limit the Committee's request to the guns stipulated in the original memorial: four cannons and two mortars captured by Jackson from the Spanish at Pensacola in 1818. The House voted to strike the provision for "other pieces of brass ordnance" and S.R. 37 was returned to the Senate for concurrence.[23]

The Senate accepted the House's emendation and passed the measure as Joint Resolution No. 25. President James K. Polk signed it on August 11, 1848:

> *Resolved by the Senate and House of Representatives of the United States of America in Congress assembled,* That the President ... be ... authorized and requested to cause to be delivered to the Jackson Monument Committee ... the brass guns and mortars captured by General Andrew Jackson at Pensacola, and referred to in a statement of the Chief of the Ordnance Office [Lt. Col. George Talcott], dated Fourteenth April, eighteen hundred and forty-six, to be used by the said committee as material for the construction of the monument to that distinguished patriot; and the said committee is hereby authorized to erect the said monument upon such portion of the public grounds in the city of Washington as may be designated for that purpose by the President of the United States.[24]

Finally, it was official. The Jackson Monument Committee would get the old Spanish guns. Suddenly, though, the members changed their mind. Perhaps the objection raised by Representative King resonated in their hearts. The artillery pieces were indeed "venerable and precious" national trophies. The Committee decided not to melt them down after all. Instead, the four cannons would be mounted on wooden carriages and displayed as part of the Jackson memorial.

Who originated the idea, Mills or the Committee, is not known. But it was unprecedented. None of the half dozen world-renowned equestrian statues in Europe was adorned with field artillery pieces seized in battle by the memorialized horseman. This change in plan, however, left the Committee with only the two mortars for metal—a scant 2,130 pounds. The members had to boost their fund-raising. They turned to Charles Fenderich.

Charles Fenderich was a preeminent lithographer.[25] Since arriving in Washington from Switzerland in 1837, he had produced many fine portraits of presidents, senators and congressmen, all lithographed in multiple copies and sold to admirers of the statesmen. In 1846 he had published a lithograph for the Washington National Monument Society that depicted Robert Mills's design for the anticipated memorial.[26] The Society offered the print to donors as a premium. Why should the Jackson Monument Committee not adopt the same stratagem? On November 10, 1848, the Richmond *Enquirer* reported:

> Mr. Fenderich, an accomplished artist, has just completed a fine lithographic view of the equestrian statue of General Jackson, designed, now in progress, and to be cast in Bronze by Mr. Clark Mills.[27]

This was the first published image of Mills's intended statue. Fenderich's drawing, "Jackson Monument in the City of Washington," lithographed by Edward Weber & Co. in Baltimore, illustrates the memorial as it was expected to look when completed.[28] It stands in the center of Lafayette Square, directly across Pennsylvania Avenue from the Executive Mansion. Evidently, President Polk had already designated that site as the "portion of the public grounds in the city of Washington" where the memorial would be erected.[29] So Fenderich's print is also the earliest published reference to the future location of the statue.

The spirited horse and rider stand on the classical pedestal that Mills envisioned for the sculpture. Eight to nine feet high, it consisted

Lithographic print by Charles Fenderich, 1848, the first depiction of Mills's proposed statue of General Jackson. Published more than four years before the work was completed, it shows the pedestal the sculptor envisioned, but never executed, as well as the four 18th-century Spanish cannons that were made a part of the memorial. (Library of Congress)

of two tiers. The upper portion was inscribed with the toast that Jackson once raised to his role model, Thomas Jefferson: "THE / FEDERAL UNION / IT / MUST BE PRESERVED."[30] In the lower portion was a bronze relief panel depicting the "Battle of New Orleans." Mills intended a second scene in bas-relief illustrating another of Jackson's exploits for the opposite side of the pedestal.[31] He planned to create the two panels himself. The statue on its pedestal occupies the center of a marble platform with stairs descending on opposite sides. Generic field cannons in wheeled carriages are positioned at the four corners, because neither the Jackson Monument Committee nor Mills nor Fenderich knew yet what the old Spanish guns actually looked like.

Fenderich took artistic liberty with the perspective of his print's background: the White House appears to the right of the Jackson equestrian and David d'Anger's pedestrian statue of Thomas Jefferson, which stood on the lawn in front of the White House, appears to the left. Printed in the lower right-hand corner is the sentence: "Mr. _____ has contributed $_____ towards the erection of this monument." The blanks were to be filled in for individual donors. It was the hope of the Jackson Monument Committee that offering a premium lithograph—as the Washington National Monument Society had done—would entice greater participation by the public.

Shortly after the *Enquirer* announced the availability of Fenderich's print, the lithographer decamped to California to pan for gold.[32] He left behind an unfinished panorama, "View of Washington City and Georgetown," to be published by the book dealer, Casimir Bohn.[33] The border surrounding the drawing contained images of 20 points of interest, including a near-identical copy, much reduced, of Fenderich's Jackson print. Bohn would have the work completed by a local artist, lithographed by Edward Weber & Co., and published in February 1849.[34]

These images were only part of the national exposure that Mills and his ambitious endeavor received. Time and again throughout the project, Mills would invite guests into his studio—newspaper reporters, government officials, actors, authors, sculptors. Time and again, he would swing open the gate of his fenced-in compound to the general public. Mills appreciated the fact that what he was doing was something new and exotic in the United States. Standing amid the strange-looking tools and raw materials of "The Sculptor," he delighted in expounding to his fellow Americans on the profession that enthralled him. He reveled in sharing the excitement that he himself felt about his calling. Moreover, showing off in the guise of an earnest, wide-eyed learner himself lent a semblance of humility to his teaching. The public exposure was perpetual. The pressure to succeed could not have been greater. Mills thrived on it.

And it brought commissions, which Mills always welcomed for income. It was about this time that he made a bust of one of the most renowned statesmen of his day:

> **Henry Clay**, U.S. Congressman and sometime Speaker of the House from Kentucky; U.S. Secretary of State; U.S. Senator; twice a candidate for the presidency.[35]

In October 1848 Mills took the life mask of the Honorable **Dixon Hall Lewis** of Alabama.[36] Congress was not in session then, but the senator "had become in a sense, by long residence, a citizen of Washington."[37] He was married to a sister of Mills's stalwart patron, Franklin Harper Elmore, who had recommended Mills so heartily to Calhoun.[38] But Lewis never got to see his likeness. Shortly after sitting for Mills, he went to New York City, where he sickened suddenly and died. The plaster bust was delivered to the senator's grieving widow.[39]

Press coverage in Washington and Charleston, guns from the government, prints by Fenderich and Bohn, steady progress on the model, and commissions for busts: Mills was on top of the world. He could not wait to unveil his fiery, larger-than-life warhorse, even without its rider. The *National Intelligencer* reported:

[T]he modeling of the horse is so nearly completed that the artist has it in contemplation to exhibit it one day in the week following the Christmas holydays.... According to the present calculations of the artist the Statue of Jackson will be entirely completed and placed in Lafayette Square in January, 1850.[40]

Mills was giving himself a year. It would take him four.

But he did, as he had predicted, finish the full-scale model of the imposing horse by Christmas. The sculpture of plaster of Paris on an iron frame weighed three tons.[41] However, Mills decided not to invite the public into his studio "in the week following the Christmas holydays." Rather, the savvy entrepreneur would hold off until March. In March, Zachary Taylor would be inaugurated president. In March, thousands of visitors from all over the country and many from abroad would be in Washington.

NOTES

1 "Ahead of the Mail, Washington, Nov. 22," [Charleston] *Courier*, Nov. 28, 1848, p. 2.
2 "The Jackson Statue," [Washington] *National Intelligencer*, Dec. 11, 1848, p. 3.
3 "The Equestrian Statue of Jackson, at Washington," *Merry's Museum and Parley's Magazine*, Jan. 1, 1853, p. 152. Italics in original.
4 [no title], [Charleston] *Courier*, June 12, 1848, p. 2.
5 "An Hour with Clark Mills," [Washington] *Evening Star*, Dec. 24, 1870, p. 1.
6 Michael Edward Shapiro, *Bronze Casting and American Sculpture, 1850–1900* (Newark, Del.: University of Delaware Press, 1985): 37–38.
7 Letter, Henry Kirke Brown to Lydia Brown, May 18, 1849; Papers of Henry Kirke Bush-Brown, vol. 3: 571; Manuscript Division, Library of Congress, Washington, D.C.
8 "The Jackson Statue," *National Intelligencer*, Dec. 11, 1848, 3.
9 See Bk. 1, Ch. 17.
10 Eleanor Lee Templeman, *Arlington Heritage: Vignettes of a Virginia County* (Arlington, Va.: self-published, 1959): 126–27; and Ludwell Lee Montague, *The Glebe of Fairfax Parish*, at http://arlingtonhistoricalsociety.org/wp-content/uploads/2020/02/1971-2-Glebe.pdf: 8-9. However, neither of these publications is reliable. Both authors write incorrectly that Mills resided at

Glebe House in Arlington County, Virginia, where, supposedly, he cast the Jackson and Washington equestrians, as well as *Freedom* for the U.S. Capitol dome. All documentary evidence contradicts that claim. See Bk. 2.
11 Gilbert Vanderwerken (1810–94), see https://en.wikipedia.org/wiki/Gilbert_Vanderwerken.
12 See, for example, "History of the Jackson Statue," [Washington] *Daily Union*, Jan. 18, 1853, p. 2; and "Clark Mills, The Sculptor," [N.Y.] *Illustrated News*, Jan. 29, 1853, p. 72; and "Sketches of Washington. By Childe Harold. Washington, March 29, 1853. An Hour with Clark Mills, the Sculptor [Concluded]," *Brooklyn Eagle*, Mar. 31, 1853, p. 2; and "Clark Mills at Home," *The Washington Post*, Feb. 7, 1880, p. 2. Regarding Mills's passion for horses, see Bk. 1, Chs. 3 and 17, and Bk. 2.
13 Regarding German ironmongers, see Bk. 1, Chs. 25 and 33.
14 For sessions of the 30th Congress, see https://en.wikipedia.org/wiki/List_of_United_States_Congresses.
15 See Bk. 1, Ch. 16.
16 Remarks of Cong. McClernand. See *Congressional Globe*, 30th Cong., 1st Sess., Aug. 7, 1848, p. 1045.
17 John Adam Dix (1798–1879), see http://bioguide.congress.gov/scripts/biodisplay.pl?index=d000365.
18 *Congressional Globe*, 30th Cong., 1st Sess., July 31, 1848, p. 1015–1016. Also *Senate Journal*, July 31, 1848, p. 513.
19 *Congressional Globe*, 30th Cong., 1st Sess., Aug. 1, 1848, p. 1025. Also *Senate Journal*, Aug. 1, 1848, p. 521.
20 *Congressional Globe*, 30th Cong., 1st Sess., Aug. 7, 1848, p. 1045. Also *House Journal*, Aug. 7, 1848, p. 1177–1179. Thomas Butler King (1800–64), see https://en.wikipedia.org/wiki/Thomas_Butler_King.
21 *Congressional Globe*, 30th Cong., 1st Sess., Aug. 7, 1848, p. 1045.
22 Ibid. Also *House Journal*, Aug. 7, 1848, p. 1177–1179.
23 *Congressional Globe*, 30th Cong., 1st Sess., Aug. 7, 1848, p. 1045. Also *House Journal*, Aug. 7, 1848, p 1177–1179.
24 U.S. Statutes at Large, vol. 9: 340, 30th Cong., 1st Sess., Aug. 11, 1848, Joint Resolution No. 25.
25 Charles Fenderich (1805–89), see https://digital.librarycompany.org/islandora/object/digitool%3A79145.
26 Charles Fenderich, "Design of the Washington Monument," lithographic print, 1846, Prints and Photographs Division, Library of Congress, Washington, D.C.; at http://hdl.loc.gov/loc.pnp/pga.03714.
27 "Mills's Statue of Jackson," [Richmond] *Enquirer*, Nov. 10, 1848, p. 2.
28 Charles Fenderich, "Jackson Monument in the City of Washington," lithographic print, 1848, Prints and Photographs Division, Library of Congress, Washington, D.C.
29 "The Jackson Statue," *National Intelligencer*, Dec. 11, 1848, 3.

30 Jackson's precise words were, "Our federal union, it must be preserved." The quotation would appear correctly in later lithographs and eventually be inscribed on the west face of the pedestal as completed.
31 "The Jackson Statue," [Washington] *Evening Star*, May 3, 1890, p. 9.
32 "View of Washington City and Georgetown," [Washington] *Daily Union*, Feb. 3, 1850, p. 4.
33 Casimir Bohn (1816–83), see https://www.findagrave.com/memorial/149270436/casimir-bohn; and C. Bohn entry, 1850 U.S. Census, 5th Ward, Washington City, D.C., p. 44 (handwritten), p. 22[b] (stamped); NARA M432, roll 56; and Edward Waite, comp. and pub., *The Washington Directory, and Congressional, and Executive Register, for 1850* (Washington, D.C.: Columbus Alexander, Printer, 1850): 8.
34 Casimir Bohn, "View of Washington City and Georgetown," lithographic print, 1849, Prints and Photographs Division, Library of Congress, Washington, D.C.; at http://hdl.loc.gov/loc.pnp/pga.03021.
35 Henry Clay (1777–1852), see https://en.wikipedia.org/wiki/Henry_Clay; and Henry Clay entry, 1850 U.S. Census, Dist. No. 2, Fayette Co., Ky., p. 445 (handwritten), p. 223 (stamped); NARA M432, roll 199: "73, Statesman, $50,000;" and Henry Clay entry, 1850 U.S. Census Slave Schedule, Dist. No. 2, Fayette Co., Ky., p. 673 (handwritten); NARA M432, roll 224; and Waite, *Washington Directory . . . for 1850*, 10. Multiple copies of the life mask survive, attributed to Mills, but not signed. Presumably, Mills made a bust from the mask. See Rosemary Hopkins, *Clark Mills: The First Native American Sculptor* (M.A. thesis, University of Maryland, 1966): 177.
36 Dixon Hall Lewis (1802–48), see http://www.encyclopediaofalabama.org/article/h-1515.
37 [no title], *New York Journal of Commerce*, Nov. 1, 1848, p. 2.
38 Franklin Harper Elmore entry, "Find-A-Grave," at https://www.findagrave.com/memorial/8066729/franklin-harper-elmore.
39 [no title], *New York Journal of Commerce*, Nov. 1, 1848, 2.
40 "The Jackson Statue," *National Intelligencer*, Dec. 11, 1848, 3.
41 "Correspondence of the Baltimore Sun, Washington, May 14, 1849," [Baltimore] *Sun*, May 15, 1849, p. 4.

CHAPTER 22

March 1849

The rooms of Mr. Clarke Mills, near the Treasury Department, have, within the last week, been visited by hundreds.

"Statue of Jackson," [Nantucket, Mass.] *Inquirer*,
Mar. 28, 1849, p. 2; reprinted from the *Baltimore Clipper*.

Mills timed the opening of his studio shrewdly. Reported the *Daily National Whig*:

It seemed as though the population of London had been poured into Washington, so thronged were the avenues and streets.[1]

Added the *Daily Union*:

In the crowd, people might be seen of many different nations, in their national costume, from the North American Indian to the Turk and Persian.[2]

It was the occasion of Zachary Taylor's inauguration as President of the United States. "Hundreds" of visitors crowded into Mills's studio to see his colossal, three-ton steed of plaster balancing on its hind legs.[3] Members of the Jackson Monument Committee, curious to view the progress of their enterprise, were surely among them. The sculptor, eager to demonstrate the stability of his rearing behemoth, delighted in alarming his guests by dangling his own 156 pounds from the horse's elevated front legs.[4]

This was most likely when Mills met two men who would figure prominently in his life. Both were in Washington City during Taylor's swearing-in and both shared a professional interest in Mills's pioneering venture: Carl Ludwig Richter and Joseph Henry.

Short in stature, fair-haired, with a florid face, high forehead and gray eyes, Carl Ludwig Richter could speak almost no English.[5] The 26-year-old was Prussian. He had just sailed into New York harbor four months earlier on board the ship *Elise*, out of Bremen. Future activities of Richter's would suggest that he had participated in the uprising of 1848, or at least espoused its republican ideals. The movement's objective was to increase popular representation in Prussia's governing body. The Kaiser, Friedrich Wilhelm IV, crushed it. Thousands of Prussian intellectuals and political activists fled to the United States.[6]

Richter's self-assurance reflected his privileged upbringing and noteworthy professional training.[7] Referring to himself in the third person, he wrote:

From early youth, he was especially educated to fit him for the pursuit of controlling and managing Foundrys, every variety of castings of compounding, mixing and working of metals.[8]

He was a metallurgist, and metallurgy as a science was more advanced in Prussia than anywhere in the world. Richter had worked at the Royal Foundry in Berlin, casting ordnance for the Prussian government and pieces of the monumental statue of Frederick the Great. Eager to advance in his adopted country, he had already filed his Declaration of Intention to become a citizen. He was working as an engineer at the dry dock in Brooklyn.

Richter had traveled to Washington for the swearing-in celebrations with a friend, William Furniss.[9] Furniss was a writer with a law degree from Harvard.[10] He had recently spent two years in Europe—"prior to the Revolutions of 1848"—including time in Prussia, and was publishing books about his travels.[11] It appears that the New Yorker knew enough German to serve as Richter's translator. The lawyer/author evidently enjoyed sufficient reputation in the nation's capital to introduce his émigré friend to men of influence, military as well as civilian. That was Richter's purpose, to make connections in Washington. He had an invention he wanted the U.S. government to buy: a revolutionary new kind of furnace for casting bronze. He summarized it this way:

> *My furnace has the advantage over all other furnaces, in this that it consumes most of its own smoke, is without a chimney, and distributes and equalizes the heat so that the whole mass of metal in the furnace is subjected to equal temperature and all melts at once, so that no part thereof is scorched and burned up whilst other portions are not in the fluid state.*[12]

Unabashedly, the newcomer proclaimed his goal:

> *I can produce cannons for the U.S. far superior to any now in America and not surpassed by any even in the Prussian Artillery.*[13]

The cannons of the Prussian Artillery were renowned as the best in the world. But Richter's aspirations were more than military. He also wanted to create works of sculpture and cast them in bronze.[14] He would have been eager to see Mills's much-publicized prancing horse and make his expertise—and availability—known to the sculptor. For his part, Mills—thanks to his rigorous self-education—was surely familiar with the outstanding international reputation of the Royal Prussian Foundry. Its castings of superior quality included not only military hardware, but works of fine art, too. Although Mills was still far from the casting stage of his project, meeting a foundryman who had worked on the colossal *Frederick the Great* would have quickened his pulse. Though not yet finished, that statue-to-be was already world famous.

It was to soar 44 feet into the air. The horse and rider, over 18 feet tall, would stand upon a granite pedestal of four tiers. Bas-reliefs of historic scenes would cover the sides of the base and numerous, life-size, standing and mounted figures in dynamic poses would encircle it. Prussia's preeminent sculptor, Christian Daniel Rauch, had

March 1849

Engraving of Christian Daniel Rauch's stupendous memorial to Frederick the Great, dedicated in Berlin in 1851. Carl Ludwig Richter assisted in casting the statue at the Royal Prussian Foundry during the 1840s. Richter emigrated to the United States in 1848 and was employed at the Washington Navy Yard. Mills met the ambitious young foundryman the following year, most likely during the inaugural festivities of President Zachary Taylor. (Alamy)

fashioned the model and in 1845 Karl Ludwig Friebel had begun casting it in bronze at the Royal Prussian Foundry.[15] One of the workers there was young Carl Ludwig Richter.

The foreign-born engineer's brief sojourn in Washington would yield quick results. Very soon afterwards, he would be hired as a draftsman in the Bureau of Ordnance and Hydrography at the Washington Navy Yard.[16] A year after that, in a letter to "Professor Henry," Richter would write:

I have had the honor of being introduced to You by Mr. William Furniss of New York who is a grad friend of Mine, at the time of the Inguration of President Taylor. At the time I was introduced I could not converse with you on account of being unable to speak the English

Language, but now I would be pleased to talk with You in regard to my Furnace.[17]

Joseph Henry, a stocky man of 51, square-jawed and clean-shaven, was the country's most revered scientist and inventor. He had come to Washington from the University of New Jersey (today's Princeton) in December of 1846, when the Board of Regents of the Smithsonian Institution invited him to be its first Secretary. Henry resided with his wife and four children on 10th Street, a few blocks southwest of the red sandstone "castle" being built to house the fledgling Institution. So far, only the east wing of the Norman Gothic building designed by James Renwick was completed. When finished in 1855, however, it was to contain an apartment for the Henry family.[18]

The Smithsonian had been chartered by Congress as an establishment dedicated to the "increase and diffusion of knowledge."[19] Secretary Henry was fulfilling that mandate with gusto. Although his own achievements lay principally in the realm of electro-magnetism, he corresponded with all manner of scientists and explorers and met with many of them personally, in Europe as well as at home. He would confer more than once with the impressive young metallurgist/inventor from Prussia.

Henry would also have multiple exchanges with Mills. The Secretary was keeping an eye on the progress of the autodidact's ground-breaking enterprise.[20]

It may have been about this time—spring of 1849—that *Joseph Henry* sat for Mills to take a plaster cast of his face and skull for a bust. Rather than adhere to the neoclassical style of depicting his distinguished subject in a toga—which Mills had always done—he represented the man of science in a coat, collar and necktie of the day.[21] It was the first expression of the naturalistic style Mills was to advocate so assertively for American sculpture. However, he did wrap the professor's shoulders in elegant drapery which, intended perhaps to evoke an academic gown, nevertheless resembled the

Mills's plaster bust of Joseph Henry, ca. 1849, the sculptor's earliest known work in a naturalistic rather than classical style. Mills represented the renowned scientist and first Secretary of the Smithsonian Institution in a coat, collar and necktie of the day. However, he wrapped Henry's shoulders in drapery that—intended perhaps to evoke an academic gown—nevertheless resembles the classical emblem of everlasting fame. (Smithsonian American Art Museum)

"classical flourish" Mills had seen on Houdon's bust of Lafayette in the Virginia capitol.

Since March 4th fell on a Sunday, Zachary Taylor's inauguration took place on the following Monday. That morning, the *Daily National Whig* reported:

> The skies were closed in by a heavy mantle of clouds, that every moment threatened snow or rain, and the wind blew keenly from the North East, the precursor of an old fashioned snow storm. The mutterings, however, of the impending storm were not heeded by the multitudes, and fortunately for the occasion, the heavens neither threw down rain or snow until after the ceremonies were ended.[22]

The rugged general, famous for his exploits in the recent war with Mexico, swore the oath of office at half past noon on the east portico of the Capitol before a throng estimated at "near thirty thousand persons."[23] His address was brief.

Then the new Chief Executive, accompanied by out-going President James K. Polk, the former vice president, and the mayor of Washington, rode in an open barouche (braving the cold) down Pennsylvania Avenue to the Executive Mansion. Thousands of cheering supporters filled the sidewalks, balconies, porches and windows along the parade route. When the procession reached the Irving Hotel, where Polk had lodgings, the ex-president descended from the carriage and bade his parting farewell.

By evening, snow was falling, thick and heavy.[24] But ticketholders were not deterred from attending the two balls. One attendee, Benjamin B. French, would enter into his diary that both events *"were numerously attended."*[25] The Grand Inaugural Ball was for members of the party of "Old Rough and Ready;" that was the Whig party. An "extensive saloon" had been erected on Judiciary Square to house the affair. Though bonfires were lit, it was the crush of bodies that kept attendees from freezing. The National Inauguration Ball Without Distinction of Party took place in the spacious assembly rooms at Jackson Hall on Pennsylvania Avenue.[26] Elbow-to-elbow, revelers perspired from the potent drink and multiple blazing stoves.

The ticket price of "ten dollars cash" was assailed in the press as outrageous; however, event managers argued that the "enormous price is necessary to secure a 'respectable audience.'" Besides, all of the proceeds, "after the payment of expenses, are to be equally divided between the two orphan asylums of the city."[27] The plethora of dishes displayed in copious extravagance on long tables at the two locations dazzled attendees, who were too numerous to partake of the feast without an indelicate struggle. Punch and champagne flowed abundantly into early morning hours. General Taylor attended both inaugural celebrations.

Whether Clark Mills or Carl Ludwig Richter or Joseph Henry attended either ball, where they may have met one another, is far from unlikely, but not recorded in any historical source. Nor can it be proven that either Richter or Henry visited Mills in his studio during his "open house"—although both men certainly did so before the end of the year. Nevertheless, documentary evidence points convincingly to Taylor's inauguration as the occasion when these two inventors with keen professional interest in Mills's undertaking entered the sculptor's life. Richter's crucial impact on Mills's career would begin within months. The important role Henry was to play, on the other hand, would not occur until long after the halcyon days of the "American Michelangelo" had faded.

The *Baltimore Clipper* report that Mills's studio had been "visited by hundreds," also predicted that the foundation stone of his already-famous statue would be laid in Lafayette Square on July fourth and that his *Jackson* would be dedicated "on the 5th of January, [1850]."[28] Evidently, Mills's work on the model of the horseman was progressing well enough for the sculptor to anticipate having the memorial finished and erected on its pedestal within ten months. The estimate was pitifully naïve. Mills knew nothing about casting bronze.

NOTES

1 "The Inauguration Ceremonies," [Washington] *Daily National Whig*, Mar. 6, 1849, p. 2.
2 "Inauguration Day," [Washington] *Daily Union*, Mar. 6, 1849, p. 3.
3 "Statue of Jackson," [Nantucket, Mass.] *Inquirer*, Mar. 28, 1849, p. 2; reprinted from the *Baltimore Clipper*.
4 "Clark Mills," [Charleston] *Courier* (quoting the *Camden* [S.C.] *Journal*), May 8, 1850, p. 2; and "Mr. Mills," [Washington] *Daily Union*, May 1, 1850, p. 3; and "The Jackson Statue," [Washington] *National Intelligencer*, Dec. 11, 1848, p. 3.
5 For full documentation on Richter, see John Philip Colletta, "'The Workman of C. Mills:' Carl Ludwig Richter and the Statue of Andrew Jackson in Lafayette Park," *Washington History*, vol. 23 (2011): 3–35. The first source note of the article catalogs the scholarly literature published about Mills and his Jackson

equestrian, late 19th to late 20th centuries. Subsequent notes correct many errors that have appeared and reappeared in that secondary literature. When this article appeared, the author had not yet found Richter's baptismal record (see n. 7).

6 "German revolutions of 1848–1849," at https://en.wikipedia.org/wiki/German_revolutions_of_1848%E2%80%931849#Prussia.

7 Baptismal record, Carl Ludwig Richter, Apr. 18, 1823, microfilmed duplicates of Evangelical Church Registers of Grossmonra, Sachsen, Prussia, 1800–74, rolls 1273424 and 1273222; Family History Library, Salt Lake City, Utah. Richter's father, Benjamin Gottfried Richter, was an economist and the leaseholder of a baronial estate. Richter's godparents were: 1) a Doctor of Medicine and Inspector of the Cabinet of Natural History in Dresden (by proxy); 2) another Doctor of Medicine; 3) the wife of a leaseholder of the Grand Duke of Weimar; and 4) the wife of the Lord Mayor of Grossmonra. The godparents of Richter's eight siblings were also members of the higher socio-economic class—schoolmasters, church pastors, court officials, government administrators, estate managers and property owners, merchants, and church cantors and musicians, or their wives. These associations, and Richter's education and training at Royal institutions, reflect an aristocratic life. The author thanks Professor Roger Minert of Brigham Young University, Provo, Utah, for finding and translating this and other records pertaining to Richter, his parents, and his siblings, 2013–14.

8 Richter's first memorial to Congress, Jan. 24, 1853; Legislative Records, 32nd Cong., 2nd Sess., box SEN 32A-H19, Committee on Public Buildings; Records of the U.S. Senate, RG 46; NARA.

9 Letter, C. Ludwig Richter to Professor Henry, Oct. 22, 1850; Joseph Henry Collection, Archives of the Smithsonian Institution, Washington, D.C.

10 William Furniss (1821–82), see https://openlibrary.org/authors/OL2442630A/William_Furniss; and W. Stewart Wallace, comp., *A Dictionary of North American Authors Deceased before 1950* (Toronto: Ryerson Press, 1951): 162; and William P. Furnace [sic] entry, 1850 U.S. Census, 12th Ward, New York City, N.Y. Co., N.Y., p. 108 (handwritten), p. 54[b] (stamped); NARA M432, roll 548.

11 William Furniss, *Landvoieglee: Or Views across the Sea* (New York: D. Appleton & Co., 1850): iv.

12 Richter's first memorial to Congress.

13 Letter, C. Ludwig Richter to Hon. Mr. Conrad, Secretary of War, Jan. 28, 1852; Special File, Inventions, Class 1A, no. 104; Records of the Office of the Chief of Ordnance, RG 156; NARA.

14 Colletta, "'The Workman of C. Mills' . . . ," 3–35.

15 "Equestrian Statue of Frederick the Great, at Berlin," *Gleason's Pictorial Drawing Room Companion*, vol. 1, no. 21 (Nov. 22, 1851): 336. See also "Equestrian Statue of Frederick the Great," at https://en.wikipedia.org/wiki/Equestrian_statue_of_Frederick_the_Great.

16 Carl Ludwig Richter (1824–66), see Colletta, "The Workman of C. Mills' . . . ," 3–35.
17 Letter, C. Ludwig Richter to Professor Henry, Oct. 22, 1850.
18 Joseph Henry (1797–1878), see https://siarchives.si.edu/history/joseph-henry; and J. Henry entry, 1850 U.S. Census, Ward 3, Washington City, Washington Co., D.C., p. 330 (handwritten), p. 165[b] (stamped); NARA M432, roll 56; and Alfred Hunter, comp. and pub., *The Washington and Georgetown Directory, Strangers' Guide-Book for Washington, and Congressional and Clerks' Register* (Washington, D.C., printed by Kirkwood & McGill, 1853): 48. For physical description of Henry, see Mills's bust of him in the Smithsonian American Art Museum, Washington, D.C., and photograph printed in Richard E. Stamm, *The Castle, An Illustrated History of the Smithsonian Building*, 2nd ed. (Washington, D.C.: Smithsonian Books, 2012): 39.
19 "Smithsonian: Our History," at https://www.si.edu/about/history.
20 Journal of Joseph Henry, entry of July 28, 1853; Joseph Henry Papers, Archives of the Smithsonian Institution, Washington, D.C. See also Bk. 1, Ch. 25, and Bk. 2.
21 Today a copy of this bust is in the Smithsonian American Art Museum, Washington, D.C.
22 "The Inauguration Ceremonies," [Washington] *Daily National Whig*, Mar. 6, 1849, p. 2.
23 "Inauguration Day," [Washington] *Daily Union*, Mar. 6, 1849, p. 3.
24 For descriptions of Taylor's inauguration, see "The 16th Presidential Inauguration, Zachary Taylor, March 05, 1849," at www.inaugural.senate.gov/about/past-inaugural-ceremonies/16th-inaugural-ceremonies/index.html#theme; "U.S. Presidential Inaugurations: Zachary Taylor," at www.loc.gov/rr/program/bib/inaugurations/taylor/index.html; and "UVA MILLER CENTER, U.S. Presidents/Zachary Taylor," at https://millercenter.org/president/taylor.
25 Donald B. Cole and John J. McDonough, eds., *Witness to the Young Republic, A Yankee's Journal, 1828–1870* (Hanover and London: University Press of New England, 1989): 209.
26 "Grand Inauguration Ball," and "National Inauguration Ball Without Distinction of Party," [Washington] *Daily National Whig*, Mar. 1, 1849, p. 3.
27 Ibid.; and "Taylor Republicanism," *New London* [Conn.] *Democrat*, Feb. 24, 1849, p. 2.
28 "Statue of Jackson," [Nantucket, Mass.] *Inquirer*, Mar. 28, 1849, 2. The text reads, "on the 5th of January, 1859," which is obviously a typographical error for 1850.

CHAPTER 23
March–May 1849

> A CARD.—*The undersigned respectfully informs the citizens of and visitors to Washington that to-day will be the last exhibition of the Equestrian Statue of Gen. Jackson until it shall have been finished, when the public will be notified of his studio being reopened to visitors.*   CLARK MILLS, *Sculptor*
>
> "A Card," [Washington] *Daily National Intelligencer*, May 12, 1849, p. 3.

The colossal horse had been on display since Zachary Taylor's inauguration. During those ten weeks of "open house," in addition to welcoming the curious public, Mills had been working on the full-scale plaster model of the rider. Asked how he managed to depict Jackson accurately when he had never seen the man, Mills explained:

> "It was done in this way: All the portraits, busts and other representations of the hero were brought to my studio. I examined all of them. I took the best features of each one. From Power's bust I got the mouth and hair. From Jevelot I got the nose and forehead. I submitted the head to Gen. Armstrong, . . . who was a bosom friend of 'Old Hickory.' He said it was perfect."[1]

From the National Museum, Mills borrowed Jackson's uniform and sword.[2] The "National Museum" was housed in the grand hall on the top floor of the U.S. Patent Office building. All manner of historical artifacts and natural curiosities were exhibited there in glass-doored cabinets.[3] Mills "stuffed out" Jackson's uniform "to give him an idea of the figure."[4]

Response to Mills's "Card" was prodigious. The Baltimore *Sun* reported:

> A large number of visitors were, on Saturday, present at the studio of Clark Mills, Esqr., for the purpose of surveying the splendid horse, intended for the "Jackson Monument." The noble animal is, at present, represented in a statue of plaster of paris over an iron skeleton, in a prancing attitude. A perfect balance is obtained by throwing the hind feet under the centre of the body. . . . Eminent judges, from all parts of the country, pronounce the form and symmetry of the "Jackson horse" to be exquisitely fine.[5]

At the close of that raucous Saturday, Mills padlocked the gate of his compound and hung a sign over his studio door: "NO ADMISSION ON ANY PRETENSE." He was facing the challenging task of mounting the ponderous, outsized horseman on the ingeniously balanced charger. Nevertheless, one afternoon—despite the terse injunction he had posted—Mills did admit an uninvited caller who, that evening, would send his wife a detailed account of his visit:

> *Washington, May 18, 1849*
>
> *Dearest Lydia,*
>
> *. . . After dinner I called on Mr. Mills, native self-made sculptor of whose works Dr. Wilson of Charleston was so much enamored and who has received $12,000 from Congress for modeling and casting in bronze the equestrian statue of Gen. Jackson. Uncle Sam provides the metal.*
>
>> [In fact, Mills was being paid by the Jackson Monument Committee, not Congress, and the amount was $12,500, not $12,000.][6]
>
> *On coming in sight of his "sanctum" I saw in large letters over the entrance: No admission on any pretense. . . . On arriving at a picket*

fence with which the place was baracaded [sic] I found the gate locked but the door of the studio was open, and a tall lean looking figure sat leaning back in his chair at the back side of the entrance. I ventured to address it to the effect that I had taken the liberty, though perhaps too great a one, to visit his studio, but hoped like Paul Pry, I did not intrude.

[Paul Pry, the protagonist of an eponymous English comedy, was mischievous and consumed by curiosity.[7]]

The figure in the chair got up and I heard it say something about "ague fits." That I know was a point made for I too had suffered with the fever and ague and as this figure emerged slowly, slowly, from the door towards the locked gate, I saw he was a victim of that shaking disease. I ventured at all hazards to hint my name and profession, thinking it might prove a passport through this very singular looking place, as in fact it did, and the figure gave me to understand, I can hardly say how, that he was Mr. Mills the sculptor; said he was glad to see me and begged that I would excuse the fever and ague, which of course I did.

Tall and striking, with an impeccable goatee, high forehead, and luxuriant, curly brown locks, Henry Kirke Brown looked more like an art patron than an artist. In fact, though, he, like Mills, was the son of a "small farmer." Born in Massachusetts, roughly 200 miles east of Mills's New York birthplace, Brown was 35, one year Mills's senior.[8] It must have taken Mills by surprise when the aristocratic-looking gentleman at his door ventured *"to hint"* at his *"name and profession."*

Mills worked outside of the social and professional network of America's preeminent sculptors: Greenough, Powers and Crawford. He did not frequent the country's leading art circles of Boston, New York and Philadelphia. Nor had he ever corresponded with any of these artists. Nevertheless, he was familiar with them and their works—some of which he had seen with his own eyes in Washington.[9] Greenough, Powers and Crawford, though residents of Italy, enjoyed the coverage of celebrities in the American press. They were

HENRY KIRKE BROWN.

American sculptor Henry Kirke Brown at age 37, two years after his visit to Mills's studio. Brown studied in Italy, but repatriated and embraced naturalism rather than classicism. His statues were among the first to depict American themes and to be cast in bronze in the United States. Achieving national prominence, Brown was Mills's arch rival and most strident critic. (*Sartain's Union Magazine of Literature and Art*, vol. VIII, no. 2 (Feb. 1851): 135)

a source of national pride. People knew their names. Lithographic prints of their works, framed behind glass, hung in parlors throughout the United States.[10] Neither had Mills ever met Henry Kirke Brown. But he would have known—from newspapers and journals—that his distinguished caller had spent four years of rigorous training in Italy, and now, rapidly, was earning a position of distinction in the art establishment of his homeland.

Brown had made a radical decision for an aspiring American sculptor. Unlike his elder compatriots who remained in Italy, he had returned to the United States to make his career here. That was in 1846. Mills was in Charleston making plaster busts at the time. What Mills may not have known yet is that he and his surprise visitor embraced the same patriotic ambition: to create an identifiably American art representing American subjects realistically, rather than "ideally" in the neoclassical mold. More than that, both sculptors sought to have their statues cast in bronze . . . in the United States.[11]

Henry Kirke Brown would become Mills's arch rival and arch critic.

Just the previous year, 1848, he had been commissioned by the American Art-Union in New York City to create a statuette, not in marble, but in bronze, and the subject was to be, not an allegorical figure or eminent statesman, but an American Indian. The request was unprecedented. Brown leased a lot in Brooklyn and built a studio, a small foundry, and a house for himself and his wife, Lydia. Then he took off for Mackinaw Island in Lake Superior to sketch American Indians.[12]

What had brought Brown to Washington this May of 1849 was to make a relief portrait of the new president, Zachary Taylor. The image would be used on a bronze peace medal to be given to native American chiefs.[13] Since Mills's studio was literally "just around the corner" from the Executive Mansion, Brown seized the opportunity to satisfy his curiosity about his fellow countryman, the self-taught ingénue who had aroused such a frenzy of praise and controversy. He wanted to see for himself the fantastic charger that balanced on two legs. His letter to Lydia continued:

> *We entered a room with one window in it and two doors one to the main studio and one to the street. In this little room were two busts, old boots, a few books, fever and ague medicines, a hat full of eggs, his sketches for the great work, and a variety of other objects. He left a moment to arrange the light in the main studio, then he showed me in and "won an unco sight,"...*

[Scottish: "What a strange sight."]

> *... this immense horse standing upon its hind legs balancing himself with an enormous tail which could not contain less than a barrel of plaster, but balance the thing did, for he had a plumb bob suspended for every one to range for themselves, and see that there was no more favor shown the head than the tail, and that there was an equal*

amount of plaster on each side of that dividing line showing clearly that they must balance. He then pointed out by measurement wherein the Parthenon marbles are wrong and wherein his is right.

[The marble frieze of the Parthenon contained depictions of horsemen that artists revered as perfect specimens of high classical art. To another visitor some years later, Mills would say: "The ancient sculptors knew very little about the horse, and their representations of that noble animal are for the most part wretched burlesques."[14]]

I could not help wondering how difficult it was to measure soul by square and rule. This sculptor, at all events, does not know the length, height, or proportion of that essential quality.

His eloquence was very striking though after all I was only convinced that he had outlined to tell Dr. Wilson he would do (i.e.) make a fool of himself, during his speech which lasted some time. My eyes wandered around the room. I saw hanging up on the walls casts from dissections of various parts of horses like beef to dry. The tools with which he works as you must know he models in plaster, not clay, they consisted of two deck scrapers, one with and one without teeth, a hatchet and hand saw, masons hods and trowels. The manner in which he uses these I am yet ignorant of.

[Inventive and uncommitted to established norms, Mills did not limit his tools to the ones traditionally used by sculptors. He employed any implement he found to be serviceable.]

I was then shown into another small apartment corresponding with the first, in this he had a cookstove and various utensils, he informed me that all his arrangements in the culinary line were under his own supervision. I could but applaud his sagacity, as otherwise some person out of solicitude for his coming into his inheritance in another world, as soon as possible might take it into his head to poison him, that he would esteem it a great loss to the arts. He also informed me that there was another small room upstairs, which was provided with a bed, that room was plastered, and he slept in it. I then, like one enchanted, followed him into the back yard, to the stable where he kept his horse from which he had modeled. Then we returned into the large studio. There I saw the boots of the old Hero Jackson. These were partly chopped out in plaster, but the hewing out he informed me was the rough part, that he kept a nigger for that.

[Mills was very likely referring to Philip Reid.]

At the feet of these boots, (so to speak) lay the half formed head of the General over which the boots seemed to be enjoying a temporary triumph, the body too stood aloof from the other members of the same family, and seemed perfectly indifferent to the decapitated poll beside it, no more than if it were in no way related to it. You must understand that these parts are roughed out in plaster and finished separately and are then to meet on their proper footing, and be joined, not again to be sundered. . . . He showed me back into the first little room, where was located a very fat Dutchman and a big dog.

[This "Dutchman" has not been identified. Needing a huge iron armature for his model, Mills had tapped into the renowned expertise of German-American ironmongers, as he would do again when searching for a founder to cast his statue.[15]]

Brown could afford to be snide; he was one step ahead of his host. He had already imported two founders from France to his little foundry in Brooklyn and had learned a lot from them. The Frenchmen had molded, cast in bronze, finished, and patinated several of Brown's works: a few miniature American Indian busts and a statuette of an Indian hunter holding a bow and reaching for an arrow. They were small pieces. They could be displayed on a parlor table. But they were unprecedented. These sculptures proclaimed Brown's determination to create bronze works of American subjects in a naturalistic style—though they did still reflect the influence of his classical training. Brown had also produced a classical figurine of a girl spinning, "filatrice" in Italian. The *Choosing of the Arrow* and the *Filatrice* would become the American Art-Union's bronze editions of 1849 and 1850. Brown, in short, was in the vanguard of fine art bronze casting in America. He had hands-on experience. Mills did not.[16]

Just two months prior to this inspection of Mills's studio, Brown had completed a model for a monumental statue of former New York State governor, DeWitt Clinton.[17] The committee that commissioned the work was now soliciting donations to have it cast in bronze. The figure would stand 10½ feet tall, a much larger statue than Brown's little foundry could handle. Eventually, therefore, he would need what Mills needed: a foundry of industrial proportion in the United States with workers capable of casting larger-than-life statuary.

Mills may have told Brown that he expected to cast his Jackson in the foundry at the Washington Navy Yard. Or, perhaps sensing a rival in his visitor, Mills opted not to mention that. Regardless, Brown's missive to his wife betrayed no fear of competition from "*the native self-made sculptor.*" Nor was his sanguine disdain of Mills's efforts groundless. Use of the Navy Yard foundry was still an assumption, not a fact. And even if the expectation were to be realized, who at the Navy Yard knew anything about casting a bronze statue?

Brown closed his account to his wife:

I cannot conceive of a worse place for a sensible person to be in than this same Washington at any time of the year.... I will continue to spoil paper [scribble letters] as long as I stay in this old hole.

H.[18]

Scarcely was Brown out the door when Mills paused his efforts to attach the larger-than-life rider to the larger-than-life horse, locked his gate, and scurried across the city to the Navy Yard. Exciting news had reached him. The naïve dreamer's education in the casting of heavy metal was about to begin.

NOTES

1. "Clark Mills at Home," *The Washington Post*, Feb. 7, 1880, p. 2. "Jevelot" should be "Gevelot;" see Bk. 1, Ch. 15, n. 14. Gen. Robert Armstrong (1792–1854), who served under Jackson in the War of 1812 and Creek War, owned Washington's *Daily Union* newspaper; see Bk. 1, Prologue. Hiram Powers had a correspondent in Washington, Boyd Reilly, who kept him abreast of matters regarding the proposed Jackson equestrian. When Powers learned that Mills had won the commission for the statue and then used his bust of Jackson as a portrait for it, he was furious. See Richard P. Wunder, *Hiram Powers, Vermont Sculptor, 1805–1873* (Newark, Del.: University of Delaware Press, 1991), vol. 1: 160. However, Wunder's account of how Mills got the commissions for the Jackson and Washington statues contains several erroneous statements, for which he cites no source. It appears that Reilly was misinformed and passed on false rumors to Powers, which the historian Wunder (like Powers) assumed to be facts. Nevertheless, it is true that Powers (like Henry Kirke Brown and other established sculptors of that time) was indignant that such important commissions went to a novice sculptor with no formal training and no important works to his credit.
2. "History of the Jackson Statue," [Washington] *Daily Union*, Jan. 18, 1853, p. 2.
3. Ernest B. Furgurson, *Freedom Rising, Washington in the Civil War* (New York: Alfred A. Knopf, 2004): 240.
4. "The Jackson Statue," [Washington] *Evening Star*, May 3, 1890, p. 9.
5. "Correspondence from Washington, May 14, 1849," [Baltimore] *Sun*, May 15, 1849, p. 4.
6. See Bk. 1, Ch. 19. "Dr. Wilson" was a member of a large South Carolina clan of well-heeled planters. See Samuel Wilson entry, 1850 U.S. Census, Parishes of St. Philip's and St. Michael's, Charleston, S.C., p. 46 (handwritten), p. 141[b] (stamped); NARA M432, roll 850; and Dr. Saml Wilson entry, 1850 U.S. Census Slave Schedule, Parishes of St. Philip's and St. Michael's, Charleston, S.C., p. [107?] (handwritten); NARA M432, roll 862.
7. "Paul Pry (play)," at https://en.wikipedia.org/wiki/Paul_Pry_(play).
8. Henry Kirke Brown (1814–86), see https://en.wikipedia.org/wiki/Henry_Kirke_Brown; and Michael Edward Shapiro, *Bronze Casting and American Sculpture, 1850–1900* (Newark, Del.: University of Delaware Press, 1984): 44–50; and Cleaveland, "Henry Kirke Brown," *Sartain's Union Magazine of Literature and Art*, vol, VIII, no. 2 (Feb. 1851): 135–38.
9. See Bk. 1, Chs. 15 and 19.

10 See Bk. 1, Chs. 9 and 16.
11 Shapiro, *Bronze Casting*, 44; and Wayne Craven, "Henry Kirke Brown in Italy, 1842–1846," *The American Art Journal*, vol. 1, no. 1 (1969): 65–77.
12 Shapiro, *Bronze Casting*, 45.
13 "Zachary Taylor Indian Peace Medal," New-York Historical Society, at https://emuseum.nyhistory.org/objects/5385/zachary-taylor-indian-peace-medal.
14 "An Hour with Clark Mills," [Washington] *Evening Star*, Dec. 24, 1870, p. 2.
15 See Bk. 1, Chs. 25 and 33.
16 Shapiro, *Bronze Casting*, 46–47; and Catherine Hoover Voorsanger and John K. Howat, eds., *Art and the Empire City: New York, 1825–1861* (New Haven and London: Yale University Press, 2000): 155.
17 Shapiro, *Bronze Casting*, 48–49.
18 Letter, Henry Kirke Brown to Lydia Brown, May 18, 1849; Papers of Henry Kirke Bush-Brown, vol. 3: 567–75; Manuscript Division, Library of Congress, Washington, D.C.

CHAPTER 24
May 1849

The horse is to be finished in bronze, from brass cannon captured by the Old Hero, which will be cast at the foundery of our Navy Yard. The vessel with these guns has just arrived.

"Correspondence from Washington, May 14, 1849,"
[Baltimore] *Sun*, May 15, 1849, p. 4.

Making his way across Washington, Mills traversed a vibrant neighborhood southeast of the Capitol that was totally unlike "the Avenue." Called Navy Yard Hill, it clustered outside the gatehouse of the military installation. Tight, two-story frame rowhouses shared city squares with kitchen gardens, fruit orchards, tethered milk cows, goats and hogs, roaming geese and chickens, natural springs, old growth trees, fields of grain and fields of weeds. Marine Corps barracks occupied a long block of 8th Street. They enclosed a parade ground with the Commandant's elegant house anchoring the northern end. In summer the residents of this working-class community gathered to enjoy the stirring patriotic airs of the Marine Band; public concerts were given weekly.

Humble houses of God met the needs of White churchgoers who were Baptist, Episcopal and Methodist. An African Methodist Episcopal Church served local residents of color. Presbyterians and Catholics had to walk a few blocks beyond Navy Yard Hill to worship. Men attended convocations in the Odd Fellows Hall and Masonic Hall, while women with baskets on their arm—every Monday, Wednesday and Friday—circulated among the stalls of the Eastern Market at 6th and E Streets. The Navy Yard was the neighborhood's employer. Wrote one visitor in 1842:

There is no commerce, and what trade there is, consists in coal and wood, and the produce of the river, fish and oyster. The houses look ancient and time worn.[1]

Mills came to the high brick wall surrounding the naval compound. Situated on the northern bank of the Eastern Branch (the Anacostia, today), it was the foremost metalworking center of the U.S. Navy. Founded in 1799 as a facility to build warships, it began developing ordnance only after disaster bloodied the deck of the U.S. Steam Frigate *Princeton* on February 28, 1844. President John Tyler and about 500 military and civilian officials, foreign dignitaries, and their families were embarked on the *Princeton* for a demonstration of a huge new naval cannon. Called the "Peacemaker," the gun was a 12-inch smoothbore muzzle loader of wrought iron. After several successful firings, it exploded, killing seven men, including the Secretaries of the Navy and State. About 20 other passengers and crewmen were injured. This catastrophe spurred the Navy to seek a more scientific system for determining the worthiness of ordnance for its ships—here at the Washington Navy Yard.[2]

And here, at last, the vessel bringing the bronze guns that Congress had given to the Jackson Monument Committee had arrived. The "Old Hero" himself had seized the four cannons and two mortars from the Spanish on the battlefield at Pensacola, Florida, in 1818. Lieutenant Colonel George Talcott had found them at the arsenal in Watervliet, New York, in 1846.[3] Since then, Mills and the Committee members had been looking forward to this day. They were eager to see the artillery pieces. Their other concern at the Navy Yard, however—use of the foundry to cast their statue—remained unsettled.

During the weeks of Mills's "open house," when Washingtonians were gaping at his huge rearing horse of white plaster and the sculptor was modeling the heroic-size general, ordnance experts at the Navy Yard were considering the Committee's request. The contract

Drawing of the Washington Navy Yard as seen from the Eastern Branch (or Anacostia River). Carl Ludwig Richter was working there as a civilian engineer in the Bureau of Ordnance and Hydrography in 1849 when Mills hired him to build a foundry to cast his statue of Andrew Jackson. (*Morrison's Stranger's Guide to the City of Washington*, 1842, p. 44)

with Mills stipulated specifically that the statue was to be "cast in Washington, D.C." That fact had already been made public over a year earlier.[4] Just recently, though, the Baltimore *Sun* had been more specific: "The horse . . . will be cast at the foundery of our Navy Yard."[5] Obviously, the Jackson devotees were pinning their hopes on the only facility in the national capital capable of casting a work as large as theirs.

The socially well-connected Committee members had taken the obvious action. Just as they had turned to the Chief of the Army's Ordnance Department for cost-free metal, they appealed to the Commandant of the Navy Yard for a cost-free foundry. The Commandant was Captain Charles S. McCauley, a decorated veteran of the War of 1812.[6] McCauley referred the Committee's request to the Chief of the Bureau of Ordnance and Hydrography, Captain Lewis Warrington.

Warrington, too, had had a long and distinguished career, including meritorious service as a commodore during the War of 1812. In 1844, when the Secretary of the Navy was killed in the Peacemaker explosion, Warrington had fulfilled temporarily the duties of that cabinet post. He was 67 years old now and all matters relating to ordnance at the Navy Yard fell within his command.[7] Warrington's subordinate officer in charge of the ordnance establishment, including its foundry, was a young lieutenant named John Adolphus Dahlgren.[8]

Dahlgren showed a genius for weapons design, production and systematic testing. Younger by a generation than his superior officers, he was a leader in the vanguard of the emerging science of metallurgy. Warrington recognized Dahlgren's brilliance and gave him liberal support for his experiments. Within a few years, Dahlgren himself would be promoted to Chief of the Bureau of Ordnance and Hydrography, and later serve as the Navy Yard's Commandant. To history, he would be remembered as "the father of American naval ordnance."[9]

Mills reached the Yard's signature gatehouse. Designed in 1804 by the preeminent architect, Benjamin Henry Latrobe, it was an amalgam of Greek revival elements. Built of brick stuccoed to resemble stone, the building housed two guardrooms, one on either side of a central 40-foot-long passageway lined with Doric columns. Surmounting the gatehouse, a large marble eagle grasped an anchor in his talons.[10] Marines much younger than Mills stood sentry to his left and right as he passed through the iron gates.

Suddenly the sights and sounds of Washington's principal industrial enterprise opened up before the civilian visitor. The Navy Yard's rolling mill, tilt hammer, foundry, factories, and workshops manufactured an array of items: anchors, block and tackle, chain cables, shot, shells and cannon balls, gun carriages, steam propulsion machinery and small arms. Large guns, however, such as cannons, the Navy Yard would not be equipped to cast for another eight years. The most prominent structures Mills saw were the two "ship sheds." Resembling gargantuan barns, they miniaturized the buildings around them. Sheltered beneath their roofs, vessels were repaired and fitted with armament. Shipbuilding operations, though, had been transferred to naval installations on the Atlantic coast years earlier.

Mills witnessed the bustle of blacksmiths, carpenters, joiners, riggers, armorers, plumbers and painters. The Navy Yard was manned by several hundred men. They were naval personnel and civilians, skilled workers—called mechanics—and laborers, White, free Black and enslaved. Monday through Saturday, the call of a trumpet proclaiming "Reveille" (known as "morning colors") summoned the men to work from Navy Yard Hill. The duty day lasted ten hours. Then the clarion signal of "Retreat" sounded ("evening colors") and the men passed through the Latrobe Gate and dispersed back into Navy Yard Hill. All of them, regardless of rank or post, shared the same brutal working conditions—ear-splitting din, smoke- and dust-filled air, cold in winter, torrid mugginess in August, and ubiquitous hazards. Ordnance testing was a dangerous business. Despite Lieutenant Dahlgren's precautions, explosions did occasionally occur, injuring a worker or even taking a life.

Fit and trim in his double-breasted blue uniform with shiny brass buttons, gold-braided epaulets and service stripes, Dahlgren was unmistakable. He had a massive forehead, side-whiskers that joined his mustache, but a clean-shaven chin. And he wore glasses, though he was only 39.[11] Dahlgren would have recognized Mills when he saw him. The sculptor was a celebrated personage of the city. Nor did the officer have to introduce Mills to his civilian draftsman, Carl Ludwig Richter. Mills and the Prussian had met earlier this year during President Taylor's inaugural festivities.[12] Richter was the only member of the "ordnance establishment" who had participated in the casting of a monumental statue. Lieutenant Dahlgren's expertise was unsurpassed, but he had no experience casting statuary of any size.[13]

Richter's English had improved greatly since March. The ambitious young engineer was eager to vaunt his credentials. Mills was about to learn more about the casting of military ordnance than he ever dreamed a sculptor needed to know.

Later Richter would describe his professional formation in a petition to Congress, called a "memorial." It was customary for the "memorialist" to refer to himself in the third person:

> *From early youth he was especialy educated to fit him for the pursuit of controling and managing Foundrys, every variety of castings, of compounding mixing and working of metals; and with his knowledge of every variety of machinery was admitted to the Polytecnick school, and school of art. And was subsequently upon an examination for proficiency and skill, admitted into the War Department of the Prussian Government. And was employed by said Government in the Ordnance and Laboratory Departments, to introduce improvements in the Casting of Cannon and all manner of castings, and to introduce and improve the machinery, furnaces, moulds, and all the methods, of accomplishing the same, and to overlook and determine, the best method of combining mixing and melting metals, to give to them, the greatest strength consistency and density.*[14]

This Richter had done at the Royal Prussian Foundry in Berlin in the 1840s. At that time Alfred Krupp was endeavoring to convince Friedrich Wilhelm IV's minister of war that guns made of steel would be superior in accuracy and reliability to those of iron or bronze. But Prussian cannons of bronze had defeated Napoleon at Waterloo; no argument of Krupp's could trump that. Steel was a new and untested alloy, more expensive than bronze and far more expensive than iron. In the United States, it was virtually unknown.[15]

In *The Arms of Krupp*, historian William Manchester describes weapon technology in 1840s Prussia. This was the environment in which Richter was formed:

> The perennial obstacle had been metallurgy. At the time of Krupp's debut, armorers were still woefully ignorant of chemical principles. The few advances they did make were largely through trial and error, and since they were experimenting with death they often returned to their drawing boards with bloody hands. No metal was reliable. Any big weapon could explode at any time. Cast iron cannon had been used effectively by Gustavus Adolphus in the Thirty Years War, yet it remained dangerously brittle because of its high carbon content; ... Wrought iron, with even less carbon than steel, was coming into use. But here the difficulty was the exact opposite. It was too soft. ... [Every accidental explosion] strengthened the innate conservatism of the gold-braided mossbacks. Bronze was the safest bet, and most of them stuck to that.[16]

In the United States, however, most heavy cannons made in the 1840s were still iron. Unlike bronze, which is an alloy, iron is a naturally occurring element and cheap. From early American colonial days, wherever iron ore was found in the earth, ironworks had risen. Foundries manufactured myriad products of cast and wrought iron: skillets and kettles, heat stoves and cook stoves, plowshares, nails, tools, building façades, columns, staircases, ornamental railings,

Depiction of an iron foundry in Berlin, Prussia, 1840s. The bronze works where Carl Ludwig Richter was employed at the time—the Royal Prussian Foundry—would have resembled this scene. Mills searched in vain for an American founder who could cast his huge statue of Jackson in bronze, before hiring Carl Ludwig Richter to build a foundry for him. (Alamy)

steam engines and boilers for riverboats, springs for coaches, gas and water pipes, rails for railroads, street lamps, and big guns.

Big guns were large cannons installed in stationary configurations in forts and on ships. They were cast by four private manufacturers holding contracts with the War Department: Tredegar Ironworks in Richmond; Fort Pitt Foundry in Pittsburgh; Cyrus Alger & Co. in Boston; and the West Point Foundry in Cold Spring, New York.

Iron working in 1840s America is described in *A Quest for Glory, A Biography of Rear Admiral John A. Dahlgren*, by Robert J. Schneller, Jr.:

> Although advances in science were beginning to affect the foundryman's craft in the mid-nineteenth century, metallurgy largely remained a mystery. Foundrymen had no explanations for such elementary operations as the reduction of ores to metal, the formation of alloys, or the conversion of cast iron into wrought iron or steel. Many knew what would make good castings, but not why. No one could explain why one iron was better than another. Founders guessed at the quality of a metal from its appearance. Most problems in iron casting arose from ignorance about what happened chemically, not thermally or mechanically.
>
> The entire process of gun-founding relied upon the knowledge of the foreman of the foundry. Ironmasters behaved like craftsmen, jealously guarding their art and skill, keeping certain knowledge in their heads, not on paper, and passing secrets and tricks of the trade by word of mouth from father to son, from master to apprentice. They also acted like modern engineers, solving practical problems and producing books filled with solid technical information and current best practice. The mid-nineteenth-century foundry foreman was a metallurgist, patternmaker, chemist—indeed, everything. With raw materials, a little equipment, common sense, and most of all experience, he blended his own

special mixture of iron ores that he "knew" would yield a strong product, tapped the furnace to pour the casting at the "right" moment, and extracted the casting from the mold when he "figured" it had cooled enough.[17]

Since the latter 1830s, however, two foundries had been supplying the U.S. Army with light field artillery of bronze: Cyrus Alger & Co. and Ames Manufacturing Co.[18] Light field artillery included small cannons on wheeled carriages that soldiers maneuvered on the battlefield. Bronze weighed less than iron. Americans were familiar with the 6-pounder "brass pieces" that Alger and Ames produced, because Major Samuel Ringgold had used them effectively in a stunning victory of the recent war with Mexico.[19] They were showcased in Independence Day parades.

Carl Ludwig Richter had brought to the United States a cutting-edge knowledge of *"every variety of castings, of compounding mixing and working of metals"*—iron, bronze, possibly even steel. His expertise in metallurgy was far advanced beyond that of his American counterparts. Lieutenant Dahlgren would have appreciated this, as did Mills now, too. The Prussian had more than merited his professional post in the Navy's Bureau of Ordnance and Hydrography. But he was pushing hard for something more: Richter had invented a new kind of furnace for casting bronze and he wanted to see it built and tested in the United States.

He had described it—through his interpreter, William Furniss—to the Secretary of the Smithsonian Institution, Joseph Henry, at President Taylor's inauguration. He may have told Mills about it at that time, too.[20] Since then, given Richter's aggressive assertiveness, surely he had explicated his invention in technical terms to his immediate supervisor, Lieutenant Dahlgren, and likely to Captain Warrington also. It was cannons of superior quality, not fine art, that the Prussian-trained engineer was promising the U.S. military. What resonated in Mills's ear, though, was Richter's boast that he had participated in the casting of the stupendous equestrian statue of Frederick the Great.

Now, at last, the old Spanish guns were here at the Navy Yard for the members of the Jackson Monument Committee and their sculptor to examine. And the sight caught the men by surprise. They had expected to see artillery pieces resembling the sober 6-pounders of the United States. These guns, on the contrary, were . . . "beautiful works of art."[21]

The four cannons were 4-pounders. They measured about five and a half feet in length and tapered from breech to lip. Baroque relief work, including heraldic devices, decorated their shafts, and the

Eighteenth-century Spanish 9-inch mortar (left) and 4-pounder cannon (right) at Castillo de San Marcos, St. Augustine, Florida. Comparable guns captured by Jackson in Pensacola in 1818 were more ornate—masterworks of the preeminent Spanish founder Joseph Barnola—and mounted on carriages with large wheels for maneuverability in the field. Four cannons seized by Jackson became part of his monument, while two mortars were very likely melted down and used in the bronze for the statue. (Castillo de San Marcos, https://en.wikipedia.org/wiki/Castillo_de_San_Marcos)

reinforcing bands encircling the tubes bore inscriptions in Latin. Each gun weighed 700 pounds and was inscribed with a name—two Visigoth kings of Spain, two gods of ancient Greece. The two 9-inch mortars were much shorter and squatter than the cannons, but weighed half again as much: 1,065 pounds each. Their barreled, belted shafts bore floral ornamentation in relief. About a hundred years old, the artillery pieces had been cast at the royal foundry in Barcelona by a virtuoso founder. Proudly, he had emblazoned his handiwork: "fecit Josephus Barnola."[22] They were flawless casts matured to a moss green patina.

Avid student of bronze casting that Mills was, he would have appreciated that these masterful specimens of the craft would not be destroyed. As Thomas Butler King of Georgia had proclaimed on the floor of the House of Representatives, they were "venerable and precious" national trophies.[23] They did indeed warrant being preserved for future generations of Americans as a part of the Jackson memorial.

Exiting the Navy Yard through Latrobe's singular gatehouse, Mills had still not laid eyes on a monumental equestrian statue. But he had learned a lot about casting heavy metal. Maybe Warrington or Dahlgren had even allowed him to step inside the naval foundry in operation. The education would have brought home to the naïve sculptor, perhaps for the first time, the magnitude of the undertaking he and the Jackson Monument Committee had set themselves. There was good reason why the master founders of Munich, Paris, Florence, Rome and Berlin were celebrated worldwide.[24]

As he traversed Navy Yard Hill on his way back to "the Avenue," Mills knew that even if the Commandant did let the Committee use his foundry, they still did not have the bronze they needed. But those matters, for the time being, were out of his hands. Mills's immediate concern was mounting his full-scale Jackson on the full-scale rearing horse.

NOTES

1 Description of Navy Yard Hill is derived from: (1) Edward Waite, ed., *The Washington Directory, and Congressional, and Executive Register, for 1850* (Washington: Columbus Alexander, Printer, 1850); (2) William M. Morrison, *Morrison's Stranger's Guide to the City of Washington, and Its Vicinity* (Washington City: William M. Morrison, 1842): 44–45; and (3) references scattered in numerous histories of Washington.
2 Description of the Washington Navy Yard is derived from: (1) Edward J. Marolda, *The Washington Navy Yard, An Illustrated History* (Honolulu, Hawaii: University Press of the Pacific, 2004): 15–17; (2) Robert J. Schneller, Jr., *A Quest for Glory, A Biography of Rear Admiral John A. Dahlgren* (Annapolis, Md.: Naval Institute Press, 1996): 74, 76–77; (3) Morrison, *Morrison's Strangers' Guide*, 44–45 and engraving; and (4) references scattered in numerous histories of Washington.
3 See Bk. 1, Ch. 16.
4 "The Jackson Monument," [Washington] *Daily Union*, Mar. 23, 1848, p. 3; and [no title], [Richmond] *Enquirer*, Mar. 28, 1848, p. 1. See Bk. 1, Ch. 19.
5 "Correspondence from Washington, May 14, 1849," [Baltimore] *Sun*, May 15, 1849, p. 4.
6 Charles Stewart McCauley (1793–1869), see https://en.wikipedia.org/wiki/Charles_Stewart_McCauley.
7 Lewis Warrington (1782–1851), see https://en.wikipedia.org/wiki/Lewis_Warrington.
8 The Navy did not have a discrete Bureau of Ordnance until 1862, when the hydrography functions of the Bureau of Ordnance and Hydrography were separated as the Bureau of Navigation. Extensive searching in the records of the Washington Navy Yard at the National Archives, including (1) Records of the Bureau of Yards and Docks, RG 71; (2) Records of Naval Districts and Shore Establishments, RG 181; (3) Records of the Bureau of Ordnance (which includes records of the antecedent Bureau of Ordnance and Hydrography), RG 74; and (4) Naval Records Collection of the Office of Naval Records and Library, RG 45, failed to uncover any correspondence about the Jackson Monument Committee's request. Tragically, much of the Navy Yard correspondence for 1849 is damaged beyond legibility. Nevertheless, that the Committee dealt with "the Commandant" is documented, and the Commandant (McCauley) would have consulted his subordinate officer in charge of ordnance (Warrington), who would have relied on the expertise of his subordinate officer in charge of the foundry (Dahlgren).
9 John Adolphus Dahlgren (1809–70), see Schneller, Jr., *Quest for Glory*, 5, 74–75, 181, 361.
10 "Main Gate, Washington Navy Yard," National Register of Historic Places Inventory—Nomination Form, at https://npgallery.nps.gov/

GetAsset/38f414df-54c0-468b-8575-fb5caee1ae59. Today Latrobe's gatehouse is scarcely discernible within the multi-story superstructure that was built around it in the 1870s.
11 Schneller, Jr., *A Quest for Glory,* 134, 183, and cover photograph.
12 See Bk. 1, Ch. 22.
13 That members of the Committee examined the Spanish guns at the Navy Yard is documented. See *Congressional Globe,* 31st Cong., 1st Sess., July 15, 1850, p. 1372. That Mills did likewise, either on his own or in their company, is not recorded, but highly probable. His future dealings with Richter reveal that the sculptor and the foundryman became well acquainted during 1849. Certainly, they met more than once. See Bk. 1, Ch. 25. It is likely, therefore, that Mills made a number of trips to the Navy Yard that year.
14 Richter's first memorial to Congress, Legislative Records, 32nd Cong., 2nd Sess., Jan. 24, 1853, box SEN 32A-H19, Committee on Public Buildings; Records of the U.S. Senate, RG 46; NARA.
15 William Manchester, *The Arms of Krupp, 1587–1968* (New York: Little, Brown and Co., 1964): 65–67.
16 Ibid., 67.
17 Schneller, Jr., *A Quest for Glory,* 60–63.
18 "M1841 6-pounder field gun," at https://en.wikipedia.org/wiki/M1841_6-pounder_field_gun.
19 "Samuel Ringgold," at https://www.nps.gov/people/samuel-ringgold.htm.
20 See Bk. 1, Ch. 22.
21 *Congressional Globe,* 31st Cong., 1st Sess., July 15, 1850, p. 1372.
22 Tim Kerr, *The History of the Equestrian Statue of General Andrew Jackson, Lafayette Park, Washington, D.C.* Typescript report prepared for the National Park Service, White House Liaison, August 1999: 35–36. Kerr states erroneously that the cannons were cast in Madrid. They were cast in Barcelona. See "General Andrew Jackson Statue," at https://www.nps.gov/places/000/general-andrew-jackson-statue.htm.
23 See Bk. 1, Ch. 21.
24 Michael Edward Shapiro, *Bronze Casting and American Sculpture, 1850–1900* (Newark, Del.: University of Delaware Press, 1984): 29.

CHAPTER 25
June–December 1849

> *Smithsonian Institution*
> *Nov. 30th 1849*
> *My dear sir*
> *Permit me to introduce to your acquaintance Mr Mills the artist whose statue of general Jackson you have seen. Mr M. wishes to exhibit some drawings to you, and confer on the employment of German in whom he is interested.*
> *I remain truly*
> *yours &c*
> *Joseph Henry*
> *Prof. A. D. Bache*
>
> Letter, Joseph Henry to Alexander Dallas Bache[1]

Mills emerged from the long passageway of the Latrobe gatehouse into the Washington Navy Yard, where the customary bustle bore a noticeable solemnity. A few days earlier—on November 13, 1849—an explosion had rattled Lieutenant Dahlgren's testing battery. The *National Intelligencer* had reported:

> [W]hilst experimenting with a large thirty-two pounder, which had been fired several times, the gun suddenly burst, and instantly killed Mr. Charles S. McLane, a gunner in the United States navy.

It is supposed that a fragment of the gun must have entered his head, as the upper part was shockingly mutilated. The deceased was a valuable officer, and generally esteemed. Several other officers narrowly escaped injury. . . . [T]he coroner's inquest, in their verdict, express the opinion "that every care and precaution were used by those who had charge of the battery, and that no blame whatever is attributable to any person."[2]

Nevertheless, Captain Warrington, Chief of the Bureau of Ordnance and Hydrography and Dahlgren's commanding officer, had immediately authorized an investigation. Although the report would exonerate the Lieutenant of any negligence, Dahlgren was deeply affected by the gruesome demise of his young gunner.[3] Warrant Officer McLane had been interred in the Congressional Burial Ground the day after the accident.[4]

Mills laced his way with a purpose through the campus of factories and workshops. He needed to talk to the civilian engineer from Prussia who worked in Dahlgren's ordnance establishment. Mills was desperate. To see his daring representation of General Jackson cast in bronze, he was willing to risk everything. He had a proposition to offer Carl Ludwig Richter.

The summer had begun with good news. The Commandant, Captain McCauley, had granted the Jackson Monument Committee permission to use the Navy Yard foundry. Although the facility was not equipped to cast a monumental statue, Richter had insisted that he could adapt it to the purpose.[5] Delighted, "The Jackson Committee informed Mills that he should have the use of the Navy Yard to build his furnaces in."[6] Then, abruptly, permission had been withdrawn.

To make the casting facility work according to Richter's plan, a large pit had to be excavated beside the furnace. That was one of the "improvements" of his revolutionary foundry: molds to be filled with bronze were positioned in a pit.[7] When Warrington and Dahlgren "found that he wanted to dig a pit 15 ft. deep, to sink his mold below the furnace level, they became alarmed for the safety of the foundations of the furnace."[8] The excavation would destabilize the building's 70-foot chimney.[9] This the Commandant could not allow. "I found it impossible," Richter was later to lament, "to test my improvements at the Washington Navy Yard."[10]

The Committee members were disheartened. Mills, though, was undaunted. He would just find another foundry to cast his statue! He "sent to different large foundries in Pennsylvania, and other places."[11]

Because of its rich deposits of iron ore, Pennsylvania was a leading iron manufacturing center of the United States. From colonial days, German settlers had built and operated foundries there. Their preeminence as ironmasters was legendary.[12] Mills had already employed at least one "Dutchman" (as Henry Kirke Brown called him), because the armature that supported his gigantic horse of plaster was forged of iron.[13] Maybe Mills hoped that the German ironmongers could adapt their expertise to casting bronze.[14]

He might have approached non-German ironworks, as well. One was the Robert Wood Foundry in Philadelphia. Robert Wood, a successful manufacturer of ornamental iron work, was interested in expanding his business into the emergent arena of casting sculpture. This he would soon do, but not in bronze.[15] Another ironworks that was not German lay farther afield: Fort Pitt Foundry in Pittsburgh. Fort Pitt was a supplier of ordnance and cannons to the U.S. War Department.[16]

Not all foundries of "Pennsylvania, and other places" were iron manufactories, though. There were bronze works, too. "Mills," an acquaintance of his was to write, "communicated with the brass-founders, for the statue was to be of bronze."[17] These factories, however, were fewer than ironworks and smaller in scale.[18]

When Mills described to seasoned founders what he proposed to do, they replied "that such a work could not be cast in their foundries, but that one could be built for the purpose for twenty thousand dollars."[19] That, of course, was out of the question. "Of all the extensive founderies to which he applied ... none of them could or would dare undertake a work which they deemed utterly impracticable!"[20]

Mills's search ended in frustration. The facility he needed simply did not exist in the United States, nor was the requisite expertise available. As the Prussian metallurgist, Richter, would later pronounce, "It is perfectly ridiculous to use the same process for casting both iron and bronze. Iron is a distinct metal by itself; bronze is a composition."[21] The summer, however, was not entirely unproductive for Mills.

In the afternoon of Thursday, August 7th—three months after Zachary Taylor had sat for Henry Kirke Brown to sculpt his relief portrait for a peace medal—the President sat for Mills to take casts of his face and skull.[22] Mills met with his august sitter in the Executive Mansion. First, he made sure the General was seated comfortably. Then he greased Taylor's craggy visage, wrapped his skull tightly in an oiled cap, inserted tubes into his nostrils, and spread warm wet plaster all over his face and scalp. After the paste cooled, dried and hardened, Mills asked the President to lean forward and flex his face muscles. Mills caught the three forms of plaster in a towel and walked out of the White House with the molds he would use to fashion the bust.[23]

He made the President's portrait in the conventional style, depicting *Zachary Taylor*, not in contemporary dress—as he had done for the scientist, Professor Henry—but swathed in a toga.[24] Evidently Mills did not yet have the temerity to abandon neoclassicism for naturalism when depicting a head of state.

Also that summer Mills continued to fill orders for copies of his famous *CALHOUN*. One he had promised to Philip Tidyman, a well-known physician and planter of Charleston, over a year earlier.[25] Tidyman was a state legislator, member of the German Friendly Society, American Philosophical Society, and South Carolina Academy of Fine Arts.[26] Mills finished the doctor's copy in August, but did not ship it immediately to Charleston. Rather, he placed it "for examination" at "Mssrs. Taylor & Maury's," a fancy, book and stationery shop that

Mills's plaster bust of President Zachary Taylor, 1849. Although by this time Mills was espousing naturalism in American sculpture, he evidently considered a "traditional" portrait most fitting for a statesman of Taylor's eminent stature. He clothed the General in a toga. (Smithsonian American Art Museum)

fronted on Pennsylvania Avenue near 9th Street, the bustling commercial center of Washington.[27] Taylor and Maury drew attention to their business by displaying artwork in their store. The practice was common among nineteenth-century merchants. It promoted patronage and the publicity was a boon for local artists. Mills would take advantage of Taylor & Maury's establishment to display other examples of his handiwork in the future.[28]

The bust reached Tidyman in December and he immediately placed it for public viewing "at the store of Messrs. Gregg, Hayden & Co., corner of King and Hasell streets."[29] "It is generally admired," the highly gratified customer wrote to Mills, "and you cannot imagine how much it has elevated your reputation. I think it cannot be excelled by Mr. Powers."[30] Like many of Mills's clients, Tidyman expected to engage the sculptor to carve the bust in marble after honing his skills in Italy.[31] But Italy no longer figured in Mills's plans.

In addition to making busts during the summer months, Mills worked on attaching the full-scale model of Jackson to the rearing steed. This entailed erecting a scaffold around the mammoth horse and adding an iron spur to its armature to support the rider, then fastening the large, weighty chunks of sculpted plaster to it. By November, the full-scale model was done. The Baltimore *Sun* reported the unprecedented feat on the 3rd:

> Mr. Mills . . . has succeeded in mounting the General on the horse—and those acquainted with the General at that period, pronounce the likeness a capitol one."[32]

Normally, at this point, the model would be removed from the sculptor's studio to a foundry, where a caster would undertake the process of duplicating it in bronze. But Mills still had no caster. He still had no foundry. Desperate, he devised an audacious plan. This is when he strode purposefully through the streets of the Navy Yard—the workers were mourning the horrific death of Warrant Office McLane—to the Bureau of Ordnance and Hydrography. There he found Carl Ludwig Richter.

By this time, Richter had shown drawings of his furnace to a colleague of his at the Navy Yard, Adelbert Pomnietzky. Pomnietzky, like Richter, was a foreign-born civil engineer. He had built several furnaces.[33] Richter asked him to assess his invention. Pomnietzky found it workable. But he was the Prussian's sole supporter.[34]

The furnace "was condemned unanimously as a scheme that could not possibly succeed," an acquaintance of Mills's would later write. "Among those who put themselves on record to that effect were Professor Joseph Henry, of the Smithsonian Institute, and Professor Page, of Washington."[35] Page was the inventor and patent attorney to whom Mills had demonstrated that a large bronze horse could stand on two legs without toppling.[36] The Washington *Union* would report:

> Of this foundry, as well as of balancing the statue, scientific men had said it was contrary to experience and to all the known rules of science.[37]

Mills was on the verge of taking the biggest gamble of his life. What choice did he have? He borrowed Richter's drawings and asked Joseph Henry for a letter of introduction to Alexander Dallas Bache.

Alexander Dallas Bache was one of America's most distinguished scientists. Formerly a professor at the University of Pennsylvania, he now resided in Washington, where he was Superintendent of the U.S. Coast Survey, a member of the Lighthouse Board, and Superintendent of the Bureau of Weights and Measures. Bache was also a founding regent of the Smithsonian Institution and a close colleague of Secretary Henry's.[38] Henry and Bache had both visited Mills's studio and marveled at his huge horse of plaster. However, while Henry had conferred with Mills and later sat for his portrait bust, Bache had not met the sculptor.[39] Therefore, on November 30, 1849, Professor Henry—in spite of his own misgivings about Richter's furnace—accommodated Mills with a terse note of introduction to Bache.

Unfortunately, no reply to Henry's letter has been found.[40] Whatever judgment Bache may have rendered, though, supportive or not, Mills forged ahead with his plan. In December he "called upon [Richter], to engage him to model, and make mouldings and cast the said equestrian Statue; proposing . . . a partnership."[41] Richter said yes. The Prussian engineer's ego was as big as the American sculptor's.

The two men agreed that Richter would construct a foundry containing his unorthodox furnace next to Mills's studio/abode in President's Park. Then he would act as Mills's—in Richter's own words—"*assistant or foreman for the completion of the Jackson Statue.*"[42] Mills echoed that understanding when he penned in a subsequent note: "*my foreman, Mr. Richter.*"[43]

The die was cast. Mills had taken the gamble of a lifetime. The audacity of the undertaking enflamed the two visionaries. Richter would come to regret, though, that he made no contract in writing with the formidable Mills.

NOTES

1. Letter, Joseph Henry to Alexander Dallas Bache, Nov. 30, 1849; Joseph Henry Papers, Correspondence, Smithsonian Institution Archives, Washington, D.C.
2. "Fatal Casualty at the Navy Yard," [Washington] *National Intelligencer*, Nov. 14, 1849; reprinted in [Washington] *Daily Union* and *The* [Washington] *Republic*, Nov. 15, 1849, p. 3.
3. Robert J. Schneller, Jr., *A Quest for Glory, A Biography of Rear Admiral John A. Dahlgren* (Annapolis, Md.: Naval Institute Press, 1996): 87–88.
4. Charles S. McLane entry at https://congressionalcemetery.org/records-search.
5. "A Visit to Clark Mills' Studio," [Washington] *Evening Star*, June 9, 1857, p. 4.
6. Sketches of Washington. By Childe Harolde. Washington, Mar. 29, 1853. An Hour with Clark Mills, the Sculptor. [Concluded]," *Brooklyn Eagle*, Mar. 31, 1853, p. 2.
7. Letter, C. Ludwig Richter to Charles M. Conrad, Secretary of War, Jan. 28, 1852; Special File, Inventions, Class 1A, no. 104; Records of the Office of the Chief of Ordnance, RG 156; NARA.
8. A[loha] Vivarttas, "The Clark Mills Furnace—A Reminiscence," *The Railroad and Engineering Journal*, vol. 63 (July 1889): 327.
9. "Correspondence of the Courier. Washington, April 14," [Charleston] *Courier*, Apr. 17, 1850, p. 2; and "A Visit to Clark Mills' Studio," *Evening Star*, June 9, 1857, 4.
10. Letter, C. Ludwig Richter to Charles M. Conrad, Jan. 28, 1852.
11. "History of the Jackson Statue," [Washington] *Daily Union*, Jan. 18, 1853, p. 2.
12. "The Pennsylvania Iron Industry: Furnace and Forge of America," at www.ExplorePAhistory.com.
13. See Bk. 1, Ch. 23.
14. "The Jackson Statue," [Washington] *Evening Star*, May 3, 1890, p. 9. See also Bk. 1, Ch. 33.
15. Michael Edward Shapiro, *Bronze Casting and American Sculpture, 1850–1900* (Newark, Del.: University of Delaware Press, 1984): 179; and Karen Chernick, "Finding Robert Wood: The Long Lost Foundry Of An Iconic Ironworker," *Hidden City, Exploring Philadelphia's Urban Landscape*, at https://hiddencityphila.org/2015/09/finding-robert-wood-the-long-lost-foundry-of-an-iconic-ironworker/.
16. See Bk. 1, Ch. 24.
17. Vivarttas, "The Clark Mills Furnace," 327.
18. See Bk. 1, Ch. 16.
19. "History of the Jackson Statue," *Daily Union*, Jan. 18, 1853, 2.
20. "The Equestrian Statue of Jackson, at Washington," *Merry's Museum and Parley's Magazine*, Jan. 1, 1853: 152.
21. Letter, C. Ludwig Richter to Charles M. Conrad, Jan. 28, 1852.

22 "[Correspondence of the Baltimore Sun.] Washington, August 8, 1849," [Baltimore] *Sun*, Aug. 9, 1849, p. 2: "yesterday afternoon."
23 "Clark Mills, the Artist," [Charleston] *Courier*, Aug. 13, 1849, p. 2; and "Correspondence Commercial Advertiser, Washington, Aug. 9, 1849," [New York] *Spectator*, Aug. 16, 1849, p. 1.
24 Today a copy of this bust is in the Smithsonian American Art Museum, Washington, D.C. Rosemary Hopkins, *Clark Mills: The First Native American Sculptor* (M.A. thesis, University of Maryland, 1966): 167, in her catalog of Mills's busts, mistakenly includes a President John Tyler bust, ostensibly in place of this one, which she does not mention. The source Hopkins cites, Anna Wells Rutledge, "Cogdell and Mills, Charleston Sculptors," *Antiques*, vol. 41 (Mar. 1942): 192–92, 207–08, makes the same error. No evidence has been found that Mills ever made a bust of Tyler.
25 [no title], *Charleston Mercury*, Feb. 22, 1848, p. 2.
26 Philip Tidyman (1776–1850), see https://library.haverford.edu/finding-aids/files/975-07-120.pdf.
27 "[Correspondence of the Baltimore Sun.]," [Baltimore] *Sun*, Aug. 9, 1849, p. 2; and "Clark Mills, the Artist," *Courier*, Aug. 13, 1849, 2. Also Edward Waite, comp. and pub., *The Washington Directory, and Congressional, and Executive Register, for 1850* (Washington, D.C.: Columbus Alexander, printer, 1850): 226.
28 See Bk. 1, Ch. 33.
29 "Mills' Bust of Mr. Calhoun," [Charleston] *Courier*, Dec. 13, 1849, p. 2.
30 "[From the Washington Union.] Mills's Bust of Mr. Calhoun," [Charleston] *Courier*, Jan. 16, 1850, p. 2.
31 "Correspondence Commercial Advertiser, Washington, Aug. 9, 1849," *Spectator*, Aug. 16, 1849, 1: "[T]o be 'done in marble' in such style as that were 'worth ambition.'" "Clark Mills, the Artist," *Courier*, Aug. 13, 1849, 2, calls the copy made for Tidyman "a marble bust." Likewise, "Mills' Bust of Mr. Calhoun," *Courier*, Dec. 13, 1849, 2, references "the new marble Bust." Both of these appear to be a misreading of the original *Commercial Advertiser* piece of Aug. 9th. Regarding the expectation that Mills would take plaster busts to Italy to be carved in marble, see [untitled], *New York Journal of Commerce*, Nov. 1, 1848, p. 2; and "Clark Mills at Home," *The Washington Post*, Feb. 7, 1880, p. 2.
32 "Correspondence of the Baltimore Sun. Washington, Nov. 2, 1849. *Jackson Monument*," [Baltimore] *Sun*, Nov. 3, 1849, p. 4.
33 Sworn deposition of Adelbert Pomnietzky, Jan. 22, 1853, appended to Richter's second memorial to Congress, Feb. 24, 1855; Legislative Records, 33rd Cong., 2nd Sess., box SEN 33A-H10, Committee on the Library; Records of the U.S. Senate, RG 46; NARA. See also Adelbers Pomnietzkey [sic] entry, 1850 U.S. Census, Ward 6, Washington, D.C., p. 127 (handwritten), p. 64 (stamped); NARA M432, roll 56.

34 All of Richter's drawings of his furnace have been lost: (1) drawings loaned to Mills in Nov. 1849 to show Prof. Bache; (2) drawings attached to a letter, Richter to Charles M. Conrad, Jan. 28, 1852; and (3) drawings attached to Richter's first memorial to Congress, Jan. 24, 1853; Legislative Records, 32nd Cong., 2nd Sess., box SEN 32A-H19, Committee on Public Buildings; Records of the U.S. Senate, RG 46; NARA.
35 Vivarttas, "The Clark Mills Furnace," 328.
36 See Bk. 1, Ch. 20.
37 "History of the Jackson Statue," *Daily Union*, Jan. 18, 1853, 2.
38 Alexander Dallas Bache (1806–67), see https://en.wikipedia.org/wiki/Alexander_Dallas_Bache.
39 For Henry, see Bk. 1, Ch. 22. For Bache, see Letter, Joseph Henry to Alexander Dallas Bache, Nov. 30, 1849.
40 "A. D. Bache Papers," Manuscript Division, Library of Congress, has been searched.
41 Richter's first memorial to Congress.
42 Richter's second memorial to Congress. Underlining in original.
43 Handwritten note, Clark Mills to Mr. Dalgreen [sic] [Lt. John A. Dahlgren], Washington, Oct. 4, 1850; annexed to Richter's second memorial to Congress. Underlining in original.

CHAPTER 26
December 1849–February 1850

And this deponent further says, that he next knew said Richter when he was inventing and constructing his furnace, which was put into operation for one Clark Mills, to cast the equestrian statue of General Jackson in Washington city. And this deponent further states, that said Mills proposed to enter into partnership with said Richter, who was acting at that time as foreman for said Mills.

Theodore Stossmeister, sworn deposition, Jan. 31, 1853, appended to Carl Ludwig Richter's second memorial to Congress, Feb. 24, 1855.

In December of 1849 Carl Ludwig Richter left the Bureau of Ordnance and Hydrography at the Washington Navy Yard to build what Mills was to call "the Jackson Monument Foundry." First, Richter engaged Theodore Stossmeister to help with the project. Stossmeister was a *"practical bronze caster."* He and Richter had met in 1845 at the Royal Cannon Foundry in Berlin, where they were both employed at the time. Three years later, they emigrated to the United States, although separately.[1] While working together on Mills's foundry, Richter and Stossmeister most likely communicated in German.

Richter also called upon two former colleagues in the Bureau of Ordnance and Hydrography for their expertise: Adelbert Pomnietzky and William Godfrey Bitner. Pomnietzky was *"a Civil Engineer and Machinist and well acquainted with such works."* He had *"directed the building of several furnaces of different kinds."* Pomnietzky calculated the number of bricks Richter needed and *"was frequently at the place while the furnace was constructing."* Bitner was a gunsmith. He would swear *"that he also saw Mr. Richter at work on said furnace."*[2] Pomnietzky, a native of Poland—perhaps Prussian Poland—and Bitner, an immigrant from Germany, probably spoke German with Richter and Stossmeister.[3]

For the brickwork of the furnace, oven and mixing vat, Mills hired Richard Sheckells, the proprietor of a masonry business in Georgetown.[4] The rest of the foundry was constructed of wood. Wood was much cheaper than brick and went up more quickly. Future accounts of Mills's compound in the White Lot would invariably describe it in terms of "a few shanty-looking buildings."[5] According to art historian Michael Edward Shapiro, writing in *Bronze Casting and American Sculpture, 1850–1900*:

> The foundry they built was located in "a small, miserable shanty" and probably consisted only of two parts: an enclosed, kiln-like furnace of brick for melting down bronze cannon and an adjacent area where the flask containing the molds would be placed or buried.... In short, it would be difficult to conceive of a more modest casting facility.[6]

"Modest" it was. Nevertheless, in light of the colossal dimensions of the statue to be cast in it, the building could not have been "small."

The season was bitterly cold. A "sheet of snow" covered the ground on the first morning of 1850 and temperatures hovered just a few degrees above freezing throughout New Year's Day.[7] Harsh weather notwithstanding, during the month of January workmen erected Mills's foundry on the back of his living quarters/studio. They shoveled out a crater 15 feet deep, mixed and churned mortar, laid the bricks of a furnace the size of a smokehouse next to the pit, built a large brick oven and vat, hauled planks and beams, measured, sawed, hammered, raised four walls, climbed up and down ladders, crisscrossed scaffolds, glazed windows, erected massive derricks and rigged them with block and tackle, installed a scale for weighing, pitched a chute from the furnace down to the pit, and roofed the building with broad ranks of shingles.

Photograph of the south façade of the White House, 1857, showing the extensive grounds designated President's Park—but commonly called the "White Lot"—that descended to the mouth of Tiber Creek and the Potomac River beyond. During the winter of 1849–50, Carl Ludwig Richter built the bronze foundry he designed for Mills next to the sculptor's studio, roughly 200 yards to the right of where the photographer of this image was standing. (Library of Congress)

No partitions disrupted the cavernous interior. An opening in one wall was tall enough and wide enough for a wagon to wheel in large molds and wheel out colossal pieces of statue. The workers furnished it with a pair of huge wooden doors hung on iron hinges.[8]

Richter "*directed*" the construction.[9] Mills observed and learned, piece by piece, the elements of a bronze foundry. It was Mills's understanding that Richter was working *for him*, period, regardless of what the disgruntled "*partner*" was later to protest.

As his foundry was taking shape, Mills was sculpting something in his studio that Richter could use to test his unique furnace. The initial trial piece had to be the simplest of forms. Mills chose a bell. He sculpted four bells in plaster and made full-scale models of them.

Three of the bells were modest in size, probably varied for experimental purposes. Cast in bronze, their total weight was to amount to 300 pounds or so. But the fourth bell stood about 30 inches high and measured 20 inches in diameter at the shoulder and 40 inches at the lip.[10] Its weight in bronze would be 1,300 pounds.[11] Sculpting and manipulating a plaster model for a casting of that size and heft required physical brawn. Mills entrusted the "rough part"—as he himself described it—the "hewing out"—to a Black worker—who was most likely Philip Reid.[12]

There it stood. The Jackson Monument Foundry. A makeshift, barn-like structure just off the south lawn of the President's House. Mills had what he needed to begin casting.

NOTES

1 Sworn deposition of Theodore Stossmeister, Jan. 31, 1853, appended to Richter's second memorial to Congress, Feb. 24, 1855; Legislative Records, 33rd Cong., 2nd Sess., box SEN 33A-H10, Committee on the Library; Records of the U.S. Senate, RG 46; NARA. Stossmeister would be employed at the Ames Manufacturing Co. in Chicopee, Mass., in 1851, when Richter would also be working there (see Bk. 1, Ch. 33). By 1853 Stossmeister would be residing in New York City, where he swore the deposition for Richter.

2   Sworn depositions of Adelbert Pomnietzky and William Godfrey Bitner, Jan. 22, 1853, appended to Richter's second memorial to Congress.
3   Adelbers Pomnietzkey [sic] entry, 1850 U.S. Census, Ward 6, Washington, D.C., p. 127 (handwritten), p. 64 (stamped); NARA M432, roll 56; and Wm Bitner entry, 1860 U.S. Census, 1st Ward, Washington, D.C., p. 150 (handwritten), p. 358 (stamped); NARA M653, roll 102.
4   Sworn deposition of Theodore Stossmeister. Also Sheckells, Richard, son, entry, Alfred Hunter, comp. and pub., *The Washington and Georgetown Directory, Strangers' Guide-Book for Washington, and Congressional and Clerks' Register* (Washington, D.C., printed by Kirkwood & McGill, 1853): 91.
5   "Sketches of Washington. By Childe Harold. Washington, March 29, 1853. An Hour with Clark Mills, the Sculptor," *Brooklyn Eagle*, Mar. 30, 1853, p. 2. The foundry Mills was to build at Meadow Bank Spa Spring in 1853 would also be frame (see Bk. 2).
6   Michael Edward Shapiro, *Bronze Casting and American Sculpture, 1850–1900* (Newark, Del.: University of Delaware Press, 1984): 38–39. Shapiro's quotation is taken from "History of the Jackson Statue," *New-York Daily Times*, Jan. 22, 1853, p. 3.
7   For the weather, see [no title], [Washington] *Daily Union*, Dec. 27, 1849, p. 3; and "The New Year," [Washington] *National Intelligencer*, Jan. 5, 1850, p. 8.
8   "[From the Washington Union.] *Mills's Bust of Mr. Calhoun*," [Charleston] *Courier*, Jan. 16, 1850, p. 2.
9   Sworn deposition of Theodore Stossmeister.
10 Author's inspection of the bell at Magnolia Cemetery, Charleston, S.C., May 2011. This is the only one of Mills's bells known to be extant. See Bk. 1, Ch. 30.
11 "Equestrian Statue of Jackson," *The* [Washington] *Republic*, Aug. 22, 1851, p.3; reprinted in many newspapers nationwide, from Boston to New Orleans to San Francisco. Thirteen hundred pounds subtracted from the 1,600 pounds of metal that Mills used leaves 300 pounds for the other three bells.
12 See Bk. 1, Ch. 23.

CHAPTER 27

March–April 1850

Mr. Mills, we are happy to perceive, has been equally successful in his experiments in casting.

"Clark Mills' Equestrian Statue of Jackson,"
The [Washington] *Republic*, Apr. 17, 1850, p. 3.

Studio work done, foundry work could begin. This is when sculptors normally handed their model over to a caster. Mills, however, wanted to learn every aspect of creating a bronze statue. As Richter progressed from one stage of the process to the next, Mills shadowed him, observing and learning every operation along the way.[1]

By this time in his rigorous self-education, Mills was apprised of the two methods of casting bronze: "lost wax" and "sand casting." In *Bronze Casting and American Sculpture, 1850–1900*, Michael Edward Shapiro explains:

> The method of bronze casting used in the classical world and revived during the Renaissance and again in the late nineteenth century is known today as the lost-wax or *cire perdue* method. However, from the early eighteenth to the late nineteenth century, sand casting or French sand casting was the primary method used for bronze casting in Europe and then in America.[2]

Sand casting is what Richter practiced. Shapiro continues:

> Sand casting involves three essential steps in producing bronze sculpture: preparing a negative mold from a plaster cast of the artist's original model, casting the bronze, and cleaning and coloring the cast.[3]

Each of these steps, though, entails a sequence of complicated procedures that call for specialized skills and an in-depth understanding of the metals. Since the Jackson Monument Foundry was in its infancy and run on an austerity budget, Mills himself and Richter and Reid handled as many of the tasks as they could. Eventually, however, Mills would be required to hire foundry workers.

"He has had but little assistance," the *Republic* was to report, "and on an average not more than three workmen in his employ."[4] There were tradesmen who specialized in every stage of the operation— molders, casters, chasers, finishers, polishers, patinators. Some were American-born, but most were immigrants from Europe. Men of color, either free or enslaved, performed the unskilled labor of the operation. They hauled barrels of plaster, sacks of sand, buckets of water, and cartloads of fuel for the furnace and mixing vat. Directed by the founder, they maneuvered models, molds, heavy iron copes and drags, sheets of copper, ingots of tin and zinc, and ponderous casts of bronze. Mills's foundry was equipped with cranes rigged with block and tackle, as well as wheelbarrows, carts and wagons, but all power was provided by workmen and beasts of burden. The animals, along with Mills's sorrel gelding, Olympus, required care and feeding, too. There was plenty of muscle work to be done.

Philip Reid, however, was an anomaly. Although African-American and enslaved, he was already a master plasterer and trusted assistant of Mills in the studio. His future collaboration with the sculptor suggests that now, while working alongside Mills and Richter in the foundry, he learned and executed a variety of skilled tasks required for the casting of bronze.[5]

Conditions in the workplace were harsh for all of the men, White and Black alike. Hazards were omnipresent. Coordinated teamwork was essential. And expenses were incessant. Mills's disbursements from the Jackson Monument Committee never lasted long.

It was March of 1850. The rare expertise that Richter had mastered in Prussia he was now about to share with Mills. This was the tutelage that would ultimately empower the visionary American to cast the first monumental bronze statue in the United States.

CREATING A BRONZE STATUE

Step 5: Cut the model into pieces and make molds from them

The mold maker ("moulder" in 19th-century parlance) usually began by making a plaster copy of the sculptor's clay model. Since Mills eschewed clay and worked directly in plaster, Richter did not have to do this. Next, the molder would saw the plaster model into as many pieces as necessary for successful casting. No large sculpture could be cast in its entirety; it had to be cast in manageable pieces—which the caster determined by size and configuration. Mills chose to begin with bells because they were simple enough to be cast in a single mold. There was no need, therefore, for Richter to saw Mills's models into pieces. Nevertheless, making a mold from a model as simple as a bell was still a complex undertaking.

Two box-like flasks of iron were needed for each mold. Richter packed moist, coarse "backing sand" into one of the flasks, called the "drag." Then he shellacked one of Mills's models and pressed it halfway into the sand. After packing a fine grade of moist, cohesive "French sand" around the exposed half of the model, Richter clamped the second flask, the "cope," on top of the drag. Then he rammed backing sand into it. Next, inverting the two iron flasks and detaching the drag, Richter repeated the procedure for the other half of the bell. He emptied the coarse sand from the cope, shellacked the exposed half of the model, and packed "French sand" around it. Then Richter extracted Mills's model, leaving negative impressions of the two halves of the bell.

For backing sand, Richter used loam, a mixture of sand and clay, rather than coarse sand alone.[6] That was one of his signature "improvements" to the process.

For reasons of economy, and because bronze is such a heavy metal, statues are cast hollow. They are not solid, but rather empty "shells." At this time, therefore, Richter constructed an inner "core" for the bell.

The core was a plug-like body of sand that fit inside the mold. It had roughly the same shape as the interior of the bell, but was slightly smaller, which left a thin membrane of air all around it. When molten bronze was poured into the mold, it would fill this membrane and thus assume the shape of the bell. That shell of metal might vary in thickness from one-eighth to three-eighths of an inch, sometimes more, depending on what that particular section of the sculpture required to retain its shape and its strength.

To hold the core in place during casting, Richter used metal rods that extended out from the core into the surrounding sand. He also positioned—strategically, this was critical—several venting tubes to release the air and toxic gases that would be forced out of the membrane as the molten metal filled it. If the tubes were not placed where needed, the cast would contain flaws, such as air bubbles, holes, or cracks. Even worse, a violent explosion might hurl chunks of flaming metal and clouds of scalding steam into the foundry. Finally, Richter reclamped the drag and cope together securely.

Workers then transported the iron flask to the oven, where it baked until the sand was hard and dry. How long this took depended on the size and complexity of the mold, but it was never less than a dozen hours. The mold maker knew from experience how much time to give it. After the men removed the iron flask from the oven, it was set aside to cool.

By early April, Richter had executed this procedure for each one of Mills's bells. He then directed the workmen in positioning the four molds in the pit, so they would be "convenient at hand" when his bronze was ready.

Step 6: Weigh out, melt down and mix the metals

Bronze is a compound of copper (roughly 90 percent), tin (roughly 8 percent), and a trace amount of zinc or lead (roughly 2 percent). The "caster" decides the precise percentage of each element he wants in his alloy. Each metal melts and hardens at a different temperature and has its own bonding characteristics. The caster, therefore, must control the heat when melting each ore individually and then, after they have been combined, when heating them together as a composite. He decides when to add each element to the mix, and when and how to stir the amalgam. He recognizes the opportune moment for pouring the molten alloy into the mold to achieve "the greatest strength, consistency and density" possible—that is, the best "tensile strength."[7] Later Richter would avow that "*he acted with said Mills . . . directing the mode of mixing the metal.*"

It reveals Richter's self-assurance, if not reckless bravado, that he chose to cast, not one, or even two or three, but all "4 Bells, at one time."[8] Given their size, that single "firing" would take about 1,600 pounds of bronze. That was an unusually large quantity, more than twice the weight of a field cannon. Such a massive quantity was unheard of in American foundries. But Richter had modified radically the traditional design of a furnace, and one of the advantages of *his* furnace, he confidently proclaimed, was that it could cast more than one cannon at a time. In addition, he made changes in the traditional way of handling the metals, which—this was later to be verified by the U.S. Army—produced bronze of a superior quality.[9]

Richter detailed in written accounts the four ways that his furnace improved upon the typical furnace in use in the United States at the time:

(1) His furnace was a hemispherical kiln. It resembled an enormous beehive, perhaps 8 feet in diameter and 5 feet high at its apex, and it was encased in a solid block of brick. Metal to be melted down was fed through an opening in one side that had an iron door some two feet square.

(2) Richter's furnace had no chimney. A flue about 8 inches square and 16 inches tall assisted in starting the fire. He explained:

In the old Furnace with a chimney in the centre, the heat passes off over the metal and escapes through the chimney, only melting the metal in the centre, while that around the sides is far behindhand in melting.

This reduced the tin (the softest of the three elements) to ashes.

My furnace is covered over and retains all the heat, which is uniformly distributed all through the metal, melts the metal uniformly, and then passes off gradually in well projected draught holes.

This kept the tin from burning up.

(3) Richter's furnace was fueled by *"fine dry and clean pine wood,"* rather than the traditional *"stone coal."* Coal burned quickly and unevenly and (because it contained sulfur) produced oxides that altered the chemical make-up of the metals. This resulted in casts that were *"crumbling and brittle,"* Richter said, *"not compact not dense."* Wood, on the other hand, provided a slower, more uniform burn and (since it contained no sulfur) did not create damaging oxides, so the metals remained in their unchanged, natural state. This produced a superior cast. The wood was fed into a chamber beneath the floor of the kiln. Maintaining an even, steady fire for just the right length of time was a critical part of the process of making bronze. Philip Reid, Mills's enslaved assistant, was to become proficient at this.[10]

(4) Richter's furnace delivered the molten alloy—at the ideal temperature—*directly* to the mold by means of a channel. To receive the molten metal, molds were positioned in a pit beside and below the level of the furnace. Richter explained:

> *The old process requires the metal when ready to be poured first into a kettle and from the kettle into the mould's; this is because the old furnaces over heat the metal, which must be reduced before pouring into the mould's. It is plain that the metal loses much by being over heated and cooled in the kettle; the tin is burned out, etc., as I said before.*

Every kettleful of alloy—several were needed to fill a large mold—brought together metals of unequal temperature.

> *[This] prevents an absolute union necessary to give the full cohesive power to the metal.*

Low on one wall of Richter's furnace, however, a trap door was opened to release the alloy down a chute and into a mold. Transferring the bronze *directly* preserved its ideal temperature, consistency, composition, and cohesive quality.

The combination of these features together—the modified equipment and the handling of the metal—gave his furnace, Richter insisted, "*the advantage over all other furnaces:*"

> *If I had my furnace alone without the knowledge of the mode of using it, my castings would fail. If on the other hand, I have the knowledge of the nature of copper, of the process of melting it, of preserving it in its natural state, but was compelled to work in the old furnace, I must fail.*[11]

The Spanish guns that the Jackson Monument Committee had secured from Congress had not yet been transported from the Navy Yard to Mills's compound. For this initial test firing of Richter's furnace, therefore, Mills had to purchase his own metal. Copper was available in sheets; tin, zinc and lead were available in blocks called ingots. Mills bought about 1,440 pounds of sheet copper, 128 pounds of tin ingots, and 32 pounds of lead ingots.[12]

On April 14th the Washington correspondent of the Charleston *Courier* reported mistakenly that Mills, in his "newly invented furnace," had succeeded in "melting some old brass cannon."[13] Likewise, the Washington *Evening Star* would print erroneously—many years later—that "the bell was made of the metal of the cannon captured by Gen. Jackson."[14] But those assertions contradict Richter's own testimony. He would later write that he melted "*sheet copper*"— not obsolete guns—for the bells.[15] Also, a *Courier* piece of April 19th, stating that Mills had "melted . . . lead and copper," corrected the earlier report."[16] Furthermore, in the near future Richter would find it impossible to use obsolete guns to make his bronze. He needed to be able to control the percentage of each element in his alloy.[17]

Richter melted the copper, tin and lead individually in his furnace. Then he combined precisely measured quantities of each molten metal in a huge vat—adding each one in a carefully timed sequence— and stirred the mix. He never allowed the lower portion of the mixture to thicken. Stirring continuously from the start kept a uniform consistency throughout the alloy:

> *Now I stir my metal with the stump of a tree 24 feet long and 8 inches thick, and it requires an experienced castor to know when is the proper time to stir the metal. How absurd it is to permit the metal to settle down, the upper part melted, and then to stir with a pipe stem or broom stick.*

What kind of machinery, horsepower or human muscle it took to operate a stirrer so much larger than the norm is hard to imagine.

Step 7: Pour molten bronze into the molds

At this point, traditionally, the caster would declare the "ideal moment" to start pouring the alloy into kettles and transporting the kettles to the mold. When that ideal moment was reached, only the caster knew. Intuition gained from experience was as valuable as technical knowledge and practical skill. But now Richter did otherwise. He transferred the alloy from the vat, not into kettles, but rather to his furnace, and there he heated it to the optimum temperature for releasing it into the mold:

> *I wait till my metal is ready, I then pour it fresh from the Furnace into the mould's which are convenient at hand.*

Richter unlatched the trap door at the base of the furnace and, sparkling, fiery orange, steaming and hissing, like a flow of lava, the bronze rolled down the chute and disappeared into the first mold, the second, the third, the fourth. The tricky procedure transpired without mishap. There was no explosion of gases. There was no shower of scalding metal fragments. Founder and sculptor sighed with relief. Then they retired to a restive night of anticipation, while the molten metal cooled and hardened in the molds.

Step 8: Extract the rough bronze casts from the molds

The next morning, they hoisted the four iron flasks out of the pit. One at a time, they unlatched the drag and cope and lifted out the rough bronze cast, carefully, breathlessly. As Mills and Richter progressed, one, two, three, four, they grew giddy. All of the bells were acceptable casts. Their surfaces were rough, but contained no holes or cracks that could not be "touched up." The delighted founders knocked the core out of each bell and, forthwith, Richter advanced to "finishing" them.

Step 9: Finish the surface of the casts

He started by "chasing" the casts. Using a saw, he cut off the protruding rods, which were formerly the venting tubes. Then, employing files ranging from coarse to fine, he smoothed mold lines, bumps and other imperfections on the exterior surfaces of the bells. Next, wielding chisels, rasps and other tools, he added or "heightened" surface details. On a portrait bust or statue, fine features such as hair, eyes and fingernails were chiseled by hand. On Mills's bells, though, only two elements in relief required heightening. Encircling the shoulder of the largest one (probably the smaller ones, too), Mills had sculpted a frieze of acanthus leaves, and just below that, the phrase: "FIRST CASTING AT THE JACKSON MONUMENT FOUNDRY AT WASHINGTON 1850." Beneath the words, "FIRST CASTING," three six-pointed stars formed a "V."[18] After finishing the casts, Richter washed the bells with water.

Step 10: Assemble the bronze pieces into a whole
In the case of a monumental statue, after the multiple pieces were finished, they would be joined together, generally using bolts and nuts or pins and welds. However, each of Mills's bells was cast in its entirety in a single mold. They required no assembly. So the American sculptor and his foreign-born founder hastened to the final task.

Step 11: Patinate the statue
At this time, the four bells were a bright, coppery-golden hue.[19] It was time to give them a desired color, that is, a patina. This process was commonly called "pickling." Richter treated the bells with a mixture of acidic chemicals, either by brushing it on or soaking them in it. How many coats were applied, or how long the bells were left in the bath—as well as the particular mix of chemicals used in the solution—determined whether the metal would turn to a shade of green or brown or black. Mills chose a rich charcoal gray, almost black, for his bells.[20] After given a patina, the bells were polished to a high sheen.

The success of the Jackson Monument Foundry on the very first trial was phenomenal. Newspapers announced that Mills had melted 1,600 pounds of metal in a single firing.[21] But that was not all. The consensus of men of science had been that a furnace without a draught

Bronze bell hanging at the entrance to Magnolia Cemetery, Charleston. An inscription encircling the shoulder of the bell reads, "FIRST CASTING AT THE JACKSON MONUMENT FOUNDRY AT WASHINGTON 1850." Weighing about 1,300 pounds, this was the largest of the four bells Mills cast to test Richter's unorthodox furnace. (photo courtesy of Kimberly Stephanian)

could not generate sufficient heat to melt such an immense mass of metal.[22] But Richter's chimneyless furnace had just done it.

But that was still not all. Scientists—including the preeminent Professor Joseph Henry—had agreed that only coal could produce the intensity of heat required to melt such a tremendous amount of metal. The Commander of the Washington Arsenal, Captain Alfred Mordecai, a key member of the Ordnance Board—which developed, tested, and approved all new weapons, ammunition, and related equipment—had asserted that "it was not possible to cast with wood."[23] Yet Richter had done just that using only "three-fourths of a cord of common pine."[24] Even Captain Mordecai would ultimately concede that Richter's furnace did indeed produce superior bronze.[25] At the conclusion of the casting process, Washington's *Daily National Intelligencer* reported, "The charcoal left was worth as much as the wood."[26] When Mills told Henry of his success, "the Professor held up both hands with astonishment."[27]

Mills's gamble on Richter was vindicated. The initial test of the Prussian's furnace was a tour de force. In *Bronze Casting and American Sculpture, 1850–1900*, Edward Shapiro writes:

> None of these procedures for casting bronze sculpture—mold making, casting, chasing, and patinating—was generally known in mid-nineteenth-century America.[28]

But Mills's European-born, -trained and -practiced foreman knew them well and shared his singular expertise with his employer. This Carl Ludwig Richter would come to regret.

NOTES

1 Richter's first memorial to Congress, Jan. 24, 1853; Legislative Records, 32nd Cong., 2nd Sess., box SEN 32A-H19, Committee on Public Buildings; Records of the U.S. Senate, RG 46; NARA: "Your memorialist further represents that he acted with said Mills for the period of nearly one year." Also Richter's second memorial to Congress, Feb. 24, 1855; Legislative Records, 33rd Cong., 2nd Sess., box SEN 33A-H10, Committee on the Library; Records of the U.S. Senate, RG 46; NARA: "[T]he greatest part of the arrangement for executing said Statue was his [Richter's] work."
2 Michael Edward Shapiro, *Bronze Casting and American Sculpture, 1850–1900* (Newark, Del.: University of Delaware Press, 1984): 16.
3 The sand casting method summarized here is derived from Shapiro, *Bronze Casting*, 16–24.
4 "Mills's Equestrian Statue of Jackson," *The* [Washington] *Republic*, Nov. 22, 1852, p. 3.
5 See Bk. 2.
6 Letter, C. Ludwig Richter to the Secretary of War [Charles M. Conrad], undated, but transmitted with a cover letter of Sen. James Shields dated Dec. 10, 1851; Special File, Inventions, Class 1A, no. 103; Records of the Office of the Chief of Ordnance, RG 156; NARA.
7 Richter's first memorial to Congress. See also John Philip Colletta, "'The Workman of C. Mills:' Carl Ludwig Richter and the Statue of Andrew Jackson in Lafayette Park," *Washington History*, vol. 23 (2011): 8.

8   Richter's first memorial to Congress; and letter, C. Ludwig Richter to Hon. Mr. [Charles M.] Conrad, Secretary of War, Jan. 28, 1852; Special File, Inventions, Class 1A, no. 104; Records of the Office of the Chief of Ordnance, RG 156; NARA.
9   Ibid.
10 See Bk. 2.
11 Letter, C. Ludwig Richter to Hon. Mr. [Charles M.] Conrad. The description of Richter's furnace and method of handling the metal described here, as well as the quotations, are derived from: (1) Richter's 1852 letter to Conrad; (2) Richter's first memorial to Congress; and (3) A[loha] Vivarttas, "The Clark Mills Furnace—A Reminiscence," *The Railroad & Engineering Journal*, vol. 63 (July 1889): 327–29, which describes, not Mills's first foundry, but the one he built in 1855 at Meadow Bank Spa Spring (see Bk. 2).
12 Author's estimate based on a 1,600-pound firing.
13 "Correspondence of the Courier. Washington, April 14," [Charleston] *Courier*, Apr. 17, 1850, p. 2.
14 "Sale of an Artist's Effects," [Washington] *Evening Star*, Jan. 27, 1885, p. 3.
15 Letter, C. Ludwig Richter to Hon. Mr. [Charles M.] Conrad, Jan. 28, 1852.
16 "Correspondence of the Courier, Washington, April 18," [Charleston] *Courier*, Apr. 19, 1850, p. 2. This report was reprinted in newspapers where the phrase, "lead and copper," appeared erroneously as "brass and copper." See, for example, "News of the Day," *Alexandria* [Va.] *Gazette*, Apr. 23, 1850, p. 2; and [no title], [Washington] *Daily National Intelligencer*, Apr. 26, 1850, p. 3; and [no title], [Little Rock] *Weekly Arkansas Gazette*, May 3, 1850, p. 2.
17 See Bk. 1, Chs. 32 and 33.
18 Author's inspection of the bell at Magnolia Cemetery, Charleston, S.C., May 2011. The three stars may have been purely decorative, or they may have held some significance for Mills. What that significance may have been, however, no one today can say.
19 Shapiro, *Bronze Casting*, 23.
20 Author's judgment based on inspection of the bell. It is difficult to determine the original patina of Mills's monumental statues, as they have been restored several times over the years. This bell, however, has received less care, ostensibly no restoration at all, so its original patina may be posited from visual inspection. See Bk. 1, Ch. 30, n. 34, and Ch. 36, n. 5.
21 "Correspondence of the Courier. Washington, April 18," [Charleston] *Courier*, Apr. 19, 1850, p. 2; and "History of the Jackson Statue," [Washington] *Daily Union*, Jan. 18, 1853, p. 2; and "A Commencement of a New Era in the Arts: Jackson Statue" in Alfred Hunter, comp. and pub., *The Washington and Georgetown Directory, Strangers' Guide-Book for Washington, and Congressional and Clerks' Register* (Washington, D.C., printed by Kirkwood & McGill, 1853): 91–94.
22 "History of the Jackson Statue," [Washington] *Daily Union*, Jan. 18, 1853, p. 2.

23 Letter, C. Ludwig Richter to Hon. Mr. [Charles M.] Conrad, Jan. 28, 1852. See also Colletta, "'The Workman of C. Mills,'" 11.
24 [no title], [Washington] *Daily National Intelligencer*, Apr. 26, 1850, p. 3. All sources state "three-fourths" except: "History of the Jackson Statue," [Washington] *Daily Union*, Jan. 18, 1853, 2, and "A Commencement of a New Era in the Arts: Jackson Statue," both of which state "three-eighths."
25 See Bk. 1, Ch. 33.
26 [no title], *Daily National Intelligencer*, Apr. 26, 1850, 3.
27 Vivarttas, "The Clark Mills Furnace," 328.
28 Shapiro, *Bronze Casting*, 24.

CHAPTER 28
April 1850

> *Mr. Clark Mills has succeeded admirably with his newly invented furnace. It is the admiration of men of science. . . . [He] contrived a furnace in the small enclosure around his studio, without any chimney, and succeeded with it, on the first trial.*
>
> "Correspondence of the Courier. Washington, April 14,"
> [Charleston] *Courier*, Apr. 17, 1850, p. 2.

Mills rode out the gate of his compound, proceeded along Pennsylvania Avenue, and ascended the hill to the Old Brick Capitol. The austere, three-story building stood at 1st and A Streets, across from the Capitol grounds. The legislature had met there while their quarters were being rebuilt after the War of 1812. Now the red brick edifice was a boarding house for members of Congress.[1] Mills had in tow a heavy satchel containing a sack of dry plaster, a bowl, wooden spoons, a straight razor, shaving cream, oil, towels, note pad, tape measure. Philip Reid likely accompanied him to assist. It was Sunday, March 31, 1850, shortly after noon. John C. Calhoun had died at half past seven this morning in his room. Mills had been summoned to take the death mask.[2]

It was five years, almost to the day, since the house plasterer-turned-sculptor had taken Calhoun's life mask at the Senator's plantation in Clemson, South Carolina.[3] During their second meeting, as Mills imparted life to the plaster bust—lifting eyelids, adjusting facial muscles, sharpening ears and hair—he had listened to the former Congressman, Secretary of War, Vice President and Senator reminisce about his experience sitting for Hiram Powers. The offhand conversation had lent a friendly spirit to their relationship. Calhoun

297

had been Mills's living, breathing link to the man who was the all-consuming focus of his labors: Andrew Jackson.

Ushered now into the chamber where the once-fearsome orator lay abed, Mills called for a pitcher of water, extracted his tools and materials, and made a plaster cast of the "serene, majestic" face—as newspapers described it. But then he did more. He took measurements of the senator's entire body. One day, Mills promised, he would create a full-length statue of the legendary "Cast-Iron Man."[4]

Then Mills carefully packed the fragile cast, bagged his implements, and withdrew from the hushed room. The singular relationship between the aspiring sculptor and the illustrious politician—whose bust in marble had assured Mills's career—had come to a fitting close. Or so it seemed. In reality, Mills's association with Calhoun was about to benefit him even more now than it already had.

After Mills (and perhaps Reid) exited the Old Brick Capitol, the remains of Calhoun were enclosed in a Fisk & Raymond

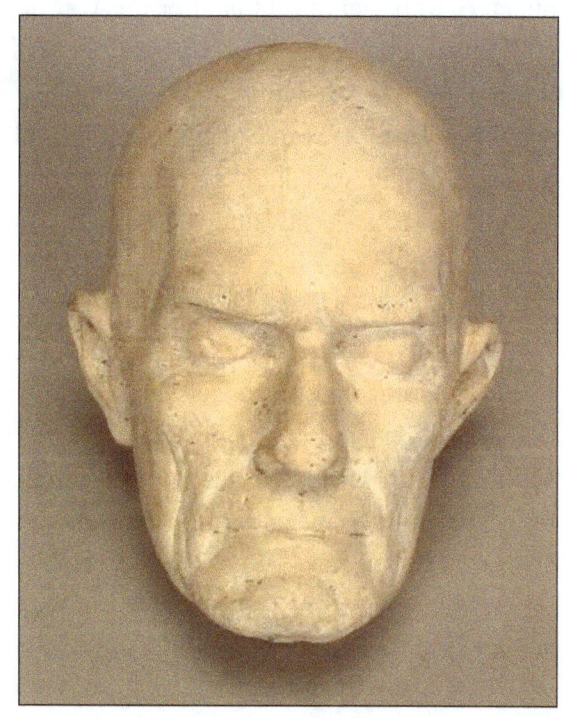

Death mask of John C. Calhoun, which Mills took on March 31, 1850, in the Senator's room in the Old Brick Capitol, a boarding house for members of Congress at the time. Calhoun, the "Cast-Iron Man," the "Lion of the South," had died earlier that morning. Participating by invitation in Calhoun's ceremonious four-day funeral procession from Washington to Charleston and the deposition of his body in a cemetery vault of St. Philip's Church enhanced Mills's reputation and furthered his career. (New-York Historical Society)

patent metallic burial case. The recent invention to preserve corpses, reported *The Wilmington Journal*, was "made of cast iron, bronzed and hermetically sealed."[5] Shaped to the human form—akin to an ancient Egyptian coffin—it was "furnished with six handles, which rendered the transfer from one conveyance to another, safe and convenient."[6] Nevertheless, its weight was considerable.

On Tuesday morning, April 2nd, six pallbearers bore the burial case solemnly across the street and into the Senate chamber of the Capitol. The 31st Congress had recessed for the day. Eulogies were delivered at noon. Then a great procession of national leaders in carriages, followed by a throng of Washingtonians on foot, Caucasian and Black, enslaved and free, conveyed the mortal remains from Capitol Hill to the Congressional Burial Ground. There, on the bluffs above the Eastern Branch, Calhoun's body was laid in the public vault, pending a funeral in Charleston.[7] The mayor of Charleston, governor of South Carolina, and U.S. Senate had all appointed committees to arrange a fitting farewell.

The South Carolina contingent was called "the Committee of Twenty-Five." Twenty-five prominent citizens of the Palmetto State were delegated by the governor to proceed to Washington and deliver the remains of Calhoun to Charleston for burial. A greater honor was beyond imagining. Chairing the committee was Daniel Ravenel, Esq., scion of one of the oldest, most prominent and wealthiest families of the state.[8] By April 20th, Ravenel and all of the members of his mission were assembled in Washington. Coincidentally, Mills had just cast his four bells and news of the success of the Jackson Monument Foundry had brought the sculptor's name anew before the public—because Mills had wasted no time trumpeting his triumph.

Right away, he had flaunted his bells before the wide eyes of men of science who had doubted that Richter's unorthodox furnace could function: Professors Henry and Page. But more than that, from the moment the furnace proved effective, Mills claimed to be its inventor. He showcased "his newly invented furnace" to the correspondent of the Charleston *Courier* on April 14th. Two days later, he exhibited the fruit of "his experiments in casting" to a reporter from the Washington *Republic*."[9] Forthwith, both the *Courier* and *The Albion, A Journal of News, Politics and Literature* published in New York City reprinted the lengthy *Republic* piece in its entirety.[10] On April 18th the *Courier* correspondent submitted another article about "the new furnace invented by the Sculptor."[11] No report mentioned Carl Ludwig Richter.

While members of the Committee of Twenty-Five were arriving in Washington, Mills was gathering information that would help him design an appropriate statue of the "Cast-Iron Man." He interviewed the distinguished South Carolinians about their departed countryman. He spoke to members of Congress about their colleague's manner in the Senate chamber. As Calhoun's widow and three sons converged on the city for the obsequies, Mills asked them about the private life of the master of Fort Hill. Mills secured "other advantages," too—perhaps photographs or personal items of some kind—to assist him in sculpting a realistic representation of Calhoun.[12] At this moment the "hometown sculptor" of the famous marble bust of Calhoun enshrined in Charleston's city hall, who had (reportedly) invented a revolutionary new way of casting bronze, who had taken Calhoun's death mask, and who was promising to create a statue of South Carolina's favorite son—Clark Mills was in the public eye. Suddenly, he received a stunning invitation.

Due to "a domestic bereavement," one member of the Committee of Twenty-Five was obliged to withdraw. Ravenel offered Mills the honor of escorting the body of Calhoun to Charleston as a guest of his committee.[13] Mills accepted.

Richter could certainly carry on without him for a week or so. For the next test of the furnace, Mills had sculpted something that was much more complex than a bell. It was a bust of the Greek god Apollo. He left the full-scale plaster model—ready for mold-making and casting—in the hands of his foreman. Evidently Richter was not aware yet of Mills's flagrant claim to his furnace.

NOTES

1 James M. Goode, *Capitol Losses: A Cultural History of Washington's Destroyed Buildings* (Washington, D.C.: Smithsonian Institution Press, 1979): 190–92.
2 "Death of Mr. Calhoun. Correspondence of the Alexandria Gazette. Washington, March 31, 1850," *Alexandria* [Va.] *Gazette*, Apr. 2, 1850, p. 3.
3 See Bk. 1, Ch. 8.
4 "Correspondence of the Courier. Washington, April 22," [Charleston] *Courier*, Apr. 27, 1850, p. 2; and South Carolina Legislature, *The Death and Funeral Ceremonies of John Caldwell Calhoun* . . . (Columbia, S.C.: Published by Order of the Legislature, Printed by A. S. Johnston, 1850): 59–60.
5 "Reception of the Remains of the Hon. J. C. Calhoun, at Wilmington, N.C.," *The Wilmington Journal*, Apr. 26, 1850, p. 2.
6 South Carolina Legislature, *Death and Funeral Ceremonies*, 58.
7 Unless otherwise cited, description of Calhoun's funeral is derived, and quotations are taken, from: (1) "South-Carolina Mourns for her Dead," [Charleston] *Courier*, Apr. 27, 1850, p. 2; and (2) South Carolina Legislature, *Death and Funeral Ceremonies*.
8 See Bk. 1, Ch. 17.
9 "Correspondence of the Courier. Washington, April 14," [Charleston] *Courier*, Apr. 17, 1850, p. 2; and "Clark Mills' Equestrian Statue of Jackson," *The* [Washington] *Republic*, Apr. 17, 1850, p. 3.
10 "Clark Mills' Equestrian Statue of Jackson," [Charleston] *Courier*, Apr. 20, 1850, p. 2; and *The Albion, A Journal of News, Politics and Literature*, vol. 9 (Apr. 20, 1850): 16.
11 "Correspondence of the Courier. Washington, April 18," [Charleston] *Courier*, Apr. 19, 1850, p. 2.
12 South Carolina Legislature, *Death and Funeral Ceremonies*, 59–60.
13 "Clark Mills, Esq.," [Charleston] *Courier*, Apr. 29, 1850, p. 2.

CHAPTER 29

April 1850

Mr. Mills remained among us on Saturday, receiving the warm congratulations and respectful attentions of his fellow townsmen, proud of the genius he is so successfully displaying and the fame he is so honorably earning, in the execution of the equestrian statue of Gen. Jackson, at Washington, and in other achievements of his noble art, in which his services, we learn, were put in requisition, even during his short sojourn in our city.

"Clark Mills, Esq.," [Charleston] *Courier*, Apr. 29, 1850, p. 2.

Two years had elapsed since the ambitious bust maker had left his wife and sons to pursue his dream in the nation's capital. Now Daniel Ravenel's invitation afforded Mills an interlude with his family that his own resources had not allowed. Perhaps, though, Mills's long absence had not been owing entirely to a lack of funds. During his "short sojourn" in Charleston for Calhoun's funeral, Mills would not spend much time at all with Eliza and the boys—although there is no evidence, not yet at this date, that he and his wife were already estranged.[1]

Early on Monday, April 22nd, the body of John C. Calhoun had been retrieved from the vault at the Congressional Burial Ground in Washington and transported to the eastern front of the Capitol.[2] The Senate Committee and Committee of Twenty-Five were assembled there to receive it. The morning was wet and cold.[3] "At 8 o'clock, punctually," the hearse containing the cast-iron casket, followed by the committee members in a reverential string of carriages, rode "on the southern side of Capitol Hill and along Maryland Ave." to the wharves on the Potomac River at the foot of 6th and 7th Streets.

Six pallbearers carried the weighty burial case aboard the steamer *Baltimore*, which was draped in "crepe decorations and other tokens of mourning." Her flag and pennant were flying at half-mast. Mills was already onboard. Whether he took Philip Reid on this trip is unknown. The enslaved man had family residing in Charleston whom he had probably not seen in two years.[4] More likely, though, Mills left the plasterer behind to assist Richter in the foundry.

The *Baltimore* pulled away from the pier at about 9:00 a.m. Churning down the Potomac, the steamer passed the port of Alexandria, slowed respectfully while in sight of Mount Vernon, and arrived at the port of Aquia Creek around noon. There the funeral party was joined by delegations from Richmond and Fredericksburg who had come with a military escort on a special train provided by the Richmond, Fredericksburg & Potomac Railroad Company. As a band measured out a dirge, the remains of Calhoun were transferred reverentially from the ship to the train's elaborately decorated funeral car. Then the gentlemen from Washington boarded for the trip to Richmond.

En route, the cars stopped in Fredericksburg for 15 minutes "to allow the citizens, who turned out in great numbers, to show their respects." The city's church bells tolled continuously during the pause. Later, reaching the town of Milford, the funeral party was served "ample refreshments . . . provided . . . by the Richmond Committee." The train pulled into the Richmond depot on Broad Street about 4:30, welcomed by Governor John B. Floyd and a suite of Virginians dressed in mourning.

Mills walked in the "large procession of citizens," accompanied by "a splendid military escort," from the train station to the Virginia capitol. The cityscape was familiar to the sculptor from his brief sojourn there three years earlier. As the official party filed into the capitol, Mills may have had the opportunity to admire once again, fleetingly, the sublime statue of Washington by Houdon. He planned to cast a bronze replica of that noble head. In the hall of the House of Delegates, the Fisk & Raymond burial case was positioned reverently under guard and a memorial service was intoned. The runaway urchin from the hinterland of upstate New York absorbed the pomp and echoing oratory of the historic occasion. During that afternoon and evening, "great numbers of both sexes visited the Hall."

Meanwhile, the Senate Committee and Committee of Twenty-Five—together with its guest, Clark Mills—were escorted to the Exchange Hotel, where they sat down to a sumptuous supper at seven-thirty. Frequently throughout the meal, men rose from their chairs to propose toasts, relate personal reminiscences of Calhoun, and proclaim their esteem for the departed colleague. "The company adjourned at an early hour." They were escorted to their apartments as guests of the city for the night.

On Tuesday morning at 10 o'clock, after savoring the copious breakfast provided by the Exchange Hotel, the committees were conducted in carriages to the Virginia capitol. There, with grave formality and florid rhetoric, Governor Floyd recommitted the body of John C. Calhoun to their charge. Then, "to the sounds of solemn music and the tolling of bells," a caravan of carriages with military escort followed the hearse down to the Richmond & Petersburg Railroad Depot on the bank of the James River. "The streets and windows were thronged with spectators while minute guns were fired during our passage through the city." The special train departed Richmond at about 11:00 a.m.

An hour later the cars stopped in Petersburg, where a solemn procession conveyed the iron coffin through the city to St. Paul's church on Walnut Street. Following an Episcopal service, municipal authorities took charge of the mortal remains of Calhoun while the two committees were driven to Jarrett's Hotel, where a feast was spread before them. After eating, they retrieved the casket at St. Paul's, rode to the depot of the Petersburg, Raleigh & Wilmington Railroad, and departed at 8:00 p.m. on an overnight train to Wilmington, North Carolina.

The cars rolled into Wilmington at half past noon on Wednesday, April 24th. A blast of cannon signaled their arrival. Stores and businesses suspended operations. Vessels in port struck their colors to half-mast. Bell ringers in the city's churches commenced a clamor of tolling. The weather was inclement and the formally attired gentlemen from Washington were groggy, achy and hungry. At the Carolina Hotel, a sumptuous dinner awaited the distinguished out-of-town guests, courtesy of Wilmington's civic leaders. But the funeral cortege was behind schedule. Foregoing the meal, the long-suffering travelers mustered posthaste into a procession at the railroad depot. Meanwhile, local citizens sat down to the feast.[5]

Minute guns fired while "the remains of the lamented deceased" were transported down Front Street to Market Dock and carried aboard the *Nina*. The steamer had been chartered specially by the City of Charleston. On deck, a delegation of notable Charlestonians (the committee delegated by the mayor) stood and removed their hats to receive the casket. A second steamer, the *Wilmington*, had been provided by the Wilmington & Raleigh Railroad. "A part of the company in attendance went in each boat; and by this arrangement, the comfort of all was greatly promoted." The two steamers left the Wilmington harbor together about three o'clock. Still other members of the committees, however, along with Mills, traveled on a third steamer, the *Gov. Dudley*.[6]

The funeral party spent that night onboard the packets as they navigated the choppy waters along the Atlantic coast. It was Thursday, April 25th, at 9:00 a.m., when the boom of a cannon on the revenue cutter *Gallatin*, lying in Charleston harbor just below Fort Sumter, announced that the *Nina* and *Wilmington* were approaching through the fog. Three boats sailed out to meet them and the entire flotilla, hung with emblems of mourning and colors at half-mast, "passed up [the Cooper River] nearly the entire length of the city to the landing place at Smith's wharf." They docked at noon. The three committees—local, state and federal—disembarked and transferred charge of "the illustrious deceased" to a Special Guard of Honor.

Mills participated in the teeming cortege—"the largest of the kind ever known in our city"—that bore the remains of the favorite son of South Carolina to Citadel Square.[7] Six horses drew the funeral car. The grooms were liveried in black. "In every street . . . the temples of religion, the public buildings of the city, and the fronts of private dwellings, were tastefully draped with the emblems of mourning." Eulogies at the Citadel were delivered by the chairman of the Senate Committee, the governor of South Carolina, the mayor of Charleston, and the Honorable Abraham Watkins Venable, a U.S. Representative and close friend of Calhoun's. They lasted about an hour.

At one o'clock the procession re-formed and bore the "Cast-Iron Man" through the gates of Citadel Square, where the palmettoes had been arrayed in black bunting, and into the streets teeming with spectators.

> The tolling of all the Church bells, the firing of minute guns, by detachments of Artillery, at various points, and by the Revenue Cutter, off the Battery, the solemn roll of the muffled drum, and the plaintive dirge of the military band, added largely to the funeral character of the occasion.

The cortege wound southward for about a mile and a half through neighborhoods Mills knew well. "A pleasant temperature prevailed," but the skies kept a gloomy overcast all day. At last the funeral party reached City Hall, across the street from the Guard House where Mills once kept a workshop, and halted. The coffin was taken from the hearse and, too heavy to be borne up the fanned staircase, was carried through the street-level entrance and "deposited under a magnificent catafalque."

> The ceremonies of the day completed, the various deputations and committees of this and other States . . . were invited to the Council

Chamber, where the hospitalities of the city were tendered by the municipal authorities.

The supper was sumptuous. The men "were afterwards escorted to the lodgings provided for them by the committees appointed for the purpose." The members of the Senate Committee, however, "repaired to the headquarters of his Excellency, Gov. Seabrooke, where they were received and entertained as the guests of South Carolina during their stay." Throughout Thursday night, an unbroken stream of citizens filed past the coffin of John C. Calhoun.

Where Mills slept that night is not recorded, whether in "the lodgings provided" or the home of his family.[8] Eliza was residing with their four boys in the house her father held in trust for her at no. 9 Atlantic Street.[9] That was not up in the Northern Neck, where Eliza's Ballentine relatives lived, but in St. Philip's and St. Michael's Parishes, down by the East Battery of the harbor. At the end of Atlantic Street flowed the Cooper River, along which the many wharves of the prosperous port city jutted out like the teeth of a comb. Eliza was 30 now. Theodore had just turned 11, Fisk was close to 10, John was seven, and Clark, Jr., three. The federal census taker who came to the house a few months after the Calhoun funeral would record that all four boys were attending school—although, for Clark, Jr., that seems unlikely.[10]

Few of Eliza's neighbors could be called "well off," but they were not poor. They included a tailor, two ship's chandlers, two riverboat pilots, many mariners, master mariners, ship captains and sail makers, a dozen merchants and shopkeepers, a sawyer who was free Black, a watchmaker, a baker, and a boot maker and carter, both mulatto. A majority of them owned slaves; most, just one or two; others, as many as nine. Only a handful—a bank officer, an attorney-at-law, four merchants and a few who practiced no profession—were wealthy plantation owners who kept their in-town residence in this neighborhood. They owned more slaves than their neighbors who plied trades, as many as 17.[11]

How the Mills family managed during the absence of their breadwinner is undocumented. Philip Reid, the "first-rate plasterer," could have supported them, had Mills not taken him off to Washington. Mills must have sent money to his wife periodically. Given the sculptor's financial circumstances, though, and his heedless management of money, those stipends would have arrived at irregular intervals that widened as the years passed. For a short time, Eliza evidently took in boarders. The year of Calhoun's funeral, three people named Ward also resided at 9 Atlantic Street, presumably a family: William, 29, Mary, 26, and William, 9.[12] But the house was not large, as the lot measured only 23 feet wide by 35 feet deep. For three adults and five boys, the accommodations would have been cramped. Within a couple of years, however, Eliza and her sons were to have the house to themselves.[13]

Eliza was not without the moral support and companionship of loved ones. She came from "a large family" who were sensitive to her situation.[14] The Ballentines were an old and sizeable clan of South Carolina.[15] Eliza also had "numerous friends."[16]

Nor was she the only wife in Charleston left to raise children on her own while her husband was away on business, or serving at a distant civil or military post, or on the high seas. No one would have blamed Mills, not yet, for earning his living far from his family, as long as he provided for them. However, future events would suggest that it dismayed Eliza to learn that—after being away for two years—her husband had not even begun to cast the Jackson statue, and that he would be staying in Washington at least another year, likely longer. Nevertheless, despite the uneasy domestic situation, it is possible that Mills spent that Thursday night with Eliza and the four boys at no. 9 Atlantic Street.

At dawn on Friday, April 26th, the tolling of Charleston's bells resumed. Businesses remained shuttered. In front of City Hall, the funeral procession formed under skies somber with clouds, though the air was warming. At 10 o'clock the iron burial case was brought out and conveyed in an elaborate carriage to St. Philip's Church. The landmark house of worship, with its three majestic Tuscan porticoes and looming tower—close to being finished now—was swathed in ornamentations of grief.[17] The galleries, pews, aisles and passages teemed with spectators.

After "an anthem richly sung by a numerous choir of male and female voices," the bishop of the Episcopal Diocese of South Carolina intoned the burial service. A eulogium based on a passage from the Book of Proverbs, "The memory of the just is blessed," reverberated down the nave. Then the coffin was transported to the Western Cemetery of St. Philip's Church (the section for non-Charlestonians) and deposited in a temporary vault. Final interment would be decided later by Calhoun's widow and sons in consultation with the State Legislature.

The gentlemen of the municipal, state and federal committees, exhausted, dispersed. But Mills lingered in Charleston. He had the remainder of Friday and all of Saturday to spend with his wife and sons. However, he could not have seen much of them, because the *Courier* reported, "[H]is services, we learn, were put in requisition, even during his short sojourn in our city."[18] That is, Mills was occupied taking face and head casts for busts.

Ever the self-promoter, he also took advantage of his stay in Charleston to broadcast the success of his initial castings in bronze. He reiterated publicly that the furnace that had been so denigrated, yet proved so successful, was his own invention. The assertion ricocheted throughout the country as fact:

> **Alexandria, Va.:** "A new furnace has been invented by the Sculptor, Mr. Clark Mills."[19] (April 23)
>
> **Camden, S.C.:** "[H]e has invented a furnace for melting the metal, which economizes the fuel and the heat."[20] (April 23)
>
> **Charleston:** "His confidence in his invention of a new furnace for casting, without a flue, is, we learn, perfect, and enthusiastic."[21] (April 29)

Little Rock: "A new furnace has been invented by Mr. Clark Mills, of Washington city. It is upon the principle of an air-tight stove."[22] (May 3)

Philadelphia: "Mr. Clark Mills . . . has invented a furnace for melting the metal."[23] (May 6)

Charleston: "In making experiments, as to building the furnace . . . Mr. Mills has made a discovery that will be of great importance."[24] (May 8)

Houston: "Mr. Clark Mills, the Charleston Sculptor, has invented a furnace which promises great improvements on those now in use."[25] (May 9)

Detroit: "Mr. Clark Mills, of South Carolina . . . has invented a furnace for melting the metal."[26] (May 13)

Not one article mentioned Carl Ludwig Richter, either as inventor or simply as Mills's "foreman." Three times while Mills was in Charleston his boast was published in Washington, D.C., where Richter was casting the bust of Apollo:

> A new furnace has been invented by the sculptor Mr. Clark Mills.[27]
> (*Daily National Intelligencer*, April 26, and *Weekly National Intelligencer*, April 27)

> [H]e has invented a furnace for melting the metal, which economizes the fuel and the heat.[28] (*Daily Union*, May 1)

Did it never occur to Mills that Richter might protest? Art historian Michael Edward Shapiro, writing in *Bronze Casting and American Sculpture, 1850–1900*, asserts, "Mills co-opted Richter's techniques and claimed them for his own."[29] Still, the historical record presents no reaction yet from Richter.

On Sunday morning, April 28th, the U.S.M. *Gov. Dudley* steamed out of the port of Charleston with Mills onboard.[30] At Wilmington, he took the cars and transferred from the rails of one company to those of another until he reached Aquia Creek, Virginia. By that time, he must have been impatient to resume his work. Participation in the funeral of Calhoun had stoked his ambition, advanced his career, and enhanced his reputation.

Five years earlier, the house plasterer's marble bust of Calhoun had bestowed upon him the status of "Clark Mills, the sculptor." Now that the "Cast-Iron Man" had passed to eternity, demand for the bust soared. Mills would make many plaster copies, not only of the bust, but of Calhoun's face and head casts, too.[31] One of the busts—in a matter of months—would make its way to the studio of Hiram Powers in Florence, Italy. The preeminent American sculptor would copy it in marble.[32]

For some time, the rumor persisted that the state of South Carolina was going to "employ Mr. Mills to erect a bronze statue of Mr. Calhoun."[33] But the commission never materialized. Mills would never use the measurements he had taken of the Senator's corpse in the Old Brick Capitol, or the information he had collected about the man from colleagues and family members. Eventually, though, he would cast the bust of the immortal advocate of states' rights and strident defender of slavery in bronze. But only once. And *that* unique treasure he would keep for himself.[34]

Traveling as a guest of the Committee of Twenty-Five had elevated Mills's repute. Masses of Charlestonians who filled the streets to see Calhoun's festooned funeral car witnessed the sculptor shoulder-to-shoulder with the most celebrated of South Carolinians. The press, too, noted his presence among the select number of elite citizens. Mills seized the occasion to rekindle ties with former patrons and forge new acquaintanceships that were to prove valuable in Washington—particularly, with Isaac Edward Holmes and **Abraham Watkins Venable**. Holmes, a U.S. Representative from South Carolina, had sat for Mills three and a half years earlier in Columbia and later introduced him to Cave Johnson.[35] Now Venable, a U.S. Congressman from North Carolina, would also sit for Mills.[36] Holmes and Venable were both Southern Democrats, and Mills was more than a casual reader of *The United States Magazine, and Democratic Review*, a national weekly magazine. The personal support that these two members of Congress were to lend Mills in the nation's capital would benefit the sculptor's career far more than two commissions for busts.

Mills's appearance in public with a civic leader of the stature of Daniel Ravenel gilded his reputation as a sculptor. But their acquaintance may have originated three years prior to Calhoun's funeral, when Mills was studying how bronze statues were made. Ravenel was Vice President of the College of Charleston, whose library Mills may have used.[37] In future years, one tradition would hold that Mills gave the "original model" of his Jackson equestrian to "his friend, Daniel Ravenel of Charleston."[38] This could be true.[39] The statuette would certainly have made a unique and personal token of Mills's gratitude. Ravenel's invitation had provided the gregarious go-getter with the ideal venue—the city that loved him—for proclaiming himself not only a sculptor, but an inventor, too.

Arriving by train in Aquia Creek, Virginia, Mills transferred to a packet steaming up the Potomac to the wharves of southwest Washington City. At last, back in his studio/foundry/abode, he met with his Prussian foreman, who presented him with the finished bust of Apollo.

NOTES

1 See Bk. 2.
2 Unless otherwise cited, description of Calhoun's funeral is derived, and quotations are taken, from: (1) "South-Carolina Mourns for her Dead," [Charleston] *Courier*, Apr. 27, 1850, p. 2; and (2) South Carolina Legislature, *The Death and Funeral Ceremonies of John Caldwell Calhoun* . . . (Columbia, S.C.: Published by Order of the Legislature, Printed by A.S. Johnston, 1850).
3 "Correspondence of the Courier. Washington, April 22," [Charleston] *Courier*, Apr. 27, 1850, p. 2.
4 For Reid's family, see Bk. 1, Ch. 4.

April 1850

5   "Reception of the Remains of the Hon. J. C. Calhoun, at Wilmington, N.C.," *The Wilmington Journal*, Apr. 26, 1850, p. 2.
6   "Passengers," [Charleston] *Courier*, Apr. 27, 1850, p. 2.
7   "Clark Mills, Esq.," [Charleston] *Courier*, Apr. 29, 1850, p. 2.
8   The Charleston *Courier* has no "hotel arrivals" column at this date and no advertisements for the city's hotels.
9   See Bk. 1, Ch. 13.
10 Clark Mills household, 1850 U.S. Census, Parishes of St. Philip's & St. Michael's, Charleston, S.C., p. 182 (handwritten), p. 91[B] (stamped); NARA M432, roll 850. Ages given in censuses are often inaccurate; ages given here are correct. See Bk. 1, Ch. 4. Also Clark Mills entry, J. H. Bagget, pub., *Directory of the City of Charleston, for the Year 1852* (Charleston: Edward C. Councell, printer, 1851): 88.
11 Data derived from the 1850 U.S. Census of neighbors enumerated around the Clark Mills entry.
12 Clark Mills household, 1850 U.S. Census.
13 A search of the *Directory of the City of Charleston, for the Year 1852* resulted in no listings other than Clark Mills at 9 Atlantic Street.
14 "Obituary," *The Charleston Daily Courier*, Aug. 30, 1855, p. 2.
15 Ballentine and variant spellings of the surname were searched in the 1850 U.S. Census for the state of South Carolina, NARA M432, rolls 848–860, and 1860 U.S. Census, NARA M653, rolls 1212–1228. The name Ballentine does not appear in the Charleston City Directory of 1852 because the volume does not include residents of the Northern Neck. The author thanks his colleague and friend, Brent H. Holcomb, professional genealogist, for his extensive research on Eliza's family ties in the South Caroliniana Library, University of South Carolina, and the South Carolina Department of Archives and History, Columbia, 2015–16.
16 "Obituary," *Charleston Daily Courier*, Aug. 30, 1855, 2.
17 "St. Philip's Church" at http://www.scencyclopedia.org/sce/entries/st-philips-church/.
18 "Clark Mills, Esq.," *Courier*, Apr. 29, 1850, 2.
19 "News of the Day," *Alexandria* [Va.] *Gazette*, Apr. 23, 1850, p. 2.
20 "Clark Mills and His Statue," *Camden* [S.C.] *Journal*, Apr. 23, 1850, p. 3.
21 "Clark Mills, Esq.," *Courier*, Apr. 29, 1850, 2.
22 [no title], *Weekly* [Little Rock] *Arkansas Gazette*, May 3, 1850, p. 2.
23 "An American Artist and a Work of Art," [Philadelphia] *Public Ledger*, May 6, 1850, p. 6.
24 "Clark Mills," [Charleston] *Courier*, May 8, 1850, p. 2.
25 [no title], *Weekly Houston Telegraph*, May 9, 1850, p. 3.
26 [no title], *Detroit Free Press*, May 13, 1850, p. 2.
27 [no title], [Washington] *Daily National Intelligencer*, Apr. 26, 1850, p. 3; reprinted in the [Washington] *Weekly National Intelligencer*, Apr. 27, 1850, p. 9.

28 "Mr. Mills," [Washington] *Daily Union*, May 1, 1850, p. 3, a reprint of "Clark Mills . . . ," *Camden Journal*, Apr. 23, 1850, 3.
29 Michael Edward Shapiro, *Bronze Casting and American Sculpture, 1850–1900* (Newark, Del.: University of Delaware Press, 1984): 39.
30 "Clark Mills, Esq.," *Courier*, Apr. 29, 1850, 2.
31 Rosemary Hopkins, *Clark Mills: The First Native American Sculptor* (M.A. thesis, University of Maryland, 1966): 141–52. See also Bk. 1, Ch. 13.
32 [no title], *Southern Press*, Mar. 20, 1851, p. 4.
33 "An Hour in the Studio of Mills," *Camden* [S.C.] *Journal*, June 4, 1850, p. 3.
34 In 1876 Mills donated the bronze bust to the Corcoran Gallery of Art in Washington, D.C. Hopkins, *Clark Mills*, missed this bust in her catalogue raisonné.
35 See Bk. 1, Chs. 12 and 16.
36 Abraham Watkins Venable (1799–1876), see https://bioguide.congress.gov/search/bio/V000084. Also "Bust of Hon. A. W. Venable," *The* [Washington] *Southern Press*, Aug. 19, 1850, p. 3.
37 See Bk. 1, Ch. 17.
38 *Maryland History Notes* (Baltimore: Maryland Historical Society, 1945), vol. 3, no. 1 (May 1945): 34.
39 For an evaluation of this tradition and a different, equally plausible account of the fate of Mills's "original model," see Bk. 1, Ch. 17.

CHAPTER 30
May–June 1850

> *The most beautiful image we have ever seen of this deity is now in our city. It is not an oil painting, nor a painting in watercolors, nor a marble bust, but bright and glorious as Apollo's self, it is a bust in bronze.*
>
> "Apollo," *The* [Washington] *Republic*, Apr. 30, 1850, p. 3.

When Mills got home from Calhoun's funeral, he found his *Apollo* cast, finished, patinated, and polished to a "bright and glorious" sheen. Richter had done it all while the sculptor was in Charleston.[1] Without delay, Mills unveiled his latest work proudly to a reporter from *The Republic*.[2]

Evidently, to be taken seriously, the self-taught artist considered it *de rigueur* to produce something classical. One of the earliest works that Henry Kirke Brown had given his two French founders to cast was a Greek figurine, *Filatrice*. The American Art-Union had just selected the statuette for its 1850 edition.[3] Might not a head of the Greek god Apollo garner comparable legitimacy for Mills? Nor was this bust his sole venture into classical themes. Three years later, a visitor to Mills's studio would write:

> I strolled round his shop, observing the different curiosities. Here lay the head of Apollo, fractured at the base; here a limb of Venus; there a small Cupid, with one arm, half a leg, and the nose broken off. In another place I found Jackson's limbless trunk, under the shavings; Jupiter's head, with the face knocked off. A perfect conglomeration of headless, limbless, trunkless Gods and Goddesses, Sylphs and Cupids—all lay here in each other's embrace, only sadly deficient as a whole.[4]

315

These fragments, most likely of plaster, show that Mills—while advocating a naturalistic "American art for Americans"—knew that aspiring artists traditionally learned by copying the ancient European masters. That's what he was doing, apparently to round out his unconventional formation as a sculptor.

The reporter from the *Republic* was captivated by Mills's *Apollo*:

> We did not know that such an effect could be produced with bronze. As you gaze upon it, the soft beauty of the richest oil painting appears to be developed. In every feature there is a delicacy and beauty entirely captivating. We confess that we have been surprised and astonished, not by the skill—for we forgot that—but by its product. This image has been produced by Mr. Mills in his experiments, ere attempting his colossal statue.[5]

Bronze statues simply were not known in America. Although engravings of European bronzes were common, they did not capture the luster of three-dimensional metalwork, or the play of light and shadow on the modeled surfaces. Keenly aware of the novelty of his profession, Mills delighted in educating—and entertaining—not only newspaper men, but the general public as well. He often unlocked his compound gate and welcomed visitors, as he did on Saturday and Sunday, May 11 and 12, 1850. Mingling with his guests, he lectured to them, answered their questions, and basked in their fascination with the trappings and products of his calling.[6]

Mills may also have had a practical motive for this "open house." He had reached the two-year due date of his contract with the Jackson Monument Committee.[7] He needed to reassure the members, not only that he was as committed as ever to keeping his word, but that progress was being made. Seeing Mills's four bells and bust of Apollo convinced the Committee to disregard the deadline. The undertaking had turned out to be enormously more complicated than any of the well-intentioned but naïve men had anticipated. They left Mills to carry on. He padlocked his gate once again and called upon his foreman to begin casting a bust of George Washington.

Mindful of what his undertaking meant for the advancement of art in the United States, and sensitive to the power of symbol, Mills had resolved early on that he would cast a bust of Washington. And *his* portrait of the *Pater Patriae*—true to his creed of realistic rather than idealized sculpture—would be historically impeccable. Vivid in Mills's memory was the statue in the Virginia capitol that had mesmerized him two and a half years earlier, and which he had just recently glimpsed again during the memorial service for Calhoun: the marble *Washington* by Jean-Antoine Houdon.[8]

It was during a stay at Mount Vernon in 1785 that the preeminent French sculptor of the age had taken measurements of the General's body and plaster casts of his face, head and shoulders to use in creating the statue. When Houdon returned to his studio in Paris with these materials, he left a parting gift: a clay bust of his host that he had modeled from life. That bust was universally acclaimed to be "the most accurate likeness of George Washington" in existence.[9] It was that likeness, therefore, that Mills wanted to copy for *his* portrait of the Father of His Country.

In October of 1849 he traveled 18 miles down the Potomac River to Mount Vernon. A great-grandnephew of Washington's, Colonel John Augustine Washington, was presiding over the Virginia plantation at that time. Mills met with him and made a request.[10] The Colonel was later to recount in a letter:

> *I allowed Mr. Clarke Mills to take a copy of it [the clay bust of Washington]. The work was done here, and I was a good deal with Mr. Mills while he was engaged on it. I witnessed his operations: these were simply to make a mask or mould over the bust, which mould was removed in pieces, these pieces were afterwards secured together and a bust cast into this mould by repeated washings of soft or liquid plaster.*[11]

Mills made two plaster copies of Houdon's bust of Washington. When he departed Mount Vernon, mimicking the gesture of the great French sculptor, he left one of them with his host as a gift. "*The first cast or bust produced by Mr. Mills in this way,*" the Colonel would later write, "*is in my possession, and I think it an excellent copy.*"[12] The other copy Mills took back to his studio to use as the model for his own *Washington*.[13]

Working with Richter in May of 1850, Mills made the mold for his bust of Washington from this model.[14] Meanwhile, he ordered a delivery of copper, tin and zinc or lead. By this time the Spanish guns that the Jackson Monument Committee had secured from Congress had been transported from the Navy Yard to Mills's compound. A visitor saw them there "lying about."[15] But the trophies of war would not be melted down; they were to be made a feature of the Jackson memorial. Mills, therefore, had to pay for the metals he needed for his bust of Washington. When the shipments of metals arrived, he weighed out the requisite amount of each one, melted them down, and mixed his alloy. By June everything was ready for casting. Mills invited guests into his foundry.

He chose this climactic moment to demonstrate to his detractors the viability of the disparaged furnace. He also summoned members of the press to witness and spread the word of his vindication. One reporter was from Camden, South Carolina. When the excited spectators had assembled in the foundry, Mills gave the signal and the trap door in the furnace was unlatched.[16] Fiery molten bronze oozed down the chute and into the mold positioned in the pit. It was a dazzling spectacle. The audience gasped. Afterwards, the *Camden Journal* man would tell his readers:

> Professors of Science laughed at the idea as utterly ridiculous. The other day, Mr. Mills invited them round to see the very species invention they had laughed at, in full operation.... A greater heat is engendered with one tenth the fuel—the fuel is charred, and worth as much when it comes out as before it went in."[17]

The beaming sculptor/founder recounted for his rapt listeners the story of how he came to conceive the principle of a chimney-less furnace. The boyhood recollection he narrated would appear in multiple publications over the years:

> This Mr. Mills was blest with a fairly good memory, and studying over the best authorities upon the subject of bronze-melting, he came to the conclusion that their plans were unnecessarily expensive. And he bethought him how, when a boy of 15, he had been with a gang of men burning charcoal, and how the lost log chain was found when the pit was burnt and emptied, it having been accidentally covered in the bottom of the pile, and lain there through the burning.
>
> But of that log chain Clark Mills also recollected that not only were the wrought-iron links melted and run together, but that pieces of brick that lay in contact with them were also melted, and so fused with the iron that they could not be separated nor distinguished from each other at the junction. . . .
>
> Anyway, Mr. Mills, wanting a bronze furnace, remembered his youth, and he took courage and said, "I will melt those guns in a charcoal pit. A coal pit burns wood; wood I can have. A coal pit uses no chimney; no chimney will I use. A coal pit is covered with earth to confine the heat and gases; I will build my furnace of brick or baked clay, that it may retain its form for another time. In that alone will I depart from the charcoal pit plan."[18]

Was Richter within earshot?

Mills led his guests on a tour of his workplace. He had mounted his 1,300-pound bell on a scaffold of hefty timbers. The Camden man would report:

> We rung a bell of large dimensions, which Mr. Mills had cast in his new furnace, which I never heard equaled for strength and euphony of tone.[19]

After the invitees departed, Mills and Richter operated the pulley system to haul the mold containing the bust of Washington up from the pit. When it cooled sufficiently, they extracted the cast. The head was stunning. The surface was rough—that was normal—but the cast did not show any visible defects. The two men rejoiced. Richter set about finishing, patinating, and polishing the sculpture.[20]

Along with his victory, Mills had apprised the public of his financial straits. No one, including the sculptor himself, had anticipated that he would have to build his own foundry and hire a foreman and a crew of workers to meet his contract with the Jackson Monument Committee. On top of that, buying metal for the bells, the Apollo, and the bust of Washington had been a burdensome outlay of capital. Copper, in particular, was very expensive. Mills was sinking in debt. One sympathetic piece appeared in the Washington *Republic*:

> It is the opinion of excellent judges of the art that Mr. Mills has, in this effort, achieved a work that will form the basis of a reputation entitling him to a position in the front rank of his profession; and yet, while the richest rewards are attending the efforts of others, he has been laboring for two years to produce a statue that can by possibility enrich him in reputation only. The price fixed upon his labor was in just keeping with his inexperience and obscurity; but he has produced a work of which the greatest adept might well be proud. In view of this, we would make the remark, that it would be but even-handed justice on the part of all who can derive gratification from witnessing a monument to Jackson, or an admirable specimen of the art, so to enhance his compensation as to enable the young artist to enter with good heart upon other tasks, and to feel that his art is to him not alone the sure pledge and guarantee of future fame, but a reliable source of present independence.[21]

The editor of the Charleston *Courier*, equally sanguine about Mills's ultimate success, put it more succinctly:

Mr. Mills has made a discovery that will be of great importance, and prove a source of profit to himself, which will be highly gratifying to his friends, for as yet his genius has not been rewarded with much of this world's goods. A very short period must only elapse, however, before his talent will be called into requisition on works that will command a remuneration worthy of this artist mind.[22]

During the summer of 1850, Mills attempted to raise some cash by selling his "test works." At first, given the press coverage he enjoyed, that entailed minimal effort. Scarcely had the bells been finished—mid-April—when the Charleston *Courier* reported, "He cast a bell, the tones of which are so sweet and rich, that it has been purchased for one of the Churches of this city."[23] The *Camden Journal* identified the buyer of "the bell of huge dimensions" as "Magnolia Seminary of South Carolina."[24] It appears, though, that these two reports actually refer to the same bell—the largest of the four, which Mills had set up in his foundry—that was bought by Magnolia Cemetery, which is located just north of Charleston.[25] In the minutes of the graveyard's Board of Directors, the entry of September 18, 1850, reads:

The Bell, as ordered from Mr. Clark Mills of Washington D.C. has arrived and is now upon the grounds. The Bill for the same will be presented at an early day for payment.[26]

The directors installed the bell in an obelisk-like housing adjoining the cemetery's gatehouse. The tower, like the gatehouse, was covered with clapboards and painted white. The bell still hangs today in the same location, but beneath a simple wooden canopy supported by two brick posts. Exposed to weather for over a century and a half, the shell of charcoal gray bronze is badly deteriorated and punched through with holes. Clearly visible, though, is the frieze of acanthus leaves that encircles the shoulder of the bell and, just below that, the words, "FIRST CASTING AT THE JACKSON MONUMENT

FOUNDRY AT WASHINGTON 1850." What payment was made for the bell "*at an early day,*" the Magnolia Cemetery minutes fail to reveal.[27] But it would be the only one of Mills's initial bronze works ever to bring him any remuneration.

One of the bells he kept for himself. He installed it at his compound in the White Lot "to call the men to work." That treasure would remain in the possession of its creator throughout his lifetime and then be sold as a part of his estate.[28]

One bell, an acquaintance of Mills's would later recall, "was sent to the Navy Yard, and one, I think, to the Smithsonian Institute."[29] Although uncorroborated, this recollection may contain at least some truth. Mills had dealings with both establishments and no source provides any other disposition of the remaining two bells.

Mills's busts of Apollo and Washington, by August 1850, were on exhibit in the "principal saloon" of the Congressional Library.[30] That large and elegant room, two stories high, occupied the middle of the west façade of the U.S. Capitol. It had a round skylight in its lofty, vaulted ceiling, and was furnished with sofas and writing tables with side chairs. More than 30 paintings and sculptures were on exhibition in the hall, most of them on loan from the owners and artists, such as Mills.[31] Four large windows and a door onto the Capitol's west portico offered library users "pleasant vantage points for admiring city and water views."[32]

Regarding Mills's *Washington*, a correspondent for the *Philadelphia Inquirer* reported:

> The bust, which is finely executed, is from a cast of Washington's living face, by Houdon, and is said by G. W. Park Custis, Esq., Gen. Washington's adopted son, to be the only correct likeness extant.[33]

Honest, noble, and devoid of any military or civilian allusion, the portrait is striking. Washington's chest and shoulders are bare. Long tresses course back from his high brow to a ponytail at the nape of

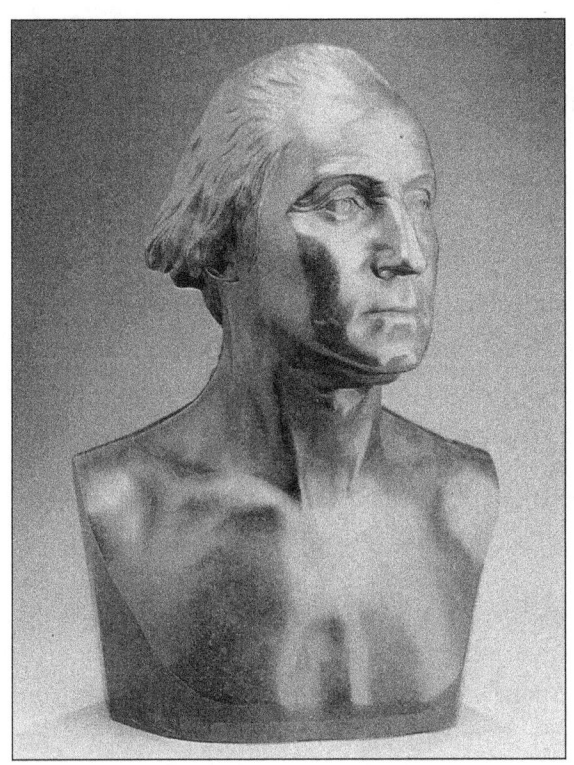

Mills's bronze bust of Washington, inscribed on the back, undated. To portray "the Father of His Country" accurately, Mills took a plaster cast of the bust of Washington at Mount Vernon, which Jean-Antoine Houdon had modeled in clay from life in 1785. Mills's original cast of this bust, made in 1850, was on display in the Congressional Library in the U.S. Capitol in 1851 when a fire damaged it. Mills then gave it to Dorothea Dix, who said the effigy had been "consecrated by fire." (courtesy of the Corcoran Gallery; now in the National Gallery of Art, Washington, D.C.)

his neck. The face peers to the left. The play of light on the modeled surface, which is a rich, charcoal gray, almost-black, imbues the figure with life. It stands 17¾ inches high, 13½ inches wide, and 9 inches deep. The inscription on the back betrays the sculptor's limited literary skills:

> This Bust is from the living face
> of Washington by Monseur Houdon
> 1785 Permission was granted to Clark
> Mills in 1849 by Col. Washington
> at Mnt Vernon to make a coppy of the
> original cast in Bronse
> Clark Mills
> Founder.[34]

The Washington correspondent of the *Philadelphia Inquirer* added:

> I understand Mr. Mills proposes to execute a number of plaster copies of it, and they will no doubt be eagerly sought after, by every one who desires to have a correct likeness of the Father of his Country. The price is, I believe, to be $10 for each copy.[35]

Indeed, they were "eagerly sought after." Mills would make many copies of his Washington bust, most of them left in plaster, but some with a patina of bronze and some cast in bronze. Unfortunately, he did not number them. In her Master's thesis, Rosemary Hopkins writes:

> So many busts of Washington were made by Mills that it is difficult to determine which particular bust is referred to [in 19th- and 20th-century sources].[36]

Mills also placed two of his plaster busts on display in the Congressional Library: Abraham Watkins Venable and **Samuel Houston**. Venable, a Congressman from North Carolina, had escorted the body of John C. Calhoun from Washington to Charleston.[37] He and Mills had become acquainted during those four days of ceremonies.[38] Houston was a Senator from the new state of Texas.[39] Mills, Venable and Houston were all members of the Democratic Party, owners of enslaved Black families, and ardent lovers of the South. Washington's *Southern Press* called Venable's bust "a very striking likeness" and Houston's "a perfect likeness."[40]

Mills offered his bronze bust of Washington to Congress for permanent display in the Capitol for $800. But the legislators did not take up the proposition in time.[41] On the morning of December 24, 1851, fire ravaged the Congressional Library, gutting the "principal saloon."[42] The *Weekly National Intelligencer* reported on the 27th:

> Of the statuary burnt and rendered worthless, we recollect . . .
> an Apollo in bronze by Mills; a very superior bronze likeness of Washington, ...[43]

The *National Era* of January 1, 1852, was more specific:

The fine busts of Jefferson, Lafayette, and General Taylor, with a bronze one of Washington, by Mills, are also rendered worthless.

John S. Meehan, the Librarian of Congress, in a letter to Senator James Alfred Pearce, Chairman of the Joint Committee on the Library, dated January 7, 1852, reiterated that "A bust, in bronze, of Gen. Washington, and a bust in bronze of Apollo" were lost in the fire.[44]

In fact, though, Mills's *Washington* had not been lost. Many months after the fire, while removing the mass of rubbish and charred chunks of stone, brick and mortar, workmen discovered the bust. It was damaged and blackened, but had survived. It was returned to Mills.[45]

Later that year—1852—Dorothea Dix, the New England humanitarian and reformer, visited Mills in his studio. Advocating improved care and more humane institutions for the mentally ill, Dix lectured extensively throughout the United States. Frequently she stopped in Washington to solicit congressional support for her cause. When she admired the rescued likeness of "the Father of our Country," Mills told her that he intended to melt it down and recast it. Dix urged him to preserve the original, as it "had been consecrated by fire."

Some months later, during another stay in Washington, Dix came again to Mills's studio. Seeing the "precious work" still there, she renewed her appeal to save it. Mills replied, "You shall have it. No one will value it as you."[46]

Dix immediately offered the damaged work to the Boston Athenaeum for permanent exhibition.[47] The *"excellence and rare beauty"* of the bust, she wrote, had *"attracted crowds of admirers"* to the Congressional Library.[48] The museum accepted the bust, but deaccessioned it just six years later. What became of it is unknown. However, later casts that Mills made from the original mold are extant.

It is surprising, given Mills's habitual silence regarding his foreman, what Dorothea Dix knew and conveyed to the Boston Athenaeum:

> *The Bronze Bust of Washington ... he [Mills] effected, assisted by a skillful worker in Bronze, of high reputation, Ludwig Richter, of Berlin, Prussia, and who conducted at that time the mechanical operations in the foundry, at Washington City.*

Mills had inscribed himself on the bust as "Founder"—not "Sculptor"—but Dix was evidently informed that Richter, conducting "*the mechanical operations*" of the foundry, had "*assisted*" Mills in its making. More than that, though, her phrase, "*at that time*," reveals that she also knew that the "*skillful worker in Bronze*" was no longer working there.[49] Even when Dorothea Dix had called at Mills's studio the first time, Richter was already gone. He had indeed been within earshot of his employer's claim to his chimney-less furnace. Or else he read Mills's boast in the newspaper.

NOTES

1 Richter's first memorial to Congress, Jan. 24, 1853; Legislative Records, 32nd Cong., 2nd Sess., box SEN 32A-H19, Committee on Public Buildings; Records of the U.S. Senate, RG 46; NARA.
2 "Apollo," *The* [Washington] *Republic*, Apr. 30, 1850, p. 3; reprinted in the [Charleston] *Courier*, May 4, 1850, p. 2.
3 Michael Edward Shapiro, *Bronze Casting and American Sculpture, 1850–1900* (Newark, Del.: University of Delaware Press, 1985): 46.
4 "Sketches of Washington. By Childe Harold. Washington, March 29, 1853. An Hour with Clark Mills, the Sculptor," *Brooklyn Eagle*, Mar. 30, 1853, p. 2.
5 "Apollo," *Republic*, Apr. 30, 1850, 3.
6 "Correspondence of the Courier. Washington, May 12," [Charleston] *Courier*, May 15, 1850, p. 2.
7 See Bk. 1, Ch. 19.
8 See Bk. 1, Chs. 14 and 29.
9 George Washington bust by Houdon, Collections, Object Number W-369, "George Washington's Mount Vernon," at www.mountvernon.org.
10 "Correspondence of the Baltimore Sun. Washington, Nov. 2, 1849. Jackson Monument," [Baltimore] *Sun*, Nov. 3, 1849, p. 4. Also Letter, Dorothea L. Dix to The President and Trustees of the Boston Athenaeum, Oct. 24, 1853; Boston Athenaeum Archive, Boston, Mass. For John Augustine Washington III

(1821–61), see https://www.mountvernon.org/library/digitalhistory/digital-encyclopedia/article/john-augustine-washington-iii/.
11 Letter, John Augustine Washington to William James Hubard, Oct. 8, 1859; ms. at Mount Vernon, Va.; quoted in Rosemary Hopkins, *Clark Mills: The First Native American Sculptor* (M.A. thesis, University of Maryland, 1966): 82–83.
12 Ibid. Also George Washington bust by Mills, Collections, Object Number H-709, "George Washington's Mount Vernon," at www.mountvernon.org.
13 In future years a controversy would erupt over whether Mills removed the original bust by Houdon from Mount Vernon and left his own copy in its place (see Bk. 2).
14 Richter's first memorial to Congress. Also letter, Dorothea L. Dix to The President and Trustees of the Boston Athenaeum.
15 "An Hour in the Studio of Mills," *Camden* [S.C.] *Journal*, June 4, 1850, p. 3, but the article bears the dateline, "Washington city, May 28, 1850."
16 Richter's first memorial to Congress.
17 "An Hour in the Studio . . . ," *Camden Journal*, June 4, 1850, 3.
18 A[loha] Vivarttas, "The Clark Mills Furnace—A Reminiscence," *The Railroad & Engineering Journal*, Vol. 63 (July 1889): 327–328. See also "An Hour with Clark Mills," [Washington] *Evening Star*, Dec. 24, 1870, p. 1; reprinted, abbreviated, in "Clark Mills Interviewed," *Chicago Tribune*, Jan. 3, 1871, p. 2. Also "Death of Clark Mills," [Washington] *Evening Star*, Jan. 12, 1883, p.4.
19 "An Hour in the Studio . . . ," *Camden Journal*, June 4, 1850, 3.
20 Richter's first memorial to Congress.
21 "Clark Mills' Equestrian Statue of Jackson," *The* [Washington] *Republic*, Apr. 17, 1850, p. 3; reprinted in *The Albion, A Journal of News, Politics and Literature*, vol. 9 (Apr. 20, 1850): 16.
22 "Clark Mills," [Charleston] *Courier*, May 8, 1850, p. 2.
23 "Correspondence of the Courier. Washington, April 14," [Charleston] *Courier*, Apr. 17, 1850, p. 2.
24 "An Hour in the Studio . . . ," *Camden Journal*, June 4, 1850, 3.
25 "Equestrian Statue of Jackson," [Charleston] *Courier*, Aug. 25, 1851, p. 2.
26 Minutes of Magnolia Cemetery, Sept. 18, 1850; Magnolia Cemetery, Charleston, S.C.
27 The author examined the bell in May 2011 and thanks Beverly M. Donald, Superintendent, Magnolia Cemetery, Charleston, for her generous research assistance. Regarding the bell's patina, see Bk. 1, Ch. 27, n. 20.
28 "Sale of an Artist's Effects," [Washington] *Evening Star*, Jan. 27, 1885, p. 3.
29 Vivarttas, "The Clark Mills Furnace . . . ," *Railroad & Engineering Journal*, vol. 63 (July 1889): 328.
30 "Bronze Bust of Washington," *The* [Washington] *Southern Press*, Aug. 2, 1850, p. 3. Also letter, John S. Meehan, Librarian of Congress, to Sen. James Alfred Pearce, Chairman of the Joint Committee on the Library, Jan. 7, 1852, itemizes the works of art lost when fire ravaged the Congressional Library on

Dec. 24, 1851; quoted in Charles E. Fairman, *Art and Artists of the Capitol of the United States of America* (Washington, D.C.: U.S. Govt. Print. Off., 1927): 380. Also Architect of the Capitol, *Art in the United States Capitol*, House Doc. No. 94-660, 94th Cong., 2nd Sess. (Washington, D.C.: U.S. Govt. Print. Off., 1978): 412–13, lists among Works of Art Lost in Fires, "Apollo, Bust or statue, Unknown artist, 1851." It does not list Mills's bust of Washington; however, the work itemized as "George Washington, Bust, bronze, David d'Angers, 1851" is, in fact, Mills's. Regarding this misattribution, see Fairman, *Art and Artists*, 90, 113 and 377. Since Mills's bust of Washington was not discovered until many months after the fire, early newspaper accounts of the fire and official reports of the art lost in it included the bust. Relying on these sources, twentieth-century scholars repeated the misinformation that a bronze bust of Washington by David d'Angers was among the destroyed artworks. In fact, it was Clark Mills's bust of Washington, and it was damaged, not destroyed.

31 Fairman, *Art and Artists,* 90, 113, 122, 377 and 380.
32 William C. Allen, *History of the United States Capitol: A Chronicle of Design, Construction, and Politics* (Washington, D.C.: U.S. Govt. Print. Off., 2001): 148.
33 "Correspondence of the Inquirer, Washington, Aug. 6, 1850," [Philadelphia] *Inquirer*, Aug. 8, 1850, p. 2.
34 In 2011 the author examined a copy of this bust that Mills gave to the Corcoran Gallery of Art, Washington, D.C., in 1883. The Corcoran's records indicate that it was chased by James D. Smith. Today, this copy is in the National Gallery of Art. See https://www.nga.gov/collection/art-object-page.176387.html #inscription. See also Hopkins, *Clark Mills*, 169. It is difficult to determine the original patina of Mills's monumental statues, as they have been restored several times over the years. His early, smaller works, however, have received less care, perhaps no restoration at all, so their original patina may be posited from visual inspection. See Bk. 1, Ch. 27, n. 20, and Ch. 36, n. 5.
35 "Correspondence of the Inquirer," *Inquirer*, Aug. 8, 1850, 2.
36 Hopkins, *Clark Mills*, 84 and 167–74.
37 "Letter from Washington. Correspondence of the Alexandria Gazette. Washington, April 13th, 1850," *Alexandria* [Va.] *Gazette*, Apr. 16, 1850, p. 3. Also South Carolina Legislature, *The Death and Funeral Ceremonies of John Caldwell Calhoun* . . . (Columbia, S.C.: Published by Order of the Legislature, Printed by A.S. Johnston, 1850): 58.
38 See Bk. 1, Ch. 29.
39 Sam Houston (1793–1863), see https://bioguide.congress.gov/search/bio/H000827.
40 "Bust of Hon. A. W. Venable," *The* [Washington] *Southern Press*, Aug. 19, 1850, p. 3; and "Senator Houston," *The* [Washington] *Southern Press*, Aug. 30, 1850, p. 3.

41 Letter, Dorothea L. Dix to The President and Trustees of the Boston Athenaeum. Also Hopkins, *Clark Mills*, 174. However, a search of the *Congressional Globe* yields no action by Congress regarding this matter.
42 "Destruction of the Congress Library," [Washington] *Weekly National Intelligencer*, Dec. 27, 1851, p. 5. Also Allen, *History of the United States Capitol*, 206.
43 "The National Library Destroyed by Fire," [Washington] *Weekly National Intelligencer*, Dec. 27, 1851, p. 7.
44 Quoted in Fairman, *Art and Artists*, 380.
45 Letter, Dorothea L. Dix to The President and Trustees of the Boston Athenaeum.
46 Ibid.
47 Correspondence between the author and Hina Hirayama, Associate Curator of Painting and Sculpture, The Boston Athenaeum, Sept.–Oct. 2010. Also Hopkins, *Clark Mills*, 174–75. Regarding Dix, see Thomas J. Brown, *Dorothea Dix, New England Reformer* (Cambridge, Mass.: Harvard University Press, 1998).
48 Letter, Dorothea L. Dix to The President and Trustees of the Boston Athenaeum.
49 Ibid.

CHAPTER 31
September 1850

OURSELVES.

We, the undersigned, subscribers to the United States Magazine and Democratic Review, feel deeply interested in its success, and recommend it to all our democratic friends. Its primary objects are to advocate and disseminate true Democracy, (such as was taught by Jefferson and Jackson,) and we feel confident, that such being the character of the work, all true democrats will feel the same interest that we do in the promulgation of those principles, and will be found to contribute to its support and development. We feel a national pride as well as duty in liberally supporting the only organ of the National Democratic Party in this great republican country; and we are confident in assuring our friends that if they will do their duty, that the editor and proprietors will make this organ, both as a literary and political Magazine, equal, if not superior, to any work published in this country or Europe. We would further add, that their general canvassing agent, Mr. THEODORE A. FOSTER, is now on his Southern and Western tour, and we earnestly recommend all good democrats to avail themselves of the present opportunity of enrolling their names on the books of the Democratic Review.

R. Jones,	Georgetown, D. C.	John S. Caskie,	Richmond, Va.
Clark Mills,	Washington, D. C.	John Wamble,	do.
Dr. McClelland,	Nashville, Tenn.	James T. Butler,	do.
N. G. Norcross,	Lowell, Mass.	Massena Beazley,	do.
W. V. Marquis,	Bellefontaine, Ohio.	Alexander Craig,	do.
T. M. Kobb,	do.	John Y. Mason,	do.
M. M. Preble,	New-Richmond, Ohio.	Dr. F. W. Roddey,	do.
E. B. Kilpatrick,	Holly Springs, Miss.	R. W. Hughes,	do.
Col. A. Dimock,	Harrisburg, Pa.	William H. Edwards,	do.
J. Buckingham, Mayor,	Alexandria, Va.	S. B. Wheeler,	Evansville, Va.
J. Lewis Kinzer,	do.	Weston E. Jones,	Richmond, Va.
William H. Irvin,	do.	R. H. Maury,	do.
Charles McCastleman,	do.	William Greuner,	do.
M. M. J. Society,	Marquette, Wis.	S. W. Glasbrook,	do.
H. S. Doggett,	Fredericksburg, Va.	R. Blankinship,	do.
Joseph Sanford,	do.	W. A. Patterson,	do.
Alfred Barratt,	N. Y. City.	R. H. Dickinson,	do.
James Montgomery, jr.	do.	Robert Lumpkin,	do.
Judge Amadeo Morel,	Assumption, La.	Benjamin Davis,	do.
H. W. Eastman,	Roslyn, N. Y.	D. S. Wooldridge,	do.
James Bennett,	Weston, Va.	Charles S. Morgan,	do.
Gov. John B. Floyd,	Richmond, Va.	T. H. Taylor,	do.
James Brown,	Wilsonville, Va.	George E. Deneal,	Harrisburg, Va.
Henry Shackleford,	Culpepper, C. H., Va.	E. Q. Fellows,	Center Sandwich, N. H.
Robert G. Scott,	Richmond, Va.	Horace Metcalf,	North Charlestown, N. H.

"OURSELVES," *The United States Magazine, and Democratic Review*, New Series, Vol. XXVII, No. 147 (September 1850): 285–88. Four pages listing 428 names.

CHAPTER 32
July–October 1850

At this point of time, the said Mills caused to be rumored abroad and actually had the audacity to claim that, he himself was the inventor, of your memorialist's furnace. . . . In consequence of this attempted wrong of said Mills, your memorialist left his employ.

Carl Ludwig Richter's first memorial to Congress, Jan. 24, 1853.[1]

Mills walked the short distance from his compound to the President's House. Swags of black crepe draped the balustrade along the roof, the pillars and every window. An attendant escorted him to the room where the body of Zachary Taylor had just been toweled dry, dressed in his uniform, and laid in a coffin. It was Friday, July 12, 1850, less than a year since the Old General had invited Mills into the Executive Mansion to take casts of his face and head. This time, however, the sculptor brought no plaster or tools, other than a tape measure, notepad and pencil.[2]

The President had died on Tuesday evening, after four days of suffering from cramping, diarrhea, nausea and dehydration. His personal physicians concluded that he had succumbed to *cholera morbus*, a bacterial infection of the small intestine. The President, they said, had eaten bad cherries at an Independence Day celebration he had recently attended.[3] The Washington correspondent of the Baltimore *Sun* reported:

> Until one o'clock to-day, the body of the venerated chief continued to be imbedded in ice. Upon removing it to the coffin the remains were found to be in a remarkable state of preservation. Clark Mills, Esq., the celebrated sculptor, was in waiting to take the exact measurement of General Taylor's form, so that if hereafter a statue should be desired, it could be executed with great precision.[4]

When Mills finished his measuring and note-taking, the casket containing the remarkably preserved corpse was borne to the middle of the East Room. The newly installed "splendid chandeliers of gas jets" and ornate tall mirrors had been swagged in black.[5] *The Southern Press* described the scene:

> The coffin was of rich mahogany, lined with white satin and covered with black silk velvet, over which was thrown the pall with heavy silver fringe and tassels. [At the President's face and shoulders, however, the casket was open.] The bier rested upon a raised platform, and over the whole a canopy of black and white, interwoven and fastened.[6]

Then the doors of the Executive Mansion were opened. Thousands of persons "gazed with admiration," the *Sun* informed Baltimore readers, "on the placid features of him who now shares the calm repose and imperishable fame of his illustrious predecessors."[7] Washington's *Daily National Intelligencer* noted:

> [A] white cravat was gracefully thrown around the neck. . . . On the coffin lay a profuse quantity of flowers, and buds, which were continually being removed by the crowds . . . and were as often renewed.[8]

Meanwhile, Mills walked back to his Spartan abode, clutching the corporeal dimensions he would need to make a life-size statue—should one be desired—of "Old Rough and Ready."

Saturday broke clear and cool for July, with a breeze.[9] At noon, the Reverend Doctor Pyne performed an Episcopal service over the casket in the presence of family members and invited guests. Then a long procession followed the remains of the late Chief Executive across the city. Led by President Millard Fillmore, it included members of both houses of Congress, heads of the federal departments and their clerks, Supreme Court justices and federal judges, the entire diplomatic corps, the mayors of Washington and Georgetown, six carriages containing 20 honorary pallbearers, military officers and aged Army veterans, local clergy and civil officeholders. Hundreds of "citizens and strangers" shuffled behind in silence.[10] The description in *The Southern Press* continued:

> The funeral car was drawn by eight large and beautiful white horses, their heads dressed in black plumes and the usual mourning accompanyments. The groomsmen were dressed in white, with flowing skirts gathered around the waist by a black sash. They wore turbans of white, with black interwoven.[11]

Behind the hearse pranced Old Whitey—"the Horse used by General Taylor in the late war," detailed the *Republic*—caparisoned for battle.[12] Military bands played funeral marches. Church bells tolled. Small guns blasted salutes from Capitol Hill, City Hall, and other public squares. Places of business were closed. Houses along the three-mile route were festooned in black crepe. The streets thronged with mute spectators. Men and boys removed their hats as the funeral car passed. The *Alexandria Gazette* apprised Virginians:

> The procession extended nearly two miles, its rear being at the President's House when the Military Escort, which occupied more than a third of its entire length, had passed the Capitol. It slowly wound its way over the high grounds East of the Capitol, pursuing the broad and lately improved avenue which heads to the Congressional Cemetery.[13]

At the burial ground, Reverend Pyne intoned a few simple words before Taylor's remains were deposited in the public vault. They were to be removed in the fall to his family's graveyard in Louisville, Kentucky. It was about four o'clock when three volleys of artillery and musketry closed the ceremonies. The pleasant weather had held all day.[14]

Monday, July 15th, the citizens of Washington resumed their occupations, Congress reconvened, and Isaac Edward Holmes rose at his desk in the House chamber to present the latest petition of the Jackson Monument Committee.[15] In light of the Congressman's personal acquaintance with Mills, it is not surprising that the members of the Committee chose him to champion their cause. A native Charlestonian, Holmes had served in the South Carolina legislature as Representative from the Parishes of St. Philip's and St. Michael's, where his family—and now Mills's wife and sons, too—resided.[16] He and close kin owned plantations worked by scores of bound African-American families.[17] After Holmes had been elected to the 28th and 29th Congresses, he sat for Mills during one of the bust maker's sojourns in Columbia.[18] Then, when Mills made his first trip to Washington, it was Holmes who introduced him to Cave Johnson, President of the Jackson Monument Committee.[19]

Subsequently, Holmes had the honor of making the official announcement of the demise of Calhoun to the House of Representatives.[20] His long encomium of the "Cast-Iron Man" was widely published and the Senate committee handling Calhoun's funeral invited him to accompany the body to Charleston.[21] During that pilgrimage, Holmes had socialized with his fellow Democrat and guest of the Committee of Twenty-Five, Clark Mills.[22]

Standing now before his colleagues in the House chamber, Holmes introduced Joint Resolution No. 21. The measure proposed granting the Jackson Monument Committee's memorial, which the Clerk read aloud:

> "To the Senate and House of Representatives of the United States, in Congress assembled:
>
> "The Jackson Monument Committee beg leave to return its thanks to the Congress of the United States for the gift of the cannon and mortars taken by General Jackson at Pensacola. These pieces were given with a view to conversion into the bronze equestrian statue, which the people have contributed to erect in

commemoration of General Jackson's achievements, but they have been found, on examination, to be themselves such beautiful works of art, and as well worthy of preservation as national trophies, that the Committee have concluded to apply to Congress for other old cannon, (condemned as unserviceable and not trophies,) enough of which are now lying useless in the arsenal at this city, to complete the construction of the statue.

"This will save the fine antiqued pieces that bear the motto of the sovereigns under whose auspices this Continent was discovered. The engraving on the breaches bears the menace of 'The thunderbolt of a violated king'—*'Violati Regis Fulmina.'*

"They should be laid at the feet of Jackson's statue to evidence to the world how harmless are the thunderbolts of kings when hurled at the men of iron, whose armor is the patriotism inspired by the Republic. These trophies should be preserved for the glory of our country, like those taken at Saratoga and Yorktown, and the batteries recently returned from Mexico, inscribed with the names of the heroes who directed them and by whom they were emblazoned with the victories of Palo Alto, Resaca, Monterey, Buena Vista, Vera Cruz, Cerro Gordo, Cherubusco, Molino del Rey, Chepultepec, and the city of Mexico.

"The Jackson Monument Committee, therefore, respectfully solicit Congress to authorize the supply of brass (which is designed to furnish to make the equestrian statue of Jackson) of such other unserviceable pieces of brass cannon, not national trophies, as may be found in its arsenals.

By order of the Jackson Monument Committee,

    Benj. B. French
    John C. Rives
    John W. Maury,

Sub-Committee of the Jackson Monument Committee, Washington, July 15, 1850."[23]

The Clerk retook his chair. The Speaker invited discussion. It was minimal. The House passed Holmes's Joint Resolution 21 and sent it to the Senate, which concurred the next day. The legislation authorized the President:

> [T]o cause to be delivered to the Jackson monument committee . . . such old brass guns, condemned as unserviceable, and not being national trophies, as may be sufficient material for casting the equestrian statue of Andrew Jackson.[24]

President Fillmore signed it into law on July 29, 1850, and promptly instructed his Secretary of War, Charles M. Conrad, to fulfill its mandate.[25] Conrad asked the Chief of the Army's Ordnance Department, General George Talcott, to locate suitable obsolete guns and deliver them to the Jackson Monument Committee. Talcott was a highly decorated officer who had worked in ordnance since the War of 1812.[26] He was already familiar with the Committee's enterprise. Four years earlier, he had found for them the Spanish field guns seized by Jackson.[27] He assigned this new search to Captain of Ordnance William Maynadier.

On August 26th, Maynadier notified John W. Maury, Secretary of the Committee, that old brass guns weighing an aggregate of 52,811 pounds had been located in Washington and New York arsenals. They would be forwarded to the Committee "*at such place within this City, as they may designate,*" by the Commandant of the Washington Arsenal, Major Alfred Mordecai. In addition, guns weighing 17,773 pounds had been found in the Watertown Arsenal near Boston and those would be shipped to Washington for the Committee, as well.[28] That much metal—70,584 pounds—was more than twice the amount Mills would ultimately need. Neither he, though, nor the Committee members, nor the Army officers were sufficiently practiced in the esoteric business of casting heroic-size public sculpture to know that.

It was thrilling news for Mills. But his delight was quickly snuffed. When the "old brass guns" reached his compound in the White Lot, they were analyzed—it must have been Richter who did it—and found to contain too much tin for a large bronze statue. They were useless to Mills. The Committee needed to secure other metal, not guns, so Richter could mix an alloy of his own composition.

Straightaway, Mills or his foreman—maybe both of them together—dashed to the Washington Navy Yard to consult Richter's former supervisor, Captain Lewis Warrington. As Chief of the Bureau of Ordnance and Hydrography, Warrington knew what metal he had on hand at the naval facility and it did include a quantity of scrap brass and old copper. The officer was sympathetic to the Jackson Monument Committee's plight. Besides, the guns already delivered to Mills, unsuitable for making a statue, if returned to the military, could be melted down and used for new castings. Warrington wrote a letter, recommending that the guns in Mills's possession be exchanged for sundry unused brass and copper lying in the Navy Yard.[29]

This time, it was not the Jackson Monument Committee, but Mills personally, who enlisted an advocate in Congress to champion their cause. He showed Warrington's letter to Abraham Watkins Venable. From their conversations during the Calhoun funeral trip, Mills knew that the Congressman from North Carolina applauded the Committee's project to memorialize Jackson.[30] He also knew that Venable, a fellow Southern Democrat, respected him as a sculptor. Returned to Washington from the funeral, Venable had had Mills make his bust, which was now on view in the Congressional Library.[31] Mills had matured into a shrewd lobbyist.

Venable took Mills's business in hand. He presented Warrington's letter to the Secretary of the Navy, William A. Graham, a fellow North Carolinian.[32] After securing Graham's blessing for the scrap-metal-for-old-guns swap, Venable drafted Joint Resolution No. 23. On September 14th he stood in the House chamber and addressed his colleagues:

> "Clarke Mills, the artist who has been employed to cast the bronze statue of General Andrew Jackson, has been much delayed for

want of proper metal for the work. He has incurred great expense by the delay, and some short time since he received from the Government a quantity of brass cannon which were useless for defence, but considered useful for the object in view. Upon an analysis of the brass it is found to contain an undue proportion of tin for the purpose of casting in bronze. There is in possession of the Government a quantity of old copper, which would be available to Mr. Mills, and the brass is precisely suitable for the purpose of casting cannon. I have a letter from Commodore Warrington recommending the exchange of metals, and called upon the Secretary of the Navy, who expressed his willingness to make the exchange should Congress approve of the arrangement. In order to prevent further delay, and as the exchange would be advantageous to all parties, I hope the House will at once adopt the resolution."[33]

Joint Resolution No. 23 passed the House without objection, then the Senate by unanimous consent.[34] President Fillmore signed it on Sept. 20, 1850.[35] The law made no mention whatever of the Jackson Monument Committee. It authorized the Secretary of the Navy:

> [T]o make such exchanges of the metal delivered to Clarke Mills ... for other brass or copper, in possession of the United States, as he may deem proper in order for the execution [of the Jackson equestrian].[36]

Mills wasted no time claiming *his* metal. On October 4th he sent Richter to the Navy Yard with a quickly scribbled note to Lieutenant John A. Dahlgren, the brilliant young ordnance expert on Warrington's staff:

> *Mr. Dalgreen will pleas deliver to my foreman Mr. Richter all the new copper first and the ballance from the old Sheete copper. And I will give you a receipt for the amount delivered. Yours with respect, Clark Mills.*[37]

This errand would be the last bidding that Richter performed for Mills. The inventor, it turns out, had known about Mills's false claim to his furnace for months. And he was outraged.

By this time, Richter had done more than construct the foundry and cast and finish Mills's bells and busts of Apollo and Washington. While Mills was waiting for free metal from the government and trying to sell his seminal bronze works, he had tasked Richter with "modeling the model of the Richmond Washington Monument."[38]

That was the colossal memorial to George Washington that Thomas Crawford was making in his studio in Rome for the Virginia State Assembly. Crawford's design had just been chosen in February, but the cornerstone had already been laid that very month with elaborate ceremony on the capitol grounds in Richmond.[39] It was by far the most ambitious sculptural work ever conceived by an American. A huge equestrian statue of the General topped a very high pedestal, around whose base stood six pedestrian figures, all larger than life, depicting eminent Virginians of the Revolutionary War era. The ensemble stood on a circular platform with six staircases leading down to ground level between pedestals surmounted by large American eagles.[40] The architecture was all of white granite, the figures were all of bronze.

Engravings of the breathtaking memorial as it was intended to look when completed were published many years before it was actually finished.[41] Mills must have obtained a picture of it for Richter to work from. Maybe he was already thinking about making an equestrian statue of Washington himself. Evidently, he was keen to study the concept of the only other American sculptor working on an equestrian statue of heroic proportion.[42]

Also while in Mills's employ, Richter had made "*two moulds of the body of General Jackson*," most probably the upper and lower portions of the torso.[43] In other words, he had contributed directly to the execution of the groundbreaking statue.

Most important, though, for Richter—the issue he was to press most stridently—was that the new way to cast bronze was of his devising, not Mills's. He was aggrieved and angry that Mills was taking all the credit for his revolutionary furnace and basking in all the glory for its success.

Richter quit.[44]

And on Saturday, October 19, 1850, Mills had an unexpected caller. Richard Wallach, the Marshal of the District of Columbia, came to his door with a subpoena. It ordered Mills to appear before the judges of the Circuit Court *"to answer unto Charles Lewis Richter in a plea of trespass."*[45]

NOTES

1. Richter's first memorial to Congress, Jan. 24, 1853: Legislative Records, 32nd Cong., 2nd Sess., box SEN 32A-H19, Committee on Public Buildings; Records of the U.S. Senate, RG 46; NARA.
2. "The Official Arrangements For the Funeral Solemnities and Interment of the late President of the United States, General Zachary Taylor," *The* [Washington] *Republic*, July 12, 1850, p. 2. Also "Correspondence of the Baltimore Sun, Washington, July 12. The Remains of the President," [Baltimore] *Sun*, July 13, 1850, p. 4.
3. Zachary Taylor (1784-1850), see https://en.wikipedia.org/wiki/Zachary_Taylor.
4. "Correspondence of the Baltimore Sun . . . ," *Sun*, July 13, 1850, 4.
5. Allan B. Slauson, ed., *A History of the City of Washington, Its Men and Institutions* (Washington, D.C.: The Washington Post, 1903): 82.
6. "Some Particulars of the Funeral Ceremonies of the late President," *The* [Washington] *Southern Press*, July 15, 1850, p. 2.
7. "Correspondence of the Baltimore Sun . . . ," *Sun*, July 13, 1850, 4.
8. "The Funeral," [Washington] *Daily National Intelligencer*, July 15, 1850, p. 3.
9. "The Funeral," *Alexandria* [Va.] *Gazette*, July 16, 1850, p. 2.
10. "The Obsequies," *The* [Washington] *Republic*, July 15, 1850, p. 2.
11. "Some Particulars . . . ," *Southern Press*, July 15, 1850, 2.
12. "The Official Arrangements . . . ," *Republic*, July 12, 1850, 2.
13. "The Funeral," *Alexandria Gazette*, July 16, 1850, 2.
14. Ibid.

15 *Congressional Globe*, 31st Cong., 1st Sess., July 15, 1850, p. 1372.
16 Isaac E. Holmes entry, 1850 U.S. Census, Parishes of St. Philip's and St. Michael's, Charleston, Charleston Co., S.C., p. 176 (handwritten), p. 88[b] (stamped); NARA M432, roll 850. Also Clark Mills household, 1850 U.S. Census, Parishes of St. Philip's and St. Michael's, Charleston, Charleston Co., S.C., p. 182 (handwritten), p. 91[b] (stamped); NARA M432, roll 850.
17 James G. Holmes, Miss Holmes and J. G. Holmes entries, 1850 U.S. Census Slave Schedule, Parishes of St. Philip's and St. Michael's, Charleston, Charleston Co., S.C.; NARA M432, roll 862.
18 See Bk. 1, Ch. 12.
19 See Bk. 1, Ch. 16.
20 *Congressional Globe*, 31st Cong., 1st Sess., Apr. 1, 1850, p. 620–21. For Isaac Edward Holmes (1796–1867), see https://bioguideretro.congress.gov/Home/MemberDetails?memIndex=H000738.
21 "Letter from Washington. Correspondence of the Alexandria Gazette. Washington, April 13th, 1850," *Alexandria* [Va.] *Gazette*, Apr. 16, 1850, p. 3. Also South Carolina Legislature, *The Death and Funeral Ceremonies of John Caldwell Calhoun* . . . (Columbia, S.C.: Published by Order of the Legislature, Printed by A.S. Johnston, 1850): 58.
22 See Bk. 1, Ch. 29.
23 *Congressional Globe*, 31st Cong., 1st Sess., July 15, 1850, p. 1372. Also *House Journal*, July 15, 1850, p. 1129.
24 *Congressional Globe*, 31st Cong., 1st Sess., July 16, 1850, p. 1389. Also *Senate Journal*, July 16, 1850, p. 451.
25 U.S. Statutes at Large, vol. 9:562, 31st Cong., 1st Sess., July 29, 1850.
26 George Talcott (1786–1862), see https://goordnance.army.mil/history/chiefs/talcott.html. See also Bk. 1, Ch. 16.
27 See Bk. 1, Ch. 16.
28 Letter, Wm. Maynadier, Capt. of Ord. in charge of Ord. Dept., to John W. Maury, Esq., Aug. 26, 1850; Misc. Letters; Records of the Office of the Chief of Ordnance, RG 156; NARA.
29 *Congressional Globe*, 31st Cong., 1st Sess., Sept. 14, 1850, p. 1811.
30 See Bk. 1, Ch. 29.
31 Ibid.
32 William Alexander Graham (1804–75), see https://en.wikipedia.org/wiki/William_Alexander_Graham.
33 *Congressional Globe*, 31st Cong., 1st Sess., Sept. 14, 1850, p. 1811.
34 *House Journal*, Sept. 14, 1850, p. 1454; and *Senate Journal*, Sept. 14, 1850, p. 630.
35 *House Journal*, Sept. 21, 1850, p. 1500; and *Senate Journal*, Sept. 21, 1850, p. 659.
36 U.S. Statutes at Large, vol. 9:563, 31st Cong., 1st Sess., Sept. 20, 1850. Curiously, the law makes no mention of the Jackson Monument Committee, which

nonetheless continued to play a role in the execution and dedication of the statue. See Bk. 1, Ch. 36 and Epilogue.
37 Handwritten note dated "Washington Oct. 4, 1850" (underscoring in original) included with Richter's second memorial to Congress, Feb. 24, 1855; Legislative Records, 33rd Cong., 2nd Sess., box SEN 33A-H10, Committee on the Library; Records of the U.S. Senate, RG 46; NARA.
38 Richter's first memorial to Congress.
39 "Virginia Washington Monument," [Washington] *Daily Union*, Feb. 9, 1850, p. 3; and "The Twenty-Second of February at Richmond, Virginia," [Washington] *Daily Union*, Feb. 27, 1850, p. 3.
40 "Equestrian Statue of Washington," *Gleason's Pictorial Drawing Room Companion*, vol. 4, no. 16 (Apr. 16, 1853): 241. The memorial as completed after the Civil War would differ slightly from the original design. See Michael Edward Shapiro, *Bronze Casting and American Sculpture, 1850–1900* (Newark, Del.: University of Newark Press, 1985): 27–28.
41 See, for example, "Equestrian Statue . . . ," *Gleason's*, vol. 4, no. 16 (Apr. 16, 1853): 241. Although no earlier engraving has been found, Mills had to have seen—prior to October 1850—some representation of what the finished work would look like for him to task Richter with making a model from it.
42 Henry Kirke Brown would not start sketching initial ideas for his *Washington* until December 1852. See Bk. 2.
43 Richter's first memorial to Congress.
44 Ibid.
45 Subpoena authorized by Judge Wm. Cranch, Aug. 5, 1850, served on Clarke [sic] Mills, Oct. 19, 1850; Case Papers, 1802–63, March Term 1856, Imparlance #32, box 811; Records of the U.S. District Court for the District of Columbia, RG 21; NARA.

CHAPTER 33
October 1850–August 1851

> *Washington City, October, 26th 1850.*
> *Honorable,*
> *Charles M. Conrad,*
> *Secretary of War,*
> *Sir,*
> *It is doubtless known to you that in the fabrication of bronze cannon and ordnance in all countries, the secret and art of perfectly combining or amalgamating the metals, have ever been the great desideratum....*
> *The object of this communication is to inform you that the art and secret mentioned, are known to me; and to that extent which enables me to make a better cannon than is made, either in America or Prussia. These facts I am desirous of proving to the Government; and to that end I would ask your cooperation....*
>
> Letter, Clark Mills to Charles M. Conrad[1]

Scarcely had Richter strode out the gate when Mills made this brash overture. Obviously, the loss of his foreman did not distress him. On the contrary, Mills was confident that he had learned enough about casting bronze to manage a foundry on his own, and more than that. His four-page missive to the Secretary of War continued:

> *What I desire is, that you would give me an order for the construction of a brass or bronze cannon, of such calibre and pattern as you may be pleased to name, to be of the same calibre and pattern of the best cannon which you can select, [whether made in America, Prussia or elsewhere] and now in the possession of the Government.—I will construct the cannon according to order,—when I propose that the*

same shall be fired,—shot for shot,— with the selected gun, until one or the other fail....

If I make good my claim, I shall ask you to make a report of the fact and results to Congress, together with such recommendations as may be warranted by those results. I shall ask these with a view to placing in the possession of Government, a knowledge of the secret and art I have mentioned and of obtaining therefor, a suitable reward....

Mills's debts had mounted. A contract from the U.S. military would relieve his financial distress and, thereby, ensure the completion of his Jackson. A less conceited supplicant would have closed the communication there. But Mills did not. He added a threat:

If my proposition be declined, or if my own Country shall refuse me that reward, my circumstances will compel me to make known my knowledge to others who will bestow it.

I am, Sir,
Very Respectfully
Your Obedient Servant,
Clark Mills[2]

The Secretary of War referred Mills's letter to General George Talcott, the Army's Chief of Ordnance, for his expert evaluation. Talcott knew who Mills was. Just three months earlier, the General had instructed Captain Maynadier to find unserviceable old guns for the Jackson Monument Committee, so the sculptor could cast a monumental statue of bronze.[3] In his three-and-a-half page reply to Conrad, dated November 15th, Talcott took issue with one declaration after the other made in Mills's long letter, then concluded:

What particular secret or art Mr. Mills possesses I know not, but I am not aware that he has ever cast, or seen cast any bronze cannon, or that there is any secret about the process. Of course, some persons have by practice acquired greater skill in it than others, but I do not think Mr. Mills is one of them, as he has had no practice in this kind of work. Finding him entirely mistaken in his assertions in other respects and not even knowing that heavy ordnance of the larger calibres are not made of bronze, but are better if made of iron, I must be permitted to doubt his assertion that he can make better bronze cannon than are made either in America or Prussia.

To give him an order to make heavy Siege or Sea Coast cannon of bronze would be to order him to make a useless experiment; and that he can make better field guns than those practically tested by our troops in the late Mexican war is extremely doubtful—certainly better guns have not been made in Europe or any other country.

Mr. Mills' letter is herewith returned.

I have the honor to be Sir,
Respectfully,
Your obd Servt
G. Talcott Br. Maj. Gen.[4]

Conrad accepted the officer's judgment and closed the matter on December 4th by instructing one of his clerks to send Mills a copy of Talcott's report.[5] Neither the Secretary of War nor the Chief of Ordnance deigned to comment on the petitioner's offensive threat. How curious it must have seemed to General Talcott: Mills's letter had come to his desk just two days after he had discussed the very same matter—casting cannons of superior bronze for the U.S. military—with a remarkable young metallurgist from Prussia named Carl Ludwig Richter.[6]

Precisely when Richter learned of Mills's claim to his furnace cannot be determined. Did he read it in the newspaper when Mills was still in Charleston? Did he hear it from Mills himself during the sculptor's open house in May? The open house in June? Certainly, though, by August Richter knew, because—behind his employer's back—the outraged inventor had acted.

First, he had called on William J. Stone, Jr. The "Attorney and Counsellor at Law" advertised in the Washington City directory:

"Will attend to the collection of debts and the prosecution of claims of every description. Office on F street, corner of Fourteenth street."[7] Richter explained his grievance to Stone, who filed the suit of "Charles Lewis Richter" versus "Clarke Mills" in the Circuit Court of the District of Columbia.[8] Mills had been subpoenaed to respond to Richter's accusation on October 19th, a week before writing his bold letter to Secretary Conrad.[9]

Next, Richter had gone to the Washington Arsenal at Greenleaf's Point and presented himself to the Commandant, Major Alfred Mordecai.[10] Mordecai was a key member of the Ordnance Board, which developed and approved all new weapons, ammunition, and related equipment for the U.S. military. In 1840 he had toured the arsenals and cannon foundries of Europe, including those in Prussia, to observe the latest advancements in arms manufacture. Returned to Washington, he was placed in charge of the Arsenal, where he was implementing the latest scientific methods for testing army ordnance. This was when Lieutenant Dahlgren was testing ordnance at the Navy Yard. Just as Dahlgren's inventions, innovations and writings would be seminal for modernizing the armament of the Navy, Mordecai's studies, experiments and reports would have a lasting impact on modernizing the armament of the Army.[11]

Richter described his furnace and its advantages to Major Mordecai. He also explained the improvements he could bring to it, now that he had the benefit of the trials made at the Jackson Monument Foundry. The officer was impressed with Richter's training and grasp of metallurgy. He urged his superior officer, the Chief of Ordnance, General Talcott, to meet with the Prussian. Talcott promptly summoned the two men to his office. The War Department occupied a federal-style red brick building immediately west of the President's House.[12]

By the end of the meeting, Talcott concurred with Mordecai that the young foreign engineer should be given a chance to prove himself. He offered Richter a one-year contract to construct his furnace

Engraving of Ames Manufacturing Company in Chicopee, Mass., a major supplier of bronze arms to the U.S. military, 1856. Carl Ludwig Richter built his unorthodox furnace here for the Army in 1851. He cast several cannons of superior quality, but failed twice to cast Henry Kirke Brown's bas-relief, *Plato and His Disciples*. Mills's proposal to cast cannons for the Army was rejected that same year. (*The New England Magazine*, new series, vol. xviii, no. 3 (May 1898): 363)

at the Ames Manufacturing Company in Chicopee, Massachusetts, and cast cannons for the Ordnance Board to test and evaluate.[13] Ames was a principal provider of bronze arms to the U.S. military. Richter departed for Chicopee within days—maybe even before Talcott received Mills's letter.

Mills had acted swiftly after Richter stormed out of his foundry. First, on October 21st, responding to the subpoena he had been served, he appeared in Circuit Court with his lawyer, Joseph H. Bradley, and denied Richter's accusations.[14] A few days after that he penned his audacious offer to Secretary Conrad. When Mills received General Talcott's peremptory refusal, he did not contest it. He was too preoccupied now to concern himself with manufacturing arms—for his own country or any other. By this time, he had the "other brass or copper" from the Navy Yard.[15] He also had the two molds of the body of Jackson that Richter had made.[16] He was eager to start casting his statue. His plan was to cast the smaller pieces of the rider before attempting the larger, heavier pieces of the horse.

It was not long, though—despite his innate brilliance and brash self-confidence—that Mills realized he was unprepared to fill Richter's shoes. He went in search of seasoned foundrymen. This time he did not head to Pennsylvania. Instead, he traveled to a center of old and reputable foundries closer to home, Baltimore. But there he encountered the same obstacle as before. The *Daily Union* would explain:

> He could find numbers of workmen capable of casting things in the ordinary way, or any small piece. He could find no one who understood casting so large a mass as his statue, which required so much skill and precision.[17]

Mills did hire one brass finisher named Philip A. McAleer, but the youth was hardly "seasoned." About 17 years of age, the native of York, Pennsylvania, had just completed his apprenticeship in Baltimore.[18] Known to everyone as "Mac," he would work for Mills "throughout the whole of the time that the [Jackson] statue was being made."[19] Interviewed many years later by an *Evening Star* reporter, McAleer would describe the challenge Mills faced trying to replace Richter:

> "Several Germans, who claimed to come from Munich, came to this city [Washington] when they heard about the statue and they agreed to cast it in one piece. Mr. Mills at once employed them, but just previous to completing the mold for pouring in the metal they wanted him to sign a contract agreeing to pay them a certain amount of money in case the casting was perfect; if not, they were to receive only days' wages. Mr. Mills saw that this was likely to take the wind out of his sails and he broke up the mold.
>
> "Then he brought over a German iron molder from Baltimore by the name of Keilholtz. He undertook the contract, but soon found that he could do nothing with it and he threw up the job.
>
> "The next man that Mr. Mills engaged was a Frenchman named LaRue and he assisted Mr. Mills in modeling and finally completed the casting in thirteen pieces, just as it is today."[20]

Of the Germans, supposedly from Munich, and the founder named LaRue, nothing further has been discovered. However, the Keilholtz of McAleer's recollection was probably David Keilholtz, co-owner of an iron foundry in Havre de Grace, Maryland, a few miles north of Baltimore. Keilholtz and his partner dissolved their business on September 2, 1850, shortly before Mills brought the molder to Washington.[21] But Keilholtz, only 22 years old, quickly found the project beyond his abilities and left.

Mills's frustrated effort to secure expert help did not bring his work to a standstill. A flattering piece in the Washington *Daily Union* would later recount:

> [Mills] trusted in himself; he took from the street ordinary laborers, and as he instructed himself, he directed them. He did nothing rashly; he made himself well acquainted with the principles

and practices of casting metals. It was impossible, however, to foresee everything. His idea of doing the work was correct, but his experience was insufficient.[22]

Mills directed the motley team of workers in weighing out, melting down, and mixing the Navy Yard scrap metal.[23] Interestingly, though, Mills himself would one day declare, "The Jackson statue contained bronze from cannon seized by the general himself in Battle."[24] Since the four 17th-century Spanish cannons captured by Jackson were set aside to be part of the memorial, it could only have been the two mortars that Mills used in his bronze. Indeed, those guns do disappear from the historical record after 1850.[25] However, their combined weight of 2,130 pounds would have constituted only about seven percent of the statue's 30,000 pounds of bronze. Even that small amount, though, would have justified Mills in asserting truthfully that the statue "contained bronze from cannon seized by the general himself."

However, his words were misunderstood to mean that the Jackson equestrian was cast *entirely* from guns captured by Jackson. The symbolism was powerful and irresistible to a nation emerging onto the world stage. Through repetition, it would become a fixed "fact" that the statue was cast from British (or Spanish) cannons captured by Jackson at the Battle of New Orleans (or in Florida).[26] For years to come, generations of writers, popular and scholarly alike, would echo the misinformation innumerable times.[27]

The figure of Jackson consisted of eight parts: (1 and 2) upper and lower torso down to the knees, which two elements would be joined at the sash girding the General's waist; (3 and 4) arms; (5) head, which fit into the General's stock, or necktie; (6 and 7) boots, which would be attached to the knees; and (8) bicorn, or cocked hat.[28] One piece after the other—each in itself a unique sculpture—Mills and his team struggled through the steps of mold-making and casting the outsized effigy of the Hero of New Orleans. Overcoming mishaps when they occurred and correcting missteps when they were made, the band of beginners improved their expertise and honed their skills as they went along.

Throughout the process, despite persistent challenges, Mills kept his enterprise before the eyes of the public. Washington's *American Telegraph* noted on April 16, 1851:

> Clark Mills' miniature model of the bronze equestrian statue of Jackson may be seen at the fancy, book and stationery store of Mssrs. Taylor and Maury. Connoisseurs regard this statue as a great curiosity, from the self-sustaining position of the horse and rider, in a rampant attitude.[29]

Mills had been displaying his busts of prominent Americans at Taylor & Maury's shop for years.[30] The free publicity was a boon for the sculptor and he continued to take advantage of it. Soon his bust of **Matthew St. Clair Clarke** would be showcased there.[31] Clarke had served as Clerk of the House of Representatives for seven Congresses prior to Benjamin Brown French.[32]

In addition to exhibiting his handiwork at Taylor & Maury's, Mills maintained public exposure by keeping the doors of his studio and foundry open. Just as he had done while creating the full-scale model of the equestrian—when callers included his arch-rival, Henry Kirke Brown—and casting the bust of Washington—when a *Camden Journal* reporter was among invited guests—Mills welcomed visitors into his studio and foundry to witness his achievements.[33] Wrote an editor of the *Daily Union*:

> We have been several times permitted to examine the details of the progress of this work, and are satisfied that its result will be not only worthy of the great subject, but place Mr. Mills on the list of the most distinguished artists.[34]

The gregarious sculptor/founder seemed to draw energy and stamina from publicity. But he never mentioned McAleer, Keilholtz,

LaRue, or any other of his workers, either by name or otherwise, just as he never mentioned Richter or Reid. He never acknowledging the assistance of anyone.

Given Mills's open door policy, news of his doings appeared continually in the nation's press, and with it, his claim that he invented the furnace.[35] This allowed Henry Kirke Brown to follow his competitor's progress. On July 28, 1851, the sculptor wrote from Chicopee, Massachusetts, to his wife in Brooklyn, New York:

> *It may be that Mills is succeeding against all obstacles, but his success will not be exactly that which I propose to myself. A monument of such enduring materials, constructed in an inferior manner, is a terrible comment upon the ambition of an artist.*[36]

Brown was in Chicopee collaborating with James T. Ames to adapt the Ames armaments foundry and train its workforce to cast bronze sculpture. The two men faced the same frustration as Mills: a lack of artisans in the United States having the requisite skills.

Coincidentally, Carl Ludwig Richter was also at the Ames Manufacturing Company at that time, building his furnace and casting cannons for the Ordnance Board to evaluate. Ames took advantage of his presence to offer him the opportunity to cast a large bas-relief by Brown, titled *Plato and His Disciples*. Richter accepted, but failed twice to produce an acceptable cast.[37] Brown wrote to his wife:

> *I could not help laughing last night, to hear Richter relating his misfortunes with the bas-relief. He speaks English very badly, after attempting in vain to account for his failure in various ways, he jumped up and said: "Py Got, I dinks one ding, dat number seven is one tam bad number." Seven, is the number of figures in the bass-relief; that seemed a new idea to him, and, for the time, seemed conclusive. Then he talked about "der tam Irishmans," who assisted him, but it seemed the hardest thing in the world for him to attribute the fault to himself.*[38]

On the other hand, three cannons that Richter cast in his furnace were judged by the Ordnance Board to contain "superior" bronze.[39] But the report submitted to the Army's new Chief of Ordnance, Colonel Henry K. Craig (Talcott had retired), stated that the improvement resulted, not from the design of the furnace, but rather from the handling of the metal. When Richter's one-year contract expired, Ames did not renew it. *"After a good deal of experiment and expense,"* the business owner informed the Army, he would not *"rebuild under his supervision."*[40]

Furious that he had been treated unfairly, Richter rushed back to Washington. To Colonel Craig and to the Secretary of War, Charles M. Conrad, he argued for a second chance. He complained that in Chicopee he had been forced to work under conditions he was powerless to control. He had had to use coal for fuel, rather than wood, and on occasion water seeped into his casting pit, which was ruinous. The success of his improvements, he protested, lay in *both* the furnace's unique configuration *and* the handling of the metals.[41]

To military and civilian leaders at the highest echelons of power, Richter repeatedly described his training and experience in the most glowing terms. And, in truth, he had enjoyed all of the advantages of being born into a privileged Prussian family.[42] But his self-promotion was counterproductive. It betrayed the young man's arrogance, which American officials found offensive. Added to this, Richter's fiery temperament alienated them. Although he observed the conventions of propriety of the day, he lacked composure and tact. To Army officers still heady with the stunning victory recently won over Mexico, Richter wrote that they should cast their cannons the way the Prussians do. Such effrontery the American victors did not care to hear.

In addition, Richter's self-importance rankled the much older, highly accomplished men whose patronage he sought. They considered the immigrant to be "assuming above his station." His English bore a heavy German accent, and the stout, florid man lacked the advantage of an imposing stature or impressive uniform. Moreover, the spelling and penmanship of his missives were abysmal, and their overall expression and appearance, sloppy. Neither the Army nor the War Department yielded to his persistent whining.

Richter, therefore, decamped to a community where he stood a better chance of realizing his ambition: the Germanic neighborhood of Manhattan's lower east side, called *Kleindeutschland*. As he gained a foothold there, his lawsuit against Mills in the Circuit Court of the District of Columbia would be continued from one term to the next. At length, it would be dropped from the docket for lack of action.[43] But Washington had not seen the last of the indignant and importunate Prussian. As soon as naturalization law allowed (five years' residency in the United States), Richter would complete the second step of the process to become a citizen. He would assume a leadership role in social and political activism in New York City and use that newfound platform to assail Mills in the press. Then, at the very moment of Mills's triumph and exaltation, Richter would reappear in the national capital to accuse his former employer before the public.[44]

Mills, meanwhile, unfazed by the clamoring of his erstwhile foreman, continued to cast the figure of Jackson. By the end of August 1851—ten months after starting—all eight parts of the General were done.[45] The achievement was hard-won and remarkable. Turning to the casting of the horse, Mills was encouraged. His spirits were high. His optimism led members of the press to publish unrealistic dates for the completion of his statue:

Jan. 9, 1850: "I learn that the statue ***will soon be completed***." ([Baltimore] *Sun*)[46]

Jan. 11, 1850: "***During the present month***, the equestrian statue of Gen. Jackson in bronze will be completed." (*Brooklyn Eagle*)[47]

Apr. 17, 1850: "[L]ittle now remains for him to do ere his admirable production shall occupy its destined place, ... *The present summer* will probably realize this." (*The* [Washington] *Republic*)[48]

Apr. 24, 1850: "Mills' Equestrian Statue of Gen. Jackson, ... will be completed *during the summer.*" (*Brooklyn Eagle*)[49]

Apr. 27, 1850: "Mr. Mills' equestrian statue of Jackson will be completed *during the approaching summer.*" ([Charleston] *Courier*)[50]

Dec. 20, 1850: "Clark Mills, Esq., the American artist, is about completing that noble work, ... so that it will be ready *by early Spring.*" ([Baltimore] *Sun*)[51]

Apr. 10, 1851: "The Equestrian statue in bronze of Andrew Jackson, ... will be ready to be placed on its pedestal, ... on *the 4th of July next.*" (*New York Journal of Commerce*)[52]

June 3, 1851: "The Equestrian Statue of Gen. Jackson ... is to be placed on the pedestal in Lafayette Square, opposite the president's House, on *the 4th of July.*" (*Brooklyn Eagle*)[53]

Aug. 22, 1851: "Unless some unforeseen accident occur, he expects to finish the statue by *the first of next January.*" (*The* [Washington] *Republic*, reprinted in newspapers of Boston, New Orleans, San Francisco, and many other cities)[54]

That was Mills's latest rosy prognostication: a finished statue by January 1852. But more than one "unforeseen accident" was indeed about to occur.

NOTES

1. Letter, Clark Mills to Charles M. Conrad, Oct. 26, 1850; Special File, Inventions, Class IX, 1–140; Records of the Office of the Chief of Ordnance, RG 156; NARA.
2. This letter was not written by Mills's own hand. For important correspondence, he routinely engaged a scribe, because his competence in spelling and grammar was rudimentary and his handwriting was labored. He did not keep a secretary, but engaged different people at different times. Mills only signed his name. Only two hastily penned notes written by Mills himself have been found that show his handwriting: (1) Note dated "Washington Oct. 4, 1850," included with Richter's second memorial to Congress, Feb. 24, 1855; Legislative Records, 33rd Cong., 2nd Sess., box SEN 33A-H10, Committee on the Library; Records of the U.S. Senate, RG 46; NARA; and (2) Receipt for payment, Dome of the U.S. Capitol to Clark Mills, dated "Washington June 2[?] 1862;" photocopy in file "Statue of Freedom;" Archives, Office of the Architect of the Capitol, Washington, D.C. (The second numeral in the date is illegible.) Examples of Mills's signature, on the other hand, are numerous, including: (1) Letter, Mills to Charles M. Conrad, Oct. 26, 1850; (2) Mills to Secretary A. H. H. Stuart, Sept. 22, 1852; Letters Received and Other Records Relating to the Extension of the U.S. Capitol, 1851–1872, A1, Entry 291, Box 3; Records of the Office of the Secretary of the Interior, RG 48; NARA; (3) Mills to Jacob Thompson, Secretary of the Interior, May 11, 1858; Letters Received and Other Records Relating to the Extension of the U.S. Capitol, 1851–1872, A1, Entry 291, box 3; Records of the Office of the Secretary of the Interior, RG 48; NARA; (4) Mills to The Hon. Jas. G. Barrett, Mayor, Sept. 13th 1858; MS 0140, Washington History Center, Washington, D.C.; (5) Mills to Hon. Jno B. Floyd, Secretary of War, Apr. 19, 1859; photocopy in file "Statue of Freedom;" (6) Mills to Sir. Capt M C Meigs in charge &c. Present, May 24, 1861; photocopy in file "Statue of Freedom;" (7) Mills to John A. Smith, Clerk of the Circuit Court of the District of Columbia, May 2, 1862; Records of the U.S. District Court for the District of Columbia Relating to Slaves, 1851–1863, NARA M433, roll 2; viewed at www.Fold3.com; and (8) Agreement to deliver "the equestrian Statue of Genl. Jackson" to Mssrs. Hoyt and Rockwell, "Washington D.C. Octo 3rd 1870."
3. See Bk. 1, Ch. 32.
4. Letter, G. Talcott, Br. Maj. Gen., to Hon. C. M. Conrad, Secretary of War, Nov. 15, 1850; Letters Sent to the War Department by the Ordnance Department; Records of the Office of the Chief of Ordnance, RG 156; NARA.
5. Letter, Geo. T. M. Davis, [illegible] clerk, to Mr. Clark Mills, D.C., Dec. 4, 1850; Letters Sent to the War Department by the Ordnance Department; Records of the Office of the Chief of Ordnance, RG 156; NARA.

6   Letter, C. Ludwig Richter to Gen. Talcott, Esq., Oct. 22, 1850; Letters Received, 1812–1894, R-194-1850; Records of the Office of the Chief of Ordnance, RG 156; NARA.
7   Edward Waite, comp. and pub., *The Washington Directory, and Congressional, and Executive Register, for 1850* (Washington, D.C.: Columbus Alexander, printer, 1850): 83 and 201.
8   Charles Lewis Richter vs. Clarke [sic] Mills, Case 424; D.C. Circuit Court, Docket Book, October Term 1850, vol. 104; Records of the U.S. District Court for the District of Columbia, RG 21; NARA.
9   Subpoena authorized by Judge Wm. Cranch, Aug. 5, 1850, served on Clarke [sic] Mills, Oct. 19, 1850; Case Papers, 1802–63, March Term 1856, Imparlance #32, box 811; Records of the U.S. District Court for the District of Columbia, RG 21; NARA.
10 James Keily, *Map of the City of Washington, D.C.* (Camden, N.J.: Lloyd VanDerveer, 1850); at https://www.loc.gov/item/88694045/.
11 Alfred Mordecai (1804–87), see https://www.ncpedia.org/biography/mordecai-and-alfred.
12 Keily, *Map of the City of Washington,* 1850.
13 Letter, J[ames] T. Ames, to Capt. Wm. Maynadier, Nov. 22, 1851; Special File, Inventions, Class 1A, no. 103; Records of the Office of the Chief of Ordnance, RG 156; NARA.
14 Subpoena authorized by Judge Wm. Cranch, Aug. 5, 1850, annotated with Mills's appearance, Oct. 23, 1850. Also Waite, *Washington Directory . . . for 1850*, 10 and 11.
15 "The Jackson Statue," [Washington] *Evening Star*, May 3, 1890, p. 9. See also Bk. 1, Ch. 32.
16 Richter's second memorial to Congress with the annexed note.
17 "History of the Jackson Statue," [Washington] *Daily Union*, Jan. 18, 1853, p. 2.
18 Biographical facts are derived from: (1) Philip McAleer entry, 1870 U.S. Census, Ward 1, Washington, D.C., p. 69 (handwritten), p. 35 (stamped); NARA M593, roll 123; (2) Philip McAleer entry, 1880 U.S. Census, Washington, County of Washington, p. 7 (handwritten), p. 154 (stamped); NARA T9, roll 121; (3) Andrew Boyd, comp., *Boyd's Washington and Georgetown Directory* (Washington, D.C.: Hudson Taylor, 1864): 206; (4) "Died at Emergency," [Washington] *Evening Star*, Jun. 28, 1893, p. 7; and (5) Death Certificate, Edward McAleer (Philip's son), Washington, D.C., Nov. 10, 1930; "District of Columbia Deaths, 1874–1961," viewed at www.familysearch.org.
19 "The Jackson Statue," [Washington] *Evening Star*, May 3, 1890, p. 9.
20 Ibid.
21 "Dissolution of Co-Partnership," [Baltimore] *Sun*, Sept. 7, 1850, p. 4. Also David Keilholtz, 1850 U.S. Census, District 2, Harford Co., Md. (Havre de Grace), p. 291 (handwritten), p. 146 (stamped); NARA M432, roll 294.
22 "History of the Jackson Statue," *Daily Union*, Jan. 18, 1853, 2.

23 See Bk. 1, Ch. 32.
24 The original source from which the author extracted this crucial quotation, unfortunately, could not be found and cited here before the book went to press.
25 No mention of the two mortars has been found after July 15, 1850, when Cong. Holmes presented the Jackson Monument Committee's memorial to Congress.
26 See, for example, among many others: (1) "Equestrian Statue of Andrew Jackson, at Washington, by Mills.—Cast from British Cannon Captured by Jackson," full-page engraving, *Illustrated* [N.Y.] *News*, Jan. 15, 1853, p. 41; and (2) "History of the Jackson Statue," *Daily Union*, Jan. 18, 1853, 2: "Government furnished the metal, which was old cannons and some of which was captured by Gen. Jackson."
27 See, for example, among many others: (1) Michael Edward Shapiro, *Bronze Casting and American Sculpture, 1850–1900* (Newark, Del.: University of Delaware Press, 1985): 39; and (2) Hametia Fielder King, *Historical Survey of Lafayette Square, Washington, D.C.* (Prepared for John Carl Warnecke & Associates, San Francisco, 1963): 2: "It was executed by Clark Mills, the sculptor, from guns captured by Jackson at New Orleans in the War of 1812."
28 The number of pieces comprising the statue has been reported variously. Rosemary Hopkins, *Clark Mills: The First Native American Sculptor* (M.A. thesis, University of Maryland, 1966): 64, puts the total at ten, as do most other authors. Tim Kerr, *The History of the Equestrian Statue of General Andrew Jackson, Lafayette Park, Washington, D.C.* Typescript report prepared for the National Park Service, White House Liaison, August 1999, p. 25, concurs, specifying that the body of Jackson is six pieces and the horse, four. This is identical to "The Equestrian Statue of Jackson," [N.Y.] *Illustrated News*, Jan. 15, 1853, p. 44. However, "The Jackson Statue," [Washington] *Evening Star*, May 3, 1890, p. 9, quotes Philip McAleer, who participated in the statue's casting and mounting, as saying that it consists of 13 pieces: eight for the rider, four for the steed, and one for the hidden base. Since the principal pieces of the statue are augmented by ancillary parts—reins, stirrups, straps holding the stirrups, spurs and saber—it appears most likely that the statue consists of 12 principal pieces, at least eight much smaller accessory pieces, and the hidden base.
29 [no title], [Washington] *American Telegraph*, Apr. 16, 1851, p. 3.
30 See Bk. 1, Ch. 25.
31 "Works of Art," *The* [Washington] *Republic*, Feb. 23, 1852, p. 4.
32 Matthew St. Clair Clarke (1791–1852), see https://history.house.gov/People/Detail/38363.
33 See also Bk. 1, Chs. 23 and 30.
34 "Mr. Mills's Equestrian Statue of General Jackson," [Washington] *Daily Union*, June 13, 1851, p. 2.

35 See, for example: (1) "Mr. Clarke [sic] Mills, the Sculptor," [Washington] *Daily Union*, Apr. 13, 1851, p. 2; (2) "Washington, April 9th," *The* [Amherst, N.H.] *Farmers' Cabinet*, Apr. 17, 1851, p. 2; (3) "Equestrian Statue of Jackson," *The* [Washington] *Republic*, Aug. 22, 1851, p. 3; reprinted in the [Charleston] *Courier*, Aug. 25, 1851, p. 2; and (4) "Native Artists," *The New England Farmer, a Monthly Journal*, vol. 3, no. 18 (Aug. 30, 1851): 295.
36 Letter, Henry Kirke Brown to Lydia Brown, July 28, 1851; Papers of Henry Kirke Bush-Brown, vol. 3: 612; Manuscript Division, Library of Congress, Washington, D.C.
37 Shapiro, *Bronze Casting*, 50–52. Also John Philip Colletta, "'The Workman of C. Mills:' Carl Ludwig Richter and the Statue of Andrew Jackson in Lafayette Park," *Washington History*, vol. 23 (2001): 12–13.
38 Letter, Henry Kirke Brown to Lydia Brown, July 28, 1851. See also Shapiro, *Bronze Casting*, 50.
39 "History of the Jackson Statue," *Daily Union*, Jan. 18, 1853, 2.
40 Letter, James T. Ames to Captain William Maynadier, Nov. 22, 1851; Special File, Inventions, Class 1A, Entry 994; Records of the Office of the Chief of Ordnance, RG 156; NARA.
41 Colletta, "'The Workman of C. Mills' . . . ," 12–13.
42 See Bk. 1, Ch. 22.
43 Charles L. Rechter [sic] vs. Clarke [sic] Mills, Case 39; D.C. Circuit Court, Docket Book, March Term 1856, vol. 115; Records of the U.S. District Court for the District of Columbia, RG 21; NARA.
44 Colletta, "'The Workman of C. Mills' . . . ," 14–25. See also Bk. 2.
45 "Equestrian Statue of Jackson," *Republic*, Aug. 22, 1851, 3.
46 "Correspondence of the Baltimore Sun. Washington, Jan. 8, 1850, The Jackson Statue," [Baltimore] *Sun*, Jan. 9, 1850, p. 4.
47 "Equestrian Statue of Jackson," *Brooklyn Eagle*, Jan. 11, 1850, p. 2.
48 "Clark Mills' Equestrian Statue of Jackson," *The* [Washington] *Republic*, Apr. 17, 1850, p. 3.
49 [no title], *Brooklyn Eagle*, Apr. 24, 1850, p. 2.
50 [no title], [Charleston] *Courier*, Apr. 27, 1850, p. 2.
51 "Correspondence of the Baltimore Sun. Washington, Dec. 19," [Baltimore] *Sun*, Dec. 20, 1850, p. 4.
52 Reprinted in "Mr. Clarke [sic] Mills, the Sculptor," [Washington] *Daily Union*, Apr. 17, 1851, p. 2, as "[Correspondence of the N. Y. Journal of Commerce.] Washington, April 9."
53 [no title], *Brooklyn Eagle*, Jun. 3, 1851, p. 3.
54 "Equestrian Statue . . . ," *Republic*, Aug. 22, 1851, 3. Reprinted in numerous newspapers.

CHAPTER 34
September 1851–August 1852

When Clark Mills had completed his preparations for the casting of his equestrian statue of Jackson, . . . he invited a number of his friends to be present and among them Forrest. In those days the casting of colossal bronze statues was not so well understood in this country as it is now, and Mill's [sic] preparations were somewhat crude.

"Anecdote of Forrest," *Fort Wayne* [Ind.] *Daily Gazette*, June 16, 1881, p. 8.

Mills began casting his one-third-larger-than-life-size horse in September of 1851.[1] The charger consisted of four parts: (1 and 2) the two sides of the body, including fore and hind legs; (3) head and neck; and (4) tail.[2] Much larger and heavier than any piece of the figure of Jackson, these casts posed new challenges and resulted in repeated failures.[3] Not all of Mills's "foundry spectacles" transpired without incident. One particularly violent explosion became the subject of newspaper accounts for many years afterwards, because it involved a guest of particular celebrity: the stage actor, Edwin Forrest. But that was not the only fiasco Mills suffered in his attempts to cast Jackson's war horse.

Early in the process, Mills's furnace burst. The *Evening Star* reported:

> He melted several tons of bronze cannon in his furnace, but, unfortunately, the brickwork was not strong enough to resist the heavy pressure. The melted bronze forged its way through the joints of the brickwork, and the melted metal was chilled.[4]

This may have happened on Mills's initial attempt to cast one of the flanks of the horse. No other part of the sculpture required as much metal. The setback cost Mills up to five or six thousand pounds of bronze, as well as time and money.[5] He needed to construct an entirely new furnace, one capable of melting larger quantities of alloy. Continued the *Evening Star* piece:

> Never daunted, Mr. Mills dug out of the ground the great conglomerated mass of bricks and bronze, and sent for another firm of bricklayers, who built him a stronger furnace, in which the metal was melted from which the Jackson statue was successfully cast.[6]

On another occasion, the tremendous weight of the side of the horse caused the cranes in Mills's foundry to snap.[7] More lost work. More delay. More expense.

Nevertheless, throughout the ordeal, Mills continued to work in the public eye. Every time he cast a piece of sculpture, he invited guests—such as Edwin Forrest—to witness the climactic moment when the molten bronze was poured into the mold. The select audience always included members of the press. The pyrotechnics never failed to draw a gasp of amazement from the spectators. Mills hosted "open houses," too, when the general public—ladies as well as gentlemen—enjoyed access to his compound. Callers were free to stroll at leisure and marvel at the strange things that filled the studio and foundry. Mills regaled his visitors with impassioned lectures on the wondrous doings of "the Bronze Founder." In between "casting shows" and "open houses," curiosity seekers showed up without warning. Mills's workplace had become a tourist attraction. South Carolina's *Camden Journal* in April of 1850 advised:

> No one should fail to visit it, in visiting or passing through Washington, especially a South Carolinian. The gentlemanly manners of Mr. Mills would make a visit pleasant in more ways than one.[8]

A visitor's guide to the nation's capital titled, "Principal Places of Attraction," appearing in the Baltimore *Sun* of February 13, 1851, urged:

> [A]nd don't forget to call at the studio of Clark Mills, the celebrated American artist who is now at work on the equestrian statue of Gen. Jackson. It is immediately at the south end of the Treasury Department, across the street.[9]

In November 1851 Mills was honored to welcome the "Father of American Sculptors," Horatio Greenough, into the Jackson Monument Foundry. The 46-year-old expatriate—ten years Mills's senior—had recently returned to the United States from Italy temporarily with his wife and children. While in Washington on business with the government, he visited the junior, self-taught sculptor/founder about whom he had heard so much. Afterwards, Greenough wrote to the secretary of the Cooper Monument Committee, which had consulted him about creating a memorial to the American novelist, James Fenimore Cooper, who had recently died:

> *I have seen the operations of Mr. Mills in bronze and have no doubt, after what I have there seen that your committe [sic] may decide upon that material without danger, and without going out of the country for workmen.*[10]

However, regarding Mills's equestrian statue, Greenough would later tell a friend that he "thought it a great mistake to make the animal superior to the rider."[11]

The following year, the New England humanitarian, Dorothea Dix, came to Mills's studio, not once, but twice, and rescued the fire-damaged bust of Washington from the furnace.[12] Professor Joseph Henry, too, visited on multiple occasions. The Secretary of the Smithsonian Institution was following Mills's endeavors with the eye of a scientist. On July 28, 1852, he noted in his journal, "*Mr. Clark*

Mills has been attempting to solder with the compound blowpipe pieces of bronze to unite the parts of his statue."[13] A compound blowpipe used jets of oxygen and hydrogen to produce a steady, intense heat.

Not all visitors, though, were famous people. Many, such as this "Tupper" mentioned in the *Daily Union*, defy identification:

> We have never seen a man more struck with the genius of another than Tupper was with that of Mr. Mills. He told us that he had spent two agreeable hours in his studio; that he had found in him a genius of high order—an inventive power of the greatest resources.[14]

Edwin Forrest, on the other hand, attracted attention wherever he went. The catastrophe that rattled the Jackson Monument Foundry when the actor stood among the spectators was widely publicized. The "ex-Bowery boy and eminent tragedian" was in the city to play an engagement. Also present in the gathering that day was Wilson MacDonald, a New York City sculptor and friend of Mills's. MacDonald was one of the witnesses who related the "Anecdote of Forrest" to the press:

> "On the day appointed for casting this statue, Mills notified Forrest, who, with other gentlemen and ladies, assembled within the enclosure. The party gathered around the pit, while Forrest placed himself on a plank laid directly across the pit. At a given signal Mills removed the plugs from the furnace, and the moulten bronze began to pour out from the furnace into the mold below. Unfortunately some water had gotten into the mold and a terrible explosion took place; the earth, sand and molten metal flew in all directions. Mills was knocked heels over head; one of the sides of the enclosure was blown out; half the guests were knocked down or covered with filth; some were scorched, the others fled in dismay. When the smoke and steam had cleared away Mills rose from the earth and discovered Forrest standing on the plank across the pit.

"'Great heavens!' exclaimed Mills, as soon as he could get his breath. 'Mr. Forrest, I hope you are not hurt.'

"'Hurt!' replied Forrest, 'what is there to hurt anybody?'

"'Thank God!' cried Mills. 'But ain't you frightened?'

"'Frightened,' replied Forrest, 'why should I be frightened? I thought this was a part o' the performance.'"[15]

Repeated accidents and failures not only cost Mills precious metal, money and time, they also called into question his prospects of success. Skepticism about the untutored artist's ability to meet his commitment intensified. Later accounts would relate:

> Men instructed in the art of statuary, with which he [Mills] had no acquaintance, continually discouraged him and predicted his failure. *Home Journal*[16]

> There were complaints strong and loud, and speculation of failure. The [Jackson Monument] committee were getting dissatisfied; . . . [they] thought the money was being wasted; they complained, his enemies thought they would triumph. *Brooklyn Eagle*[17]

> The world said he would never do it. Where could he borrow money under such obstacles? *Daily Union*[18]

Two months into casting the horse, Mills had exhausted his resources.[19] The Jackson Monument Committee was broke. The Secretary, John Walker Maury, estimated that "about two thousand five hundred dollars more" was needed to complete the statue, and "about four or five thousand dollars" would be required for the pedestal. The organization renewed its national subscription drive. In response, another group of admirers of the "Hero of New Orleans," the Jackson Democratic Association, offered to join in the fundraising effort. Maury accepted:

The kind offer of your Association to aid in procuring additional pecuniary aid for the work is therefore most opportune and is received with thanks.[20]

The new "joint campaign" to raise money to finish the memorial was announced "To the People of the United States" in multiple newspapers, beginning with Washington's *Daily Union* on Nov. 27, 1851. Maury informed potential donors:

> Mr. Mills has now succeeded in casting all of its parts, with the exception of three, and of these three the moulds for two are ready for the metal, or will be in a few days. The pieces which have been cast are those from which he expected the most difficulty, but in every instance the casts were made successfully, and they are specimens that would not discredit any foundry. The parts remaining to be cast, or at least two of them, are the heaviest pieces; but, being of simple form, he does not expect any difficulty with them. ... [I]t will require about two thousand five hundred dollars more to enable him to complete the work.[21]

The public, however, did not rally to the cause as enthusiastically as the two societies had hoped. Mills was compelled to solicit personal loans. A *Brooklyn Eagle* reporter would later report, "But he had one good, firm friend, who advanced him money, . . . and who defended him against all the attacks levelled against him."[22] That "good, firm friend" was John Walker Maury.

A Virginia-born attorney of illustrious and prosperous lineage, Maury had brought his wife and captive house servants to Washington City as a young man. He became a major player in local politics and the administration of the national capital. Elected first to the Common Council, then the Board of Aldermen, in 1852 he entered the office of mayor. A founding member and secretary of the Jackson Monument Committee, Maury was to be one of Mills's most loyal and liberal champions.[23] Years later, Maury's son, William, would write:

> Clark Mills, the sculptor, who had been employed to execute the statue of Jackson, having used up the money collected for that purpose, with the work only partially done, my father came to his relief and supplied every pay day the money needed to carry on the work, without requiring a particle of security. This I had from the sculptor himself for the first time, a few days after my father's death, when he told me of it with tears in his eyes.[24]

Incrementally, Maury would lend Mills a total of $4,907.27.[25]

As the sculptor's exertions dragged on, his debts mounted. Three other founding members of the Jackson Monument Committee were to loan him several hundred dollars each: Francis Preston Blair and John Cook Rives—co-founders and editors of the *Congressional Globe*—and Benjamin Brown French—former Clerk of the U.S.

Portrait of John Walker Maury, 1855. The Virginia-born attorney of illustrious and prosperous lineage became a major player in Washington politics, serving as mayor, 1852-54. He was a founding member and secretary of the Jackson Monument Committee. As Mills fell deeper and deeper into debt struggling to cast the Jackson equestrian, Maury personally loaned him a total of $4,907.27, roughly $190,000 in 2025 dollars. (Alamy)

House of Representatives, soon to be appointed the city's new Commissioner of Public Buildings.[26]

Meanwhile, Mills persevered. Six times he failed to cast the largest section of his statue: the side of the horse with the fore and hind legs.[27] Six times, something went wrong.

One matter that would have bedeviled Mills was determining the width of the cast. How thick did the bronze need to be in order to retain its shape without cracking or buckling under the weight? The horse's forelegs supported nothing; the hind legs had to support 15 tons of statue, so the amount of bronze in them necessarily differed. Yet, the fore and hind legs had to be cast in the same mold as the horse's flank to ensure the over-all integrity of the sculpture. The only way for Mills to arrive at the optimum thickness of the bronze shell was through trial and error—which proved to be time-consuming, expensive, and discouraging.

After each failed casting, he had to modify the core of the mold to widen or narrow, as necessary, from one point to another, the membrane of air to be filled with molten metal. Some modifications required repositioning the venting tubes. The iron flask encasing the mold (the cope and drag clasped together) measured perhaps nine by five by two feet. It weighed about nine or ten thousand pounds and was not easily maneuvered.[28] Every new attempt required melting down the faulty cast, reheating the bronze to the ideal temperature, and pouring it into the new mold. Moreover, the altered weight of each cast changed the variables at play. That was just one of the issues Mills had to resolve to achieve a perfect cast.

> [H]e was becoming disheartened.... Mr. Mills says that sometimes he felt like committing suicide. *Brooklyn Eagle*[29]

> Every one of his attempts cost him $400, and he made six successive trials.... "I have been ready," he says, "to throw myself in the Potomac." *Washington and Georgetown Directory*[30]

Still, he persevered.

NOTES

1. "Equestrian Statue of Jackson," *The* [Washington] *Republic*, Aug. 22, 1851, p. 3.
2. Regarding the number of pieces comprising the statue, see Bk. 1, Ch. 33, n. 28. All sources agree that the horse is made of four pieces.
3. "History of the Jackson Statue," [Washington] *Daily Union*, Jan. 18, 1853, p. 2.
4. "Death of Clark Mills," [Washington] *Evening Star*, Jan. 12, 1883, p. 4. This incident was reported in several newspapers.
5. Author's estimate, based on the statue's total weight of 30,000 pounds and assuming none of the bronze fused with bricks was salvageable.
6. "Death of Clark Mills," *Evening Star*, Jan. 12, 1883, 4.
7. "A Great Sculptor Gone," *The Washington Post*, Jan. 13, 1883, p. 4. This incident was reported in several newspapers.
8. "Clark Mills and His Statue," *Camden* [S.C.] *Journal*, Apr. 23, 1850, p. 3; reprinted in "Mr. Mills," [Washington] *Daily Union*, May 1, 1850, p. 3.
9. "Correspondence of the Baltimore Sun. Washington, Feb. 13, 1851. Principle Places of Attraction," [Baltimore] *Sun*, Feb. 14, 1851, p. 4.
10. Letter, Horatio Greenough to Rev. Rufus W. Griswold, Nov. 19, 1851, published in Nathalia Wright, ed., *Letters of Horatio Greenough, American Sculptor* (Madison, Wis.: University of Wisconsin Press, 1972): 395–97.
11. Diary of Mann S. Valentine, Jr., entry of Jan. 14, 1852; The Valentine Richmond History Center, Richmond, Va.
12. See Bk. 1, Ch. 30.
13. Journal of Joseph Henry, entry of July 28, 1852; Joseph Henry Papers, Smithsonian Institution Archives, Washington, D.C.
14. "Mr. Clarke [sic] Mills, the Sculptor," [Washington] *Daily Union*, Apr. 13, 1851, p. 2.
15. "Casting a Statue," *The American Artisan*, vol. 11, no. 26 (Dec. 25, 1886): A-19. Also "Clark Mills at Home," *The Washington Post*, Aug. 7, 1879, p. 1; and "Anecdote of Forrest," *Fort Wayne* [Ind.] *Daily Gazette*, June 16, 1881, p. 8.
16. "Personal," *Home Journal*, Mar. 18, 1854: 423.
17. "Sketches of Washington. By Childe Harold. Washington, March 29, 1853. An Hour with Clark Mills, the Sculptor. [Concluded.]," *Brooklyn Eagle*, Mar. 31, 1853, p. 2.
18. "History of the Jackson Statue," *Daily Union*, Jan. 18, 1853, 2.
19. "The Jackson Statue," [Washington] *Evening Star*, May 3, 1890, p. 9.
20. "To the People of the United States," [Washington] *Daily Union*, Nov. 27, 1851, p. 2.
21. Ibid.
22. "Sketches of Washington . . . ," *Brooklyn Eagle*, Mar. 31, 1853, 2.
23. See Bk. 1, Ch. 9. Also "John W. Maury" entry, 1840 U.S. census, Washington City, D.C., p. 99; NARA M704, roll 35.

24 William A. Maury, "John Walker Maury, His Lineage and Life," *Records of the Columbia Historical Society*, Washington, D.C., vol. 19 (1916): 167.
25 "History of the Jackson Statue," *Daily Union*, Jan. 18, 1853, 2; and Rosemary Hopkins, *Clark Mills: The First Native American Sculptor* (M.A. thesis, University of Maryland, 1966): 77, who cites her source: "United States Archives, Washington, D.C., MS., Statement of Clark Mills, April 28, 1854, located in Auditor's Reports of this year, in the records of the Treasury Department." Equivalent to roughly $190,000 in 2025 dollars.
26 "History of the Jackson Statue," *Daily Union*, Jan. 18, 1853, 2. Also B. B. French, "The Jackson Statue—Its Origin, &c," [Baltimore] *Sun*, Jan. 11, 1853, p. 4. See Bk. 1, Ch. 9.
27 "Mills's Equestrian Statue of Jackson," *The* [Washington] *Republic*, Nov. 22, 1852, p. 3; and "Sketches of Washington...," *Brooklyn Eagle*, Mar. 31, 1853, 2.
28 Author's estimate based on the total weight of the statue, 30,000 pounds.
29 "Sketches of Washington...," *Brooklyn Eagle*, Mar. 31, 1853, 2.
30 "A Commencement of a New Era in the Arts. Jackson Statue," in Alfred Hunter, comp. and pub., *The Washington and Georgetown Directory, Strangers' Guide-Book for Washington, And Congressional and Clerks' Register* (Washington: printed by Kirkwood & McGill, 1853): 92–93.

CHAPTER 35
September–November 1852

For the purpose of erecting a pedestal in Lafayette Square for the equestrian statue of Andrew Jackson, on such plan as may be approved of by the artist for that work, five thousand dollars.

U.S. Statutes at Large, vol. 10:95 (Ch. CVIII),
32nd Cong., 1st Sess., Aug. 31, 1852.

Mills was sitting with the Secretary of the Interior, Alexander High Holmes Stuart. It was Tuesday, September 21, 1852. Congress had recently authorized $5,000 for a pedestal for the Jackson statue and Stuart had invited Mills into his office in the Patent Building to discuss the matter.[1] The sculpture came within the jurisdiction of an agency of the Secretary's Department, the Office of Public Buildings and Public Parks of the National Capital. On the morning following their meeting, Mills penned a letter to "Sec. A. H. H. Stuart:"

Dear Sir,

Since my interview with you yesterday regarding the construction of the pedestal on which my equestrian statue of Gen. Jackson is to be placed, I have reflected more upon the subject and upon our conversation in reference to it, and I feel more strongly the importance, not to say necessity, of the entire work being placed in my hands.

. . .[I]n a work of art like mine, which is original in the balancing of the horse on his hind feet upon the nicest calculation of the centre of gravity, it is of the utmost importance that the foundation and whole pedestal be of the most solid character. . . .

Under these circumstances, I trust and believe, that you, in your kind consideration will find a way, consistent with public duty, to put the work entirely in my hands.[2]

Eight days later, Mills had Stuart's reply:

Sir,

[I] have concluded, inasmuch as the success of your experiment will depend somewhat upon the proper erection of the pedestal, to place the whole matter under your exclusive direction and control. You are therefore authorized to proceed with the execution of your plan for the pedestal with the single injunction that the expenses thereof shall be kept within the sum appropriated by Congress for that purpose.[3]

Now, in addition to the tribulations dogging Mills in his foundry, he was committed to accomplishing another task for which he had no training: mounting a 15-ton statue on a pedestal. The task had never been attempted by anyone in the United States. As usual, Mills sought out the expert who could teach him what he needed to know. He found Matthew Glascoe, "one of the most finished mechanics in the country," residing in Baltimore.[4] The 45-year-old had trained as a civilian machinist at the Washington Navy Yard and "was well known in the District." Mills brought Glascoe to Washington to help him "put up the statue of Jackson." The experience was such a high point of Glascoe's career that it would be cited many years later in his obituary.

However, another man proud of his association with the Jackson equestrian would state, "I had full charge of putting up the horse and rider in their present position."[5] That was Philip A. McAleer, the young Pennsylvanian, better known as "Mac," whom Mills had brought to his foundry after Richter quit.[6] But Mac's boast of having "full charge"—shared with an *Evening Star* reporter nearly 40 years later—was likely an exaggeration. Although he was eventually to advance from brass finisher to machinist, work at the Navy Yard and the Bureau of Engraving and Printing, and invent two devices, "Mac" in 1852 was still only about 19 years old. It is unlikely that Mills would have given him "full charge" when Matthew Glascoe brought so much more experience to the operation.

Whoever it was who directed the pioneering feat, Mills acquired the engineering information he needed to design the pedestal—that is, how to affix the colossal rampant horse securely to the base. He then started purchasing the materials and sundry services he would need for the job. By October of 1852 he was overseeing "seven stone masons and nine laborers" in constructing the pedestal in Lafayette Square.[7] But it was not the neoclassic marble base that Mills had originally conceived, with bronze bas-reliefs on two sides, centered on a raised platform with stairs at either end.[8] That could not be built for $5,000. Mills had to simplify it.

It would be a stark rectangular pier of solid bluestone cement faced with marble, 16 feet 4 inches long, 9 feet 8 inches wide, and 8 feet 6 inches high.[9] The sides would cant inward slightly and bear three inscriptions: on the west face, "**J A C K S O N**" and "OUR FEDERAL UNION / IT MUST BE PRESERVED" (the toast Jackson once gave at a banquet in honor of a former president whom he admired, Thomas Jefferson); and on the south face, in an upper corner, much smaller, "CLARK MILLS, SCULPTOR."[10] The stripped-down pedestal would stand on a low granite foundation.

Andrew Jackson Downing, the foremost landscape architect in America, had redesigned Lafayette Square in 1851, designating an elliptical plot of ground in the middle of the park for the anticipated statue of his namesake, General Jackson. Although Downing had just died suddenly in July 1852, his plan for paved paths meandering amid beds of saplings and shrubbery was being executed as Mills built the pedestal.[11]

His workers started by raising a mound in the oval designated by Downing.[12] Then they laid the granite foundation. Roughly 24½ feet by 17½ feet and a few inches thick, it would give the pedestal a stable "apron" of four feet all around.[13] Finally, the men mixed and cast the pedestal's core of bluestone cement. The large slabs of marble for facing the structure were ordered from Symington's Quarry in Baltimore County, Maryland.

In September of 1852, when Mills took charge of constructing the pedestal, more old guns had arrived at his foundry. Weighing a total of 17,773 pounds, they had been found at the arsenal in Watertown, Massachusetts, back in 1850 and promised to the Jackson Monument Committee by the Secretary of War, Charles M. Conrad.[14] The cannons had been forwarded to the Washington Arsenal, but the Committee had not applied for them until recently—prompted, maybe, by Mills.[15] Conrad authorized their delivery to his compound. However, whether Mills ever made use of the guns is not known. For sure he did not melt down all of them, because about 1862 he would be photographed sitting on one of the cannons beside his studio.[16]

By November, against all odds, finally, in his make-shift foundry, Mills completed the casting of the warhorse. When he extracted from the mold the latest cast of the last piece . . . it was flawless.[17] While the bronze shell of most of the statue was not more than a half inch thick, the horse's sides, in places, were up to an inch and a quarter—perhaps five times the thickness of Mills's bust of Washington. To ensure that the segments joined properly and to proceed with patination, Mills assembled the huge statue in his studio. The brazen General astride his rearing charger soared to a height of nine feet. It was twelve feet long from the horse's raised forehoofs to the tip of its flowing tail. The aggregate weight came to about 30,000 pounds, that is, 15 tons.[18]

Astounding. Mills had done it. Astounding! Ahead of Henry Kirke Brown, Clark Mills had cast a monumental bronze statue in the United States. Right away, he dispatched an invitation to his closest neighbor, who showed up a little too late. The amusing anecdote would be related years later by "Mac:"

> "I remember that when the horse was first put up on his feet
> Mr. Mills invited President Fillmore down to inspect it. He did
> not come that day. The next day Mr. Mills said to me: 'Mac, let no
> one, not even the President himself, see that statue now.' He had

hardly disappeared when I saw Mr. Fillmore coming down toward the building. I went out and told him what my orders were. He did not seem to like it a bit, for he drew himself up and said to me as though he meant it, 'Tell Mr. Mills that Mr. Fillmore, the President of the United States, was here to see his work.' Then he stalked off, but he did not see the statue, not that day at least, though he afterward officiated at the unveiling."[19]

Mills could not abide waiting for the official dedication. Forthwith, he unlatched the padlock on his gate. During that third week in November, wrote a reporter from the *Republic*, "ladies and gentlemen, in large numbers" came to see the work of art, "although not entirely finished."[20] The statue was probably not yet patinated. It would have been a bright copper color.

The *Republic* reporter, in awe of the colossus, was no less in awe of its creator:

> The shortest time occupied in Europe for the creation of a similar work has been eight years. But Mr. Mills has been engaged only four or five years, and during that period has encountered many embarrassments, having much prejudice to overcome, and without experience. Notwithstanding six successive failures in modelling, each involving a loss of four hundred dollars, the artist, on the seventh trial, succeeded in producing the desired result; thus affording another example of what genius, unaided, can do by the force of perseverance.... The contract price was twelve thousand dollars; an inconsiderable sum considering the magnitude of the work, causing an actual loss to the artist of upwards of six thousand dollars, exclusive of his loss of time.[21]

As soon as he could, however, Mills would pay back in full all of his creditors, John Walker Maury first of all.[22]

NOTES

1. Letter, Clark Mills to Sec. A. H. H. Stuart, Sept. 22, 1852; Letters Received and Other Records Relating to the Extension of the U.S. Capitol, 1851–1872, A1, Entry 291, Box 3; Records of the Office of the Secretary of the Interior, RG 48; NARA. Also "History of the Department of the Interior," at https://www.doi.gov/about/history.
2. Letter, Clark Mills to Sec. A. H. H. Stuart, Sept. 22, 1852.
3. Letter, Sec. A. H. H. Stuart to Clark Mills, Sept. 30, 1852; Letters Sent, 1849–1906, A1, Entry 186, vol. 1: 125–26; Records of the Office of the Secretary of the Interior, RG 48; NARA. Searching the Records of the Office of Public Buildings and Public Parks of the National Capital, NARA RG 42, has not yielded a formal contract for this job.
4. Biographical facts are derived from: (1) "Death of Matthew Glascoe," [Washington] *Evening Star*, May 18, 1869, p. 1; (2) "Mysterious Death," [Washington] *Daily National Republican*, May 19, 1869, p. 5; (3) Matthew Glasgow [sic] entry, 1850 U.S. Census, Baltimore City, 14th Ward, p. 805 (handwritten), p. 403 (stamped); NARA M432, roll 285; and (4) Glascow [sic] Matthew entry, *Matchett's Baltimore Directory for 1849–'50* (Baltimore: R. J. Matchett, 1849): 150.
5. "The Jackson Statue," [Washington] *Evening Star*, May 3, 1890, p. 9.
6. See Bk. 1, Ch. 33.
7. Senate document, "Payroll for the workmen employed on the Pedestal for Jackson Monument, Lafayette Square," October 1852; cited in Rosemary Hopkins, *Clark Mills: The First Native American Sculptor* (M.A. thesis, University of Maryland, 1966): 70. Periodic disbursements made to Mills to cover his payroll, supplies, sundry services, and pay him for his "superintendency," are recorded in Cashbooks, Mar. 19, 1851–Jun. 11, 1861, vol. 1, "Mar. 19, 1851–Jun. 30,1853," and vol. 2, "1853–1854;" Records of the Commissioner of Public Buildings, Financial Records; Records of the Office of Public Buildings and Public Parks of the National Capital, RG 42; NARA.
8. See Bk. 1, Ch. 21. Also "The Jackson Statue," *Evening Star*, May 3, 1890, 9.
9. Tim Kerr, *The History of the Equestrian Statue of General Andrew Jackson, Lafayette Park, Washington, D.C.* Typescript report prepared for the National Park Service, White House Liaison, August 1999, p. i.
10. For a detailed explication of the monument's inscriptions, see Kerr, *History of the Equestrian Statue*, 35–39. Lithographers took liberties in depicting the inscriptions in their prints of the monument. See Bk. 2.
11. Kerr, *History of the Equestrian Statue*, 31; and "The Jackson Statue," *Evening Star*, May 3, 1890, 9. In Charles Pierre L'Enfant's 1791 plan for Washington City, surveyed by Andrew Ellicott and Benjamin Banneker, the President's House was situated amid extensive grounds which came to be designated, "President's Park." When Pennsylvania Avenue was cut through President's

Park north of the Executive Mansion (supposedly at the behest of Thomas Jefferson), the mansion was separated from the northernmost portion of the park. After the visit of the Marquis de Lafayette to Washington in 1824, that northernmost portion of President's Park was named in honor of the revered visitor. Since then, cartographers, newspaper reporters, popular and scholarly historians, and the general public have used both "Lafayette Square" and "Lafayette Park" to denote that place across Pennsylvania Avenue from the White House. Lucinda Prout Janke, in "The President's Park (Give or Take a Few Acres)," *White House History*, A journal published by the White House Historical Association, no. 27 (spring 2010): 68–77, writes: "Formally, the park is still Lafayette Park; the term "Lafayette Square" refers to the houses facing the park" (p. 72). This distinction, however, while logical, has never been universally observed. For consistency throughout this book, the designation "Lafayette Square" is used. President's Park south of the White House came to be called, "the Ellipse." For an authoritative history of the Ellipse, see: Peter R. Penczer, "The Ellipse: The Nineteenth-Century Evolution of the White Lot," *White House History*, no. 38 (summer 2015): 12–21.

12 "Sketches of Washington. By Childe Harold. Washington, March 29, 1853. An Hour with Clark Mills, the Sculptor. [Concluded.]," *Brooklyn Eagle*, Mar. 31, 1853, p. 2.
13 Kerr, *History of the Equestrian Statue*, 39 and 52.
14 See Bk. 1, Ch. 32.
15 Letter, H. K. Craig, Col. of Ord., to C. M. Conrad, Sec. of War, Sept. 4, 1852; Letters Sent to the War Department; Records of the Office of the Chief of Ordnance, RG 156; NARA.
16 See Bk. 2.
17 "History of the Jackson Statue," [Washington] *Daily Union*, Jan. 18, 1853, p. 2.
18 Dimensions and weight are from Kerr, *History of the Equestrian Statue*, p. i. However, "Mills's Equestrian Statue of Jackson," *The* [Washington] *Republic*, Nov. 22, 1852, p. 3: "The horse measures fourteen feet from the front hoofs to the tail, and the height of the statue, from the ground line to the highest point of the figure of the rider, is fourteen and a half feet."
19 "The Jackson Statue," *Evening Star*, May 3, 1890, 9.
20 "Mills's Equestrian Statue of Jackson," *Republic*, Nov. 22, 1852, 3; reprinted in the [Charleston] *Courier*, Nov. 27, 1852, p. 1.
21 Ibid. However, "Death of Clark Mills," [Washington] *Evening Star*, Jan. 12, 1883, p. 4: "It was completed at a loss to him of $7,000."
22 Hopkins, *Clark Mills*, 77; and William A. Maury, "John Walker Maury, His Lineage and Life," *Records of the Columbia Historical Society*, Washington, D.C., vol. 19 (1916): 167.

CHAPTER 36
December 1852–January 7, 1853

INAUGURATION
OF THE
Equestrian Statue of Andrew Jackson.

The Equestrian Statue of General Jackson will be inaugurated on the Eighth day of January next, when the arrangements will be as follows: All those either specially or generally invited, will assemble in front of the City Hall, at ten o'clock, A. M., on the Eighth of January, 1853. Colonel George W. Hughes, a member of the Jackson Monument Committee, has been selected as Chief Marshal, and will appoint his own Aids. The Military escort, consisting of the Regiment of Volunteers of the Militia of the District of Columbia, with such detachments from the Army and Marine Corps as may be within convenient distance, and the Military Companies from other cities, who may attend, will be under the command of Colonel William Hickey.
The procession will be formed as follows:

. . . .

Committee of Arrangements,
B. B. French
John C. Rives
John W. Maury

[Washington] *Daily Globe*, Dec. 31, 1852, p. 3.

Mills was out of time. Congress had set the date for the unveiling ceremony. It was to be on the 38th anniversary of Jackson's victorious rout of the British forces at New Orleans.[1] An announcement ran in all of the city's newspapers. In a list 47 lines long, it named the individuals and groups participating in the planned procession. Immediately, civic, governmental and military organizations posted notices in the *Globe, Daily National Intelligencer, Daily Union, Evening Star* and *Republic*, rallying their members to prepare for the big event.[2]

By this time, Mills and his crew had finished the pedestal's core of bluestone cement and installed the veneer of marble from Symington's Quarry on the two short sides. But the two immense slabs of marble for the long sides were still on order.[3] Mills could wait no longer. He had to get the huge statue up now.

First, he had his workers enclose the pedestal within a large wooden shelter.[4] This may have been a precaution against foul winter weather. However, it would also serve to shield the statue-in-the-making from the eyes of the public. Next, inside the protective housing, the men erected derricks rigged with block and tackle for hoisting the parts of the statue into place. Wooden scaffolding would be built up around the sculpture as it rose.

Then, back in his foundry, Mills directed his crew in disassembling the statue into its constituent parts. Just in time, he had managed to patinate it to a dark gray-green color—"bronze green"—and polish it to a glossy sheen.[5] In the last days of December, wagons drawn by teams of mighty draft horses hauled the disjointed parts of the Jackson equestrian to Lafayette Square: four pieces comprising the charger, eight for the rider, and at least eight accessories—reins, stirrups, straps holding the stirrups, spurs, and saber.[6] Their aggregate weight totaled about 15 tons. In addition, one wagon carried a solid plate of bronze, to which the statue would be secured. Eight feet long, three feet wide and three inches thick, it weighed more than two tons. Transporting all these ponderous and variously shaped forms up 15th Street—a steady incline—then over Pennsylvania Avenue and into the square required multiple trips. The process created an entertaining spectacle for bystanders caught unawares.

The Spanish cannons that Jackson had captured, however, remained at Mills's compound. The four national trophies would not be removed to Lafayette Square and mounted on carriages there until some months after the dedication.[7]

For a while the fair weather held, then incessant rain drenched Christmas day. But that was a holiday, followed by Sunday, so no work time was lost.[8] Monday the 27th was inclement, though, and that night "cold winds, cold rain, and a little sprinkling of snow came together."[9] Fortunately, since the worksite was enclosed, Mills could press on. After that, he and his men enjoyed working conditions that were tolerable for winter.

The Washington correspondent for the Charleston *Courier* informed his newspaper on January 2, 1853:

> The statue has been already carried to its pedestal, and is about being elevated to its intended place. This is done under cover of a frame building around the pedestal.[10]

In future years, Mills would insist that the statue stood unattached to the pedestal:

> "All the statements in newspapers and guidebooks about my horse's front parts being hollow and hind parts solid to adjust it in position, is simply false. Another false report is that it is bolted down, and that when the bolts rust away the horse will pitch over on his nose—go to grass, as the saying is. There is not a bolt about it. It simply stands upon its feet, balanced."[11]

That was Mills's greatest point of pride. And, indeed, it was true that the sculpture could stand on its own, because its center of gravity was directly over the horse's rear hooves and passed up through the figure of Jackson. Nevertheless, on occasion Mills himself would nuance his brash assertion. He would tell a *Washington Post* reporter:

"My horse is placed on the pedestal without any fastening whatever. Only a bronzed rim around the hind feet to keep some fool from using a crowbar and thrusting the horse forward."[12]

To an *Evening Star* man, Mills would say:

"[T]he only fastening of the feet to the pedestal is that used to prevent mischievous persons from throwing off the statue with a crowbar."[13]

How Mills got the Jackson equestrian to stand with no external support, and whether or not it was attached to the pedestal, would be topics of speculation from the moment the colossus was unveiled. One scholar, John R. Hewett, would write in 1875 to "Prof. Joseph Henry, SS.D., Smithsonian Institute, Washington, D.C.:"

I cannot conceive it to be possible for the said statue to be in a state of stability without some fastening to the pedestal, or else a counterpoising weight within the pedestal connected with the statue through the two touching points.[14]

Hewett was a resident of the National Military Home in Hampton, Virginia. He identified himself simply as, "Ex student from Michigan University by reason of feeble health contracted in my Country's Service." A newspaper article appearing 15 years later would prove that the disabled veteran's deduction was spot on. There was indeed a "*counterposing weight*" within the pedestal.

It was in 1890 that the *Evening Star* interviewed Mills's brass finisher, Philip A. McAleer. "I think I am the only man who knows about this," Mac told the reporter, "for the rest, so far as I know, are all dead."[15] He spoke "from the actual experience he had in helping to construct the statue and erect it on the site." The detailed narrative that Mac gave the *Evening Star* reporter is the only known account of how the Jackson statue was mounted. It reveals that Mills—relying, presumably, on the engineering expertise of Matthew Glascoe—devised not one, but a set of measures that, combined, insured the stability of the monumental sculpture:[16]

> "In the first place, the horse does not stand directly upon the rough stone surface of the pedestal, as it appears to do.... [T]he legs of the horse are fastened directly, so that it is not merely the balancing of the horse that keeps it up in position."[17]

Mac divulged the existence of the "*counterpoising weight*:" the solid plate of bronze eight feet long, three feet wide and three inches thick, weighing more than two tons. Mills had cast it to anchor his colossal statue. It had a raised round platform several inches high in the center. Mills had his workmen secure this plate to the top of the bluestone cement pedestal. Then the rear hoofs of the horse—first one side, then the other—were fastened to the round platform with a rivet or key. Also affixed to the platform were the tufts of hair dangling from the horse's ankles. Having four points of contact at the base of the statue's center of gravity—rather than just two—contributed to the stability of the whole.

Another statement published in newspapers and guidebooks that Mills would deny was that the statue stayed upright because the "horse's front parts [were] hollow and hind parts solid."[18] "The casts are hollow," Mills would insist, "except the tail."[19] But this point, too, Mac would clarify in his recollection of how the statue was mounted. The charger's rear legs were solid iron up as far as the thigh. Mills had had these elements cast at the Navy Yard to his explicit specifications. He then coated the iron legs with a thin veneer of bronze, like stockings. When the two sides of the horse were mounted and secured, harness hid the long seam that ran between the two pieces.

Then the workers attached the tail. Mills had made it unusually large and long, streaming rather than limp, and filled it, too. A fanciful tradition would evolve that the tail was "full of cannon balls."[20] More likely, though, Mills filled it with iron, as he had the two hind legs. On the other hand, if Mills did use bronze from the two old Spanish mortars, this is where that metal could have been used, regardless of its composition. The horizontal stretch of the tail and its prodigious weight counterbalanced the forward weight of the statue. To keep the tail from breaking off at its base, Mills embedded a long iron rod in it. This rod ran up the tail and into the body of the horse, where Mills's men fastened it by means of a large nut.

Next, the workers hoisted the steed's head. Harness encircling the horse's neck (imitating leather decorated with stars) concealed the seam where the head joined the body. Mac asserted:

> "If the statue were ever to be taken apart, the head would have to be taken off first and then the tail unscrewed from the inside, so as to get the weight off the legs."[21]

At this point, the charger was ready to receive the Hero of New Orleans. The lower portion of Jackson's torso, from the broad sash girding his waist to his knees, was hoisted carefully and lowered onto the saddle. Once that piece was bolted in position, Mills may have attached the boots. Their rigid tops camouflaged where they joined the knee. Or he may have continued to build up the statue's vertical line of gravity first by fixing the rider's upper torso into the sash around the waist, and then attached the boots. After that, the workers secured Jackson's arms in the epaulets on his shoulders, and his head in the stock around his neck.

The last of the 12 principal pieces to be fastened in place was probably the bicorn. Standing on the highest level of the scaffold, Mills's men bolted the cocked hat to Jackson's gauntleted right hand. Then the crew attached the elements of harness, screwed spurs into the boots, and secured the saber.

Finally, Mac explained, "The rough stone top was placed on afterward and was merely a stone mason's task.... The rough stone was built... up... flush with the hoofs." It was the culminating element of Mills's masterful illusion. "It was no easy job, you may be sure,"

Mac told the newspaper man, "and it would not be an easy job either to take them apart and down again."

On Wednesday, January 5, 1853, the *Evening Star* informed Washingtonians, "The Jackson statue now stands firmly in its position in Lafayette Square. It will remain housed until the 8th instant."[22] Mills had met the deadline—not a moment too soon. The previous evening a "severe gale of wind . . . accompanied with snow and rain" had pummeled the city.[23]

NOTES

1 *Congressional Globe*, 32nd Cong., 2nd Sess., Dec. 30, 1852, p. 173 and 178.
2 "Inauguration of the Equestrian Statue of Andrew Jackson," [Washington] *Daily Globe*, Dec. 31, 1852, p.3; printed simultaneously in the *Daily National Intelligencer, Daily Union, Evening Star* and *Republic*; reprinted in subsequent issues.
3 Tim Kerr, *The History of the Equestrian Statue of General Andrew Jackson, Lafayette Park, Washington, D.C.* Typescript report prepared for the National Park Service, White House Liaison, August 1999, p. 36–37.
4 "Correspondence of the Courier. Washington, Jan. 2," and "The Jackson Statue," [Charleston] *Courier*, Jan. 7, 1853, p. 1 and 2, respectively.
5 It is difficult to determine the original patina of Mills's monumental statues, as they have been restored several times over the years. The best guess is that it was dark gray-green—"bronze green." Mills's early, smaller works, however—his bells and busts of Apollo and Washington—have received less care, perhaps no restoration at all, so their original patina may be posited from visual inspection. See Bk. 1, Ch. 27, n. 20, and Ch. 30, n. 34.
6 "Anniversary of the Battle of New Orleans," *The New York Herald*, Jan. 9, 1853, p. 1, publishes a letter from Washington dated Dec. 15, 1852, stating, "This statue is now elevated in the workshop of the artist, Clark Mills." Also "Correspondence of the Courier," and "The Jackson Statue," *Courier*, Jan. 7, 1853, 1 and 2. Regarding the number of pieces comprising the statue, see Bk. 1, Ch. 33, n. 28.
7 A visitor to Mills's studio in March 1853 would record seeing, "some old Spanish cannon from which the [Jackson] statue was made." Also "Sketches of Washington. By Childe Harold. Washington, March 29, 1853. An Hour with Clark Mills, the Sculptor," *Brooklyn Eagle*, Mar. 30, 1853, p. 2.
8 [no title], [Washington] *Evening Star*, Dec. 27, 1852, p. 3.

9   "Sixth Lecture of Dr. Baird," [Washington] *Evening Star*, Dec. 30, 1852, p. 2. And [no title], [Washington] *Evening Star*, Dec. 30, 1852, p. 2; and [no title], [Washington] *Evening Star*, Jan. 4, 1853, p. 3.
10   "Correspondence of the Courier," *Courier*, Jan. 7, 1853, 1.
11   "Clark Mills at Home," *The Washington Post*, Aug. 7, 1879, p. 1.
12   "Clark Mills at Home," *The Washington Post*, Feb. 7, 1880, p. 2.
13   "An Hour with Clark Mills," [Washington] *Evening Star*, Dec. 24, 1870, p. 2.
14   Letter, John R. Hewett to Prof. Joseph Henry, SS.D., Mar. 25, 1875; Joseph Henry Papers, Correspondence, Smithsonian Institution Archives, Washington, D.C.
15   "The Jackson Statue," [Washington] *Evening Star*, May 3, 1890, p. 9.
16   Description of the mounting of the statue is based on: (1) McAleer's account in "The Jackson Statue," *Evening Star*, May 3, 1890, 9; (2) National Park Service, "Classified Structure Field Inventory Report," Dec. 2, 1975, and NPS borescopic tests, 1993, both summarized in Kerr, *History of the Equestrian Statue*, 58–59; and (3) photographs taken for the author by the NPS during maintenance of the statue in 2017. The description given here provides additional detail to the one given in John Philip Colletta, "'The Workman of C. Mills:': Carl Ludwig Richter and the Statue of Andrew Jackson in Lafayette Park," *Washington History*, A Publication of the Historical Society of Washington, D.C., vol. 23 (2011): 26.
17   "The Jackson Statue," *Evening Star*, May 3, 1890, 9.
18   "Clark Mills . . . ," *Washington Post*, Aug. 7, 1879, 1.
19   "An Hour with Clark Mills," *Evening Star*, Dec. 24, 1870, 2.
20   See, for example, "New Age Group Tackles Capital's Problems," *The Washington Post*, Nov. 18, 1962.
21   "The Jackson Statue," *Evening Star*, May 3, 1890, 9.
22   "Local Matters," [Washington] *Evening Star*, Jan. 5, 1853, p. 3.
23   "Local Items," *Alexandria Gazette and Virginia Advertiser*, Jan. 5, 1853, p. 3.

EPILOGUE
January 8, 1853

I have seen all the great statues in Europe, and I unhesitatingly say that none of them can approach in point of merit near the one inaugurated to-day. Of Clark Mills, therefore, gentlemen, we may well be proud; for to-day the work upon which he has been engaged for years has been consummated—a work which places him at the head of the list of the artists of the world, and stands not only as a monument to the memory of Jackson, but an evidence of the genius of Mills.

Col. George W. Hughes, quoted in "Banquet of the Jackson Democratic Association," [Washington] *Daily Union*, Jan. 14, 1853, p. 3.

In the obscurity of pre-dawn, the indistinct mound in the middle of Lafayette Square looked like a huge, lumpy tent. Peaking at about 18 feet, with an oblong spread of about 17 by 10 feet, the white canvas form stood directly across Pennsylvania Avenue from the President's House. Nearby, a makeshift frame platform would serve as a stand for the speakers and guests of honor. Workers of African descent, maybe free, maybe enslaved, maybe both together, were unloading wooden chairs from wagons, toting them up the stairs of the platform, and arranging them in ranks. A supervisor pointed to where the cushioned armchairs for President Fillmore and the other dignitaries should form a front row. On the ground, another crew of Black laborers was lining up chairs for the ladies.[1]

Shadowy figures stirred around the gates of the wrought iron fence surrounding the park and moved silently along its elliptical paths. The beds of saplings and baby shrubs were all freshly planted, so the hulking structure in the center loomed large from any vantage point.[2] The first long rays of sunshine flashed golden in the window panes on the west side of Lafayette Square. The most important day in the life of "Clark Mills, the Sculptor" was dawning.

It was the 38th anniversary of the Battle of New Orleans, when U.S. troops under General Andrew Jackson's command won a stunning victory over the most formidable British expedition of the War of 1812. That triumph had laid the foundation of "Old Hickory's" enormous popularity and political career, which culminated in the presidency. This day's *Daily Evening Star* would devote three columns of the front page to a "Narrative of the Battle of New Orleans."[3]

Every year, to commemorate the victory and the victor, the Jackson Democratic Association hosted a grand dinner. Today's observances, however, far surpassed one club's traditional banquet. Today was the much-publicized and eagerly anticipated unveiling of the monumental equestrian statue of the "Hero of New Orleans" in bronze—the miraculous creation of Clark Mills.

Ten blocks down the Avenue, at the National Hotel, the Chief Marshal of the day's ceremonies, Colonel George Wurtz Hughes (retired), met with his civilian aides and assistant marshals. Resplendent in the trappings of his rank, the 46-year-old Colonel wore a yellow scarf with white rosettes.[4] His nine aides wore white scarves with yellow rosettes. The 52 assistant marshals, who also reported to the hotel as instructed, "as early as possible," wore cherry scarves with white rosettes. Hughes himself—renowned for his "gallant and meritorious conduct" in the late war with Mexico—had prescribed the fanciful attire for the occasion. From his Army training he knew that from Roman times the rosette had decorated military medals. Wearing ribbons matching their scarves and carrying batons, the Chief Marshal, his aides, and his assistant marshals proceeded from the hotel to Judiciary Square.

Judiciary Square took its name from the neoclassical edifice that stood at its southern end, the seat of Washington's municipal administration and courts: City Hall. Grounds surrounding the building would serve this day as the staging area for the grand procession.

Detachments of foot soldiers, following colorful banners, tramped through Washington's streets with the cadenced thump of hundreds of boots. Horsemen, too, clattered through the city in clouds of dust and a jangle of harness and swords. Arriving at City Hall, officers in dress uniform reported to Colonel William Hickey and saluted. Hickey had command of all the parade's military contingents. One by one, he directed the officers to their assigned places, where each unit posted its colors as a beacon to late-arriving comrades.

From Fort McHenry in Baltimore, Ringgold's U.S. Flying Artillery had hauled four 6-pounder brass cannons to Judiciary Square the previous day. The decorated soldiers and their guns had won the acclaim of the nation for their decisive participation in the war with Mexico. The servicemen now toted buckets of water to their waking horses and hung bags of feed around their necks. Shortly, they would rehitch the teams to the limbers for the procession.

Members of the U.S. Marine Band rehearsed tricky passages and held their horns close to keep them warm. A drum rattled rat-a-tat-tat above the bustle.

The preparations of Benjamin B. French, John W. Maury and John C. Rives had been meticulous. For weeks these three members of the Jackson Monument Committee had spared no effort—or personal expense—to ensure that this would be the grandest event in Washington since the triumphant visit of General Lafayette in 1824. Today would disclose to the eyes of the world the realization of the grandiose vision the Committee had conceived seven years earlier. Today was the goal to which the 13 members—who included Colonel Hughes—had clung with dedication and hope through all the years of obstacles and uncertainty.

On December 29, 1852, French, Maury and Rives, acting as the Committee of Arrangements, had formally invited both houses of the 32nd Congress to attend the dedication ceremony.[5] They had selected the military and civilian organizations that would participate, chosen the orator, named the guests, distributed invitations, decided the order of the procession, and planned the seating on the speakers' platform. In the *Daily Union* and *Daily Evening Star*, they had publicized the date of the celebration, the composition and itinerary of the procession, and the program of the ceremony. Their notice had extended an invitation:

> The Jackson Democratic Association, fraternities of Free and Accepted Masons, Odd-Fellows, and Red Men, Temperance Societies, and all other organized societies in the District, and the citizens generally, are earnestly and respectfully invited to be present at the ceremonies of the occasion.[6]

Now the sun was rising on Saturday, the "Eighth of January," 1853. The editor of the *Daily Union* would report:

> At an early hour . . . it was perceptible that the citizens of Washington were intent on something beyond the ordinary routine of business. The sky was clear, and the air soft and bland like that of the Indian summer, and not like that of mid-winter. The occasional boom of a gun, and the pavements thronged with persons moving toward Lafayette Square, would have indicated to an utter stranger that some interesting ceremony engaged the public attention.[7]

Places of business shuttered for the day.[8] Public offices closed. Aloof on its eminence, the U.S. Capitol stood abandoned, construction derricks at either end motionless, work sheds unpeopled, beasts of burden at rest. The Senate did not convene. The House adjourned early so members could attend.[9] The correspondent of the *Illustrated News* would inform his readers in New York:

> Persons of leisure, taste, and fashion, from a distance, . . . poured into Washington in crowds. All the representatives of foreign governments, stationed at Washington, were in and around the vast throng, their dresses making them even more conspicuous than the military.[10]

Residents and visitors alike scurried to make it to City Hall by ten o'clock. Excited folks claimed viewing spots along the parade route. "*By eleven,*" Benjamin B. French would write in his diary, "*the space in front of the Hall and the streets leading therefrom were filled.*"[11]

As the morning air lost its nip, spectators appeared in the upper windows and on the roofs of the elegant residences lining Lafayette Square. Along H Street, carriage traffic was no longer possible. Curious citizens were amassing all the way to the white-painted stuccoed walls of Saint John's Episcopal Church and the wrought-iron fence enclosing the mansion and gardens of William Wilson Corcoran. The millionaire banker/art connoisseur and his guests enjoyed a privileged vantage point for observing the unfolding festivity: Mr. Corcoran's roof terrace.

On the south side of the square, at the Executive Mansion, carriages rolled under the lofty North Portico and halted. President and Mrs. Fillmore welcomed their guests. The Commander in Chief of the Army, Lieutenant General Winfield Scott, stepped down. Enormous and fastidious, "Old Fuss-and-Feathers" had gained fame and the affection of the nation by winning the war with Mexico. Members of the President's cabinet alighted, as well as distinguished officers of the Army and Navy. Meanwhile, their drivers kept the carriages at the ready in a queue along the horseshoe drive.

At about eleven-thirty, Colonel Hughes gave the signal and the long column of military units and civilian officials started filing from Judiciary Square down the gentle descent of 4½ Street. First, riding superb chargers, came:

Colonel William Hickey
three high-ranking military aides

Behind them, marching in broad ranks:

Ringgold's U.S. Flying Artillery
(lumbering four of their illustrious 6-pounder brass guns)

> U.S. Marine Corps Band
> U.S. Marine Corps
> Washington Light Infantry
> National Greys
> Another military band
> Continental Guards
> Walker Sharpshooters
> Another military band
> German Yeagers
> Boone Riflemen

The pageantry of the trim young men stepping in unison and wearing a variety of dapper uniforms—brown, blue, gray, even scarlet (the German Yeagers)—stirred the public to cheers and applause. Turning onto Pennsylvania Avenue, the units strode with pride between cheering crowds. "Every available position along the route was filled with ladies and gentlemen—the balconies, and in many instances the house-tops, being filled with spectators."[12] Onlookers leaned out of upper-story windows and stood on roofs. Red, white and blue bunting festooned hotels, banks, business establishments, restaurants, boarding houses, and the stalls of Center Market. Stars and Stripes draped everywhere, limp in the motionless air, but bright with patriotism. Rousing martial airs pulsated down the Avenue. Bayonets flashed silver lightning.

On horseback came:

> Colonel George W. Hughes, the Chief Marshal
> Aides of the Chief Marshal
> Assistant Marshals
> Benjamin B. French and John C. Rives
> Other members of the Jackson Monument Committee
> Aides of members of the Jackson Monument Committee

Then, unaccompanied, on foot:

Clark Mills

Following mounted military in dazzling dress uniform and preceding a caravan of carriages full of dignitaries in shiny black top hats, Mills trod the cobbles of Pennsylvania Avenue. Five feet, ten inches tall, with sunken cheeks and prominent chin, whiskerless as a boy, but his wavy locks graying prematurely, the thirty-seven-year-old was a familiar figure to the thousands of spectators. They loved him. He radiated vigor and a comfortable decorum.

Behind Mills rolled a line of carriages bearing:

> The Honorable Stephen A. Douglas, Orator of the Day
> Chaplain of the Senate
> Chaplain of the House of Representatives
> U.S. Senators and their officers
> U.S. Representatives and their officers
> All nine Judges of the Supreme Court
> Judges of other courts (a flock of billowing black robes)

The sober attire of the civil authorities and raven gowns of the judges contrasted with the flashy uniforms of the military personnel.

Next, three elegant barouches carried:

> The Honorable John W. Maury, Mayor of Washington
> The Honorable Henry Addison, Mayor of Georgetown
> The Honorable Lawrence Berry Taylor, Mayor of Alexandria

Finally:

> Members of the Jackson Democratic Association
> Delegations from Baltimore
> Representatives of numerous fraternal societies.

As the last contingent passed by, spectators scrambled to join the parade. The stream of festive Washingtonians and visitors grew longer and longer.

Reaching 15th Street, the procession faced the gate to President's Park. Mills's crude, unpainted, wooden studio/abode/foundry showed clearly just beyond it, south of the carriage way leading to the President's House. For five years the publicity-loving sculptor had opened his compound to visitors and regaled them with his yarns. Was there a soul in the city unapprised of his unorthodox furnace? Even while Carl Ludwig Richter was still in his employ, Mills had boasted that he himself was the inventor of the revolutionary furnace in which he had cast his revolutionary statue.

Before turning up 15th Street, the marchers could glance southward and behold the stunted Washington Monument beyond the mouth of Tiber Creek. A lack of funds had recently halted its progress. Then, filing past Robert Mills's stupendous colonnade of the Treasury Department building (another grand project in mid-construction), the column of civil and military elements rounded back onto Pennsylvania Avenue. "The procession entered the grounds of the Executive Mansion, passing around the semi-circle in front, and saluting the President, who was attended by the members of his cabinet and distinguished officers of the army and navy." Presently, the buoyant cortege was enlarged by carriages bearing:

> President and Mrs. Millard Fillmore
> All seven Members of the President's cabinet,
> their wives and children
> Lieutenant General Winfield Scott
> Staff Officers of the Commander in Chief
> Oldest Commodore of the Navy
> Officers of the Army and Navy

From plumed bicorn to polished boot, the military escort was all sparkly gold braid, brass buttons, beribboned medals, glittering sashes and bright white dress gloves.

Local residents, out-of-towners and civil dignitaries dispersed into Lafayette Square through the south gate. Military personnel paraded around the square and marched in through the H Street gate. The sinuous walkways designed by Andrew Jackson Downing were scarcely finished; the plantings of trees and shrubs were all fresh and immature. The winter sun in the southern sky cast long shadows across the panorama of human choreography. The bell in St. John's tower tolled 12 times.

For a long time, spectators—excited, yet decorous—flowed into Lafayette Square. *"There were at least 20,000 people present at the ceremonies,"* the observant diarist, Benjamin B. French, would note, *"and I should think as many more on the pavements, at the windows and on the housetops along the Avenue."*[13] Parents held children firmly by the hand, lest they lose them. Only a few dozen guests, though, enjoyed the privilege of a seat: speakers and dignitaries in the elevated stand, ladies on chairs ranged on the parterre. Everybody else remained standing, elbow to elbow. Caucasian faces beneath fringed parasols and glistening top hats predominated, but Black citizens were also in evidence. Free people of color were stylishly turned out and enslaved men, women and children inhaled deeply the day's reprieve from masters' bidding. All eyes were fixed on the outsized tent that loomed in their midst.

It was almost half past noon before Colonel Hughes, satisfied that everyone was in place, rose from his armchair. He presented the Chaplain of the Senate, the Reverend Doctor Clement C. Butler. The well-known pastor of Trinity Church stood, approached the lectern, removed his hat, bowed his head (every man did likewise), and intoned a Christian invocation. Then the Chief Marshal introduced the Honorable Stephen A. Douglas. The "Little Giant" from Illinois was famed for his oratory. The mass of spectators gaped in soundless expectation.

The Senator rose to his feet and stepped forward. Not yet 40, Douglas' round face was clean-shaven, his massive brow was crowned with a billowing wave of dark brown hair.[14] His trim five feet, four inches proclaimed a force about to erupt. He unfolded his notes. He began:

"All nations have marked the period of their highest civilization and greatest development by monuments to their illustrious men."[15]

Projecting his voice to the far corners of the square, Douglas praised the ancient monuments of Trajan, Constantine and Marcus Aurelius before acknowledging the towering white canvas tent at his side.[16]

"The statue before you is the work of a man exalted by his enthusiasm for the glorious deeds and wise acts of a hero and statesman. It is the work of a young, untaught American. I cannot call him an artist. He never studied nor copied. He never saw an equestrian statue, not even a model. It is the work of inborn genius aroused to energy by the triumphant spirit of liberty which throbs in the great heart of our continent—which creates the power of great conceptions, the aspiration and the will, the mental faculty and the manual skill, to eternize the actors who ennoble the country, by giving their forms and expressions to imperishable materials."[17]

In longwinded, elaborate phrases, the statesman compared Mills's handwork to the most celebrated bronze equestrian statues of the day—Peter the Great in St. Petersburg, Frederick the Great in Berlin, the Duke of Wellington in London—and found those European memorials wanting. They all required "the unsightly contrivance" of an external support. Mills's brazen steed did not. Then, his tone stentorian, his gestures restrained, the "Little Giant" orated an unabashed encomium of Andrew Jackson. For nearly an hour, he eulogized the life and career and character of the man, from impoverished childhood to the presidency of the United States.

The cadence of the Senator's rhetoric, ornamented with many classical allusions, mesmerized the multitude of 20,000 listeners. They stood transfixed—the affluent and the erudite, tradesmen with wives and children, unlettered laborers, men and women and children of color. For close to an hour, they stayed on their feet, necks straining, ears pricked. Douglas was rousing good entertainment! Nevertheless, on the fringes of the crowd, beyond earshot, there were distractions. A Sicilian organ grinder was performing. He had obviously lost his right hand; the other one was doing the cranking. His rambunctious monkey snatched coins from appreciative listeners.[18]

At about half past one, the Senator gathered up his notes and retook his seat. The throng burst into shouts and applause, riotous hollering and clapping. At length, Benjamin B. French stood, led Clark Mills forward on the stage, and introduced him to the immense audience. "*He was received,*" French would later write in his journal, "*with that enthusiastic and soul-stirring applause which he so richly merited, by three times three heartfelt cheers.*"[19]

Mills's "searching bluish-gray eyes" scanned the dignitaries on the platform, the ladies ranged in the gallery below, the ranks of military men in dress uniform, figures leaning out of windows, perched on rooftops, the clamorous and adoring mass of humanity sprawled before him. Silence came. Clark Mills, always quick to opine, always the raconteur, always the incessant seeker of the spotlight, was tongue-tied. He turned, raised an arm toward the huge tent, and the canvas collapsed.[20]

Suddenly, there he loomed: the "Hero of New Orleans," larger than life, astride a warhorse balancing on its hind legs! The afternoon sunshine striking the polished contours of the sculpture animated the horse and rider.[21] The dynamic figure of bronze green, nine feet tall and twelve feet long, looked alive![22]

Gasps and cheers, whistling and shouting, tumultuous clapping, thunderous and echoing and reverberating, rocked Lafayette Square. The New York *Illustrated News* reporter was overwhelmed:

> Never will the writer forget the shout that went up from the assembled multitude, when . . . the attendants suddenly unveiled the statue. . . . In appealing directly to the sympathies of the

Mills's *Jackson*, 2024. (Alamy)

American people, in his design, [Clark Mills] has struck a chord in the popular breast which will associate his work with cherished reminiscences of our country's history, so long as that history shall remain on the memory of man. He presents the hero just as the mass of American people have pictured his appearance to have been at the battle of New Orleans, in their own minds. There is nothing of allegory or myth, no foreign or ancient embellishment, or allusion, woven into the composition. No feature embraced which might, possibly, prevent ... hailing it, at a glance, as a heart-reaching representation of ANDREW JACKSON LEADING HIS COUNTRYMEN TO VICTORY AT NEW ORLEANS.[23]

The General's long, craggy face was unmistakable. Bareheaded, but dressed in the military regalia of an officer, saber dangling from his sash, Jackson was heralding his troops with a wave of his bicorn. The fifteen-ton charger was straining in mid-motion, poised to leap from its perch and whisk the victor home to Tennessee. "Horse and rider," one writer would opine, "were stamped with the truthfulness of life."[24]

It was a first in the history of world sculpture. Newspapers from Maine to Florida, as far west as Chicago and St. Louis, proclaimed the statue an achievement of international significance.[25]

And it was.

Sharp orders from Colonel Hickey sliced the air and Army, Marine Corps and D.C. militiamen snapped to attention in their ranks and presented arms. A clarion salute burst from the trumpets and trombones of multiple bands. Major Taylor shouted, "Fire!" and blasts from Ringgold's four famed cannons rippled the ground and vibrated in 20,000 human bodies. Smoke billowed above the square like incense. In rowdy exuberance, the crowd clapped and hollered. Even the officious gentlemen ranged across the dais sprang to their feet.

At length, the people exhausted themselves. The din subsided. Mills returned to his chair. The Reverend Mr. Gallaher, Chaplain of the House of Representatives, rose and delivered the closing benediction. Finally, the president of the Jackson Democratic Association, Jonah D. Hoover, pronounced the proceedings concluded. The morning's *Daily Union* would report:

> [T]he various military companies filed off amidst cheers and the music of their bands, many citizens lingering in admiration of the matchless work which the hands of a man of the people had fashioned.[26]

Late-afternoon sunbeams spotlighted the Georgian façades lining the east side of Lafayette Square. Dusk carried a chill. Silence.

That evening the Jackson Democratic Association hosted its annual "Eighth of January" banquet in Jackson Hall at 339 Pennsylvania Avenue. Inside the Greek revival building, in the spacious upper room, richly festooned, aglow with gaslight and warmed by stoves at either end, a conclave of esteemed civic and military leaders sat at four long rows of tables. One after the other, they stood and intoned regular toasts, then complimentary toasts, and lastly volunteer sentiments. Over and over, amidst the orgy of adulation, a glass was raised to the guest of honor, the autodidact American genius, Clark Mills.[27] It was after midnight when the lauded sculptor descended the long staircase, walked out into the serene and lamplit Avenue, and headed toward the Willard Hotel.

Back in his room, the events of the most momentous day of his life replaying in his head, did Mills perceive what was missing? Had he noticed the ominous absence at the banquet tables that evening? Not one sculptor was there. Not one artist was there. Mills had won the hearty embrace of the public. He was the unassailable darling of the Democrats. The country's cultural establishment, however, would never grant him its imprimatur. In New York, Philadelphia and Boston, the arbiters of Art would disparage his *Jackson* as clumsy and ill-conceived. They would deprecate Mills as an overbearing, albeit very clever, artisan. Forthwith, Henry Kirke Brown would spearhead a national campaign to prevent Congress from appropriating federal monies for works of art by amateurs, such as Clark Mills. And Carl Ludwig Richter, raging with indignation, would reappear in Washington armed with a petition to Congress that railed against Mills's perfidy. The furnace that had brought forth the nation's first monumental bronze statue, the aggrieved immigrant would proclaim, was *not* Mills's invention. It was *his*.

And it was.

The career of "Clark Mills, the Sculptor," had dawned in a spectacular way. Ferocious willpower and shameless egotism had brought him from a most inauspicious starting point to this airy eminence. But the climb to the lofty *professional* repute Mills coveted was still ongoing. Biting winds would continue to buffet his efforts, and with all the defiant self-confidence of his youthful days in upstate New York, the renegade would continue to lean headlong into the gale. The loyal backing of "the slaveholding South" in Washington would enable him to persevere.

The timing had been propitious for Mills. The forging of his creative life had transpired during years when the forced, unrecompensed service of myriad Black domestics, tradesmen, laborers and field hands made it possible for their lawful owners to support a struggling artist. Mills had been able to realize the potential of his natural gifts of intelligence, imagination, and physical endurance because southern men of fierce sectional pride used their wealth, their positions, and their influence to foster the efforts of their "home boy." As they would now continue to do. Mills's story was far from over. Still ahead lay the crowning handiwork of "Clark Mills, the Sculptor," poised high above the nation's capital.

NOTES

1. Description of the dedication ceremony is derived from: (1) "Inauguration of the Equestrian Statue of Andrew Jackson," [Washington] *Daily Union*, Jan. 5, 1853, p. 4; reprinted in the [Washington] *Daily Evening Star*, Jan. 6, 1853, p. 3; (2) "Inauguration of the Statue of General Jackson at the City of Washington," [Washington] *Daily Union*, Jan. 8, 1853, p. 3; (3) "Inauguration of the Jackson Equestrian Statue," [Washington] *Daily Evening Star*, Jan. 8, 1853, p. 2; (4) "The Celebration Yesterday," [Washington] *Daily Union*, Jan. 9, 1853, p. 2; (5) "Oration of the Hon. Stephen A. Douglas, On the Inauguration of the Jackson Statue," [Washington] *Daily National Intelligencer*, Jan. 11, 1853, p. 1–2; (6) "Inauguration of the Jackson Statue," [Washington] *Daily National Intelligencer*, Jan. 11, 1853, p. 3; and (7) "Congress," *Brooklyn Eagle*, Jan. 11, 1853, p. 2.
2. Regarding the state of Andrew Jackson Downing's landscape plan and the use of the terms "Lafayette Square" and "Lafayette Park," see Bk. 1, Ch. 35, n. 11.
3. "Narrative of the Battle of New Orleans," [Washington] *Daily Evening Star*, Jan. 8, 1853, p. 1.
4. George Wurtz Hughes (1806–70), see https://en.wikipedia.org/wiki/George_Wurtz_Hughes.
5. *Congressional Globe*, 32nd Cong., 2nd Sess., Dec. 30, 1852, p. 173 and 178.
6. "Inauguration of the Equestrian Statue of Andrew Jackson," [Washington] *Daily Globe*, Dec. 31, 1852, p. 3; printed simultaneously in the *Daily National Intelligencer, Daily Union, Daily Evening Star* and *Republic*; reprinted in subsequent issues.
7. "The Celebration Yesterday," *Daily Union*, Jan. 9, 1853, 2.
8. "Inauguration of the Jackson Statue," *Daily National Intelligencer*, Jan. 11, 1853, 3.
9. "Congress," [Washington] *Daily Evening Star*, Jan. 7, 1853, p. 2.
10. "The Equestrian Statue of Jackson," [N.Y.] *Illustrated News*, Jan. 15, 1853, p. 44.
11. Donald B. Cole and John J. McDonough, eds., *Witness to the Young Republic, A Yankee's Journal, 1828–1870* (Hanover and London: University Press of New England, 1989): 228.
12. "The Celebration Yesterday," *Daily Union*, Jan. 9, 1853, 2.
13. Cole and McDonough, *Witness to the Young Republic*, 228.
14. For description of Douglas, see https://www.essentialcivilwarcurriculum.com/stephen-a.-douglas.html.
15. "Oration of the Hon. Stephen A. Douglas . . . ," *Daily National Intelligencer*, Jan. 11, 1853, 1.
16. Tim Kerr, *The History of the Equestrian Statue of General Andrew Jackson, Lafayette Park, Washington, D.C.* Typescript report prepared for the National Park Service, White House Liaison, August 1999, p. 33: "[I]t would seem that

Douglas and the honored guests occupied a low platform on one side of the pedestal with the statue as a backdrop."

17 "Oration of the Hon. Stephen A. Douglas . . . ," *Daily National Intelligencer*, Jan. 11, 1853, 1.
18 "The Letters of an Oxonian. Addressed to the Poet Laureate of England. LETTER VIII. The Fine Arts. Lines to Clark Mills," *Alexandria* [Va.] *Gazette*, June 25, 1853, p. 3.
19 Cole and McDonough, *Witness to the Young Republic*, 228.
20 "History of the Jackson Statue," [Washington] *Daily Union*, Jan. 18, 1853, p. 2; and "Sketches of Washington. By Childe Harold. Washington, March 29, 1853. An Hour with Clark Mills, the Sculptor. [Concluded.]," *Brooklyn Eagle*, Mar. 31, 1853, p. 2; and "Clark Mills and His Equestrian Statue," *DeBow's Review*, vol. 16 (Jan. 1854): 44.
21 See Bk. 1, Ch. 36, n. 5.
22 Dimensions are from Kerr, *History of the Equestrian Statue*, i.
23 "The Equestrian Statue of Jackson," *Illustrated News*, Jan. 15, 1853, 44.
24 "Sketches of Washington . . . ," *Brooklyn Eagle*, Mar. 30, 1853, 2.
25 See Bk. 2.
26 "The Celebration Yesterday," *Daily Union*, Jan. 9, 1853, 2.
27 See Bk. 1, Prologue.

Acknowledgments

I thank the many people who shared with me, affably and unstintingly, their time and expertise, so that this account of Clark Mills's life from 1815 to 1853 might be as accurate as possible. I am deeply grateful for their assistance. I apologize that I cannot acknowledge every person who responded to an inquiry of mine, but I can at least name the archivists, curators, librarians, genealogists, colleagues, and friends whose contributions were most substantial.

South Carolina

Christina Rae Butler, of Butler Preservation, L.C., Charleston, performed extensive research for me in land and tax records and provided in-depth reports that drew from other records as well. Katharine Allen and Keith Mearns of Historic Columbia supplied descriptive detail about the Hampton-Preston House and its gardens. Beth Bilderback and McKenzie Lemhouse, at the South Caroliniana Library, University of South Carolina, Columbia, sent me photographs of the seven Mills busts in their collection, and Laura K. Mina of the Charleston Library Society reported on the six Mills busts owned by her Society. Email exchanges with Valerie Perry, Assistant Museums Director at the Historic Charleston Foundation, contained valuable context regarding the state of marble carving in Charleston in the 1840s. Beverly M. Donald, Superintendent, Magnolia Cemetery, Charleston, gave me excerpts from the cemetery's records of 1850 about the bell cast by Mills, as well as old photographs of it. Throughout the research and writing of this book, for questions about "all things South Carolina," I turned repeatedly to my friend, Brent Howard Holcomb, a professional genealogist in Columbia. Brent was not only generous with his own vast knowledge of the history of his native state, but readily referred me to associates of his who were helpful.

Washington, D.C.

Catherine Dewey and Lindy Gulick, Architectural Conservators, National Capital Region, National Park Service, at my request, took photographs of details of the Jackson equestrian when it was undergoing conservation in 2017. They also put at my disposal earlier NPS studies and reports on the statue. Cecilia H. Chin and Doug Litts of the Smithsonian American Art Museum/National Portrait Gallery Library, Smithsonian Institution, helped me navigate their collections. Deborah Shapiro at the Smithsonian Institution Archives assisted with the correspondence of Joseph Henry and microfilmed records of the Ames Manufacturing Company. Anne McDonough and Alex Aspiazu of the Kiplinger Research Library, Washington Historical Society (now the D.C. History Center), led me to Mills materials found nowhere else. I am particularly fortunate to have had the abiding support of Peter R. Penczer, author of multiple books and articles about Washington history. Peter offered his time and wide-ranging knowledge generously; his comments helped me fine-tune many passages. Another writer of Washington history, John DeFerrari, also critiqued the final draft and his observations spurred improvement to the narrative.

Other Expertise

Skip Duett, a professional genealogist of New York State, conducted extensive research for me on Mills's birth, parentage and first 20 years. His reports were meticulously thorough. Brigham Young University professor Roger Minert translated the scarcely legible German script of Carl Ludwig Richter's 1823 baptismal record. William J. Forsyth, former Senior Product Manager at ProQuest, put the entire website of digitized historical materials at my disposal. This enabled me to access original sources I would not otherwise have consulted. Colleague and friend, Judy Russell, J.D., "The Legal Genealogist," explicated Mills's 1837 marriage contract and subsequent court documents. During my years of researching Mills and his world, archivists at the National Archives and Records Administration and librarians at the Library of Congress helped me access a plethora of diverse original and published materials. Elizabeth Nilson at the Maryland Historical Society (now the Maryland History Center) pulled Mills's maquette of the Jackson statue from storage for me to examine. The thoughtful comments of a friend of mine who read the final draft, David Bernstein, instigated substantial rewriting throughout the book. Another friend who critiqued the final draft was Jared Freeman, whose masterful editing brought increased clarity throughout the text. LaBrenda Garrett-Nelson, national authority on researching African American families of South Carolina, graciously read the final draft to ensure its accuracy. From initial concept to finished product, I benefited from the unflagging encouragement and keen proofreading skills of two friends and colleagues of many years, Stuart and Tammy Nixon. My brother Thomas, the artist TR Colletta, provided valuable assistance in the preparation of illustrations. Finally, innumerable discussions with my life partner, James Douglas Walker—himself a son of the Deep South—about the pre-Civil War society of Clark Mills inspired me to reappraise and understand better the content of many sources.

To all these helpers, and to the many others acknowledged in end-of-chapter notes and courtesy lines of illustrations, Thank you!

Index

Note: Names in ***bold italic*** indicate busts by Mills; page numbers in *italics* indicate an image.

A

Addison, Henry, 391
Aiken, Joseph Daniel, 106n23
Albion, A Journal of News, Politics and Literature, 300
Alexandria Gazette, 333
Allston, Washington, 115, 122–123
American Art-Union, 89, 248, 251, 315
American Farmer Magazine, 223
American Indians, 168, 248, 250–251
American Telegraph, 351
Ames, James T., 352
Ames Manufacturing Company, 263, 347–348, 352
"An Admirer of the Arts" *(Courier)*, 84–85, 89, 97
"An Honored Sculptor" *(Saturday Evening News)*, 161
Andrei, Giovanni, 169
"Anecdote of Forrest" *(Fort Wayne Daily Gazette)*, 360, 363–364
Apollo, 315–316, 322, 325
Apollo Hall, 108, *109*–110, 113
Apprentices' Library Society, 87, 103, 191
architecture
    classical, neoclassical, 372, 398
    Gothic Revival, 129, 134, 144, 238
    Greek Revival, 60, 157, 162, 214, 258, 398
Arlington Heritage: Vignettes of a Virginia County (Templeman), 223
The Arms of Krupp (Manchester), 260
Armstrong, Robert, 11
artists/artisans
    "An Admirer of the Arts," 84–85, 89, 97
    American Art-Union, 89, 248, 251, 315
    artisan vs. artist, 97, 169, 398
    celebrities, 246–247
    ironworking, 224, 250, 260, 262, 270
    Jackson statue banquet, 398
    metallurgy, 235, 237, 260, 262, 263
    Mills not artist? 14, 89, 103, 398

sculptors
    Antonio Capellano, 168, 170
    Benjamin Harris Kinney, 105n18
    Enrico Causici, 168
    Giovanni Carlo Micali, 166
    Horatio Greenough, 34, 104, 123, *165*–166, 176, 246–247, 362
    Italy and, 103–104, 121–123, 166–170
    John Frazee, 34, 97
    John Henri Isaac Browere, 34, 97
    Joseph Daniel Aiken, 106n23
    Luigi Persico, 167
    Nicholas Gevelot, 168
    Noah Parker, 33–41
    See also Brown, Henry Kirke; Houdon, Jean-Antoine; Mills, Clark; Powers, Hiram
stonecutters, 98–99, 169, 372, 378, 382–383

B

Bache, Alexander Dallas, 274
Bachman, John, 86, 102
Ballentine, Alexander, 48, 50, 54, 75, 148, 151
Ballentine, John, 55
Ballentine [Mills], Eliza Susanna Tucker
    children, 55, 58, 60–61, 88, 101, 148
    dowry, prenup, 48–49, 52n20, 54–55
    family, 308
    marriage strained? 4, 8, 191, 302
    owns house, 148, 151, 306, 308
    Phillip, enslaved boy, 54–56
    weds Clark, 48, 50
Baltimore (ship), 303
Baltimore Clipper, 241
Baltimore *Sun*, 331–332, 362
Baltimore Washington monument, 181
"Banquet of the Jackson Democratic Association" *(Daily Union)*, 385
Barnola, Joseph, 264

405

Battle of New Orleans, 2–14, 193, 229, 377, 386, 388, 398
Bitner, William Godfrey, 278–279
Black servants, workforce, 5, 11, 56, 393, 399
　See also Reid, Philip; slavery
Blair, Francis Preston, 111–112, 180, 217, 366
bluestone cement, 372, 378
Bohn, Casimir, 3, *163*, 229
Bomford, George, 179
Boston Athenaeum, 325–326
Boston Evening Transcript, 149
Boston Journal, 72
Botanic Family Physician (Thomson), 88
Brackett, Edward Augustus, 115
Bradley, Joseph H., 348
bronze
　Apollo bust, 315–316, 325
　bells, 281, 282n11, 285–287, 290–*293*, 319, 321–322
　"brass," 178, 186n14, 254, 263, 290, 336–337
　cannons, 236, 260, *264*–265, 343–345, 350, 353, 379, 387
　casting, 7, 283, 291, 294, 316, 360, 367, 373
　composition of, 103, 108, 113, 116, 177, 287, 290
　creating statue, step-by-step, 192–198, 221–224, 285–294
　European statues, 177
　"French sand," 285
　furnace for casting
　　excavating pit, 269–270
　　explodes, 360–361, 363–364
　　invented by Richter, 236–238, 263, 273, 346–348, 399
　　Mills claims credit, 25, 73, 297, 299–300, 309–310, 318–319, 331, 345–346
　　superiority of, 287–289
　　testing pieces in, 281
　　"unscientific" design, 273, 292–293
　"imperishable," 108, 113, 116

　iron vs., 271
　lost wax, 283
　Mills's foundry, 274, 278–281, 284, 292, 360–364
　patinating, "pickling," 292
　"recycling" trophies, weapons, 178–180, 224–226, 337, 350
　sand casting, 283, 285
　statue costs, 119n35, 178, 205, 320–321
　statue-creating, step-by-step, 192–196, 221–224, 285–293
　Thomas Jefferson statue, 164
　Washington bust, 322–326, 327n30, 339
Bronze Casting and American Sculpture, 1850–1900 (Shapiro), 178, 222, 279, 283, 294, 310
Brooklyn Daily Eagle, 21–22, 44, 365, 367
Browere, John Henri Isaac, 34, 72, 97, 103, 151, 158
Brown, Alexander H., 59
Brown, Henry Kirke
　campaign to limit amateur's funding, 399
　Choosing of the Arrow, 248, 250–251
　experience in bronze, *247*, 251
　"Father of American Sculpture," 200n13
　Filatrice, 251, 315
　Jackson statue, 176–177, 211n29, 245–246
　Mills's rival, 193, 194, 248–251, 352
　portrait of, *247*
　questions Mills's methods, 216, 222
Buchanan, James, 109
Buckingham, Charles W., 189, 198–199
Bulkley, Erastus, 99, 100
busts, statues
　allegorical, literal portrayals, 166–167, 169–170, 248, 397
　attire of, 95, 164, 172, 271–*272*
　bust-creating, steps for, 33–34, 74, 95, 98, 132
　classical, neoclassical designs, 157–159, 181, 203–*204*, 238–239, 386
　clay, 34, 71, 85, 150

Index

cost of, 33–34, 36, 42n15, 87, 150
death masks, 35, 84–85, 297–*298*
European equestrian, 177
experiencing procedure, 74–75
Italian Renaissance, 177
life masks, 72, 97, 151, 230, 322, 323
marble, 34, 98–99, 105n18, 116, 166
mechanical process? 85, 89, 97
Mills begins creating, 33–41, 44–47, 85, 99
naturalistic, 166, 238–239
neoclassical, 150, *165*–166, 169–170, 172, 271–*272*, 386
plaster versatility, composition, 45, 47
See also plaster, casting heads in
Butler, Andrew Pickens, 141, 161
Butler, Clement C., 393

C

C. &. J. Gibbes v. Clark Mills, 49
Calhoun, John C. (Vice President)
   bust of, 97, 99, 101–103, 122–*124*, 141, 149, 311
   "Cast-Iron Man," 95, 129, 298, 306
   Committee of Twenty-Five, 299–300, 302, 304, 311, 334
   death mask, 297–*298*
   funeral, interment, 199, 299, 308–309
   idol, representative of S.C., 103
   Mills requests he sit, 89, 93–94
   Mills's supporter, 76
   slavery defender, 28, 311
   vice presidency, 23, 27–28
Camden Journal, 44, 61, 62, 103, 318, 361
Cameron, Simon, 180
cannons
   brass, 254, 290
   bronze, 236, 260, *264*–265, 343–345, 350, 353, 379, 387
   iron, 255, 260, 262–265, 271
Capellano, Antonio, 168, 170
Capitol building (D.C.), 161–172, 183, 214, 298–299, 339

See also Washington, D.C.
Capitol building (S.C.), 129, 135
Capitol building (Va.), 155, 157
Car of History, 168
Carr, Charles D., 208
"Cast-Iron Man," 95, 129, 298, 306
   See also **Calhoun, John C.** (Vice President)
Causici, Enrico, 168
cement, bluestone, 372, 378
Charles Lewis Richter v. Clarke Mills, 346
Charleston, S.C.
   Athena goddess, protector, 125
   Charleston Friendly Botanic Thomsonian Society, *82*–*83*, 88
   Charleston Light Dragoons, 195–196
   Charleston Observer, 48
   cholera outbreak, 45
   demographics, 45
   "Great Fire," 50, 55, 58
   Guard House, 59–61, 77, 88
   libraries, 191
   Mills's residence, 44–45, *96*, 302
   Northern Neck, 55–56, *96*
   slavery, 45, 58, 307
   view from harbor, *46*
   yellow fever outbreak, 58
Cheves, Langdon, 86–87
cholera, 45, 331
Choosing of the Arrow, 250–251
church corbels, 134–135, 144
Cichi, Francisco, 116
City Hall (Washington, D.C.), 125, 161, 306, 308, 333, 377, 386–387
   See also Washington, D.C.
City Hall (Richmond, Va.), 157
Clark Mills: The First Native American Sculptor (Hopkins), 150
Clark Mills v. R. R. Hunt, 50
Clarke, Matthew St. Clair, 351
Clay, Henry, 115, 230
Clinton, DeWitt, 251
Collins, John, 36, 37

Columbia, S.C., 129–133, 135, 137n16, 138n32, 139–145
Columbus, Christopher, *167*
Conflict between Daniel Boone and the Indians, 168
Congressional Library, 322, 324
 See also Washington, D.C.
Conner, Henry Workman, 122, 189–190
Conrad, Charles M., 336, 343–345, 373
Corcoran, William Wilson, 389
Courier
 "An Admirer of the Arts," 84–85, 89, 97
 church corbels, 144
 Jackson statue progress, 108, 115, 193–195, 198, 220, 320–321, 379
 melting brass cannon, 290
 Mills plans Italy visit, 121, 122
 Mills praised, 78–79, 88, 95, 102, 125, 128, 302, 309
 Mills's methods, "new furnace," 73, 297, 300
 Mills's move, 99–100
 Mills's reward for vandal info, 49
 phrenology, 70–71
 slave auction, 54
Craig, Henry K., 353
Crawford, Thomas, 115, 116, 176, 246–247, 339
Crittenden, John Jordan, 171
Custis, G. W. Park, 322
Cyrus Alger & Co., 263

D
daguerreotypes, *167*
Dahlgren, John Adolphus, 257, 258–259, 262–263, 269, 338
Daily Evening Star, 386
Daily Globe, 377
Daily National Intelligencer, 220, 230–231, 244, 268, 293–294, 310, 332
Daily National Whig, 234, 239
Daily Union
 Jackson statue

banquet tickets, 2, 14
commissioned, 206–207
estimated cost, 114
foundrymen search, 348
funds requested, 365
Jackson Monument Committee, 110, 176
Mills obsessed with, 191–192
praised, 12, 385
revealed to crowd, 4, 388, 398
unscientific design, 273
Mills and Europe, 205
Mills claims invention, 310
Mills in his studio, 234, 363
Mills's experience, 349–351
David d'Angers, Pierre-Jean, 164, 166, 172, 185, 229
Davidson, James, 58
Davis, Louise Penelope, 133
death masks, 35, 84–85, 297–*298*
DeBow's Review, 121–122, 203
Deming, Bulkley & Co., 98
Democratic Association, Party, 112, 114, 312, 324, *330*
Devoe, William M., 12
Discovery of America, 167
Dix, Dorothea, 323, 325–326, 362
Dix, John Adam, 225
Donelson, Andrew Jackson, 182
Douglas, Stephen A., 4, 10–11, 13, 391, 393–395
Dow, Jesse Erskine, 111
Downing, Andrew Jackson, 372, 393
Duke of Wellington, 177

E
Edgefield Advertiser, 144
Edward Weber & Co., 227
"Eighth of January" banquet, 2–14, 377, 388, 398
 See also Jackson, Andrew (President)
Ellipse, 212, *215*
Elmore, Franklin Harper, 76, 94, 208, 230
Enquirer, 62, 206, 227

Erie Canal, 23–*24*, 25–26
Evening News, 101
Evening Star
    furnace explosion, 360–361, 363–364
    Jackson statue, 1, 221–222, 290, 371, 380–383, 388
    Mills on togas, *165*–166
    Mills replaces Richter, 349
Exchange Reading Room, 84, 90
Executive Mansion, 23, 109, 248, 271, 331–332, 389, 392
    See also Washington, D.C.

F

Fame and Peace Crowning George Washington, 168
Family Magazine, 46
Fenderich, Charles, 227–228
Filatrice, 251, 315
Fillmore, Millard (President), 332, 336, 338, 373–374, 389, 392
Fisk & Raymond burial case, 298–299, 303–304
Floyd, John B., 303, 304
Forrest, Edwin, 360, 363–364
Fort Wayne Daily Gazette, 360, 363–364
foundries
    foreign, 205, 346
    for Jackson statue, 274, 278–281, 284, 292, 360–364
    national, 156
    War Department's, 262
    Washington Navy Yard, 251, 255–257, 269–271
Franklin, Benjamin, 115
Franzoni, Carlo, 168
Franzoni, Giuseppe, 169
Frazee, John, 34, 97, 103, 151, 158, 169
Frederick the Great, 177, 235, 236, *237*, 264
French, Benjamin Brown
    Jackson statue, 112, 181, 366–367, 387, 389–390, 393, 395
    Taylor inauguration, 240

Friebel, Karl Ludwig, 237
Frost, Edward, 208
furnace, bronze-casting. *See* bronze
Furniss, William, 235, 237–238, 263

G

Gadsden, James, 191, 208
Gall, Franz Joseph, 68
Gallaher, James, 5, 398
Gallatin (ship), 305
Gardner, Charles Kitchell, 111
General Post Office building, 84, 90, *113*–114, 162, 181, 203
    See also Washington, D.C.
"Genius and Phrenology" (*Southern Patriot*), 67
Genius of America, 167
George W. Olney v. Clark Mills, 49, 59
Gevelot, Nicholas, 168
Gilman, Samuel Foster, 86
Gilmore, Robert, Jr., 104
Girard, Stephen, 115
Glascoe, Matthew, 371
Gold Rush, 204
Gourdin, Henry, 208
Gov. Dudley (ship), 305, 310
Graham, William A., 337
Greek Slave, 116, 203–*204*
Greenough, Horatio, 34, 104, 123, *165*–166, 176, 246–247, 362
Gregg, Hayden & Co., 272
Guard House, 59–61, 77, 88

H

Hammond, James Henry, 143
Hampton, Caroline Martha, 132
Hampton, Catharine P., 133
Hampton, Wade, II, 133, 141, 191, 196, 197, 223
Hampton daughters, 133
Hampton-Preston Mansion, *130*–131, 133–134
Handy, R. J. H., 12–13

Harold, Childe, 18, 21, 68
Harris, Jeremiah G., 108
Harris, William Alexander, 111
Hayne, Arthur Perroneau, 191
Hayne, Rebecca Brewton Alston, 86–87
Hayne, William Alston, 86–87
Henry, Joseph, 216, 238–*239*, 263, 273, 274, 293–294, 362
Hewett, John R., 380
Hickey, William, 377, 387, 397
"History of the Jackson Statue" *(Daily Union)*, 176
Hoban, James, Jr., 110, 111, 113, 129
Holmes, Isaac Edward, 143, 183, 311, 333–334
Hoover, Jonah D., 5, 398
Hopkins, Rosemary, 150, 324
Houdon, Jean-Antoine
  Lafayette bust, 158–159, 166
  Washington statue, 72, 116, 154–*155*, 317, *323*
  work inspires Mills, 159, 172
Houston, Samuel, 324
Howard, Douglas, 13
Howe, George, 142
Huard, Caroline P., 100
Huger, Francis Kinloch, 142, 208
Hughes, Clara Marie Balderston, 189, 198
Hughes, George Wurtz
  background, 182, 386
  Jackson statue inauguration, 377, 386, 389, 390, 393
  praises Mills, 385
  slave "owner," 11, 182

I

Illustrated News, 7, 32, 388, 395, 397
Inquirer, 234
ironworking, 224, 250, 260, 262, 270

J

Jackson, Andrew (President)
  death of, eulogies/toasts for, 6, 10–12, 108
  "Hero of New Orleans," 11, 112, 176, 205, 364–365, 386, 395
  Jackson Democratic Association, 1–14, 364–365, 385, 386, 388, 391, 398
  Jackson Hall, 1–2, 4, 15n1, 240, 398
  "Old Hickory," 4, 108, 191, 203, 224, 244, 386
  presidency, 23, 27–28
  slave "owner," 11, 28
  See also Battle of New Orleans
Jackson equestrian statue
  casting issues, 7–8, 360, 361, 367, 373
  composition, materials
    brass, bronze, 186n14, 201n33, *264–265*
    old weaponry, 178–180, 224–226, 334–338, 350
    parts of, 273, 350, 360
  described, 1–4, 8, 115–116, 244, 397
  design questioned, 216–217, 220–221, 273, 367, 379–383
  funding
    backers' bios, 207–208
    collecting funds, 184
    donations dry up, 364–365
    estimated costs, 119n35, 178, 205, 320–321
    with lithograph, 229
    voluntary national subscription, 108, 109, 178, 180–181
  inaugurated, 377–383, 386–395
  Jackson Monument Committee, 110–114, 172, 176–185
  Jackson Monument Foundry, 274, 278–281, 284, 292, 360–364
  "Jackson Monument in the City of Washington," 227–*228*
  Lafayette Square, 227, 231, 370, 383, 388–389, 395–396
  lithographs, 3–4, *163*, 227–*228*, 229
  maquettes/miniatures of, 189–*190*, 192, 194–199, 203, 205, 312, 351

Mills contracted, 205–207, 255, 257, 316, 367
Mills obsessed with, 9–14, 191–192
Mills praised for, 394–395, 398
Mills researches, sketches, 181–182, 190–191, 192–193, 222
Mills's work doubted, criticized, 364, 398–399
pedestal, 272–273, 370–374, 378, 379–380, 384n16
previews, 234–235, 241, 244, 245, 255, 374
promised completion, 230–231, 344, 354–355
Richter as foreman, 274
today, *396*
Washington Navy Yard, 205, 237, 254–258, 268–270
Jackson, S. A., 14
James E. Walker & Brothers, 99
Jefferson, Thomas, 72, 164, 229
Johnson, Cave, 112, 114, 172, 183–*184*, 193, 203
Johnson, David, 142
Johnson, Joseph, 87, 191
Justice and Young America, 168

K

Keilholtz, David, 349
Kendall, Amos, 110
Key, Philip Barton, 2, 7
King, Mitchell, 76
King, Thomas Butler, 225
Kinloch, George, 148, 208
Kinney, Benjamin Harris, 105n18
Kirkham, Samuel, 70
Krupp, Alfred, 260

L

LaBorde, Maximilian, 142
Lafayette bust, 158–159, 166
Lafayette Square
   architecture, design of, 372, 398

Jackson statue, 227, 231, 370, 383, 388–389, 395–396
Landing of the Pilgrims on Plymouth Rock, 168
Latrobe, Benjamin Henry, 157, 169, 257–258
Laval, Jacint, 191
Letters of Gov. Benjamin Franklin Perry to His Wife (Perry), 139, 140
Levy, Uriah Phillips, 164
Lewis, Dixon Hall, 230
Lewis, S. L., 13
Liberty, 168
libraries, 191, 322, 324
life masks, 72, 97, 151, 230, 322, 323
   See also plaster, casting heads in
Lippincott's Magazine, 196
lithographs, *3*, *163*, 227–*228*, 229, 247
Longworth, Nicholas, 103–104

M

MacDonald, Wilson, 363
Magnolia Cemetery, 321–322
Manchester, William, 260
Manning, John Laurence, 141
maquettes/miniatures, 189–*190*, 192, 194–199, 203, 205, 312, 351
marble, 34, 98–99, 105n18, 116, 166
   See also busts, statues
Maryland Center for History and Culture, 189, 198
Maury, John Walker, 14, 111, 205–206, 336, 364–*366*, 387, 391
Maury, William, 366
Maynadier, William, 336
McAleer, Philip A. ("Mac"), 348–349, 371, 373–374, 380–383
McCalla, John Moore, 182
McCauley, Charles S., 257, 269
McClernand, John Alexander, 179–180, 225–226
McCord, David James, 86–87
McCord, Louisa Susannah, 86–87
McDowell, Susanna Smith Preston, 170

McDuffie, George, 85, 103, 149, 161
McLane, Charles S., 268–269
McNerhany, Francis, 5
Meehan, John S., 325
Merry's Museum and Parley's Magazine, 221
metallurgy, 235, 237, 260, 262, 263
Mexican–American War, 140–141, 204, 263
Micali, Giovanni Carlo, 166
Mills, Clark
  Apollo bust, 315–316, 322, 325
  assistant to Noah Parker, 33–41
  awards, recognition, 4–14, 125–126, 394–395, 398
  background/bio sketches, 8, 18–28, 28n5, 32–33
  benefactors, patrons
    aristocratic clients, 47
    biographies of, 16n16
    David James McCord, 87
    A. G. Rose, 122–123, 189–190, 207
    Henry Workman Conner, 122–123, 189–190
    John C. Calhoun, 76, 300
    John Schnierle, 59–60, 77, 122–123, 189–190, 207
    John Smith Preston, 129, 135, 145
    John Walker Maury, 364–366
    Langdon Cheves, 87
    subscribers, 90, 121
    surety bonds, 8
  business savvy, 87, 234 235
  Calhoun's death, funeral, 300, 302–304
  capitol visits, 129, 135, 155, 157, 161–172
  carves church corbels, 134–135, 144
  celebrity, 103, 136, 149, 300, 302, 309–311, 361–363
  children
    Clark Jr., 61, 101, 307
    deaths of, 61
    John Schnierle, 60, 77, 101
    live with Eliza, 148
    Theodore Augustus, 61, 101
    Theophilus Fisk, 18, 21, 25, 26, 61, 101

  Columbia, S.C. visit, 129–133, 137n16, 138n32, 139–145
  competition, predecessors, 9, 58, 151, 193–194, *247*–251, 352
  cost of pieces, 33–34, 36, 42n15, 87, 150
  described
    analytical mind, 9
    appearance, 6–7, 18, 395
    "artist"? 14, 79, 89, 103, 398
    embellisher, storyteller, 18–19, 25, 67–68
    generous, 27, 76, 103
    "indomitable old man," 18
    inventive, 9, 61, 73
    "a lunatic," 212
    per neighbor "T," 19, 20, 26–28
    per Perry, 142
    plain manner, dress, 171
    scoundrel, "tremendous liar," 33, 38
    sculpting "genius," 9, 125–126
    self-absorbed/egotistical, 18–19, 62, 399
    self-taught, 9, 102
    steals credit due others, 9–11, 351–352
    See also Richter, Carl Ludwig
  early employment, 20, 23, 25–26, 45, 47
  Eliza Susanna Tucker Ballentine Mills (wife)
    dowry, prenup, 48–49, 52n20, 54–55
    family, 308
    marriage strained? 4, 8, 191, 302
    owns house, 148, 151, 306, 308
    Phillip, enslaved boy, 54–56
    wedding, 48, 50
  enslaved assistant. *See* Reid, Philip
  exhibits work
    Athenaeum Gallery, Boston, 149
    Capitol rotunda, 170
    Congressional Library, 322, 324
    Taylor & Maury's, 271–272, 351
    See also Jackson equestrian statue
  female companions, 4, 8

financial difficulties
  family grows, 88–89
  fires, economy, 58–59, 324–325
  home purchase, loss, 50–51, 53n32, 58, 64n20, *96*
  lawsuits, 49–50, 59, 345–346
  Philip Reid supports family? 129, 151, 191
  premarital debt, 48–50, 52n20, 54–55
  self-absorption, 62
  sells "test works," 321
Frazee similarities, 169
gives away busts, 76, 103
Guard House contract, 59–61, 88
horses and, 47–48, 128, 133, 194–198, 222–224, 249
Italy and, 121–124, 184–185, 199n2, 203
letter to/from Secretary of War Talcott, 343–345
marble sculpting, 98–99
mold replicas, 78, 123, 149, 151
Olympus (horse), 224
parents, siblings, 20, 21, 27, 30n16
patents, 73–74, 102, 149, *202*
petitions to incorporate botanic society, *82–83*, 88
phrenology and, 9, 67–69, 79, 142–143
plaster work begins, 33–41, 44–47
portrait, *32*
Preston's protégé, 104, 130–132, 135, 145, 155, 170–171, 183
"The Punishment and the School Boy's Revenge," 22
residences, 32–33, 40, 44–45, 49–50, 55–56, *96*, 302
Richmond, Va., visit, 154–159
Richter partnership, 9–10, 274, 278, 285–294, 318, 348
Richter's furnace, claims as own, 25, 73, 297, 299–300, 309–310, 318–319, 331, 345–346
Schnierle friendship, 59–60, 77, 189–190
studios/workshops

Jackson statue previews, 234–235, 241, 244, 245, 255, 374
  moves, *96*, 99–*101*, 213–*215*
  open houses, tours, 229–230, 249–250, 316, 351, 361–363
  tools of trade, 77–78
  window displays, 78–79, 97
supports brothers, niece, 27
Taylor's death, 331–332
thoughts on togas, *165*–166
Virginia capitol visit, 155
Washington bust, 317–318, 322–326, 327n30, 339, 362
Washington monument, Baltimore, 181
Whitaker bust affair, 36–38
worksite vandalized, 49–50
See also Jackson equestrian statue
Mills, Clark, Jr., 61, 101
Mills, Emory, 20, 27
Mills, John, 20
Mills, John Schnierle, 60, 77, 101
Mills, Lovisa, 27
Mills, Phineas Gurley, 20, 27
Mills, Robert (architect)
  buildings in Charleston, S.C., 157
  buildings in Richmond, Va., 157
  buildings in Washington, D.C., 162, 214
  Washington Monument (Washington, D.C) 162, 212, 217
Mills, Theodore Augustus, 61, 101
Mills, Theophilus Fisk, 18, 21, 25, 26, 61
Minnix, John N., 13
Minnix, William H., 13
Mordecai, Alfred, 293, 336, 346
"Muse of History," 168

N

Napoleon, 68, 178, 225, 260
"Narrative of the Battle of New Orleans" *(Daily Union)*, 386
National Era, 325

National Intelligencer, Daily/Weekly, 220, 230–231, 244, 268, 293–294, 310, 324, 332
National Museum, 244
Navy Yard Hill, 254, 258
　See also Washington, D.C.
New Guide to Health (Thomson), 88
New York Evening Post, 39
New-York Gazette, 36, 39, 40
Nina (ship), 305
Northrop, C. B., 208

O

"Old Hickory," 4, 108, 191, 203, 224, 244, 386
　See also Jackson, Andrew (President)
Olney, George W., 49, 59
O'Sullivan, John L., 108–114
Owner, James, 13

P

Page, Charles Grafton, 216–217, 273
"Palmetto Regiment," 140–141
Panic of 1837, 55
Parker, George, 182
Parker, Noah, 33–41, 42n4, 68
Parkman, George, 104
Patent Office, 162, 181
　See also Washington, D.C.
Peace, 167
Pearce, James Alfred, 325
Perry, Benjamin Franklin, 67, 139, 140, 142, 150, 155–156
Persico, Luigi, 115, 116, *167*
Peter the Great, 177
Petigru, James Louis, 85, 88, 122–123
Philadelphia Inquirer, 322, 324
Phrenological Almanac, *69*
phrenology, 9, 67–71, 79, 142–143
Pierce, Franklin, 2
plaster, casting heads in
　"bronzing," 77
　clay, 34, 71, 85, 150
　dangers of, 72–73
　death masks, 35, 84–85, 297–*298*
　life masks, 71–73, 97, 151, 230, 322, 323
　Mills begins, 33–41, 44–47, 85, 99
　step-by-step, 71–72, 78
　See also busts, statues
Plato and His Disciples, 352
Polk, James Knox (President), 12, 109, 141, 184, 217, 226, 240
Pomnietzky, Adelbert, 273, 278–279
Porter, N. M., 208
Powers, Hiram
　baptismal font, 134
　busts of plaster, marble, 34, 116, 150, 311
　celebrity, 246–247
　Greek Slave, 116, 203–*204*
　Jackson equestrian statue, 181–182
　prices bronze statue, 108, 114, 115, 178
　protégé of Preston, 104, 132, 135, 140–141
　studies in Italy, 104, 123
Poyas, James, 51, 58
prenuptial agreements, 48–49, 52n20, 54–55
Preservation of Captain John Smith by Pocahontas, 168, 170
Preston, John Smith, 104, 129–132, 134–135, 140–141, 161, 183
Preston, Louise Penelope Davis, 104, 133
Preston, William Campbell, 104, 130–132, 135–*136*, 145, 155, 161, 170–171
Princeton (ship), 255
Prussia, 235–237, 259–*261*

Q

A Quest for Glory, A Biography of Rear Admiral John A. Dahlgren (Schneller), 262–263

R

R. R. Hunt v. Clark Mills, 50
Rauch, Christian Daniel, 236, 237
Ravenel, Daniel, 199, 299, 300, 302, 312
Reid, Philip
　bronze work, 284, 288
　family, 56, 58

Jackson statue, 209, 211n29, 212, 250, 281, 288, 297
master plasterer, 54, 151, 284, 308
Mills's enslaved assistant, 8, 54–59, 61–62, 78, 100
Reid/Reed, 56, 64n13
residence, 213–214, 303
supports Mills's family? 129, 151, 191
Republic, 283–284, 300, 315, 320, 333, 374
Richmond, Va., 62, 154–159, 206, 227, 303–304, 339
Richter, Carl Ludwig
    background, 235, 242n7, 354
    bronze work, 236–*237*, 271
    Charles Lewis Richter v. Clarke Mills, 346
    invents furnace, 236–238, 263, 273, 309–310, 346–348, 353, 399
    Jackson statue, 339
    metallurgist, 235
    Mills claims furnace invention, 25, 73, 297, 299–300, 309–310, 318–319, 331, 345–346
    Mills's partnership, 9–10, 274, 278, 285–294, 318, 340
    Royal Prussian Foundry, 259–*261*
    temperament, 353–354
    Washington Navy Yard, *256*
Ringgold, Samuel, 263
Ringgold's U.S. Flying Artillery, 387, 397
Rist, John, 31, 36–37, 38
Ritchie, Thomas, 12, 111, 113
Rives, John Cook, 111–112, 366, 387, 390
Robinson, John, 197, 223
Rose, A. G., 122, 189–190, 207
rosettes, 386
Ross, Robert, 36, 37, 42n4
Round Table, 20–26, 97, 99, 166

S

sand casting, 283
Saturday Evening News, 161
Schneller, Robert J., Jr., 262–263
Schnierle, John, 59–60, 77, 122, 189–190, 207

Schultz, Henry, 88
Scott, Winfield, 389, 392
sculptors. *See* artists/artisans
Sengstack, Charles P., 111
Sewell, James, 48
Shand, Peter J., 134, 135
Shapiro, Michael Edward, 178, 222, 279, 283, 294, 310
Sheckells, Richard, 279
Simons, Benjamin Bonneau, 84
slavery
    auctions, *57*, 59
    Charleston, 45, 58, 307
    Jackson statue and, 183, 207, 284, 393
    plantations, 11, 128, 131, 139–140, 158, 307, 334
    Richmond, 158
    slave "owners"
        Ballentine, 48, 56
        Calhoun, 28, 311
        Democrats, 324
        Hughes, 11, 182
        inherit enslaved, 86
        Jackson, 11, 28
        Maury, 365
        Schnierle, 60
        Whitaker, 35
        See also Mills, Clark
    unremunerated Black workers, 8–9
    See also Reid, Philip
Southern Patriot, 59, 67, 115, 125, 206
Southern Press, 245, 254, 273, 324, 331, 332, 333
St. Philip's Church, 309
"Statue of Jackson" *(Inquirer)*, 234
statues. *See* busts, statues; *specific work*
Stone, William J., Jr., 345
stonecutters, 98–99, 169, 372, 378
    See also artists/artisans
Stossmeister, Theodore, 278–279
Stuart, Alexander High Holmes, 370–371
Sun, 331–332, 362
Symington's Quarry, 372, 378
Syracuse Daily Standard, 23

T

Talcott, George, 179–180, 255, 336, 344–345, 346
Taylor, Benjamin Franklin, 141
Taylor, Lawrence Berry, 391
Taylor, Zachary (President), 141, 234, 239–241, 271–*272*, 276n24, 331–333, 397
Taylor & Maury, 272, 351
Telegraph newspaper, 150
Templeman, Eleanor Lee, 223
"The Dead Sculptor16. Clark Mills" *(Washington Post)*, 197
Thomson, Samuel, 88
Tidball, Scott, 224
Tidyman, Philip, 271–272
"To the People of the United States" *(Daily Union)*, 365
Treasury Department, 181, 214
  See also Washington, D.C.
"Tribute to a Native Artist" *(Courier)*, 125, 128
Trinity Church, 48, 50, 129, 134–135, 144, 393
Tripoli Monument, 166
Troy Weekly Times, 23–24
Turf, Field and Farm, 224
Tyler, John (President), 255

U

United States Magazine, and Democratic Review, 330
Utica Morning Herald, 19

V

Valaperti, Giuseppe, 169
Van Ness, John Peter, 110
Vanderwerken, Gilbert, 223
Venable, Abraham Watkins, 306, 311, 337
"A Vindication of the Whitaker Family" *(New-York Gazette)*, 31, 39–40

W

Walker, Thomas, 98
War, 167
War Department foundries, 262
Warrington, Lewis, 257, 269, 336–338
Washington, D.C.
  Capitol building, 161–172, 183, 214, 298–299, 339
  City Hall, 125, 161, 306, 308, 333, 377, 386–387
  Congressional Library, 322, 324
  Exchange Reading Room, 84, 90
  Executive Mansion, 23, 109, 248, 271, 331–332, 389, 392
  General Post Office building, 84, 90, *113*–114, 162, 181, 203
  map of, *215*
  Patent Office, 162, 181
  powerful men of, sit for Mills, 143
  Treasury Department, 181, 214
  Washington Navy Yard, 205, 237, 254–258, 268–270
  White House, 161, 197, 213, 229, *280*
  "White Lot"/President's Park, 212, *215*, 279, *280*, 322, 375n11
  See also *Jackson* equestrian statue
Washington, George
  bronze equestrian statue, 115
  Fame and Peace Crowning George Washington, 168
  Washington bust, 317–318, 322–326, 327n30, 339, 362
  Washington Enthroned, *165*–166, 176
  Washington Monument (D.C.), 162, *163*, 212, 392
  Washington monument (Baltimore), 181
  Washington statue, 72, 116, 154–*155*, 317, *323*
Washington, John Augustine, 317–318
Washington and Georgetown Directory, 367
Washington Post, 18, 20, 72, 154, 197, 212, 379–383
Waterloo, 175, 225, 260
Watervliet Arsenal, 179
Webster, Daniel, 103, 171–172
Weekly National Intelligencer, 310, 324
Whitaker, Warren C., 35–36, 39–40

Whitaker, Washington, 31, 35–41
"The Whitakers" (Parker), 40
White, John Blake, 86, 98–99
White House, 161, 197, 213, 229, *280*
"White Lot"/President's Park, 212, *215*, 279, *280*, 322, 375n11
Wilhelm, Friedrich, IV, 260
William Penn's Treaty with the Indians, 168
Wilmington (ship), 305
Wilmington Journal, 299

Y

Yeadon, Richard, 74–75, 85, 89, 95, 97, 103, 193–195
yellow fever, 58

www.ingramcontent.com/pod-product-compliance
Lightning Source LLC
Chambersburg PA
CBHW052042220426
43663CB00012B/2408